**Clashing Views
on Controversial Issues
in Drugs and Society**

## Clashing Views
## on Controversial Issues
## in Drugs and Society

**Edited, Selected, and with Introductions by**

**Raymond Goldberg**
*State University of New York*
*College at Cortland*

**The Dushkin Publishing Group, Inc.**

*To Norma, Tara, and Greta*

**Photo Acknowledgments**

Part 1   UNITED NATIONS/JOHN ROBATON
Part 2   Pamela Carley
Part 3   Sara Krulwich/NYT PICTURES

**Library of Congress Cataloging-in-Publication Data**

Main entry under title:
  Taking sides: clashing views on controversial issues in drugs and society
    1. Drug abuse—Social aspects. I. Goldberg, Raymond, *comp.*
      HV5800                                                         362.29
      ISBN: 1–56134–103–7                                            92–74286

 Printed on Recycled Paper

*The Dushkin Publishing Group, Inc.*
*Sluice Dock, Guilford, CT 06437*

# PREFACE

One of the hallmarks of a democratic society is the freedom of its citizens to disagree. This is no more evident than on the topic of drugs. The purpose of this book is to introduce drug-related issues that (1) are pertinent to the reader and (2) have no clear resolution. In the area of drug abuse, there is much difference of opinion regarding drug prevention, causation, and treatment. For example, should drug abuse be prevented by increasing enforcement of drug laws or by making young people more aware of the potential dangers of drugs? Is drug abuse caused by heredity, personality characteristics, or environment? Is drug abuse a public health, medical, legal, or social problem? Are individuals who inject drugs best served by the provision of clean needles or treatment? Are self-help groups the most effective treatment for drug abusers?

There are many implications to how the preceding questions are answered. If addiction to alcohol or other drugs is viewed as hereditary rather than as the result of flaws in one's character or personality, then a biological rather than a psychosocial approach to treatment may be pursued. If the consensus is that the prevention of drug abuse is achieved by eliminating the availability of drugs, then more money and effort will be allocated for interdiction and law enforcement than education. If drug abuse is viewed as a legal problem, then prosecution and incarceration will be the goal. If drug abuse is identified as a medical problem, then abusers will be given treatment. However, if drug abuse is considered to be a social problem, then energy will be directed at underlying social factors, such as poverty, unemployment, health care, and education. Not all of the issues have clear answers. One may favor increasing penalties for drug violations *and* treatment services. And it is possible to view drug abuse as a medical *and* public health *and* social *and* legal problem.

Many of the issues debated in this volume have an immediate impact on the reader. For example, the discussion in Issue 3, *Does Drug Testing Violate Civil Rights?* is pertinent because the majority of large corporations in the United States now test job applicants for drugs. Issue 8, *Is Passive Smoking Harmful to Nonsmokers?* is relevant to smokers as well as nonsmokers because legal restrictions on passive smoking are discussed. And the question *Should Medical Patients Be Permitted to Use Marijuana?* (Issue 2) may become relevant for many readers or their loved ones someday.

**Plan of the book**   In this first edition of *Taking Sides: Clashing Views on Controversial Issues in Drugs and Society,* there are 34 articles dealing with 17 issues. Each issue is preceded by an *introduction* and followed by a *postscript.* The purpose of the introduction is to provide some background information and to set the stage for the debate as it is argued in the YES and NO

i

selections. The postscript summarizes the debate and challenges some of the ideas brought out in the two readings, which can enable the reader to see the issue in other ways. Included in the postscript are additional suggested readings on the issue. The issues, introductions, and postscripts are designed to stimulate readers to think about and achieve an informed view of some of the critical issues facing society today. At the back of the book is a listing of all the *contributors to this volume*, which gives information on the physicians, professors, and policymakers whose views are debated here.

*Taking Sides: Clashing Views on Controversial Issues in Drugs and Society* is a tool to encourage critical thought. In reading an issue and forming your own opinion you should not feel confined to adopt one or the other of the positions presented. Some readers may see important points on both sides of an issue and may construct for themselves a new and creative approach. Such an approach might incorporate the best of both sides, or it might provide an entirely new vantage point for understanding.

**A word to the instructor** To facilitate the use of *Taking Sides*, an *Instructor's Manual With Test Questions* (multiple-choice and essay) and a general guidebook called *Using Taking Sides in the Classroom*, which discusses methods and techniques for implementing the pro-con approach into any classroom setting, can be obtained through the publisher.

**Acknowledgments** A number of people have been most helpful in putting together this book. Assisting in the writing of the introductions and postscripts were Christine Wiegers and Nancy Wicklin. Their perceptions and understanding of the different drug issues resulted in a book that is not only informative but intellectually stimulating. Their dedication has certainly enhanced the quality of this edition. Without the editorial staff at The Dushkin Publishing Group, this book would not exist. The contributions of Mimi Egan, program manager, cannot be overstated. Her insights and encouragement were most appreciated. The efforts of David Dean, administrative assistant, and David Brackley, copy editor, were also instrumental to this book. In no small way can my family be thanked. I am grateful for their patience while I secluded myself in the study and monopolized the computer.

Raymond Goldberg
State University of New York College at Cortland

# CONTENTS IN BRIEF

# CONTENTS

Professor Ethan A. Nadelmann feels that current drug control policies are costly and ineffective in combating drug problems, and he argues that more emphasis should be put on drug education, prevention, and treatment instead of on drug prohibition. Criminologist James Q. Wilson argues that legalizing drugs is fundamentally unprincipled and inappropriate, and he feels that legalization would increase drug use and addiction and pose great risks to society.

---

Speaking as a mother, Mae Nutt describes the physical and emotional relief that marijuana provided her son while he was undergoing cancer treatment and argues that patients should be allowed to use marijuana while in treatment. John C. Lawn, director of the Drug Enforcement Administration, contends that medical patients should not be permitted to use marijuana because there is a lack of reliable scientific evidence showing marijuana's safety and its usefulness in the treatment of medical conditions.

---

Professor of health law Leonard H. Glantz argues that random drug testing violates civil liberties and sacrifices citizens' Fourth Amendment rights for the sake of the war on drugs. Physician and psychiatrist Robert L. DuPont contends that the dangers of illicit drug use warrant mandatory random drug testing.

---

Research associate Richard J. Goeman points out that consumption of alcohol among young adults accounts for a disproportionate number of automobile accidents, fatalities, and other alcohol-related problems. He argues that maintaining the current minimum drinking age is necessary to prevent further alcohol-related problems. David J. Hanson, a professor of sociology, argues that minimum-age drinking laws are unnecessary because they fail to prevent underage drinking and alcohol-related problems.

---

Public health specialists James F. Mosher and Karen L. Yanagisako argue that drug problems should come under the province of public health and not the criminal justice system. They believe that too much emphasis is placed on controlling illegal drugs and not enough on legal drugs, like alcohol and tobacco. The Office of National Drug Control Policy feels that not only should drug users be prosecuted but that efforts should be directed toward disrupting and dismantling multinational criminal organizations.

---

Professors Merrill Singer and Jean J. Schensul and drug treatment specialist
Ray Irizarry believe that the tremendous rise in the incidence of AIDS
necessitates exploring needle exchange programs for intravenous drug users
as a prevention strategy. The Office of National Drug Control Policy sees
needle exchange programs as an admission of defeat and a retreat from the
ongoing battle against drug use.

Paul A. Logli, a prosecuting attorney, argues that pregnant women who use
drugs should be prosecuted because they risk harming their unborn children. Professor of criminal justice Alida V. Merlo asserts that the prosecution
of pregnant drug users is unfair and discriminatory because such prosecution primarily affects poor, minority women who lack access to quality
prenatal care and drug treatment facilities.

Richard G. Schlaadt, director of the University of Oregon Substance Abuse
Program, concludes that the evidence regarding passive smoking shows that
it poses a great risk to nonsmokers. Physicians Gary L. Huber, Robert E.
Brockie, and Vijay K. Mahajan contend that claims about the adverse effects
of passive smoking are not based on scientific fact, because the level of
exposure to secondhand smoke cannot be measured.

Free-lance writer Janis A. Work argues that the consumption of caffeine, even at low levels, can have adverse physical effects. Dr. Diederick E. Grobbee and associates from the Department of Epidemiology and Nutrition at Harvard University's School of Public Health report on a study in which caffeine use did not increase the risk for cardiovascular disease.

---

The U.S. Department of Health and Human Services maintains that heredity is the major risk factor contributing to alcoholism. Social and clinical psychologist Stanton Peele and health care activist Archie Brodsky argue that research studies claiming a genetic basis for alcoholism ignore personal values and environment as factors contributing to alcoholism.

---

Falcon Baker, a director of delinquency programs, argues that drug education is a viable avenue for dealing with drug problems. Professor of psychology Harry H. Avis highlights many of the inadequacies of drug education and argues that schools are unfairly being asked to address problems that exist in all of society.

---

Don Cahalan, an emeritus professor of public health, discusses the link between tobacco companies advertising to certain audiences and the increase in tobacco use among these populations and argues that such advertising should be restricted. Professor of philosophy John Luik argues that individual autonomy is solely responsible for the desire to smoke and that prohibiting tobacco advertisements infringes on freedom of speech.

---

Professor of philosophy Herbert Fingarette asserts that proof for labeling alcoholism a disease is lacking and that identifying alcoholism as a disease is a great disservice to heavy drinkers. Professor of anthropology William Madsen claims that research showing that alcoholics can be moderate drinkers is faulty and that promoting the idea may prove fatal to the problem drinker.

---

Patricia Taylor, director of the Alcohol Policies Project of the Center for Science in the Public Interest, argues that banning alcohol advertisements aimed at youths and minorities will help eliminate alcohol-related problems. Harold Shoup and Christine Dobday, executives of the American Association of Advertising Agencies, contend that research does not support singling out advertising as a major controlling cause of alcohol abuse.

---

Psychotherapist Jeffrey A. Schaler contends that addicts always have control over their addiction and that they must therefore assume responsibility for their behaviors. Addiction, he says, is a matter of the addict's free volition. Lecturer and certified chemical dependency therapist Craig Nakken argues that once an addictive personality has been established, the addict has no control over his or her addiction.

---

Ray Hoskins, an alcoholism and drug abuse counselor, advocates total abstinence for the successful treatment of addiction, and he argues that controlling addiction through moderation is impractical. Harry H. Avis, a professor of psychology, criticizes the 12-step model of Alcoholics Anonymous and other self-help groups because it is not applicable to many addicts, and he argues that alternatives to lifelong recovery need to be explored in helping people deal with their addictions.

---

Medical writer Virginia S. Cowart asserts that the long-term consequences of anabolic steroid use has yet to be determined because this type of research has not been scientifically conducted. The National Institute on Drug Abuse identifies many short-term physical and psychological problems and potential long-term problems linked to the unregulated use of anabolic steroids.

# INTRODUCTION

## Drugs: Divergent Views
Raymond Goldberg

### AN OVERVIEW OF THE PROBLEM

Very few topics generate as much debate and concern as drugs. Drugs are evident in every aspect of life. There is much dismay that drug use and abuse cause many of the problems that plague society. Many are concerned that individuals, families, and communities are being destroyed by drug use and that moral decay will continue to fester because of drugs. The news media are replete with horrible stories of people under the influence of drugs committing crimes against others, of senseless drug-related deaths, of men and women who compromise themselves for drugs, and of women who deliver babies that are addicted or impaired by drugs.

From the fetus to the elderly, no one is untouched by drugs. In some cases, stimulants are prescribed for children so that they may learn or behave better in school. Sometimes students take stimulants on their own so that they can stay up late to study for a test or lose a few pounds. Many teenagers take drugs because they want to be accepted by their friends who take drugs. They also take drugs to deal with daily stress. For many people, young and old, their elixir for relaxation may be sipped, smoked, swallowed, or sniffed. Some people who live in poverty-stricken conditions anesthetize themselves from their environment with drugs. On the other hand, some individuals who seem to have everything also immerse themselves in drugs, possibly out of boredom. To cope with the ailments that come with getting older, the elderly often rely on drugs. Many people use drugs to confront their pains, problems, frustrations, and disappointments. Others take drugs simply because they like the effects or are curious about the effects.

### BACKGROUND ON DRUGS

Despite one's feelings about drug use, drugs are an integral part of society. Understanding the role of drugs in society is critical to our being able to address the problem of drugs. It is also helpful to place drugs in a historical context. Drugs have been used extensively throughout history. Alcohol's role in the early history of the United States was significant. According to

Lee (1963), the Pilgrims landed at Plymouth Rock because they ran out of beer. Marijuana use dates back nearly 5,000 years ago, when the Chinese emperor Shen Nung prescribed it for medical ailments like malaria, gout, rheumatism, and gas pains. Hallucinogens have existed since the beginning of humankind. About 150 of the estimated 500,000 different plant species have been used for hallucinogenic purposes (Schultes and Hofmann, 1979).

Opium, from which narcotics are derived, was alluded to often by the ancient Greeks and Romans; opium is referred to in Homer's *Odyssey* (circa 1000 B.C.). In the Arab world, opium and hashish were widely used (primarily because alcohol was forbidden). The Arabs were introduced to opium through their trading in India and China. Arab physician Avicenna (A.D. 1000) wrote an extremely complete medical textbook in which he describes the benefits of opium. Ironically, Avicenna died from an overdose of opium and wine. Eventually, opium played a central role in a war between China and the British government.

Caffeine is believed to be the most commonly consumed drug throughout the world. More than 9 out of every 10 Americans consume caffeine. Coffee dates back to A.D. 900 in Arabia, where, to stay awake during lengthy religious vigils, Muslims drank coffee. However, coffee was later condemned because the Koran, the holy book of Islam, described coffee as an intoxicant (Brecher, 1972). Drinking coffee became a popular activity in Europe, although it was banned for a short time. In the mid-1600s, coffeehouses were primary locations where men would converse, relax, and do business. Medical benefits were associated with coffee, although England's King Charles II and English physicians tried to prohibit its use.

One function of coffeehouses was that they served as places of learning: For a one-cent cup of coffee, one could listen to well-known literary and political leaders (Meyer, 1954). Lloyd's of London, the famous insurance company, started around 1700 from Edward Lloyd's coffeehouse. However, not everyone was pleased with these "penny universities," as they were called. In 1674, in response to the countless hours men were spending at the coffeehouses, a group of women published a pamphlet titled *The Women's Petition Against Coffee*, which criticized coffee use. Despite the protestations against coffee, its use has proliferated. Now, over 300 years later, the adverse effects of caffeine are still being debated.

Coca leaves, from which cocaine is derived, had been chewed before recorded history. Drawings found on South American pottery showed that coca chewing was practiced before the rise of the Incan Empire. The coca plant was held in high regard: It was considered to be a present from the gods, and it was used in religious rituals and burials. When the Spaniards arrived in South America, they tried to regulate coca chewing by the natives but were unsuccessful. Cocaine was later included in the popular soft drink Coca Cola. Another stimulant, amphetamine, was developed in the 1920s. Amphetamines were originally used to treat narcolepsy, and they were later prescribed for treating asthma and for weight loss.

Minor tranquilizers, also called "antianxiety agents," were first marketed in the early 1950s. The sales of these drugs were astronomical. Drugs to reduce anxiety were in great demand, principally because people felt they were under much stress. Are people's lives much different today than they were 40 years ago? Another group of antianxiety agents are benzodiazepines. Two well-known benzodiazepines are Librium and Valium. Valium ranks as the most widely prescribed drug in the history of American medicine. Minor tranquilizers are noteworthy because they are legally prescribed to alter one's consciousness. There were mind-altering drugs prior to minor tranquilizers, but they were not prescribed for that purpose.

## COMBATING DRUG PROBLEMS

The debates in *Taking Sides: Clashing Views on Controversial Issues in Drugs and Society* confront many important drug-related issues. It is an understatement to say that drugs are a problem in society; recognizing the problem is essential. However, what is the most effective way to reduce drug abuse? Should laws preventing drug use and abuse be more strongly enforced, or should drug laws be less punitive? How can the needs of individuals be met while serving the greater good of society? Should drug use be seen as a public health problem or a legal problem? This debate is addressed in Issue 5. One could argue that the individual is best served by a public health approach and that society benefits most from a legal approach.

One of the oldest debates concerns whether or not drug use should be legal. Issue 1 deals with this question. In recent years this debate has become more intense because well-known individuals such as political analyst William F. Buckley, Jr., and economist Milton Friedman have come out in support of legalization. The issue is not whether drug use is good or bad but whether or not people should be punished for taking drugs. One question that is basic to this debate is whether drug legalization causes more or less harm than drug criminalization. A related issue concerns needle exchange programs, in which clean needles are provided to individuals who inject themselves with drugs (Issue 6). There are obvious inherent dangers to injecting drugs; yet, does the provision of sterile needles help these people? Should people be given equipment that is used for an illegal act? What has been the effect of needle exchange programs in cities in which they have been instituted?

In a related matter, if drugs have the potential for abuse, should they be restricted even for medical purposes? There is concern that drugs that are used for medical reasons may be illegally diverted. Yet, most agree that patients should have access to the best medicine available. Is the federal government consistent in allowing drugs to be used that are potentially harmful? For example, narcotics are often prescribed for pain relief. Is there a chance that patients who are given narcotics will become addicted? The debate regarding whether or not marijuana has a legitimate medical use is the focus of Issue 2.

Many of the issues discussed in this book deal with drug prevention. As with most controversial issues, there is a lack of consensus regarding how to prevent drug-related problems. For example, Issue 7 debates whether or not prosecuting women who use drugs during pregnancy will affect drug use by other women who become pregnant. Many drugs damage the fetus; will prosecuting pregnant women who use drugs help prevent others from using drugs during pregnancy? Will pregnant women who do use drugs avoid prenatal care because they fear prosecution? Will newborns be better served if pregnant women who use drugs are charged with child abuse? Are these laws discriminatory, since most cases that are prosecuted involve poor women?

Some contend that drug laws not only discriminate according to social class but also according to age and ethnicity. Many drug laws in the United States were initiated because of their association with different ethnic groups. Numerous stories were circulated throughout the country describing the effects of drugs on various ethnic groups: Opium was made illegal after it was associated with Chinese immigrants (Musto, 1991); cocaine became illegal after it was linked with blacks; and marijuana was outlawed after it was linked with Hispanics.

Besides ethnicity, drug laws demonstrate an age bias also. This is no more evident than with alcohol. One assumption is that young people gain wisdom and maturity as they get older, which is why alcohol consumption is prevented until age 21—to reduce problems with alcohol. The value of maintaining 21 as the legal age for drinking alcohol is discussed in Issue 4.

Some maintain that educating young people about drugs is one way to prevent drug use and abuse. Studies show that by delaying the onset of drug use, the likelihood of drug abuse is reduced. In the past, however, drug education had little impact on drug-taking behavior. Some programs actually resulted in an increase in drug use because they stimulated curiosity. Does this suggest that drug education is worse than no education or that more effective programs need to be developed? Issue 11 focuses on current drug education programs and their effectiveness as vehicles for deterring drug abuse.

One of the problems with drug education is identifying the goals to be achieved. Should drug education stress preventing drug use? Drug abuse? Should drug education strive to stop individuals from harming themselves or from harming society? Should responsible drug use be the goal? Should the emphasis be on altering attitudes or behaviors? It is clear that drug education imparts knowledge, and if one has knowledge about the potential effects of drugs, then the consequences of their use may be minimized. Issues 9 and 17 discuss the potential physical effects of caffeine and anabolic steroids, respectively.

## DRUG TREATMENT

Besides addressing the legal aspects of drug use and the effectiveness of drug prevention efforts, this book looks at several treatment issues. Despite a sagging economy, one growing industry is drug treatment. Drug treatment is expensive, and consumers need to be aware of the different modalities. However, before deciding on the best course of treatment action to take, the causes of drug abuse need to be determined. Issue 15 examines whether drug addiction stems from personality traits that may be inherited or from weaknesses in one's character. The latter would portend that addiction is a matter of free will. The answer to this question has many legal ramifications.

One of the few areas that drug experts agree on is that alcoholism is a serious problem. There are an estimated 10 million alcoholics in the United States. Treatment experts, however, disagree in terms of the most effective approach for treating alcoholism. Traditionally, alcoholics have been told not to drink for the remainder of their lives, that there is no cure for their condition, and that recovery is a lifelong process. Issue 16 carefully scrutinizes the need for alcoholics to be permanently abstinent. Tied into this debate is the origin of alcoholism. The theories that alcoholism can be hereditary or a disease are discussed in Issues 10 and 13, respectively.

## DISTINGUISHING BETWEEN DRUG USE, MISUSE, AND ABUSE

Although the terms *drug, drug misuse,* and *drug abuse* are commonly used, they may have different meanings to different people. Defining these terms may seem simple at first, but many factors affect how they are defined. Should the definition of a drug be based on its behavioral effects, its effects on society, its pharmacological properties, or its chemical composition? One simple, concise definition is that a drug is any substance that produces an effect on the mind, body, or both. One could also define a drug by how it is used. For example, if watching television or listening to music are forms of escape from daily problems, then they may be considered drugs.

Legal drugs cause far more death and disability than illegal drugs, but society appears to be most concerned with the use of illegal drugs. The potential harms of legal drugs tend to be minimized. By viewing drugs as illicit substances only, we may fail to recognize that commonly used substances like caffeine, tobacco, alcohol, and over-the-counter preparations are drugs. If these substances are not perceived as drugs, then we may not acknowledge that they can be misused or abused. Definitions for misuse and abuse are not affected by a drug's legal status. Drug misuse refers to the inappropriate or unintentional use of drugs. Someone who smokes marijuana to improve his or her study skills is misusing marijuana because it impairs short-term memory. Drug abuse alludes to either physical, emotional, financial, intellectual, or social consequences arising from chronic drug use. Using this definition, can a person abuse food, aspirin, soft drinks, or chocolate?

## THE COST OF THE WAR ON DRUGS

The U.S. government spends more than $10 billion each year to curb the rise in drug use (Herman, 1991). The major portion of that money goes toward drug enforcement. Vast sums of money are used by the military to intercept drug shipments, while foreign governments are given money to help them with their own wars on drugs. A smaller portion of the funds is used for treating and preventing drug abuse. One strategy being implemented to eliminate drug use is drug testing. Currently, men and women in the military, athletes, and others are subject to random drug testing.

The expense of drug abuse to industries is staggering: Experts estimate that almost 20 percent of workers in the United States use dangerous drugs while at work; the cost of drug abuse to employers is approximately $120 billion each year (Brookler, 1992); as compared to nonaddicted employees, drug-dependent employees are absent from their jobs 16 times as often (Wrich, 1986); and drugs users are less likely to maintain stable job histories than nonusers (Kandel, Murphy, and Kraus, 1985). In its report "America's Habit: Drug Abuse, Drug Trafficking and Organized Crime," the President's Commission on Organized Crime supported testing all federal workers for drugs. It further recommended that federal contracts be withheld from private employers who do not implement drug-testing procedures (Brinkley, 1986).

A prerequisite to being hired by many companies is passing a drug test. On the positive side, many companies have reported a decrease in accidents and injuries after the initiation of drug testing (Angarola, 1991). However, most Americans consider drug testing to be degrading and dehumanizing (Walsh and Trumble, 1991). One important question is, What is the purpose of drug testing? Drug testing raises three other important questions: (1) Does drug testing prevent drug use? (2) Is the point of drug testing to help employees with drug problems or to get rid of employees who use drugs? and (3) How can the civil rights of employees be balanced with the rights of companies? These and other questions are addressed in Issue 3.

How serious is the drug problem? Is it real, or is there simply an excess of hysteria regarding drugs? There has been a growing intolerance toward drug use in the United States during the last 20 years (Musto, 1991). Drugs are a problem for many people. Drugs can affect one's physical, social, intellectual, and emotional health. Ironically, some people take drugs because they produce these effects. Individuals who take drugs receive some kind of reward from the drug; the reward may come from being associated with others who use drugs or from the feelings derived from the drug. If these rewards were not present, people would likely cease using drugs.

The disadvantages of drugs are numerous: They interfere with career aspirations and individual maturation, and they have been associated with violent behavior, addiction, discord among siblings, children, parents, spouses and friends, work-related problems, financial troubles, problems in school, legal predicaments, accidents, injuries, and death. Yet, are drugs the cause or the symptom of the problems people have? Perhaps drugs are one aspect of a larger scenario in which society is experiencing much change and in which drug use is merely another thread in the social fabric.

## GATEWAY DRUGS

A type of drug that is popular with many young people is inhalants. Like tobacco and alcohol, inhalants are considered to be "gateway drugs," which are often used as a prelude to other, usually illegal, drugs. Inhalants are comprised of numerous products, ranging from paints and solvents to aerosol sprays, glues, petroleum products, cleaning supplies, and nitrous oxide (laughing gas). Inhalant abuse is a relatively new phenomenon. It seems that until the media started reporting on the dangers of inhalant abuse, its use was not particularly common. This raises a question regarding the impact of the media on drug use.

Advertisements are an integral part of the media. Two issues in this book deal with the advertising of alcohol and tobacco. Issue 12 addresses whether or not there should be limits on tobacco advertisements, while Issue 14 discusses alcohol advertising. One argument is that if young people were better educated about the hazards of drugs and were taught how to understand the role of the media, then limits on advertising would not be necessary.

One final issue that is currently under debate concerns the potential effects that tobacco smoke may have on nonsmokers. In the 1880s, cigarette use began to escalate in the United States. One of the most important factors contributing to cigarettes' popularity at that time was the development of the cigarette-making machine (previously, cigarettes could be rolled at a rate of only four per minute). Also, cigarette smoking, which was considered an activity reserved for men, began to be seen as an option for women. By marketing cigarettes for women, cigarette smoking became more widespread. Today, the debate regarding the hazards of tobacco to the smoker is moot. The current debate focuses on whether or not passive smoking, also called "involuntary smoking" and which involves the release of "environmental tobacco smoke," is harmful to nonsmokers. This is discussed in Issue 8.

## REFERENCES

R. T. Angarola, "Substance-Abuse Testing in the Workplace: Legal Issues and Corporate Responses," in R. H. Coombs and L. J. West, eds., *Drug Testing: Issues and Options* (Oxford University Press, 1991).

E. M. Brecher, *Licit and Illicit Drugs* (Little, Brown, 1972).

J. Brinkley, "Drug Use Held Mostly Stable or Better," *The New York Times* (October 10, 1986).

R. Brookler, "Industry Standards in Workplace Drug Testing," *Personnel Journal* (April 1991), pp. 128–132.

E. S. Herman, "Drug 'Wars': Appearance and Reality," *Social Justice* (vol. 18, no. 4, 1991), pp. 76–84.

D. B. Kandel, D. Murphy, and D. Kraus, "Cocaine Use in Young Adulthood: Patterns of Use and Psychosocial Correlates," in N. J. Kozel and E. H. Adams, eds., *Cocaine Use in America: Epidemiologic and Clinical Perspectives* (National Institute on Drug Abuse, 1985).

H. Lee, *How Dry We Were: Prohibition Revisited* (Prentice Hall, 1963).

H. Meyer, *Old English Coffee Houses* (Rodale Press, 1954).

D. F. Musto, "Opium, Cocaine and Marijuana in American History," *Scientific American* (July 1991), pp. 40–47.

R. E. Schultes and A. Hofmann, *Plants of the Gods: Origins of Hallucinogenic Use* (McGraw-Hill, 1979).

J. M. Walsh and J. G. Trumble, "The Politics of Drug Testing," in R. H. Coombs and L. J. West, eds., *Drug Testing: Issues and Options* (Oxford University Press, 1991).

J. T. Wrich, "Some National Statistics: The Impact of Substance Abuse at the Workplace," in H. Axel, ed., *Corporate Strategies for Controlling Substance Abuse* (Conference Board, 1986).

# PART 1

## Drugs and Public Policy

*Most people recognize that drugs are a problem in society: The psychological and physical effects on drug use can be devastating; drugs can be addictive, and they can disrupt families; disability and death are caused by drug overdoses; and drugs are often implicated in crimes, especially violent crimes. Identifying drug-related problems is not difficult. What is unclear is the best course of action to take in dealing with these problems.*

*Three scenarios exist for dealing with drugs: Policies can be made more restrictive, less restrictive, or remain the same. The position taken depends on whether drug use is seen as a legal, social, or medical problem. The issue is not whether drugs are good or bad but how to minimize the harm of drugs. These questions are discussed in the following debates.*

Should Drugs Be Legalized?

Should Medical Patients Be Permitted to Use Marijuana?

Does Drug Testing Violate Civil Rights?

Should the Drinking Age Remain at 21?

Is the War on Drugs Misdirected?

Should Needle Exchange Programs Be Promoted?

Should Drug Use by Pregnant Women Be Considered Child Abuse?

# ISSUE 1

# Should Drugs Be Legalized?

**YES: Ethan A. Nadelmann,** from "America's Drug Problem: A Case for Decriminalization," *Bulletin of the American Academy of Arts and Sciences* (December 1991)

**NO: James Q. Wilson,** from "Against the Legalization of Drugs," *Commentary* (February 1990)

## ISSUE SUMMARY

**YES:** Professor Ethan A. Nadelmann supports drug legalization in America because he feels that current drug control policies are costly and ineffective in combating drug problems. He argues that more emphasis should be put on drug education, prevention, and treatment instead of on drug prohibition.
**NO:** Criminologist James Q. Wilson argues that legalizing drugs is fundamentally unprincipled and inappropriate. He feels that legalization would increase drug use and addiction, decrease the positive effects of drug treatment and drug education, and pose great risks to society.

The war on drugs pervades every level of society. Every year, the U.S. government spends vast sums of money to control drug use and to enforce laws enacted to protect society from the dangers caused by drug use. Some people believe that the war on drugs has been effective, but they contend that government agencies and communities are not fighting hard enough to stop drug use and that laws are too few and too lenient. Others argue that a fight against drugs is not needed—that society has already lost the war on drugs and the only way to remedy the problem is to end the fighting altogether by ending the criminalization of drug use.

Many conflicting views exist on whether or not legislation has had the intended result of reducing the problems of drug use. Many argue that legislation and the criminalization of drugs have been counterproductive in controlling drug problems. Some suggest that the criminalization of drugs has actually contributed to and worsened the social ills associated with drugs. Proponents of drug legalization argue that the war on drugs, not drugs themselves, is damaging to American society.

Proponents of drug legalization argue that the strict enforcement of drug laws damages American society because it drives people to violence and crime, creates corrupt law enforcement officials, and overburdens the court system, thus rendering it ineffective. They also contend that the criminalization of drugs fuels organized crime, allows children to be pulled into the drug business, and makes illegal drugs themselves more dangerous because they are manufactured without government standards or regulations. Hence, drugs may be adulterated or of unidentified potency. Legalization advocates also argue that legalization would take the profits out of drug sales, thereby decreasing the value and demand of drugs.

In addition to the tangible costs, some legalization advocates argue that drug prohibition on the part of the federal government is an immoral and impossible objective. To achieve a "drug-free society" is self-defeating and a misnomer because drugs have always been a part of human culture. In addition, prohibiting drug use is unprincipled and amoral: Prohibition efforts indicate a disregard for the private freedom of individuals because they are employed under the assumption that individuals are unable to make their own choices.

People who favor legalizing drugs feel that legalization would give the government more control over the purity and potency of drugs and that it would allow the international drug trade to be regulated more effectively. Legalization, they argue, would also take the emphasis off of law enforcement and allow more effort to be put toward education, prevention, and treatment. Advocates for decriminalization assert that most of the negative implications of drug prohibition would disappear.

Opponents of this view maintain that legalization is not the solution to the drug problem and that it is a very dangerous idea. Legalization, they argue, will drastically increase drug use. They contend that if drugs are more accessible, more people will turn to drugs, and this upsurge in drug use will come at an incredibly high price: American society will be overrun with drug-related accidents, loss in worker productivity, and hospital emergency rooms filled with drug-related emergencies; drug treatment efforts would be futile since users would have no legal incentive to stop taking drugs; users may prefer drugs rather than rehabilitation; and education programs may be ineffective in dissuading children from using drugs. The feeling is that despite their potential health risks, drug use would be allowed by law, and that would have a bigger impact than education. Legalization opponents argue that regulations to control drug use have a legitimate social aim to protect society and its citizens from the harm of drugs. Maintaining criminalization is not immoral, nor is it a violation of personal freedom; rather, criminalization allows a standard of control to be established in order to preserve human character and society as a whole.

In the following selections, Ethan A. Nadelmann explains what he sees as the benefits of legalizing drugs, while James Q. Wilson warns of the dangers to society that would result from such a move.

# YES

Ethan A. Nadelmann

## AMERICA'S DRUG PROBLEM: A CASE FOR DECRIMINALIZATION

Legalization of drugs, or decriminalization, means different things to different people. For some it means taking the crime or the money out of the drug business. For others it has become a rallying cry, in much the same way that "repeal prohibition" was sixty years ago—one that brings together people from across the political spectrum, with very different views about what is wrong with our current policy of drug prohibition, and very different notions about what should replace it. Consider the wide range of prominent individuals who have expressed support for legalization. On the one hand are conservatives such as Milton Friedman, George Shultz, William F. Buckley, Gary Becker, and others associated with the Chicago school of law and economics, as well as the editorial boards of the *Economist* and many other conservative newspapers in Europe. On the other hand are Democrats and liberals such as Ira Glasser of the American Civil Liberties Union, as well as a number of leading black politicians—Kurt Schmoke, the mayor of Baltimore; Carrie Saxon Perry, the mayor of Hartford, Connecticut; and state legislative figures from New York, Missouri, Pennsylvania, and elsewhere—even one Congressman who dared to say the word *decriminalization* shortly before he retired—George Crockett of Michigan, a former judge. In this nation, so intensely divided on the issue, it is significant that the few politicians willing to take the brave step of proposing decriminalization have been African Americans. But this alternative is also supported by people in medicine, law, law enforcement, and education; by older people and younger people. The notion has a much broader base of support across America than might be supposed.

Legalization also implies something else. It means evaluating our current drug-prohibition policies in terms of their costs and benefits, and comparing them on this basis with the wide array of what could be called drug-legalization policies. I must stress that these alternatives are best understood not as polar opposites but as a variety of points across a spectrum, with the most prohibitionist policies at one extreme and the most libertarian ones at

From Ethan A. Nadelmann, "America's Drug Problem: A Case for Decriminalization," *Bulletin of the American Academy of Arts and Sciences* (December 1991). Copyright © 1991 by The American Academy of Arts and Sciences. Reprinted by permission.

the other. If we use the word *legalization* in this sense, then we can begin to appreciate which policy leads to the best mix of costs and benefits.

The conclusion I come to is that when such an analysis is done, the best policy looks more like something called legalization or decriminalization than like something called prohibition. The trouble with calling it legalization is that the model itself often looks libertarian, and hence there is a tendency on the part of some to conclude that what is being advocated is a libertarian alternative. The libertarian model is in fact a fascinating one, in that it poses interesting and difficult questions about the vulnerability of a society to a free market in psychoactive drugs, as well as about the basic need for drug control. But it is not, in the end, the policy solution advocated by most of those who support legalization or decriminalization.

Legalization also has a much more moderate meaning—the one that political figures often use. Let me quote Mayor Schmoke. He said, "If we're going to have a war against drugs, it shouldn't be headed by the attorney general; it should be headed by the surgeon general." I am largely in agreement with that. This is an area of public policy in need of government intervention, as well as other forms of intervention. The question is, Which forms of intervention should be taken? Look, for instance, at what we are doing to reduce cigarette consumption, and how we could be doing much more. Or look at what other nations have done with their alcohol policies. If only we could turn the notion of a public health approach into a verb, "to public-health-ify" drug policy, maybe we would have a more acceptable, if less catchy, label for what many mean by legalization.

Before proceeding with the analysis of costs and benefits, we need to begin by asking a question that is rarely asked: what is the objective of U.S. drug policy? I would argue that the mainstream objective, the government's objective, the objective to which most people will instinctively relate, is that of creating a "drug-free society." That rhetoric has come to dominate the formulation of policy. But what is a drug-free society? In one sense the notion, if you take it literally, is ludicrous. No society in civilized human history has not used psychoactive drugs in one form or another. Some people say there is one possible exception—the Eskimos because they could not grow anything. Otherwise, every society has used drugs for a variety of reasons: ritual, religious, recreational, and medicinal. When people talk about a drug-free society, they do not really mean a society without psychoactive drug use, because current U.S. policy is not typically aimed at alcohol, tobacco, or caffeine, all of which are psychoactive substances. The objective really seems to be to prohibit the use of restricted psychoactive substances without the authorization of a doctor, irrespective of whether or not that use causes any harm. I would argue that this is the wrong objective—one that is ludicrous, ahistorical, misguided, and even dangerous.

U.S. drug policy should have two objectives. First, it should aim to reduce the extent of drug abuse in American society. Note that I did not specify illegal drug abuse, because I think we need to be concerned as well about legal drug abuse involving alcohol and tobacco. These drugs kill far more people than illegal drugs do, and this has more to do with the nature of these products than with the fact that they are legal. Note also that I said abuse, not use. As far as I am concerned, the use of psychoactive substances per se is not a problem. The second objective is equally important: we need to minimize the negative consequences of drug-control policies.

The only way to explain the divergence between the government's policy objectives and those I propose is by reference to fundamentally different moral notions about drug use and drug policy.

What are the moral notions underlying the ideal of a drug-free society and the drug-prohibition model? One notion is that drug use—better still, the use of prohibited drugs—is immoral. Another is that addiction itself is fundamentally immoral. These are key assumptions underlying the current U.S. drug policy, and I do not agree with them. Now, I am not arguing that addiction is good, but I am suggesting that addiction is an inevitable fact of life—one that well describes how many human beings relate not just to illicit drugs or alcohol and tobacco but also to coffee, food, work, exercise, money, and one another. To call it immoral because it happens to be associated with certain substances is wrong.

What moral assumptions do I make? When you analyze the costs and benefits of our current drug policy and consider which mix of costs and benefits represents the optimal policy, you cannot get away from some very basic value claims. One has to do with the notion that individuals, or at least adults, ought to be able to make their own choices—even stupid choices. The private sovereignty of individuals ought to be respected, not just for utilitarian reasons but for its own sake. I take it that this value is, in and of itself, a moral good. It is not an absolute good; it is not something to which all policy must defer. But when you add up the costs and benefits of competing policies, this value needs to be considered.

Reducing criminal-justice controls, which is what legalization and decriminalization are all about, requires us to rely on other forms of control. It means moving along the continuum of policy options, away from the more severe drug-prohibition policies we now follow—but it does not mean going to the opposite extreme. We need to deemphasize the reliance on criminal-justice approaches while trying to change the conditions that lead people to abuse drugs. We need to shift resources away from prohibition efforts and toward other programs, including some that are directed not specifically at drug abuse but rather at the conditions that spawn drug abuse.

We know that removing criminal-justice controls—that is, implementing a policy of legalization—will mean three things: the price of drugs will go down, the availability of drugs will go up, and the deterrent power of criminal sanctions will be diminished. All three of these results suggest negative developments in terms of drug use and abuse. However, for a number of reasons, I would argue that legalization is advisable, that it can be implemented in a controlled fashion, and that we need to consider taking these risks, none of which are as great as many people fear.

In terms of a criminal-justice approach to the drug problem, everything we have done in the past, are doing now, and are talking about doing in the future is inherently limited in its effectiveness against the fundamental problem of drug abuse. This is especially true in a country like the United States, which has certain legal and other societal values and principles that keep us from going to extremes in law enforcement. That is the first reason for trying legalization, but it is the least important.

More important is the fact that most of what people identify as components of the drug problem are actually the results of drug-prohibition policies. Most people tend not to recognize this causal relationship. We tend to talk about the drug problem as one great big hodgepodge of drug-related problems without distinguishing between those associated with the misuse of drugs and those that stem from prohibition. By contrast, Americans sixty years ago were highly cognizant of this distinction. They knew that the irresponsible consumption of alcohol was to blame for a host of society's ills—which was why they had imposed prohibition in the first place. But then they began to distinguish these from other problems: organized crime; rising levels of violence and corruption in urban areas; tens of millions of people being labeled criminals for their involvement in the business of alcohol; police being killed; bootleggers becoming role models for children and taking over towns and cities; and tens, if not hundreds, of thousands of people being blinded, poisoned, and killed by bad bootleg liquor. Alcohol was more dangerous than ever, precisely because it was illegally produced and unregulated. At some point Americans, for a great variety of reasons, said enough is enough and turned away from prohibition. The analogy with today's drug problem is totally apropos. We need to make the distinction between problems of drug abuse and those that result from drug prohibition.

First, however, it is necessary to identify the five principal components of America's prohibition policy and to assess their potential for solving our drug-related problems. These components are (1) international drug control (that is, the suppression of drug production overseas); (2) interdiction efforts; (3) domestic drug enforcement directed at major drug dealers; (4) domestic drug enforcement directed at street-level dealers; and (5) drug testing.

*International control efforts.* The drugs in question are grown virtually everywhere. Opiates and marijuana can be grown almost anywhere in the world, and coca can be grown in a far broader area of Latin America and other parts of the world than is currently the case. As a result, we have what is called the push-down/pop-up effect. We pushed down on heroin coming out of Turkey in the early seventies, and it popped up in Mexico. We pushed down on it in Mexico, and it popped up in Southeast Asia. We pushed down on it there, and it popped up in Southwest Asia. We've pushed down in so many places that it's popped up everywhere. The United States is now a multiple-source heroin-importing country. If there is demand, there will be supply.

These drugs are so cheap that even when we do all sorts of things overseas to raise the cost of production, we have no impact on consumer prices in the United States. This is because the export price of drugs from Latin America and Asia is only a small fraction (1, 3, or 4 percent) of the final street price in the United States.

The drug-exporting business brings in good money overseas—billions of dollars each year—much of which trickles down to hundreds of thousands of peasants and other poor people. Not entirely in jest, somebody once said that the current American drug policy, with its combination of prohibition and ineffectual enforcement measures, is probably the best means ever devised for exporting the capitalistic ethic to potentially revolutionary third-world producers. One negative consequence of legalization might be that production would largely be controlled by big producers, as opposed to being a business for hundreds of thousands of small producers.

And of course, not everyone shares the same moral perspective on the drug traffic. U.S. officials go to these producers overseas and say, "Don't you see what you are doing? You are producing these drugs that are killing Americans. Don't you see how immoral this is?" And what the producers say is, "Let me tell you what my moral obligation is. My moral obligation is not to keep some stupid gringo from shoving white powder up his nose or sticking a needle into his arm. My moral obligation is to do the best I can for myself, my family, and my community. If it means growing these products, then so be it. That is what I am going to do. And meanwhile, you North Americans, who are you to speak of moral obligations, when your special trade representatives fly around Asia and the Third World, pushing down barriers to your tobacco exports?" When all is said and done, the whole notion of international control has no effectiveness as a drug-control device, no matter how much the politicians may insist otherwise.

*Interdiction.* The use of the military, the Air Force, the Coast Guard, the Navy, Customs, AWACS (the Air Force's airborne warning and control system), satellites, and radar satellite balloons to try to keep drugs from coming into the United States is not working. Trying to catch the six to ten tons of heroin and the hundred or two hundred tons of cocaine coming into this country during each of the last few years makes looking for a needle in a haystack seem like child's play. If there were a market for a hundred tons of heroin in the United States instead of six to ten tons, a hundred tons would come in. Interdiction efforts cannot keep that from happening.

Having said this, let me acknowledge that interdiction has worked to some extent with respect to marijuana. We have reduced the amount of foreign marijuana coming into the United States. And what has happened? One consequence is that marijuana trafficking has been replaced by cocaine trafficking. Marijuana is bulky; cocaine is compact. Another consequence of our interdiction efforts vis-à-vis marijuana is that the United States has now emerged as perhaps the number-one producer of marijuana in the world.

*Domestic law enforcement.* Can efforts at apprehending major drug dealers make a difference? As long as the laws are what they are, we should invest our law-enforcement resources in going after the most egregious violators of the drug laws. When we seize their assets, we should use them to help pay for drug-abuse prevention programs. But can this effort make any difference in the availability of drugs or in the fundamental drug-abuse problems we have in this country? The answer is no. Because every time you arrest number one, number two is going to step into his shoes, and every time you get number two, number three is going to step into his shoes. Ask any law enforcement officer. I personally think that the Colombian government should be extraditing those miserable human beings who are shipping drugs and killing people. But will it make any difference? Once again, no. In fact, in the case of Colombia, if you buy the cartel theory of cocaine exports (that is, that a small number of people control the supply to the United States), and if you arrest the heads of the cartel, you will have even more cocaine coming into the United States because there would be no controls. So arresting high-level drug traffickers is not the answer.

What about going after street-level drug dealers and users? That was big in the sixties and has now become big again in the late eighties and early nineties. Consider the intensive law-enforcement operations such as Pressure Point and Clean Sweep. We are arresting thousands and thousands of drug users and dealers, running them through the criminal justice system, increasingly incarcerating them, and keeping them in prison for longer periods of time. Some evidence suggests that this may work in certain small neighborhoods, but can it make a difference in large cities? The answer is no, because of the same phenomenon you have internationally—the push-down/pop-up effect. You push down on drug dealing in Washington Square in New York City, it pops up in the alphabet streets. In Washington, D.C., you push down on dealing at one street corner, and it pops up on another. Some users, they say, will not go the extra blocks to get drugs, but most do. So street-level law enforcement is not making the drugs less accessible. Rather, it is opening up vast job opportunities for new generations of young people, often young black and Latino men in the inner cities. Some of them are individuals who might not otherwise have pursued lives of crime but who unfortunately have few other economic opportunities.

*Drug testing.* Evidence suggests that drug testing could be the wave of the future. More and more companies are doing it. The government is pushing it. There are judges who say it is constitutional. Presumably, there are limits as to how far this effort can be pursued. But to some extent it does seem to be working. My guess is that if I were to tell my Princeton students that they could not graduate unless they passed a periodic urine test, most of the very few who use illicit drugs would stop.

In ten years or so a nearly perfect drug-testing system may be technologically feasible. Would this go very far toward eliminating drug abuse in the United States? I think the answer is yes. Do I think we should do drug testing? The answer is no. Why? I come back to the issue of values and to the question of how far government and employers should go in policing the lives of citizens and employees. Where do we draw the line on the slippery slope of drug testing? We begin, presumably, with illicit drugs, but it can be shown that higher rates of absenteeism are associated with cigarette smoking. Why not test for cigarettes, and then alcohol, because alcohol is dangerous too? Indeed, if the ultimate objective is to enhance the productivity of Americans in the workplace or, better still, to maximize the length of time that they live, then there is no sensible point at which to stop such testing. It all becomes oriented toward more and more powerful forms of social control, justified by very simple, and seemingly defensible, objectives. I do not think we should be sliding down this slippery slope—but for moral reasons, not strictly on grounds of public policy.

My ANALYSIS OF THE CURRENT CRIMINAL-justice approach to the drug problem in this country is that some of these efforts work to some extent. They deter some people, keep the price of drugs high, and keep availability relatively low. But as law-enforcement authorities are the first to admit, this approach is not the only answer. Where I differ from those authorities is in insisting that we should rely less on the criminal-justice approach and much more on education, prevention, and treatment.

Now let's consider the direct and indirect costs of drug prohibition in the United States. Some of these costs can be calculated in tax dollars. The federal government spent $1 billion on drug enforcement in 1980 and about $8 billion in 1990. State and local governments spent between $3 and $4 billion in 1980; they may now be spending $10 billion. Nobody knows for sure.

Where the costs, measured in dollars and scarce resources, are most apparent is in such areas as the court system and prison operations. Prisons are a very easy place to get a handle on the issue because we have solid figures. Last year the United States had over one million people behind bars in federal and state prisons and local jails, and another two-and-a-half million under other forms of criminal-justice supervision. That figure is double what it was ten years ago, almost triple what it was fifteen years ago. It is the highest percentage of the American population to be incarcerated in American history. It is the highest percentage of the population of any democratic nation to be incarcerated in human history. And it is not cheap. Prison cells cost anywhere from $12,000 to $52,000 per person, per year. In many states, building and maintaining prisons is the fastest-growing item in the budget. A large portion of this has to do with drug-law violations. In virtually every major state in the country, over 20 per-

cent of the people sentenced to prison last year had violated drug laws. In Florida in 1980, 785 people were sentenced for violating drug laws; in 1989 the number was 15,000. The figures in California were 1,063 in 1980 and 10,445 in 1988. In New York the figures are much the same. That is a ten-fold, in some cases fifteen-fold, increase in the number of people sent to prison for violating drug laws. These violators now represent between 30 and 45 percent of all the people being sent to prisons in the major states. They represent well over 50 percent of the federal prison population. Yet studies uniformly show that those incarcerated for drug-law violations are less likely than other inmates to have a prior history of violating the law and are less likely to be involved in violent behavior. These people may not be model citizens, but should we send them to prison?

Among the indirect costs of prohibition are the tremendous benefits derived by organized crime. The President's Commission on Organized Crime estimated that half of all organized crime revenue comes from drug dealing. Why? Because drug prohibition is the greatest boondoggle that organized crime has ever seen—far better than alcohol prohibition. Drug prohibition in effect imposes a de facto value-added tax on the sale of drugs, enforced by the government and collected by the criminals. Take it away and organized crime may get into other kinds of activity, but nothing will replace this source of revenue.

Now let's consider the five connections between drugs and crime. First, on billions of occasions each year, people buy, sell, and consume drugs in violation of the law. This drug-crime connection is the essence of drug prohibition, and it is responsible for other connections between drugs and crime. Second, criminals and drug abuse tend to go together. In many respects it is impossible to point out the causal relationship, but in most societies, historically, there have been higher levels of drug abuse among criminals than among noncriminals. Third, we have the problem of drug addiction "causing" crimes such as robbery, theft, and burglary. Two or three years ago the surgeon general of the United States pointed out that nicotine was as addictive as, if not more addictive than, cocaine or heroin. How many of you have ever worried about being mugged by a nicotine addict? Very few, I would guess. Why? Because cigarettes are cheap—too cheap, as far as I'm concerned. We could raise the price considerably without having to worry about nicotine-related crime. Both cigarettes and alcohol are addictive, but people can maintain those habits for only a few dollars a day. Heroin and cocaine habits cost fifty to two hundred dollars a day. Why? Do heroin and cocaine cost any more to produce than alcohol or cigarettes? No. But prohibition inflates their prices dramatically. Even if these drugs were legalized and heavily taxed, prices would be lower than they are now, and the need for addicts to steal to support their habits would be much reduced.

Fourth, there is the notion that drugs make people violent. Paul Goldstein did a study of drug-related homicides in New York. He tried to determine what the relationship was between drug use and violence, and found that only a small percentage of homicides, under 10 percent, could be called psychopharmacologically related. Most of the homicides resulted from the fifth connection between drugs and crime—what he called the "systemic" sources of drug-related violence. Most drug-related killings—whether they involve drug dealers killing one another or killing cops or killing innocent people or killing witnesses or killing children in crossfire—are associated with drug prohibition. In Colombia this drug-crime connection virtually defines the drug problem. Why? One reason is that people tempted into drug dealing often are violently inclined. Another reason is that drug dealers need to protect their turf and resolve disputes, and they do so with violence. If we were to criminalize alcohol again, we would have the same alcohol-associated violence we had during prohibition. If we were to criminalize cigarettes we would surely have immense violence. In fact, the criminalization of drugs is the chief source of drug-related violence, and it breeds all sorts of other problems.

In the inner city, drug dealers—not teachers, lawyers, or politicians—are often the role models for kids. The drug dealers have the money, the lovers, the nice cars. At the same time, the drug-prohibition system creates strong incentives for kids to get involved in drug dealing. When New York and other states imposed draconian penalties for selling crack a few years ago, they might just as well have called them measures for improving child employment in the illegal drug trade. Why? Because toughening penalties for adults inevitably pulls children into the business.

The foregoing are the costs that are conventionally associated with drug prohibition. But there is another, quite severe one: drugs are more dangerous when they are illegal. Heroin won't kill you. You might get addicted to it, but you can live a long life as a heroin addict. It doesn't destroy the internal organs. It doesn't do what cocaine does to your body or what alcohol does to your liver or what cigarettes do to your lungs. So why do people "overdose" on illegal drugs? The simple reason is that illegal drugs are often adulterated, impure, and of unknown potency. Someone who thinks he is getting 4 percent heroin may actually be getting 40 percent. Or people buy what they think is heroin but is actually a more potent synthetic opiate. Imagine buying wine without knowing whether it is 8 percent alcohol or 80 percent alcohol or whether it is methyl or ethyl alcohol. Imagine taking an aspirin without knowing whether you are taking a dose of 5 milligrams or 500 milligrams. Life would be a little more dangerous. Fewer people would drink wine or take aspirin, but more of those who did would get sick or die.

What of needle-exchange programs, which are being implemented in Europe, Australia, Canada, and the United States? Basically, they involve setting up places where addicts can exchange their dirty needles for clean ones. While there, addicts may be given information about treatment or about how to use needles safely. We need to ask two basic questions about needle-exchange programs. The first is, Do these programs encourage more people to become intravenous drug users? So far the evidence indicates that the answer is no. The second is, Do these programs work? That is, do they help reduce the transmission of AIDS? Do they help lure people into treatment? The answer seems to be yes. Most addicts who participate in these programs change their injecting habits and reduce or stop their needle-sharing. Ready access to clean needles does make a positive difference. In Europe, accepting as a given that people will use and abuse

drugs and trying to reduce the negative consequences is associated with something called the harm-reduction philosophy. In America, we hear a tremendous outcry that needle-exchange programs are wrong and immoral, and that they condone drug abuse. But it seems to me that the only message that the opponents of these programs are sending is, "If you're an intravenous drug user and you can't stop, then die—and before you die, put whoever you have sex with or share needles with at risk of AIDS." Even prominent public officials have equated AIDS with drug addiction—forgetting that one is deadly and that the other, in most cases, is not.

In our country today we increasingly see an alliance between the people (largely public health officials) who are trying to introduce needle-exchange programs and what is probably the most politically powerless and disorganized constituency in America—the roughly one million intravenous drug users in the nation. On the other side of the issue we find an alliance that is somewhat more bizarre—that between those indifferent, sometimes callous, white middle-class people who say, "Let the drug users kill themselves," and certain members of the nation's black political leadership, who maintain that the operation of needle-exchange programs is the equivalent of genocide. As I see it, when Mayor Dinkins of New York City took office and obliged prominent black leaders in his city by canceling rather than expanding needle-exchange programs, he effectively signed a death warrant for thousands of people.

This leads me to what may be perhaps the most fundamental argument against drug prohibition. It is a moral one. First, the point has to be made that it is impossible to make any sort of legitimate, intellectually honest distinction between the morality of alcohol and tobacco use on the one hand and the morality or immorality of cocaine and opiate use on the other. What may be the morality of today was not the morality of the past. Go back in U.S. history to the turn of the century and slightly before, and alcohol was illegal in hundreds of towns and cities and a number of states—we were on the way toward a national prohibition of alcohol. Cigarettes were prohibited in a dozen states. Marijuana, however, was legal. Cocaine was legal. The opiates— opium, morphine, heroin—were legal, except for use by Chinese people in California. The drug-related morality of today and of the last few decades is just that—the drug-related morality of *today*. It is not the morality of the past, and it need not be the morality of the future.

Consider, as well, how drug laws are enforced. Prohibition makes drug dealing essentially a crime of vice. There is generally no victim who reports the crime to the authorities. Therefore you need very interventionist, intrusive measures to control it, such as wire-tapping, informants, and undercover operations. All these tactics are necessary, even in a democratic society, for dealing with organized crime, corruption, terrorism, and the like—but the use of these tactics should be kept to a minimum. Nonetheless, the majority of court-authorized wiretaps in this country involve investigations of drug-law violations. The same is true of the recruitment of informants, and not just from the criminal milieu but from all walks of life. Increasingly we hear of children turning their parents in to the police, and vice versa—precisely the sort of behavior we have traditionally associated with the totalitarian

states that we now see crumbling around the world. Beneath this whole issue, moreover, is a key principle that we cannot avoid dealing with. It is a principle we do not talk about much in American discourse, especially political discourse. Still, it is one that I think rings true for the civil libertarians of Stanford and the northeast as well as for the "rednecks" of South Texas. It is the notion that people who do no harm to others should not be harmed by others— and especially should not be harmed by the state. The fact remains that when you look at the seventy million Americans who have violated the drug laws in the last twenty years or so and the millions of Americans who continue to do so, the vast majority of them are doing no harm to anybody else. In most cases they are not even doing much harm to themselves. So from my point of view, saying to those people, "Because you use these forbidden substances, you lose your job, your driver's license, your money, your freedom," strikes me as a far greater immorality than any immorality associated with the use of these drugs.

Once again, this is strictly a moral argument, not a "value-free" public-policy argument. My position is that if people use these drugs and do not hurt others, it is no business of the state. If they become addicted to these drugs, then they deserve help—not just from their families but also from the state— and should not be first placed in prison. And if they use these drugs and hurt others, whether they are under the influence of these substances at the time or not, they deserve to be punished. People who directly hurt others should not be giving up their jail cells to people who engage in crimes of vice.

If the present drug-prohibition policy is a failure, what should be put in its place? I think we can, to a certain degree, move away from the prohibition side of the continuum and incur minimal risk. Education, drug-abuse prevention programs, needle-exchange programs, drug-maintenance programs of the type one sees in England and the Netherlands—these things do make a positive difference. We could have them all in this country. Lower-potency drugs could be legalized, as they were in the United States a hundred years ago, when we had not just cocaine powder but also coca colas and coca teas and coca tonics. Conditions then were much healthier than they are today in this respect. We could legalize or decriminalize individual possession of all drugs. We do not need the mandatory minimum sentences that are sending people, sometimes first offenders, to prison for extensive periods of time.

Ask what ought to be our drug policy, without any ideological or moral obligation to the notion of legalization, if our basic objective is to reduce death, suffering, and pain. My argument is that it will be a lot closer to the legalization model than to the prohibition model. It will be a policy that relies much more on the public health system than it does on the criminal justice system.

# NO                         James Q. Wilson

# AGAINST THE LEGALIZATION
# OF DRUGS

In 1972, the President appointed me chairman of the National Advisory
Council for Drug Abuse Prevention. Created by Congress, the Council was
charged with providing guidance on how best to coordinate the national
war on drugs. (Yes, we called it a war then, too.) In those days, the drug we
were chiefly concerned with was heroin. When I took office, heroin use had
been increasing dramatically. Everybody was worried that this increase
would continue. Such phrases as "heroin epidemic" were commonplace.

That same year, the eminent economist Milton Friedman published an
essay in *Newsweek* in which he called for legalizing heroin. His argument
was on two grounds: as a matter of ethics, the government has no right to
tell people not to use heroin (or to drink or to commit suicide); as a matter of
economics, the prohibition of drug use imposes costs on society that far
exceed the benefits. Others, such as the psychoanalyst Thomas Szasz, made
the same argument.

We did not take Friedman's advice. (Government commissions rarely do.)
I do not recall that we even discussed legalizing heroin, though we did
discuss (but did not take action on) legalizing a drug, cocaine, that many
people then argued was benign. Our marching orders were to figure out
how to win the war on heroin, not to run up the white flag of surrender.

That was 1972. Today, we have the same number of heroin addicts that we
had then—half a million, give or take a few thousand. Having that many
heroin addicts is no trivial matter; these people deserve our attention. But
not having had an increase in that number for over fifteen years is also
something that deserves our attention. What happened to the "heroin
epidemic" that many people once thought would overwhelm us?

The facts are clear: a more or less stable pool of heroin addicts has been
getting older, with relatively few new recruits. In 1976 the average age of
heroin users who appeared in hospital emergency rooms was about twenty-
seven; ten years later it was thirty-two. More than two-thirds of all heroin
users appearing in emergency rooms are now over the age of thirty. Back in

From James Q. Wilson, "Against the Legalization of Drugs," *Commentary*, vol. 89, no. 2
(February 1990). Copyright © 1990 by The American Jewish Committee. Reprinted by
permission of *Commentary*. All rights reserved.

the early 1970's, when heroin got onto the national political agenda, the typical heroin addict was much younger, often a teenager. Household surveys show the same thing—the rate of opiate use (which includes heroin) has been flat for the better part of two decades. More fine-grained studies of inner-city neighborhoods confirm this. John Boyle and Ann Brunswick found that the percentage of young blacks in Harlem who used heroin fell from 8 percent in 1970–71 to about 3 percent in 1975–76.

Why did heroin lose its appeal for young people? When the young blacks in Harlem were asked why they stopped, more than half mentioned "trouble with the law" or "high cost" (and high cost is, of course, directly the result of law enforcement). Two-thirds said that heroin hurt their health; nearly all said they had had a bad experience with it. We need not rely, however, simply on what they said. In New York City in 1973–75, the street price of heroin rose dramatically and its purity sharply declined, probably as a result of the heroin shortage caused by the success of the Turkish government in reducing the supply of opium base and of the French government in closing down heroin-processing laboratories located in and around Marseilles. These were short-lived gains for, just as Friedman predicted, alternative sources of supply—mostly in Mexico—quickly emerged. But the three-year heroin shortage interrupted the easy recruitment of new users.

Health and related problems were no doubt part of the reason for the reduced flow of recruits. Over the preceding years, Harlem youth had watched as more and more heroin users died of overdoses, were poisoned by adulterated doses, or acquired hepatitis from dirty needles. The word got around: heroin can kill you. By 1974 new hepatitis cases and drug-overdose deaths had dropped to a fraction of what they had been in 1970.

Alas, treatment did not seem to explain much of the cessation in drug use. Treatment programs can and do help heroin addicts, but treatment did not explain the drop in the number of *new* users (who by definition had never been in treatment) nor even much of the reduction in the number of experienced users.

No one knows how much of the decline to attribute to personal observation as opposed to high prices or reduced supply. But other evidence suggests strongly that price and supply played a large role. In 1972 the National Advisory Council was especially worried by the prospect that U.S. servicemen returning to this country from Vietnam would bring their heroin habits with them. Fortunately, a brilliant study by Lee Robins of Washington University in St. Louis put that fear to rest. She measured drug use of Vietnam veterans shortly after they had returned home. Though many had used heroin regularly while in Southeast Asia, most gave up the habit when back in the United States. The reason: here, heroin was less available and sanctions on its use were more pronounced. Of course, if a veteran had been willing to pay enough—which might have meant traveling to another city and would certainly have meant making an illegal contact with a disreputable dealer in a threatening neighborhood in order to acquire a (possibly) dangerous dose—he could have sustained his drug habit. Most veterans were unwilling to pay this price, and so their drug use declined or disappeared.

## RELIVING THE PAST

Suppose we had taken Friedman's advice in 1972. What would have happened? We cannot be entirely certain, but at a minimum we would have placed the young heroin addicts (and, above all, the prospective addicts) in a very different position from the one in which they actually found themselves. Heroin would have been legal. Its price would have been reduced by 95 percent (minus whatever we chose to recover in taxes.) Now that it could be sold by the same people who make aspirin, its quality would have been assured—no poisons, no adulterants. Sterile hypodermic needles would have been readily available at the neighborhood drugstore, probably at the same counter where the heroin was sold. No need to travel to big cities or unfamiliar neighborhoods—heroin could have been purchased anywhere, perhaps by mail order.

There would no longer have been any financial or medical reason to avoid heroin use. Anybody could have afforded it. We might have tried to prevent children from buying it, but as we have learned from our efforts to prevent minors from buying alcohol and tobacco, young people have a way of penetrating markets theoretically reserved for adults. Returning Vietnam veterans would have discovered that Omaha and Raleigh had been converted into the pharmaceutical equivalent of Saigon.

Under these circumstances, can we doubt for a moment that heroin use would have grown exponentially? Or that a vastly larger supply of new users would have been recruited? Professor Friedman is a Nobel Prize-winning economist whose understanding of market forces is profound. What did he think would happen to consumption under his legalized regime? Here are his words: "Legalizing drugs might increase the number of addicts, but it is not clear that it would. Forbidden fruit is attractive, particularly to the young."

Really? I suppose that we should expect no increase in Porsche sales if we cut the price by 95 percent, no increase in whiskey sales if we cut the price by a comparable amount—because young people only want fast cars and strong liquor when they are "forbidden." Perhaps Friedman's uncharacteristic lapse from the obvious implications of price theory can be explained by a misunderstanding of how drug users are recruited. In his 1972 essay he said that "drug addicts are deliberately made by pushers, who give likely prospects their first few doses free." If drugs were legal it would not pay anybody to produce addicts, because everybody would buy from the cheapest source. But as every drug expert knows, pushers do not produce addicts. Friends or acquaintances do. In fact, pushers are usually reluctant to deal with non-users because a non-user could be an undercover cop. Drug use spreads in the same way any fad or fashion spreads: somebody who is already a user urges his friends to try, or simply shows already-eager friends how to do it.

But we need not rely on speculation, however plausible, that lowered prices and more abundant supplies would have increased heroin usage. Great Britain once followed such a policy and with almost exactly those results. Until the mid-1960's, British physicians were allowed to prescribe heroin to certain classes of addicts. (Possessing these drugs without a doctor's prescription remained a criminal offense.) For many years this policy worked well enough because the addict patients were typically middle-class people who had become dependent on opiate painkillers while undergoing hospital treatment. There was no drug culture. The British system worked for many years, not because it prevented drug abuse, but because there was no problem of drug abuse that would test the system.

All that changed in the 1960's. A few unscrupulous doctors began passing out heroin in wholesale amounts. One doctor prescribed almost 600,000 heroin tablets—that is, over thirteen pounds—in just one year. A youthful drug culture emerged with a demand for drugs far different from that of the older addicts. As a result, the British government required doctors to refer users to government-run clinics to receive their heroin.

But the shift to clinics did not curtail the growth in heroin use. Throughout the 1960's the number of addicts increased—the late John Kaplan of Stanford estimated by fivefold—in part as a result of the diversion of heroin from clinic patients to new users on the streets. An addict would bargain with the clinic doctor over how big a dose he would receive. The patient wanted as much as he could get, the doctor wanted to give as little as was needed. The patient had an advantage in this conflict because the doctor could not be certain how much was really needed. Many patients would use some of their "maintenance" dose and sell the remaining part to friends, thereby recruiting new addicts. As the clinics learned of this, they began to shift their treatment away from heroin and toward methadone, an addictive drug that, when taken orally, does not produce a "high" but will block the withdrawal pains associated with heroin abstinence.

Whether what happened in England in the 1960's was a mini-epidemic or an epidemic depends on whether one looks at numbers or at rates of change. Compared to the United States, the numbers were small. In 1960 there were 68 heroin addicts known to the British government; by 1968 there were 2,000 in treatment and many more who refused treatment. (They would refuse in part because they did not want to get methadone at a clinic if they could get heroin on the street.) Richard Hartnoll estimates that the actual number of addicts in England is five times the number officially registered. At a minimum, the number of British addicts increased by thirtyfold in ten years; the actual increase may have been much larger.

In the early 1980's the numbers began to rise again, and this time nobody doubted that a real epidemic was at hand. The increase was estimated to be 40 percent a year. By 1982 there were thought to be 20,000 heroin users in London alone. Geoffrey Pearson reports that many cities—Glasgow, Liverpool, Manchester, and Sheffield among them—were now experiencing a drug problem that once had been largely confined to London. The problem, again, was supply. The country was being flooded with cheap, high-quality heroin, first from Iran and then from Southeast Asia.

The United States began the 1960's with a much larger number of heroin addicts and probably a bigger at-risk population than was the case in Great Britain. Even though it would be foolhardy to suppose that the British system, if installed here, would have worked the same way or with the same results, it would be equally foolhardy to suppose that a combination of heroin available from leaky clinics and from street dealers who faced only minimal law-enforcement risks would not have produced a much greater increase in heroin use than we actually experienced. My guess is that if we had allowed either doctors or clinics to prescribe heroin, we would have had far worse results than were produced in Britain, if for no other reason than the vastly larger number of addicts with which we began. We would have had to find some way to police thousands (not scores) of physicians and hundreds (not dozens) of clinics. If the British civil service found it difficult to keep heroin in the hands of addicts and out of the hands of recruits when it was dealing with a few hundred people, how well would the American civil service have accomplished the same tasks when dealing with tens of thousands of people?

## BACK TO THE FUTURE

Now cocaine, especially in its potent form, crack, is the focus of attention. Now as in 1972 the government is trying to reduce its use. Now as then some people are advocating legalization. Is there any more reason to yield to those arguments today than there was almost two decades ago?*

I think not. If we had yielded in 1972 we almost certainly would have had today a permanent population of several million, not several hundred thousand, heroin addicts. If we yield now we will have a far more serious problem with cocaine.

*I do not here take up the question of marijuana. For a variety of reasons—its widespread use and its lesser tendency to addict—it presents a different problem from cocaine or heroin. For a penetrating analysis, see Mark Kleiman, *Marijuana: Costs of Abuse, Costs of Control* (Greenwood Press, 217 pp., $37.95).

Crack is worse than heroin by almost any measure. Heroin produces a pleasant drowsiness and, if hygienically administered, has only the physical side effects of constipation and sexual impotence. Regular heroin use incapacitates many users, especially poor ones, for any productive work or social responsibility. They will sit nodding on a street corner, helpless but at least harmless. By contrast, regular cocaine use leaves the user neither helpless nor harmless. When smoked (as with crack) or injected, cocaine produces instant, intense, and short-lived euphoria. The experience generates a powerful desire to repeat it. If the drug is readily available, repeat use will occur. Those people who progress to "bingeing" on cocaine become devoted to the drug and its effects to the exclusion of almost all other considerations—job, family, children, sleep, food, even sex. Dr. Frank Gawin at Yale and Dr. Everett Ellinwood at Duke report that a substantial percentage of all high-dose, binge users become uninhibited, impulsive, hypersexual, compulsive, irritable, and hyperactive. Their moods vacillate dramatically, leading at times to violence and homicide.

Women are much more likely to use crack than heroin, and if they are pregnant, the effects on their babies are tragic. Douglas Besharov, who has been following the effects of drugs on infants for twenty years, writes that nothing he learned about heroin prepared him for the devastation of cocaine. Cocaine harms the fetus and can lead to physical deformities or neurological damage. Some crack babies have for all practical purposes suffered a disabling stroke while still in the womb. The long-term consequences of this brain damage are lowered cognitive ability and the onset of mood disorders. Besharov estimates that about 30,000 to 50,000 such babies are born every year, about 7,000 in New York City alone. There may be ways to treat such infants, but from everything we now know the treatment will be long, difficult, and expensive. Worse, the mothers who are most likely to produce crack babies are precisely the ones who, because of poverty or temperament, are least able and willing to obtain such treatment. In fact, anecdotal evidence suggests that crack mothers are likely to abuse their infants.

The notion that abusing drugs such as cocaine is a "victimless crime" is not only absurd but dangerous. Even ignoring the fetal drug syndrome, crack-dependent people are, like heroin addicts, individuals who regularly victimize their children by neglect, their spouses by improvidence, their employers by lethargy, and their co-workers by carelessness. Society is not and could never be a collection of autonomous individuals. We all have a stake in ensuring that each of us displays a minimal level of dignity, responsibility, and empathy. We cannot, of course, coerce people into goodness, but we can and should insist that some standards must be met if society itself—on which the very existence of the human personality depends—is to persist. Drawing the line that defines those standards is difficult and contentious, but if crack and heroin use do not fall below it, what does?

The advocates of legalization will respond by suggesting that my picture is overdrawn. Ethan Nadelmann of Princeton argues that the risk of legalization is less than most people suppose. Over 20 million Americans between the ages of eighteen and twenty-five have tried cocaine (according to a government survey), but only a quarter million use it daily. From this Nadelmann concludes that at most 3 percent of all young people who try cocaine develop a problem with it. The implication is clear: make the drug legal and we only have to worry about 3 percent of our youth.

The implication rests on a logical fallacy and a factual error. The fallacy is this: the percentage of occasional cocaine users who become binge users when the drug is illegal (and thus expensive and hard to find) tells us nothing about the percentage who will become dependent when the drug is legal (and thus cheap and abundant). Drs. Gawin and Ellinwood report, in common with several other researchers, that controlled or occasional use of cocaine changes to compulsive and frequent use "when access to the drug increases" or when the user switches from snorting to smoking. More cocaine more potently administered alters, perhaps sharply, the proportion of "controlled" users who become heavy users.

The factual error is this: the federal survey Nadelmann quotes was done in 1985, *before* crack had become common. Thus the probability of becoming dependent on cocaine was derived from the responses of users who snorted the drug. The speed and potency of cocaine's action increases dramatically when it is smoked. We do not yet know how greatly the advent of crack increases the risk of dependency, but all the clinical evidence suggests that the increase is likely to be large.

It is possible that some people will not become heavy users even when the drug is readily available in its most potent form. So far there are no scientific grounds for predicting who will and who will not become dependent. Neither socioeconomic background nor personality traits differentiate between casual and intensive users. Thus, the only way to settle the question of who is correct about the effect of easy availability on drug use, Nadelmann or Gawin and Ellinwood, is to try it and see. But that social experiment is so risky as to be no experiment at all, for if cocaine is legalized and if the rate of its abusive use increases dramatically, there is no way to put the genie back in the bottle, and it is not a kindly genie. . . .

## THE BENEFITS OF ILLEGALITY

The advocates of legalization find nothing to be said in favor of the current system except, possibly, that it keeps the number of addicts smaller than it would otherwise be. In fact, the benefits are more substantial than that.

First, treatment. All the talk about providing "treatment on demand" implies that there is a demand for treatment. That is not quite right. There are some drug-dependent people who genuinely want treatment and will remain in it if offered; they should receive it. But there are far more who want only short-term help after a bad crash; once stabilized and bathed, they are back on the street again, hustling. And even many of the addicts who enroll in a program honestly wanting help drop out after a short while when they discover that help takes time and commitment. Drug-dependent people have very short time horizons and a weak capacity for commitment. These two groups—those looking for a quick fix and those unable to stick with a long-term fix—are not easily helped. Even if we increase the number of treatment slots—as we should—we would

have to do something to make treatment more effective.

One thing that can often make it more effective is compulsion. Douglas Anglin of UCLA, in common with many other researchers, has found that the longer one stays in a treatment program, the better the chances of a reduction in drug dependency. But he, again like most other researchers, has found that drop-out rates are high. He has also found, however, that patients who enter treatment under legal compulsion stay in the program longer than those not subject to such pressure. His research on the California civil-commitment program, for example, found that heroin users involved with its required drug-testing program had over the long term a lower rate of heroin use than similar addicts who were free of such constraints. If for many addicts compulsion is a useful component of treatment, it is not clear how compulsion could be achieved in a society in which purchasing, possessing, and using the drug were legal. It could be managed, I suppose, but I would not want to have to answer the challenge from the American Civil Liberties Union that it is wrong to compel a person to undergo treatment for consuming a legal commodity.

Next, education. We are now investing substantially in drug-education programs in the schools. Though we do not yet know for certain what will work, there are some promising leads. But I wonder how credible such programs would be if they were aimed at dissuading children from doing something perfectly legal. We could, of course, treat drug education like smoking education: inhaling crack and inhaling tobacco are both legal, but you should not do it because it is bad for you. That tobacco is bad for you is easily shown; the Surgeon General has seen to that. But what do we say about crack? It is pleasurable, but devoting yourself to so much pleasure is not a good idea (though perfectly legal)? Unlike tobacco, cocaine will not give you cancer or emphysema, but it will lead you to neglect your duties to family, job, and neighborhood? Everybody is doing cocaine, but you should not?

Again, it might be possible under a legalized regime to have effective drug-prevention programs, but their effectiveness would depend heavily, I think, on first having decided that cocaine use, like tobacco use, is purely a matter of practical consequences; no fundamental moral significance attaches to either. But if we believe—as I do—that dependency on certain mind-altering drugs *is* a moral issue and that their illegality rests in part on their immorality, then legalizing them undercuts, if it does not eliminate altogether, the moral message.

That message is at the root of the distinction we now make between nicotine and cocaine. Both are highly addictive; both have harmful physical effects. But we treat the two drugs differently, not simply because nicotine is so widely used as to be beyond the reach of effective prohibition, but because its use does not destroy the user's essential humanity. Tobacco shortens one's life, cocaine debases it. Nicotine alters one's habits, cocaine alters one's soul. The heavy use of crack, unlike the heavy use of tobacco, corrodes those natural sentiments of sympathy and duty that constitute our human nature and make possible our social life. To say, as does Nadelmann, that distinguishing morally between tobacco and cocaine is "little more than a transient prejudice" is close to saying that morality itself is but a prejudice.

## THE ALCOHOL PROBLEM

Now we have arrived where many arguments about legalizing drugs begin: is there any reason to treat heroin and cocaine differently from the way we treat alcohol?

There is no easy answer to that question because, as with so many human problems, one cannot decide simply on the basis either of moral principles or of individual consequences; one has to temper any policy by a common-sense judgment of what is possible. Alcohol, like heroin, cocaine, PCP, and marijuana, is a drug—that is, a mood-altering substance—and consumed to excess it certainly has harmful consequences: auto accidents, barroom fights, bedroom shootings. It is also, for some people, addictive. We cannot confidently compare the addictive powers of these drugs, but the best evidence suggests that crack and heroin are much more addictive than alcohol.

Many people, Nadelmann included, argue that since the health and financial costs of alcohol abuse are so much higher than those of cocaine or heroin abuse, it is hypocritical folly to devote our efforts to preventing cocaine or drug use. But as Mark Kleiman of Harvard has pointed out, this comparison is quite misleading. What Nadelmann is doing is showing that a *legalized* drug (alcohol) produces greater harm than *illegal* ones (cocaine and heroin). But of course. Suppose that in the 1920's we had made heroin and cocaine legal and alcohol illegal. Can anyone doubt that Nadelmann would now be writing that it is folly to continue our ban on alcohol because cocaine and heroin are so much more harmful?

And let there be no doubt about it—widespread heroin and cocaine use are associated with all manner of ills. Thomas Bewley found that the mortality rate of British heroin addicts in 1968 was 28 times as high as the death rate of the same age group of non-addicts, even though in England at the time an addict could obtain free or low-cost heroin and clean needles from British clinics. Perform the following mental experiment: suppose we legalized heroin and cocaine in this country. In what proportion of auto fatalities would the state police report that the driver was nodding off on heroin or recklessly driving on a coke high? In what proportion of spouse-assault and child-abuse cases would the local police report that crack was involved? In what proportion of industrial accidents would safety investigators report that the forklift or drill-press operator was in a drug-induced stupor or frenzy? We do not know exactly what the proportion would be, but anyone who asserts that it would not be much higher than it is now would have to believe that these drugs have little appeal except when they are illegal. And that is nonsense.

An advocate of legalization might concede that social harm—perhaps harm equivalent to that already produced by alcohol—would follow from making cocaine and heroin generally available. But at least, he might add, we would have the problem "out in the open" where it could be treated as a matter of "public health." That is well and good, *if* we knew how to treat—that is, cure—heroin and cocaine abuse. But we do not know how to do it for all the people who would need such help. We are having only limited success in coping with chronic alcoholics. Addictive behavior is immensely difficult to change, and the best methods for changing it—living in drug-free therapeutic communities, becoming faithful members of Alcoholics Anonymous or Narcotics Anonymous—require great personal commitment, a quality that is, alas, in short supply among the very persons—young people, disadvantaged people—who are often most at risk for addiction.

Suppose that today we had, not 15 million alcohol abusers, but half a million. Suppose that we already knew what we have learned from our long experience with the widespread use of alcohol. Would we make whiskey legal? I do not know, but I suspect there would be a lively debate. The Surgeon General would remind us of the risks alcohol poses to pregnant women. The National Highway Traffic Safety Administration would point to the likelihood of more highway fatalities caused by drunk drivers. The Food and Drug Administration might find that there is a non-trivial increase in cancer associated with alcohol consumption. At the same time the police would report great difficulty in keeping illegal whiskey out of our cities, officers being corrupted by bootleggers, and alcohol addicts often resorting to crime to feed their habit. Libertarians, for their part, would argue that every citizen has a right to drink anything he wishes and that drinking is, in any event, a "victimless crime."

However the debate might turn out, the central fact would be that the problem was still, at that point, a small one. The government cannot legislate away the addictive tendencies in all of us, nor can it remove completely even the most dangerous addictive substances. But it can cope with harms when the harms are still manageable.

## SCIENCE AND ADDICTION

One advantage of containing a problem while it is still containable is that it buys time for science to learn more about it and perhaps to discover a cure. Almost unnoticed in the current debate over legalizing drugs is that basic science has made rapid strides in identifying the underlying neurological processes involved in some forms of addiction. Stimulants such as cocaine and amphetamines alter the way certain brain cells communicate with one another. That alteration is complex and not entirely understood, but in simplified form it involves modifying the way in which a neurotransmitter called dopamine sends signals from one cell to another. . . .

Whatever the exact mechanism may be, once it is identified it becomes possible to use drugs to block either the effect of cocaine or its tendency to produce dependency. There have already been experiments using desipramine, imipramine, bromocriptine, carbamazepine, and other chemicals. There are some promising results.

Tragically, we spend very little on such research, and the agencies funding it have not in the past occupied very influential or visible posts in the federal bureaucracy. If there is one aspect of the "war on drugs" metaphor that I dislike, it is its tendency to focus attention almost exclusively on the troops in the trenches, whether engaged in enforcement or treatment, and away from the research-and-development efforts back on the home front where the war may ultimately be decided.

I believe that the prospects of scientists in controlling addiction will be strongly influenced by the size and character of the problem they face. If the problem is a few hundred thousand chronic, high-dose users of an illegal product, the chances of making a difference at a reasonable cost will be much greater than if the problem is a few million chronic users of legal substances. Once a drug is legal, not only will its use increase but many of those who then use it will prefer the drug to the treatment: they will want the pleasure, whatever the cost to themselves or their families, and they will resist—probably successfully—any effort to wean them away from experiencing the high that comes from inhaling a legal substance.

## IF I AM WRONG . . .

No one can know what our society would be like if we changed the law to make access to cocaine, heroin, and PCP easier. I believe, for reasons given, that the result would be a sharp increase in use, a more widespread degradation of the human personality, and a greater rate of accidents and violence.

I may be wrong. If I am, then we will needlessly have incurred heavy costs in law enforcement and some forms of criminality. But if I am right, and the legalizers prevail anyway, then we will have consigned millions of people, hundreds of thousands of infants, and hundreds of neighborhoods to a life of oblivion and disease. To the lives and families destroyed by alcohol we will have added countless more destroyed by cocaine, heroin, PCP, and whatever else a basement scientist can invent.

Human character is formed by society; indeed, human character is inconceivable without society, and good character is less likely in a bad society. Will we, in the name of an abstract doctrine of radical individualism, and with the false comfort of suspect predictions, decide to take the chance that somehow individual decency can survive amid a more general level of degradation?

I think not. The American people are too wise for that, whatever the academic essayists and cocktail-party pundits may say. But if Americans today are less wise than I suppose, then Americans at some future time will look back on us now and wonder, what kind of people were they that they could have done such a thing?

# POSTSCRIPT

## Should Drugs Be Legalized?

Nadelmann asserts that utilizing the criminal justice system to eradicate drug problems simply does not work. He argues that international control efforts, interdiction, and domestic law enforcement are ineffective and that most problems associated with drug use are the consequences of drug regulation policies. He also contends that drug prohibition imposes on personal liberties. He maintains that decriminalization is a feasible and desirable means of dealing with the drug crisis.

Wilson charges that the advantages of maintaining illegality far outweigh any conceivable benefits of decriminalization. He professes that keeping the drug problem contained through regulation "buys time for science to learn more about it [addiction] and perhaps to discover a cure." Wilson argues that the government is coping adequately with the drug situation. He feels that to take away regulation would greatly increase drug abuse and drug-related accidents and that it would destroy all of the current efforts to control drug use.

Legalization proponents argue that drug laws have not worked and that the drug battle has been lost. They believe problems would disappear if legalization were implemented. Despite potential risks, advocates believe legalization is worth considering. Opponents contend that anyone who values human life would not regard legalization as acceptable. Citing alcohol and tobacco as examples, legalization opponents argue that decriminalizing drugs would not decrease profits from the sale of drugs (the profits from cigarettes and alcohol are incredibly high). Moreover, using the same examples, opponents argue that legalizing a drug does not make its problems disappear (alcohol and tobacco still have extremely high addiction rates as well as a myriad of other problems associated with their use).

Many European countries have systems of legalized drugs, and most have far fewer addiction rates and lower incidences of drug-related violence and crime than the United States. This does not mean that the European experience can be generalized to the United States. Legalization in the

United States could still be a tremendous risk since its drug problems could escalate and recriminalizing drugs would be difficult. This was the case with Prohibition.

Another aspect of this debate revolves around the moral considerations of drug criminalization. Legalization advocates believe that adults should be allowed to make their own decisions regarding drug use and that criminalization is a violation of personal freedom. Should adults be allowed to use drugs even though the serious health, social, and economic risks are known? On the other hand, should the government be allowed to police the personal habits of its citizens? Are drug users really criminals? Should they be kept in prisons alongside murderers and on taxpayers' money? As America's drug problem continues, these and other questions persist.

There are many good articles and books that debate drug legalization. Some of these include "Drug Policy: Striking the Right Balance," *Science* (September 28, 1990), by Avram Goldstein and Harold Kalant; Morton Kondracke's "Don't Legalize Drugs: The Costs Are Still Too High," *The New Republic* (June 1988); *The Drug Legalization Debate* (Sage Publications, 1991), by James Inciardi; and Sam Staley's *Drug Policy and the Decline of Cities* (Transaction Publishers, 1992).

# ISSUE 2

## Should Medical Patients Be Permitted to Use Marijuana?

**YES: Mae Nutt,** from "In the Matter of Marijuana Rescheduling Petition," U.S. Department of Justice, Drug Enforcement Administration (May 13, 1987)

**NO: John C. Lawn,** from "Their Government Tells Them All to Get Lost," *The Federal Register* (December 29, 1989)

### ISSUE SUMMARY

**YES:** Speaking as a mother, Mae Nutt describes the physical and emotional relief that marijuana provided her son while he was undergoing cancer treatment. She argues that marijuana eliminates the painful side effects of chemotherapy and that patients should be allowed to use marijuana while in treatment.

**NO:** John C. Lawn, director of the Drug Enforcement Administration, contends that medical patients should not be permitted to use marijuana because there is a lack of reliable scientific evidence showing marijuana's safety and its usefulness in the treatment of medical conditions.

Marijuana, or cannabis, has never achieved the medical status of other drugs, like morphine or opium. Nonetheless, its medicinal qualities have been recognized for centuries. Marijuana was utilized as far back as 2737 B.C. by Chinese emperor Shen Nung and then some 2,900 years later in A.D. 200 by a Chinese physician who mixed cannabis resin with white wine to make a surgical anesthetic. By the 1890s some medical reports had stated that cannabis was useful as a pain reliever. However, despite its historical significance, the use of marijuana for medical treatment has been a widely debated and controversial topic.

Marijuana has been tested in the treatment of glaucoma, asthma, and convulsions, and in the reduction of nausea, vomiting, and the loss of appetite associated with chemotherapy treatments. Many medical professionals and patients believe that marijuana shows promise in the treatment of these disorders and others, including spasticity in amputees and multiple sclerosis. Yet, others argue that there are other medical drugs and treatments available that are more specific and effective in treating these disorders than marijuana and that marijuana cannot be considered a medical replacement.

Because of the conflicting viewpoints and what many people argue is an absence of reliable, scientific research supporting the medicinal value of marijuana, the drug and its plant materials remain in Schedule I of the Controlled Substances Act. The Controlled Substances Act of 1970 established five categories, or schedules, under which drugs are classified according to their potential for abuse and their medical usefulness, which in turn determines their availability. Drugs classified under Schedule I are those that have a high potential for abuse and no scientifically proven medical use. Many marijuana proponents have called for the Drug Enforcement Administration (DEA) to move marijuana from Schedule I to Schedule II (which classifies drugs as having a high potential for abuse but also having an established medical use), to legally allow physicians to utilize the drug and/or its components in certain treatment programs. However, to date, the DEA has refused.

Currently, marijuana is used medically, but not legally. Most of the controversy concerns whether or not marijuana and its plant properties are indeed of medical value and whether or not the risks associated with its use outweigh its proposed medical benefits. Research reports and scientific studies have been inconclusive. Some physicians and many cancer patients claim that marijuana greatly reduces the side effects of chemotherapy—that it has antiemetic qualities (which prevent vomiting) that are greater than other prescribed chemotherapy buffers. Many glaucoma patients also believe that marijuana use has greatly improved their conditions. In light of these reports by patients, as well as recommendations by some physicians to allow the inclusion of marijuana in treatment, many expectations have been raised with regard to marijuana's medical usefulness and to its being made a bona fide medical treatment.

Marijuana opponents argue that the evidence in support of marijuana as medically useful suffers from far too many deficiencies and that, therefore, marijuana should not be defined as medically beneficial. Additionally, much of what marijuana proponents offer in support of their position is labelled by the DEA as outdated. The DEA believes that the studies are scientifically limited, based on biased testimonies of individuals and their families and friends who have used marijuana, and grounded in the unscientific opinions of certain physicians, nurses, and other hospital personnel.

In the following affidavit to the Drug Enforcement Administration, Mae Nutt provides a detailed account of her son's painful struggle with cancer and how the negative side effects of chemotherapy subsided after he used marijuana. Because of the way marijuana improved her son's physical, emotional, and mental condition, she argues that seriously ill patients should have legal access to quality-controlled supplies of marijuana. John C. Lawn argues that marijuana cannot be used for legal medical purposes because the federal government has found the current research on marijuana's medicinal value to be insufficient and in many cases based upon unreliable, misconducted scientific studies.

# YES

## IN THE MATTER OF MARIJUANA RESCHEDULING PETITION

Mae Nutt, being first duly sworn, states as follows:

1. My name is Mae Nutt. I was born June 28, 1921. My husband is Arnold Nutt, who was born Dec. 21, 1919. We reside in Beaverton, Mich.

2. We were married on June 13, 1953. We had three children: Keith Earl, who was born Dec. 21, 1955; Dana, who was born June 4, 1958; and Marc, who was born Oct. 3, 1959.

3. In July, 1963, shortly after his fifth birthday, Dana complained he couldn't breathe, and then he passed out. He was rushed to our local hospital, then taken to the Henry Ford Hospital in Detroit.

4. My husband and I were told Dana had Ewings Sarcoma. Emergency surgery was performed the following day, July 3, 1963. During the surgery, doctors removed a 1-pound tumor which was attached to one of Dana's ribs. The rib was also removed.

5. Dana remained hospitalized for nearly a month. Then he came home. For the next three years, Dana received chemotherapy and radiation treatments. He was often hospitalized at the Henry Ford Hospital for additional treatments.

6. The chemotherapy treatments made Dana very ill. When the cancer spread to his brain, he began receiving radiation treatments. These made him violently angry and difficult to manage. The therapy also made Dana listless and destroyed his appetite and, eventually, his personality.

7. Despite the powerful therapies which caused these severe adverse effects, the cancer continued to spread and began affecting other organs. In July, and in December 1964, additional surgical procedures were performed on Dana. During these procedures, portions of his lungs were removed.

8. For the remainder of Dana's life, he remained seriously ill.

9. Dana died Jan. 5, 1967.

10. Dana's protracted illness drained our financial resources. The emotional strain was extremely difficult on us and our other children.

Affidavit of Mae Nutt, "In the Matter of Marijuana Rescheduling Petition," Dkt. 86-22, U.S. Department of Justice, Drug Enforcement Administration (May 13, 1987).

11. In the spring of 1978, our eldest son Keith, who was living in Columbus, Ohio, phoned home to tell us that he had testicular cancer.

12. On April 19, 1978, we were in Columbus during Keith's first operation. During the operation, the diseased testicle was removed. After a biopsy, which found the tissue to be malignant, the surgeons removed a large number of lymph nodes between Keith's pelvic bone and breast bone in an effort to remove all of the cancer.

13. Keith was a very independent young man and he decided to remain in Columbus following his recovery from surgery. He made a determined effort to resume a normal life. He also discussed possible anti-cancer therapies with his physicians in Columbus. The doctors felt they had removed all of the cancer and thought no extensive chemotherapy or radiation treatments were warranted. However, Keith was unable to maintain his energy and in the fall of 1978, he returned home to live with us.

14. After returning home, Keith made a determined effort to remain active and vital. He quickly found a new job and started working. All appeared to be going well.

15. On the evening of Jan. 1, 1979, after a wonderful holiday season, Keith told us that his other testicle was hard and enlarged. He thought it might be cancerous.

16. The next morning we accompanied Keith to a urologist in Midland, the nearest large community.

17. After a brief examination, the doctor told us Keith's condition was serious and he needed another operation immediately. Keith was hospitalized later that day.

18. During the operation, surgeons removed Keith's remaining testicle.

19. Following the operation, our son was seen by an internist. He explained the cancer was spreading and told us Keith would require extensive chemotherapy treatments.

20. As soon as his surgical wounds healed, Keith was placed on a new, highly toxic form of chemotherapy called Cisplatin.

21. Keith's chemotherapy began in February 1979. The treatments made him extremely ill. After receiving his injections, he would vomit violently for 8–10 hours. Then he would become profoundly nauseated to the point he could neither bear to look at nor smell food.

22. In an attempt to curb Keith's nausea and vomiting, Compazine and other anti-emetic drugs were prescribed. These drugs did not provide any noticeable relief.

23. This combination of intense vomiting and debilitating nausea quickly took a toll on our son. Unable to eat or to keep down any food he managed to swallow, Keith rapidly began to lose weight. In less than two months, our son lost at least 30 pounds.

24. Keith's vomiting was so violent it became a heaving retch. Because he could not eat, he began to vomit bile. When there was nothing to vomit, he would simply retch and convulse. It was horrible for us to watch our child suffer such anguish.

25. My husband and I were alarmed by the intensity of Keith's vomiting and by his sudden, dramatic loss of weight. We felt Keith's weight loss to be an indication of just how rapidly he was being overwhelmed by his cancer and by the chemotherapy he was receiving to

combat it. Together, the disease and treatment were a deadly combination.

26. Keith was suffering terribly. His treatments were wearing him down. At one point, he approached me and said he did not want to become like his deceased brother, Dana—so sick he could not take care of himself, completely incapacitated and a burden on the rest of the family. He told me when things got that bad, he wanted to be able kill himself, in order to escape his misery. Then Keith made me promise when there was no more hope, I would help him end his life.

27. One evening, while reading the newspaper, I read an article about a cancer patient who had received a brown bag of marijuana on his doorstep. The article noted there was medical evidence which showed smoking marijuana helped to reduce the severe nausea and vomiting caused by many anti-cancer therapies.

28. At first I laughed at the story. It seemed unlikely that marijuana would just suddenly appear on someone's doorstep. The idea marijuana had medical benefit was a new one to my husband and me. Later, however, we told Keith what we had read. We were desperate.

29. Keith told us that while he was in the hospital in Columbus he had met other cancer patients who were receiving chemotherapy. These patients told him about smoking marijuana to reduce the side effects of chemotherapy. According to Keith, these other cancer patients said marijuana really helped reduce the vomiting.

30. As a parent, I was strongly opposed to marijuana and other illegal drugs. My husband and I made sure our sons knew exactly how we felt. We told them we never wanted them to use such drugs for any reason. We do not doubt our sons may have tried smoking mari-

juana at one time or another while growing up, but we were also sure our sons had no drug problems and no illusions about our stern opposition to drug use.

31. It was hard to believe an illegal drug could be of any help. We thought the government would know if marijuana had medical value and, if so, would make it legally available to patients by prescription. We made a few calls. One of the people we contacted was our State Representative, Robert Young. We asked Representative Young if there was any way we could legally obtain marijuana so our son Keith could try it and see if it helped.

32. I was surprised when Representative Young told me a bill to legalize marijuana for the treatment of glaucoma and cancer was scheduled to come before the Michigan legislature. Representative Young also gave me the name and phone number of Mr. Roger Winthrop, a man who was working with a number of Representatives and Senators to help enact the Michigan "Marijuana as Medicine" legislation.

33. I then contacted Mr. Winthrop. He provided my husband and I with information on marijuana and on the drug's medical use, including its anti-emetic effects relative to cancer chemotherapy treatments. We learned physicians and patients in a number of states had already succeeded in passing state laws to make marijuana available to seriously ill patients like Keith.

34. Shortly after my husband and I read these materials, Keith had to be hospitalized for another round of chemotherapy and observation. As always, the chemotherapy made him dreadfully sick.

35. We could not stand by and watch our son suffer. After a short discussion,

we decided we had to get some marijuana for Keith. My husband and I are an older couple and we did not have the slightest idea where to find marijuana. In desperation, we contacted a close friend, an ordained Presbyterian minister. He worked with a number of local youth groups and we thought he might have some contacts. He listened quietly while we explained our problem and asked for his help.

36. Several days later, at 10:30 P.M., this minister showed up at our door. He told us he had managed to obtain some marijuana. It was the first time we had ever seen marijuana.

37. The next day we took the marijuana to Keith in the hospital. After Keith smoked the marijuana, there was a dramatic improvement in his nausea.

38. Before smoking marijuana, Keith would vomit and retch for at least eight hours following his chemotherapy injection. Then he would vomit less frequently but would become overwhelmingly nauseated and unable to eat. This inability to eat would continue until the beginning of his next chemotherapy session, when he again would start to vomit. The process would repeat itself.

39. Marijuana broke this cycle. After Keith smoked marijuana, his vomiting abruptly stopped. It was amazing to see. None of the anti-emetic drugs prescribed by the doctors had been effective. Now, with just a few puffs of marijuana, Keith was no longer vomiting. It was a sudden, abrupt change.

40. Marijuana also put an end to Keith's nausea. When he smoked marijuana, he was constantly hungry and could eat. He actually began to put on weight. His mental outlook also underwent a startling improvement.

41. Prior to smoking marijuana, Keith would go to his chemotherapy, come home and rush upstairs. He would shut himself in his bedroom and stuff towels under the door to keep out the smell of dinner cooking. He would not join us for dinner and would remain in his room or the bathroom vomiting for the rest of the evening. The cancer and chemotherapy made Keith act like a wounded animal—timid and retiring. He would stay in his room and vomit. He would have intense hot and cold flashes, his joints became swollen and painful, his hair fell out and he felt sick all over. The anti-cancer drugs were so toxic Keith could pull off large pieces of skin where the chemotherapy injections had been given.

42. Smoking marijuana dramatically changed all of this. Immediately before chemotherapy Keith would smoke one marijuana cigarette. Following chemotherapy he would smoke all or part of a second marijuana cigarette if he felt queasy. On good days Keith didn't have to remain in the hospital after his chemotherapy treatments. When we got home, Keith would stay in the living room and talk with his brother and father. He would join the family for dinner, where he would eat more than his share. He became outgoing and talkative. Keith became part of our family again because marijuana controlled the debilitating symptoms of his chemotherapy.

43. Once my husband and I saw the dramatic improvement in Keith's condition, we made certain all of his doctors and nurses were aware of the situation. None objected, and some clearly approved.

44. We made arrangements with the hospital for Keith to smoke marijuana in his hospital room. This would save him

from having to smoke in the parking lot before chemotherapy and allow him to smoke in his room after chemotherapy.

45. Even though use of marijuana is illegal, many people at the hospital supported Keith's marijuana therapy. No one at the hospital doubted marijuana was helpful and no one discouraged Keith from smoking marijuana to control the adverse effects of his anti-cancer therapies. In effect, reasonable people apparently decided the law did not match the reality of Keith's—and other patients'—needs.

46. My husband and I came to resent the fact Keith's marijuana therapy was illegal. We felt like criminals. We are honest, simple people and we hated having to sneak around. I was uncomfortable with our closest friends, our minister, and our other son, Marc, having to risk arrest in order to provide Keith with the marijuana he so obviously needed. I also wondered about other parents who might have a child suffering from chemotherapy who might now know marijuana could help end their child's misery, or who did not know how to obtain marijuana.

47. My husband and I approached Keith and asked him if we could tell his story to the newspaper. I told him it might help other cancer patients. He agreed, on one condition: that we not give the newspaper details about the nature of his cancer or of the surgical procedures which resulted in the removal of his testes. As a young man in his twenties, Keith wanted at least this much of his life to remain private. We quickly agreed to this condition.

48. A reporter for the local paper (*The Bay City Times*) came to our house, listened to our story and wrote an article which appeared on March 11, 1979. The story began:

> Keith Nutt of Beaverton doesn't care who knows he uses marijuana. It is the only thing that relieves the terrible nausea that follows chemotherapy treatments for cancer, says the 23-year-old man. Right now, Keith is still able to drive to his sources of marijuana. If the time comes when Keith can't get out of the house to buy the illegal drug, his mother, Mae Nutt, 58, says, "that's where I come in! But it shouldn't be necessary to break the law to get help for a child who is very, very ill."

49. On the same day this article appeared, we went to Lansing to testify before the Michigan Senate Judiciary Committee. The hearings were on a bill to legalize marijuana's medical use by Michigan glaucoma, cancer, and multiple sclerosis (MS) patients.

50. During our testimony, one senator asked Keith if his doctors knew he was smoking marijuana. Keith, in an effort to protect his doctors and the hospital, said his doctors did not know he was smoking marijuana.

51. Doctor Barnett Rosenberg, the inventor of the new chemotherapeutic drug Cisplatin, which Keith was taking, also testified at the hearings and spoke in favor of the legislation.

52. Following the hearings, we spoke privately with Dr. Rosenberg. He was strongly supportive and encouraged Keith to keep smoking so he would continue with his chemotherapy treatments. Dr. Rosenberg told us many of the cancer patients in his test programs smoked marijuana while receiving chemotherapy.

53. Several reporters also spoke with Dr. Rosenberg. One story, which appeared after the hearings in a local newspaper,

*The Gladwin County Record,* quoted Dr. Rosenberg at length. A portion of the story notes:

> The Nutt family was backed up by Dr. Barnett Rosenberg, a Michigan State University biophysicist, credited with the discovery of a new platinum-based cancer treatment. Rosenberg told the committee cancer treatment drugs and radiation therapy induce intense vomiting and nausea. Although the research isn't complete yet, Rosenberg said it appears marijuana is the most effective drug for eliminating the painful side effects of cancer treatments. Rosenberg said doctors can now treat cancer patients with marijuana if they get federal Food and Drug Administration approval. But the process is time consuming and requires extensive research and study of each patient involved. Because of federal restrictions the Michigan bill may not make it easier for doctors to obtain marijuana for cancer patients, he noted. [Rosenberg] said he testified to increase public awareness of marijuana's potential [benefits] for cancer patients.

54. Following the Senate hearings, there was considerable publicity about Keith. We began receiving phone calls from other cancer patients in Michigan and throughout the United States. Many were seeking help. Keith often spoke with these patients late into the night, sharing information and trying to help.

55. Cancer patients and their relatives who lived close to us called and asked Keith for help and advice regarding how to smoke properly, how much to use, and how often. On several occasions Keith went on "house calls" to teach patients how to roll the cigarettes or properly inhale the smoke. This involvement with other seriously ill patients gave Keith great joy. He loved being able to help his fellow patients escape the dreadful side effects of their anti-cancer treatments.

56. One day, shortly after the hearings, we found a small brown bag of marijuana in our mailbox. There was no note, no identification, just an ounce or so of marijuana. Soon we received more marijuana in the mail. An Episcopal priest brought marijuana to our house. He told us he wanted to put it to good use and felt we would know who might benefit from it.

57. Most of the people who sent marijuana to us did not identify themselves. As news spread through the grapevine, however, we heard from some familiar folks. For example, we received a call one day from a woman who had attended elementary school with Arnold. She asked us to her home. When we arrived, she told us she had something for us and produced a cigar box filled with marijuana. She explained that her husband, recently deceased, had smoked marijuana to help control his pain. She had no use for the marijuana but did not want to throw it away.

58. It seemed to me many cancer patients were smoking marijuana. In my experience, most patients made an effort to inform their doctors. Most physicians, wanting to avoid the pitfalls of "a political issue," knew their patients were smoking marijuana and approved. Like Dr. Rosenberg, these physicians accepted that marijuana was therapeutically helpful in reducing nausea and vomiting. Unlike Dr. Rosenberg, most doctors were not willing to say in public what they told their patients in their offices: "Get some marijuana."

59. Throughout the spring and summer of 1979, Keith continued his chemotherapy treatments and smoking

marijuana. He continued to assist other patients.

60. In early October 1979, my husband and I returned to Lansing, Mich., for additional hearings before the House Committee on Public Health. Keith was not with us. He was back in the hospital. Despite his continuing chemotherapy treatments his cancer was spreading and growing worse.

61. We testified again. On this occasion we were joined by another family, the Negens, from Grand Rapids, Mich. The Negen family had testified at the earlier hearings before the Senate, but had not given their names. At the time of the Senate hearings their daughter, Deborah, then 21, was in remission from her leukemia. At the second hearing, however, her leukemia was no longer in remission and she was receiving chemotherapy treatments again.

62. The Reverend Negen is pastor of the very conservative Dutch Christian Reform Church in Grand Rapids. He spoke of how he had prayed for guidance and had come to realize if getting marijuana to help his daughter through the terrors of chemotherapy offended his congregation he would leave his church. He knew he was breaking the law. But his daughter was suffering. He spoke movingly about having to send his own young sons into the streets of Grand Rapids to purchase marijuana for his daughter's use. Marijuana was, he emphasized to the committee, the only drug that provided his daughter with any relief from the debilitating side effects of her chemotherapy treatments. It was easy for us to identify with Reverend Negen's obvious distress. He was being forced to break the law in order to provide for his daughter's medical needs. In the same way, we had to break the law to meet Keith's medical needs.

63. Deborah Negen was even more eloquent as she testified about how marijuana helped her cope with the vomiting and nausea caused by her chemotherapy treatments. She pleaded with the committee for help and asked them to consider that other seriously ill people were needlessly suffering. We were deeply moved by this family's anguished testimony. The story was so familiar, so close to home. We knew exactly how Reverend Negen felt about having to break the law. It is not something we did lightly, but something we were compelled to do by circumstances beyond our control.

64. Following the hearings in the House, my family received even more calls from newspapers, television and radio stations asking for more information. Cancer patients continued to call us seeking help or asking how they could help get the legislation enacted. We also received more marijuana in the mail from people trying to help Keith. Keith continued to distribute the marijuana he could not use to other cancer patients. He also continued to speak with patients who called for help, but he was very weak.

65. A week later, on Oct. 10, 1979, the Michigan House voted 100–0 in favor of making marijuana available to patients like Keith who suffered from life- or sense-threatening diseases like cancer and glaucoma.

66. On Oct. 15, 1979, the Michigan Senate concurred with the House and voted 33–1 in favor of making marijuana medically available to Michigan cancer and glaucoma patients for use under medical supervision. The following day *The Detroit Free Press'* Lansing Bureau

Chief, Hugh McDiarmid, wrote, "Compassion Wins In Marijuana Vote."

67. On the evening of Sunday, Oct. 21, 1979, my husband went to say goodnight to Keith. We told Keith the Michigan Marijuana-as-Medicine bill would be signed into law the next day. Keith was happy his effort had made a difference. He smiled and said goodnight.

68. Early on the morning of Oct. 22, 1979, Keith died. Later that day Michigan's Lieutenant Governor, James Brickley, signed the Michigan Controlled Substances Therapeutic Research Program into law.

69. During the time Keith smoked marijuana to alleviate the adverse side effects of his chemotherapy treatments he never once experienced an adverse effect from marijuana. It was clear to us marijuana was the safest, most benign drug he received during the course of his battle against cancer. Certainly marijuana was immeasurably safer than the lethal chemotherapeutic agents which were supposed to prolong our son's life.

70. Following Keith's death, there was a tremendous outpouring of comment. People we did not know and had never met sent us touching cards and letters praising Keith's efforts to help others. We continued to receive calls from newspapers and other media sources asking about Keith. It was clear to me Keith had deeply touched many people throughout the country. Despite my grief, I felt extremely proud of Keith for having had the courage to publicly discuss his disease and to fight to legalize medical access to marijuana so other patients could benefit.

71. In recognition of Keith's efforts, the Michigan legislature passed a Joint Resolution declaring in part: "Be it resolved by the Senate that our sincerest tribute be accorded in memory of Keith Nutt."

72. Several months after Keith's death, I went to see the oncologist who had helped treat Keith. I asked if he needed any volunteer help. He accepted the offer, and I helped to care for other cancer patients.

73. A short time after I began work, the doctor sent a patient to see me. The patient was suffering from debilitating nausea and vomiting and had threatened to stop taking her chemotherapy because of the adverse side effects.

74. I remembered how my son had reached out to other patients. We still continued to receive marijuana in the mail, though not as much as before Keith's death. The Michigan legislature had authorized marijuana's medical use, but acknowledged it would be at least 90 days before the state could begin to distribute federally approved supplies.

75. After some soul searching, my husband and I decided to use the marijuana Keith left behind for the benefit of other cancer patients. The doctor and his staff quickly learned if a patient was having a bad time they could send the patient to us for help. We would provide the patient with marijuana.

76. Before long we had a booming clinic. As more people became aware of what we were doing, we began receiving more marijuana in the mail or we would find a bag of it on our porch. The more marijuana we collected the more patients we could supply.

77. Within a very short time, I became known as the Michigan "Green Cross," and I was nicknamed "Grandma Marijuana." Doctors in several surrounding counties began sending patients to me for help. On occasion, patients who tried to get into the state program, which was

not yet operational, were referred to me. I never asked these patients who in the State Department of Public Health was referring them to me. I simply did what I could to help anyone who had a legitimate medical need for marijuana. I never ran into any jokers; it is hard to fake cancer.

78. Most of the time patients quickly understood how to smoke marijuana. On some occasions, however, we had to provide them with help. I do not smoke. I found a woman in her mid-40s who had smoked marijuana at one time. Together we would make house calls to teach uninitiated patients the basics of marijuana therapy.

79. The "Green Cross" continued throughout the spring and summer of 1980. On several occasions I received calls from patients in the southern part of Michigan or from out-of-state. I occasionally mailed marijuana to such patients.

80. I also tried to adapt marijuana so patients who could not or would not smoke marijuana could also benefit from the drug's medicinal properties. I soon learned I could boil marijuana and butter in a kettle of water for several hours, then let the mixture cool and use the butter which floated to the top.

81. Patients could either eat the butter on bread or bake it into cookies or brownies. However, dosage problems led me to start putting the butter into capsules.

82. I obtained the capsules from a hospital pharmacy. The pharmacy knew what we were doing and did not object in any way. The capsules made it simpler for those patients who did not want to smoke and who could not stand the smell or taste of food to get relief.

83. On one occasion a mother called. Her young daughter, around five, was undergoing chemotherapy treatments. The little girl could not smoke. Her mother had made brownies and these worked. But, on occasion, the little girl had fallen asleep after getting her chemotherapy and eating a brownie. Her parents did not wake her up to take another brownie. As a result, when the little girl did wake up, she began retching and vomiting. The mother wanted to know if there was some other way to use marijuana other than smoking or eating.

84. After speaking to some doctors and nurses, we decided to put pinholes in the capsules so they could be used as suppositories. We quickly discovered that this proved to be a highly effective alternative. While the relief was not as fast or as predictable when marijuana butter was used in this manner, patients did get relief from nausea and vomiting. Interestingly, we learned several years later federal drug agencies had attempted to develop a THC suppository and failed.

85. Despite promises from the Michigan Department of Public Health, the state marijuana program took far longer to develop than expected. Legislators, patients, physicians, researchers, and others throughout the state were pressing for action.

86. It seemed federal agencies were undermining the intent of the Michigan law. Instead of a compassionate program of patient care, research, and treatment, the federal agencies wanted to create a highly structured, very limited program of pure research. Instead of allowing physicians to treat patients and reach their own judgments, the FDA demanded detailed, complex, and standardized physician reporting procedures.

87. FDA and the Michigan Department of Public Health took nearly one year to implement the Michigan program.

88. The program that emerged from this constant bureaucratic friction was an administrative nightmare for doctors and patients alike. Instead of providing seriously ill patients with compassionate, legal access to quality controlled supplies of marijuana, the program became a research project in the hands of a limited number of physicians at the larger cancer centers. The welfare of patients did not seem to be a criteria under the federal government's procedures.

89. I realized the program my son, Keith, had worked so hard to enact was in serious trouble when the doctor who treated Keith, who knew about marijuana's medical benefits, and who was anxiously awaiting his chance to sign up, decided to drop out. I was furious. He, of all people, was abandoning the state program.

90. He explained he was practicing medicine. The conditions, regulations, reporting, and other requirements of the state program had grown so dense and restrictive he felt they would intrude on his practice of medicine. He said he simply did not have the administrative staff or the time necessary to handle all of the paperwork involved.

91. In 1982, after two years of conflict between the Michigan Department of Public Health and FDA, the program continued to have problems. Patients and physicians throughout the state informally boycotted the program. Physicians and patients decided it was easier to get marijuana on the streets than to deal with the complex paperwork and reporting requirements.

92. In an effort to maintain marijuana's Schedule I classification, federal agencies have failed to aggressively pursue information on marijuana's medicinal properties and have blocked state efforts to make the drug available for medical applications.

93. In response to the conduct of federal agencies, the Michigan legislature enacted a Resolution detailing these concerns. In part, this Resolution of the Michigan legislature declares:

> Federal agencies have . . . through regulatory ploys and obscure bureaucratic devices, resisted and obstructed the intent of the Michigan legislature. . . . Glaucoma and cancer patients, promised medical access to marijuana under the laws of Michigan, are being deprived of such access by federal agencies.

94. After outlining a series of complaints, the Resolution then calls on the president and the Congress to seek appropriate legislative or administrative remedies. In part, the Michigan Resolution calls for systemic reform. The Resolution reads:

> That the Congress of the United States be urged to seek to remedy federal policies which prevent the several States from acquiring, inhibit physicians from prescribing, and prevent patients from obtaining marijuana for legitimate medical applications, by ending federal prohibitions against the legitimate and appropriate use of marijuana in medical treatments.

95. As the Michigan program became more and more bureaucratic, there were fewer and fewer physicians or patients willing to tolerate the regulatory excesses federal agencies demanded. After several years of work, and despite the efforts of many individuals, we realized

there was little more we could do. We lost interest in the Michigan state program. I think it has become virtually useless to the doctors and patients that I set out to help.

96. It has been seven years since Michigan enacted a law to make marijuana legally available to patients with glaucoma and cancer. I still work occasionally at the doctor's office and for the last five years I have also worked in a local hospital's cancer ward. Doctors are still telling violently ill patients to smoke marijuana to relieve their nausea and vomiting and the patients are still getting marijuana off the streets. People who work closely with cancer patients know patients are smoking marijuana.

97. Marijuana is being used medically, but not legally. I know many doctors who quietly support marijuana's medical use. Yet, I do not know one doctor who is actively participating in the Michigan Marijuana Therapeutic Research Program. In fact, I have yet to meet a single Michigan cancer patient who ever obtained marijuana legally, through a doctor.

98. Despite its problems, it appears that Michigan fared better than most states in dealing with marijuana's inappropriate Schedule I classification. The doctors in Michigan who did participate in the limited programs that were developed reported great success. It is my understanding nearly 300 cancer patients in Michigan received marijuana during their chemotherapy treatments. Marijuana successfully reduced nausea and vomiting for the vast majority of these patients. Equally significant, there were almost no adverse effects reported.

99. I am saddened the compassionate intent of the law my son helped enact has not been realized because of federal policies. However, I know that Keith, through his efforts, helped hundreds of desperately ill cancer patients in Michigan and throughout the country to become aware of marijuana's medical benefits.

100. The available studies show marijuana is medically safe for therapeutic use.

101. Michigan and more than 30 other states have legislatively recognized marijuana's medical utility. Hundreds of physicians throughout the country are telling their patients to smoke marijuana. Thousands, if not tens of thousands, of patients with glaucoma, cancer, multiple sclerosis and other disorders are gaining relief from smoking marijuana. As a parent, I once had to confront a stark choice—obey the law and let my son suffer or break the law and provide my son with genuine relief from chemotherapeutically induced misery. I chose to help my son. Faced with the same choice again, my husband and I would help our son again. We are confident any parents confronting such circumstances would make the same decision.

# NO

John C. Lawn

# THEIR GOVERNMENT TELLS THEM ALL TO GET LOST

This is a final order of the Administrator of the Drug Enforcement Administration denying the petition of the National Organization for Reform of Marijuana Laws [NORML] to reschedule the plant material marijuana from Schedule I to Schedule II of the Controlled Substances Act. . . .

The two issues involved in a determination of whether marijuana should be rescheduled from Schedule I to Schedule II are whether marijuana plant material has a currently accepted medical use in treatment in the United States, or a currently accepted medical use with severe restrictions; and whether there is a lack of accepted safety for use of marijuana plant material under medical supervision. After a thorough review of the record in this matter, the Administrator rejects the recommendation of the administrative law judge to reschedule marijuana into Schedule II and finds that the evidence in the record mandates a finding that the marijuana plant material remain in Schedule I of the Controlled Substances Act.

The pro-marijuana parties advocate the placement of marijuana plant material into Schedule II for medical use in the treatment of a wide variety of ailments, including nausea and vomiting associated with chemotherapy, glaucoma, spasticity in amputees and those with multiple sclerosis, epilepsy, poor appetite, addiction to drugs and alcohol, pain, and asthma. The evidence presented by the pro-marijuana parties includes outdated and limited scientific studies; chronicles of individuals, their families and friends who have used marijuana; opinions from over a dozen psychiatrists and physicians; court opinions involving medical necessity as a defense to criminal charges for illegal possession of marijuana; state statutes which made marijuana available for research; newspaper articles; and the opinions of laypersons, including lawyers and associations of lawyers. The Administrator does not find such evidence convincing in light of the lack of reliable, credible, and relevant scientific studies documenting marijuana's medical utility; the opinions of highly respected, credentialed experts that marijuana does not have an accepted medical use; and statements from the American

From John C. Lawn, "Their Government Tells Them All to Get Lost," *The Federal Register*, vol. 44, no. 249 (December 29, 1989), p. 53767.

Medical Association, the American Cancer Society, the American Academy of Ophthalmology, the National Multiple Sclerosis Society, and the Federal Food and Drug Administration that marijuana has not been demonstrated as suitable for use as a medicine.

The record contains many research studies which have been published in scientific journals and many unpublished studies conducted by individual states. . . .

Both the published and unpublished research studies submitted by the pro-marijuana parties in this proceeding to support marijuana's medical use suffer from many deficiencies. They are, in essence, preliminary studies. None of these studies has risen to the level of demonstrating that marijuana has an accepted medical use for treatment of any medical condition. . . .

## NAUSEA AND VOMITING

Five studies were presented by the pro-marijuana parties to support the medical use of marijuana as an antiemetic. . . .

The research studies presented by the pro-marijuana parties in this proceeding do not support a conclusion that marijuana has a therapeutic use for treatment of nausea and vomiting associated with chemotherapy.

The pro-marijuana parties presented many testimonials from cancer patients, their families, and friends about the use of marijuana to alleviate nausea and vomiting associated with chemotherapy. These stories of individuals who treat themselves with a mind-altering drug, such as marijuana, must be viewed with great skepticism. There is no scientific merit to any of these accounts. . . . The accounts of these individuals' suffering

and illnesses are very moving and tragic; they are not, however, reliable scientific evidence, nor do they provide a basis to conclude that marijuana has an accepted medical use as an antiemetic.

There were many physicians and other medical experts who testified in this proceeding. In reviewing the weight to be given to an expert's opinion, the facts relied upon to reach that opinion and the credentials and experience of the expert must be carefully examined. The experts presented by the pro-marijuana parties were unable to provide a strong scientific or factual basis to support their opinions. In addition, many of the experts presented by the pro-marijuana parties did not have any expertise in the area of research in the specific medical area being addressed. The pro-marijuana parties presented the testimony of five psychiatrists to support the use of marijuana as an antiemetic. None of these individuals is an oncologist, nor have they treated cancer patients. Three of the psychiatrists, Drs. Grinspoon, Ungerlieder and Zinberg, are current or former board members of NORML or ACT [the Alliance for Cannabis Therapeutics]. . . .

Two pharmacologists, Drs. Morgan and Jobe, presented testimony on behalf of the pro-marijuana parties. Dr. Morgan is a professor at the City College of New York. He does not treat patients, nor is he an oncologist. His opinions are based upon a review of scientific studies and stories told to him by others. He has ties to NORML and is in favor of legalizing marijuana. Dr. Jobe is a pharmacologist and psychiatrist. He testified that his knowledge of marijuana's effects as a drug are based upon a review of the literature and stories from individuals undergoing chemotherapy. . . .

Two general practitioners, Drs. Weil and Kaufmann, also provided testimony on behalf of the pro-marijuana parties, neither are oncologists, nor do they treat cancer patients. Dr. Weil is a wellness counselor at a health spa, and Dr. Kaufman is an officer of a company that audits hospital quality control programs. . . .

Four oncologists presented testimony on behalf of the pro-marijuana parties. They were Drs. Goldberg, Silverberg, Bickers, and Stephens. Dr. Goldberg is a board certified oncologist, but practices primarily internal medicine. She only administers chemotherapy to one or two patients a year. In her career, she has administered chemotherapy to no more than 10 patients whom she believed to be using marijuana. On cross-examination, she could not recall any studies regarding marijuana. Dr. Goldberg was a member and financial contributor to NORML. Dr. Silverberg has practiced oncology for 20 years. He is a Professor of Clinical Oncology at the University of California at San Francisco, but is not a board certified oncologist. . . .

Although Dr. Silverberg has advised patients to use marijuana to control nausea and vomiting associated with chemotherapy, he has never been involved in any research nor has he documented any of his observations. Dr. Bickers is an oncologist in New Orleans and is a Professor of Medicine at the Louisiana University School of Medicine. Although Dr. Bickers claims that young patients have better control over nausea and vomiting after using marijuana, he has never documented this claim. Dr. Stephens, an oncologist professor of Medicine and Director of Clinical Oncology at the University of Kansas, characterized marijuana as a "highly effective, and in some cases, critical drug in the reduction of chemotherapeutically-induced emesis."

During cross-examination, Dr. Stephens stated that he was unaware of any scientific studies which had been done with marijuana, and that he had never done research or treated patients with marijuana. He indicated that he received his information about the patient's use of marijuana from the nursing staff or the patient's family. . . .

The pro-marijuana parties presented cases in which courts did not convict individuals of a crime associated with possession and use of marijuana based upon a legal defense of "medical necessity." These cases have no relevance to this proceeding which relates to marijuana's possible medical use. The courts found only that these individuals, who were seriously ill and believed that marijuana would help them, did not have criminal intent in possessing or using marijuana. . . .

The pro-marijuana parties also presented evidence that 34 states passed laws permitting marijuana's use for medical purposes in those states. These laws provided that marijuana should be available for medical research. The term "research" is essential to a reading of these statutes. These laws made marijuana available for research and, in some states, set up research programs to study marijuana's safety and effectiveness as a medicine. These statutes are read for what they are, encouraging research involving marijuana. They are not an endorsement by state legislatures that marijuana has an accepted medical use in treatment.

The numerous testimonials and opinions of lay persons which were presented in this proceeding by the pro-marijuana parties are not useful in determining whether marijuana has a medical use. While experiences of individuals with medical conditions who use marijuana may provide a basis for research, they cannot be substituted for reliable scientific evidence. For the many reasons stated in the previous discussion of scientific evidence, these statements can be given little weight. Similarly, endorsements by such organizations as the National Association of Attorneys General, that marijuana has medical use as an antiemetic are of little persuasive value when compared with statements from the American Cancer Society and the American Medical Association.

## GLAUCOMA

The pro-marijuana parties presented several studies to support their contention that marijuana has a medical use for treatment of glaucoma. In order for a drug to be effective in treating glaucoma it must lower the pressure within the eye for prolonged periods of time and actually preserve sight or visual fields. The studies relied upon by the pro-marijuana parties do not scientifically support a finding that marijuana has a medicinal use for treatment of glaucoma. Five of the studies presented by the pro-marijuana parties are pure THC studies. As previously noted, THC is only one constituent among hundreds found in marijuana. Therefore, the consequences of an individual ingesting pure THC as compared to smoking marijuana are vastly different. A few of the studies presented do document that heavy doses of marijuana over a short time period reduce eye pressure in most individuals. However, there are no studies which document that marijuana can sustain reduced eye pressure for extended time periods.

The acute, or short-term, studies also show various side effects from marijuana use. . . .

The pro-marijuana parties presented testimonials of individuals who suffer from glaucoma and believe their condition has benefited from the use of marijuana. Most of these individuals used marijuana recreationally prior to discovery of their illness. Chief among the individuals presenting statements was Robert Randall. Mr. Randall is president of ACT, and has been on NORML's Board of Directors since 1976. He has been a strong advocate for medical use of marijuana. Mr. Randall also has glaucoma. Mr. Randall began smoking marijuana as a college student in 1966, long before he was diagnosed in 1972 as having glaucoma. At that time Mr. Randall was treated with standard glaucoma medications. In the mid-1970s Mr. Randall was involved in a preliminary research study conducted by Dr. Robert Hepler. Dr. Hepler conducted some of the first published short-term marijuana studies relating to glaucoma. Dr. Hepler told Mr. Randall that he believed that marijuana in combination with other standard glaucoma medications would be helpful in reducing his eye pressure. In 1975, Mr. Randall was arrested for growing and possessing marijuana. His defense was medical necessity. Subsequently, he began receiving marijuana under an Investigational New Drug (IND) protocol sponsored by his physician. He also continued to receive standard glaucoma medications. Since 1976, Mr. Randall has been treated by Dr. North. Mr. Randall receives marijuana from the federal government and continues to take standard glaucoma medications. Two physicians who treated Mr. Randall, including Dr. North, testified that Mr. Randall's eye pressure appears to have been controlled and his vision kept stable for the last several years.

Mr. Randall smokes approximately 8–10 marijuana cigarettes a day. Since Mr. Randall continues to take other glaucoma medication, his controlled eye pressure cannot be attributable solely to marijuana use. In fact, Dr. North testified that Mr. Randall needs the standard medications as well as marijuana, and that the marijuana itself is not totally effective in decreasing Mr. Randall's eye pressure. Mr. Randall's experience with marijuana, although utilized under a physician's directions, is not scientific evidence that marijuana has an accepted medical use in treatment of glaucoma. Dr. Merritt, one of Mr. Randall's physicians, responded to the question of why he did not publish the results of Mr. Randall's treatment by saying, "A single isolated incident of one person smoking marijuana is not evidence for other ophthalmologists who may want to use the drug."

. . . The pro-marijuana parties rely primarily on the opinions of two of Mr. Randall's physicians, Drs. North and Merritt, in supporting their contention that marijuana has a medical use in treatment of glaucoma. Dr. North indicated that his conclusion that marijuana has a medical use in treatment of glaucoma is based solely on his observations of Mr. Randall. Dr. Merritt is a board-certified ophthalmologist and researcher who has authored many articles on the use [of] marijuana and cannabinoids to reduce eye pressure. Dr. Merritt based his opinion that marijuana has a medical use in treatment of glaucoma on published scientific studies, treatment of Mr. Randall, and treatment of other glaucoma patients. As previously stated all the available studies concern high doses of marijuana taken over short periods of time. Even Dr. Merritt admitted that there are no studies to show that marijuana repeatedly lowers eye pressure over long time periods. The maintenance of lowered eye pressure is crucial in treating individuals with glaucoma. . . .

## SPASTICITY

In support of their contention that marijuana has a medical use in treatment of spasticity in amputees and those with multiple sclerosis, the pro-marijuana parties presented three studies involving THC, testimonials of individuals with spasticity who use marijuana, medical opinions, and state court decisions on the medical necessity defense. The three studies presented by the pro-marijuana parties were very small studies. All three totaled 17 patients, and used THC, not marijuana, to treat spasticity. There are no studies using marijuana to treat spasticity. . . .

With regard to marijuana's safety for use under medical supervision, the administrator must again rely on the scientific evidence. While the pro-marijuana parties argue that no one has died from marijuana use, and individuals who use it have testified that they have not experienced adverse effects, there is little or no scientific evidence to support their claims. For example, while Robert Randall claims marijuana smoking has had no adverse effect on his health or respiratory system, he has not had a physical examination or pulmonary function in over 10 years.

In order to be effective, a drug's therapeutic benefits must be balanced against and outweigh its negative or adverse effects. This has not been established with marijuana. As the previously discussed evidence has demonstrated, there is as yet no reliable scientific evidence to support marijuana's therapeutic benefit. It is therefore, impossible to balance the benefit against the negative effects. The negative effects of marijuana use are well-documented in the record. Marijuana smoking, the route of administration advocated by many witnesses presented by the pro-marijuana parties, causes many well-known and scientifically documented side effects. These include decreased blood pressure, rapid heart rate, drowsiness, euphoria, disphoria and impairment of motor function, not to mention various negative effects on the respiratory and pulmonary systems. Therefore, the only conclusion is that marijuana is not safe for use under medical supervision, because its safety has not been established by reliable scientific evidence.

In summary, the Administrator finds that there is insufficient and in many instances no, reliable, credible, scientific evidence, supported by properly conducted scientific research, to support a conclusion that marijuana is safe for use under medical supervision. This agency, and the government as a whole, would be doing the public a disservice by concluding that this complex psychoactive drug with serious adverse effects has a medical use based upon anecdotal and unreliable evidence. . . .

## CONCLUSION

The Administrator finds that the administrative law judge failed to act as an impartial judge in this matter. He appears to have ignored the scientific evidence, ignored the testimony of highly credible and recognized medical experts and, instead, relied on the testimony of

psychiatrists and individuals who use marijuana. The administrative law judge relied heavily on ancedotal accounts of marijuana use by both physicians and seriously ill persons. The administrative law judge's findings of fact ignored any evidence presented by the government. For example, in his findings regarding marijuana and nausea and vomiting associated with chemotherapy, Judge Young cites many of the physicians presented by the pro-marijuana parties by name as accepting marijuana as "medically useful." Not once in his findings or discussion does the judge acknowledge or mention the government's experts. Not once does the judge mention why he chose to find the pro-marijuana parties' evidence more credible. . . .

The Administrator rejects the administrative law judge's findings and conclusion. They were erroneous; they were not based upon credible evidence; nor were they based upon evidence in the record as a whole. Therefore, in this case, they carry no weight and do not represent the position of the agency or its Administrator. The inadequacy of Judge Young's analysis of the case is duly noted and so are the irrational statements propounded by the pro-marijuana parties. Such statements include the following: "Marijuana is far safer than many of the foods we commonly consume. For example, eating ten raw potatoes can result in a toxic response. By comparison, it is physically impossible to eat enough marijuana to induce death." That such a statement would come from the proponents of marijuana is understandable. To give it the weight of an administrative law judge's finding is appalling. . . .

As a final note, the administrator expresses his displeasure at the misleading accusations and conclusions leveled at the Government and communicated to the public by the pro-marijuana parties, specifically NORML and ACT. These two organizations have falsely raised the expectations of many seriously ill persons by claiming that marijuana has medical usefulness in treating glaucoma, spasticity and other illnesses. Their statements have probably caused many people with serious diseases to experiment with marijuana to the detriment of their own health, without proper medical supervision, and without knowing about the serious side effects which smoking or ingesting marijuana may cause. These are not the Dark Ages. The Congress, as well as the medical community, has accepted that drugs should not be available to the public unless they are found by scientific studies to be effective and safe. To do otherwise is to jeopardize the American public, and take advantage of desperately ill people who will try anything to alleviate their suffering. The Administrator strongly urges the American public not to experiment with potentially dangerous, mind-altering drugs such as marijuana in an attempt to treat a serious illness or condition. . . . NORML and ACT have attempted to perpetrate a dangerous and cruel hoax on the American public by claiming marijuana has currently accepted medical uses.

# POSTSCRIPT

## Should Medical Patients Be Permitted to Use Marijuana?

Nutt contends that her son's experiences with marijuana in which his side effects from chemotherapy were relieved by the drug were very positive. For Nutt, his experiences more than adequately prove marijuana's vital role in the treatment of painful medical conditions. Therefore, she strongly advocates the legalization of marijuana for medical treatment. Nutt argues that the delay in the medicalization of marijuana stems from the arduous, restrictive, and purely research-oriented procedures of the federal government and that the government blocks the ill from getting a "compassionate program of patient care." Nutt's testimony is moving. However, should the government's policies be predicated on personal accounts?

Lawn believes that the federal government cannot ignore the qualified medical testimonies of physicians and other researchers who do not recommend marijuana for medical use. Lawn takes the position that promarijuana reports suffer from unscientific methodology as well as other deficiencies. The results of previous research, he contends, do not lend strong credence to marijuana's medicinal value. A related concern is that if marijuana is approved for medicinal use, would it then become more acceptable for nonmedical uses? There is also a possibility that some people would misinterpret the government's message and think that marijuana cures cancer when, in fact, it is used only to reduce the side effects of chemotherapy.

A central question is, If physicians feel that marijuana use is justified to properly care for seriously ill patients, should they promote medical treatment that falls outside the law? Does the relief of pain and suffering for patients warrant going beyond what federal legislation says is acceptable? Also, should physicians be prosecuted if they recommend marijuana to their patients? What about the unknown risks of using an illegal drug? Is it worthwhile to ignore the possibility that marijuana use may produce harmful side effects in order to alleviate pain or to treat ailments?

Many marijuana proponents contend that the effort to prevent the legalization of marijuana for medical use is purely a political battle. Detractors argue against marijuana's legalization for medical use on the basis that the data are inconclusive and scientifically unsubstantiated. Although a recommendation was made to the Drug Enforcement Administration (DEA) by its chief administrative law judge to change the status of marijuana from a

Schedule I to a Schedule II classification, the DEA and other federal agencies are not compelled to do so, and they have resisted any change in the law.

In his essay "Legalizing Drugs for Medical Purposes," in Arnold Trebach and Kevin Zeese, eds., *New Frontiers in Drug Policy* (Drug Policy Foundation, 1991), psychiatrist Lester Grinspoon argues against the government's ban on the medical use of marijuana. Grinspoon describes the potential medical benefits of marijuana in addition to its role in reducing the side effects of chemotherapy. In this same publication, Richard Doblin and Mark Kleiman, "Marijuana as Medicine: A Survey of Oncologists," report on a study in which they found that almost half of the oncologists surveyed recommended marijuana to their patients to help them deal with the side effects of chemotherapy. The DEA's refusal to legalize marijuana for medical purposes is discussed in Michael Conlan's "Top Drug Cop Weighs Use of Marijuana as Rx Drug," *Drug Topics* (1988). In a critique supporting the medical ban on marijuana, Gabriel Nahas, *Marijuana in Science and Medicine* (Raven Press, 1984), contends that the research is inconclusive and that better drugs are available.

# ISSUE 3

## Does Drug Testing Violate Civil Rights?

**YES: Leonard H. Glantz,** from "A Nation of Suspects: Drug Testing and the Fourth Amendment," *American Journal of Public Health* (October 1989)

**NO: Robert L. DuPont,** from "Mandatory Random Testing Needs to Be Undertaken at the Worksite," in Ruth C. Engs, ed., *Controversies in the Addiction's Field, Volume One* (Kendall/Hunt, 1990)

### ISSUE SUMMARY

**YES:** Professor of health law Leonard H. Glantz argues that random drug testing violates civil liberties and sacrifices citizens' Fourth Amendment rights for the sake of the war on drugs.
**NO:** Physician and psychiatrist Robert L. DuPont contends that the dangers of illicit drug use warrant mandatory random drug testing and that testing at the workplace is the fairest and most cost-effective means of preventing illicit drug use.

In 1986, President Ronald Reagan first called for a drug-free federal workplace, ordering all federal employees in "sensitive" jobs to submit to random drug testing. The goal was to begin attacking the drug problem from the demand side and to involve all employees, both public and private, in the fight against drugs. As a result of this effort, government agencies, including the military, adopted the practice of random urine testing to screen employees for illicit drugs. More than 60 percent of the major corporations in the United States also require drug testing as a condition of employment.

The impetus for random drug testing stems from a 1987 collision between an Amtrak train and a Conrail train near Baltimore, Maryland, which claimed the lives of 16 people. Because both the Conrail engineer and brakeman had used marijuana just prior to the wreck, the cause of the crash was immediately tied to drug use, even though the warning indicators on the Conrail train were malfunctioning at the time. This was a strong indication to many that drug testing was needed—if not for the sake of deterring employees from using illicit drugs for their own well-being, then to ensure the safety of others.

The Fourth Amendment of the U.S. Constitution guarantees citizens the right to be protected from unreasonable searches and seizures. With regard to drug testing, this should protect citizens from being tested unless probable cause, or a reason to suppose that an individual is engaged in criminal behavior, is shown. Many people feel that random drug testing is unreasonable because it involves testing even those employees who are not drug users and who have shown no cause to be tested. In addition, drug tests may not clearly differentiate between on-the-job drug use and off-duty drug use. Many people contend that an infringement of personal liberties and an unwarranted invasion of privacy for the sake of the government's drug battle agenda are at stake.

Others believe that all people suffer from individuals' use of illicit drugs. For example, the public pays higher prices due to lost productivity from work-related accidents and job absenteeism caused by drug use. Also, innocent people are often directly victimized by individuals on drugs who inadvertently make dangerous mistakes. Thus, from this perspective, random drug tests are not unreasonable searches. Proponents for drug testing contend that the inherent dangers of drug use, particularly while on the job, necessitate drug testing. Accidents and deaths can and do occur due to drug-induced losses of awareness and judgment. The fact that 70 percent of the 14.5 million Americans who use illicit drugs are employed has convinced many that random drug testing at the workplace should be mandatory.

In the following selections, Leonard H. Glantz argues that the arbitrary nature of drug testing transforms innocent as well as guilty individuals into suspects and requires all citizens to prove their innocence. He maintains that the Constitution grants individual liberties over government agendas and that drug testing sacrifices the American public's right to protection under the Fourth Amendment. Drug use is a problem in society, but Glantz feels that drug testing is not the fairest and most efficient way of dealing with this problem.

Robert L. DuPont argues that when drug use affects the safety of others, it is indeed appropriate to implement random drug testing at the workplace. He also believes that a surefire way to combat the overall problem of illicit drug use is to start with employers testing employees for drug use. He contends that random drug testing at the workplace achieves the principal goal of preventing drug use and problems caused by drugs because it provides the strongest incentive for employees to stop using drugs—if they do not stop, they will lose their jobs.

# YES
Leonard H. Glantz

# A NATION OF SUSPECTS: DRUG TESTING AND THE FOURTH AMENDMENT

As concern about illegal drug use in the United States has escalated, increasingly draconian measures have been suggested or implemented. Boats and airplanes have been seized when only very small amounts of illegal drugs have been found under a "zero tolerance policy." New rules are being proposed for the simplified eviction of families from public housing if a member of the family has been charged with drug possession, even outside the public housing grounds. Legislators in Texas and Delaware have introduced bills that would punish drug dealers with amputation of fingers and flogging.[1] The legislators who introduced these bills have made it clear they were not joking.

One of the weapons in the drug war arsenal is drug testing in the workplace. The pretext is often detection of worker impairment, but this is seldom the true motivation. Much of the impetus for the current drug testing rage comes from the 1986 President's Commission on Organized Crime report, *America's Habit: Drug Abuse, Drug Trafficking and Organized Crime*, which recommended that "Government and private sector employers who do not already require drug testing of job applicants and current employees should consider the appropriateness of such a testing program."[2] In the context of a report on organized crime, workplace drug testing becomes a tool for attacking the drug problem from the demand side. If users can be stopped, then the drug traffickers and dealers will have no one to whom to sell their drugs. President Ronald Reagan underscored this approach in ordering a drug-free federal workplace, declaring that illegal drug use on or off duty by federal employees is not acceptable for a variety of reasons, and directing the head of each executive agency to establish programs to test for the use of illegal drugs by employees in "sensitive positions."[3] One of the goals is to recruit employers, both public and private, into the war on drugs. Former Attorney General Edwin Meese even suggested that employers "undertake surveillance of problem areas, such as locker rooms, parking lots, shipping and mailroom areas, and nearby taverns if necessary."[4]

As a result of this fervor, the pace of workplace drug testing has notably increased. Workers from groups as diverse as firefighters, police officers, nuclear power plant employees, school bus aides, probationary school teachers, and computer programmers have been subjected to mandatory drug testing. There has understandably been a complementary increase in the number of lawsuits brought by workers to halt what they feel is a demeaning and intrusive procedure. The courts have been divided in their determination of the legality of mandatory drug tests. The vast majority of the cases have been brought by governmental employees, since their employers are subject to the restrictions against unreasonable searches and seizures found in the Fourth Amendment of the US Constitution:

> The right of the people to be secure in their persons, houses, papers, and effects, against unreasonable searches and seizures, shall not be violated, and no Warrants shall issue, but upon probable cause, supported by Oath or affirmation, and particularly describing the place to be searched, and the persons or things to be seized.

Not *all* searches are forbidden by the Fourth Amendment—only unreasonable ones. Where a search warrant is secured upon probable cause from a judicial officer, a search becomes reasonable. Over the years, however, the courts have carved out exceptions to both the warrant and probable cause requirements and have, at times, looked at other circumstances to determine if a search is reasonable and, therefore, lawful.

The initial question was, is a urine test a search or seizure at all? In one case, which upheld drug testing of police officers in limited circumstances, a concurring judge argued that requiring a person to urinate on demand could not be a search or seizure since a person could not "retain a privacy interest in a waste product that, once released, is flushed down a drain" and that one could not have a "subjective expectation of privacy in a body waste that must pass from his system."[5] However, no majority of any court has reached this conclusion, and all that have decided the issue have concluded that a mandatory urine, blood or breath test constitutes a search under the Fourth Amendment. The focus of the courts, therefore, has been on the "unreasonableness" of the "search" that is involved in drug testing.

Drug testing can be conducted in a variety of ways. It can be done by examining the urine, blood, or breath of an individual. The urine can be collected by allowing the person to urinate privately, while someone listens for the normal sounds of urination, or under direct observation. People can be tested randomly, as a result of behavior that indicates impairment due to drug use, as part of pre-employment or annual physicals, as a result of known procedures, or through sheer whim and surprise. A positive test can lead to a re-test, a warning to stop drug use, voluntary or mandatory drug treatment programs, termination of employment, or criminal prosecution. Given the possible various combinations of these factors, it is not surprising that courts have split on the "unreasonableness" of drug testing in various situations.

The depth of a court's feeling that mandatory drug screening is demeaning, intrusive, or a violation of a person's general right to be free from governmental intrusions, also affects its decision. For example, in one case the Plainfield, New Jersey Fire Department entered a city firehouse at 7:00 AM, secured and locked all the station doors, awoke all the firefighters on duty and ordered them to submit a urine sample while under surveillance.[6] There was no notice of any intent to require urinalysis, there was no written directive, policy or procedure, and nothing in the collective bargaining agreement regarding drug tests. All firefighters who tested positive for "controlled substances" were immediately terminated without pay. They were not told of the particular substance found in their urine or its concentration, nor were they provided with copies of the actual laboratory results. The city had no reason to suspect that any of the tested firefighters had used drugs or were impaired in any way. There were no complaints from the public about inadequate fire protection and no increase in the incidence of accidents. In short, there was no reason for this surprise raid.

The court cited several concerns in invalidating this testing process. First, the court noted that while public employees' liberty interests may be somewhat diminished while on the job, that they are not extinguished and are entitled to constitutional protection. It was also found that "mass round-up urinalysis" casually sweeps up the guilty and the innocent and "willingly sacrifices each individual's Fourth Amendment rights in the name of some larger public interest." As the court pointed out, the city essentially presumed each firefighter was guilty, and the burden was shifted to these individuals to submit to a highly intrusive test to vindicate his or her innocence. Such a presumption of guilt is contrary to the Constitution.

Perhaps even more important than the details of the constitutional analysis was the court's perception of the intrusiveness of mandatory urine screening:

> We would be appalled at the spectre of the police spying on employees during their free time and then reporting their activities to their employers. Drug testing is a form of surveillance, albeit a technological one. Nonetheless, it reports on a person's off-duty activities just as surely as someone had been present and watching. It is George Orwell's "Big Brother" society come to life.[6]

Some courts have taken the approach that certain public employees, particularly police officers, have a more limited constitutional right to be free from searches and seizures than private citizens because of the dangerous nature of their work and the "paramilitary" nature of the police force. These courts have thus found that a search via urinalysis can be required in the absence of "probable cause" as that term is strictly applied, but that the supervisory personnel ordering the test must have a "reasonable, objective basis to suspect that a urinalysis will produce evidence of illegal drug use."[5] This reasonable basis must be "related to the police officer's fitness for duty."[5] Random or mass testing is not permitted, but if the officer, by his or her actions, shows some job impairment that would be related to drug use, testing would be allowed.

The courts have balanced the Constitutional right to be free from intrusive searches against the need for public safety. The question is always, how far should the balance tip away from the right to be free from governmental intrusion—how weighty must the public interest be to abridge their rights? In 1986, one of the first federal courts of appeal to deal with the issue of drug testing tipped the balance powerfully in favor of governmental testing.[7] Jockeys had asked the court to strike down a rule of the New Jersey Racing Commission that required, among other things, the random drug urine screening of jockeys after a race. The state's interest in invading a jockey's Constitutional rights could, of course, in no way be related to public safety. Rather, the court upheld the testing on the basis of the state's interest in "the protection of the state's fisc by virtue of the wagering public's confidence in the integrity of the industry."[7] This is a remarkably thin thread on which to support the abridgement of Constitutional rights. It is hard to know just what the public opinion is regarding the integrity of the horse-racing industry; but it seems unlikely that post-race testing of jockeys would have much of an effect on it.

Even more disturbing was the rest of the court's reasoning. It based its holding on the fact that horse racing was an intensely regulated industry and, therefore, the industry is subject to the "administrative search" exception to the Fourth Amendment. It is certainly true that because some industries are highly regulated, their *premises* may be searched either without a warrant,[8] or with a much lower requirement for a search warrant than "probable cause."[9] Thus, certain warehouses, or coal mines can be easily inspected for violations of health and safety laws. However, the administrative search exception has been used to search places in highly regulated industries, not persons. The court was aware of the distinction, it just did not find it important. Not only is the result shocking, the reasoning is frightening. To abridge essential Constitutional rights to be free from governmental searches for the reasons this court gave meant the virtual destruction of the Fourth Amendment as it pertained to drug testing. If government agents can test jockeys for the reasons the court stated, who couldn't the state order tested?

A number of courts have cited this opinion in upholding drug testing, but others have rejected it. The Massachusetts Supreme Judicial Court struck down a more limited jockey testing regulation, holding that the state cannot abridge constitutional rights "to insure the integrity of betting on horses."[10] Another federal Court of Appeals case involved the department-wide testing of all firefighters without reasonable cause to believe that any individual used controlled substances.[11] The court forcefully rejected the idea that because an industry was heavily regulated, individuals who worked in that industry could have their Constitutional rights easily abridged, stating such an approach is "simplistic and intellectually indefensible."[11] The court noted that the creation of the administrative search exception was founded on the basis that such searches were not personal in nature, and found it "incredible" that it could be used to uphold searches of persons. The balancing test was much more strictly applied.

The court noted that a very different magnitude of harm would occur if a single air traffic controller or nuclear plant employee was impaired from drug use, than if a single firefighter were impaired: " . . . there is a continuum of employment categories that are defined by the degree of suspicion that a drug problem exists and the potential harm to society of an impaired employee operating in that employment sector."[11] The court struck down the testing rule because there was no evidence of a drug problem in the fire department.

Given the diversity of opinions and approaches used by various courts across the country, it was only a matter of time before the United States Supreme Court would enter the fray. On March 21, 1989, the Court handed down the first two of what is likely to be a series of opinions on drug testing.

The first case, *Skinner v. Railway Labor Executive Association*,[12] involved the constitutionality of a drug testing scheme directed at railway workers. While the tests were to be performed by private railways on their employees, the tests implicated Fourth Amendment concerns because they were either mandated or authorized by the Federal Railroad Administration (FRA). In 1985, the FRA promulgated regulations addressing alcohol and drug use by certain railway employees. The regulations forbid these employees from using or possessing alcohol or any controlled substance while on the job, and prohibit employees from reporting to work while under the influence of, or impaired by, controlled substances or alcohol, or having a blood alcohol level of .04 or higher. These regulations were issued in response to evidence that a significant proportion of railroad workers report to work impaired by alcohol or got drunk while working, that 23 percent of operating personnel were "problem drinkers," and that from 1972 to 1983 at least 21 significant accidents resulting in fatalities, serious injury and multimillion dollar property damage involved alcohol and drug use as a probable cause or contributing factor."[12]

In addition to the prohibition on drug or alcohol use, the regulations provided for drug testing in two circumstances. First, after any accident which involves a fatality, the release of hazardous material accompanied by an evacuation or reportable injury, or damage to railroad property in excess of $500,000, or a collision that results in a reportable injury or damage to railroad property in excess of $50,000, all crew members and other covered employees are required to be transported to an independent medical facility where both blood and urine samples are to be obtained. The samples are then shipped to an FRA laboratory which is to detect any presence of drugs or alcohol using "state-of-the-art" equipment and techniques. Employees who refuse to provide blood or urine samples may not perform certain services for nine months, and are entitled to a hearing concerning their refusal.[12]

A second part of the regulation provides for permissive testing of employees in instances where supervisors have a "reasonable suspicion" that an employee is under the influence of drugs or alcohol or where an employee appears to be impaired. In these circumstances, the railroad may require breath or urine tests. If the railroad plans to use the results of these breath or urine tests in a disciplinary hearing, it must give the employee an opportunity to provide a blood sample to an independent laboratory. If the employee refuses to do so, the railroad may presume impairment from the results of the urine test.[12] The US Court of Appeals that heard this case struck down all the testing provisions that did not require "individualized suspicion" prior to testing. Such a standard, that court said, would impose no insuperable burden on the government and would ensure that "the tests are confined to the detection of current impairment" rather than discovering the metabolites of various drugs that may remain in the body for days or weeks, and which do not provide evidence of current impairment.[13] The Supreme Court reversed, and upheld FRA's drug testing scheme by a 7 to 2 vote.

In its analysis, the Court recognizes that blood, urine and breath testing are an invasion of employee privacy interests and are a "search" for the purposes of the Fourth Amendment. The Court also recognizes that to perform a search, a warrant or at least probable cause is usually required. But at times, as the Court has held in the past, the government may have "special needs" beyond normal law enforcement that may justify departures from the usual warrant and probable cause requirements. The opinion then discusses the "special needs" in this case. First, the employees to be tested are engaged in "safety-sensitive tasks." Second, the purpose of the tests are not to aid in prosecution of employees, but rather to prevent accidents. Third, those charged with administering the test have minimal discretion and, therefore, there is only a minimal chance of arbitrary or unfair use of the testing procedure. Fourth, railroad investigators are not familiar with the Fourth Amendment or warrant requirements. Fifth, if a warrant was required, the delay in obtaining the warrant might allow the needed evidence to be dissipated. Sixth, although urine tests invade an "excretory function traditionally shielded by great privacy," the regulations do not require the direct observation of a monitor, and it is not unlike similar procedures performed in the context of a "regular physical examination." Seventh,

the expectations of privacy of employees is "diminished by reason of their participation in an industry that is pervasively regulated to ensure safety." Eighth, the interests of the government to test are "compelling" because the employees can cause "great human loss before any other signs of impairment become noticeable to supervisors." Ninth, the regulations will be an effective means of deterring employees from using alcohol or drugs. Finally, the testing procedures will help railroads obtain "invaluable information about the causes of major accidents."[12]

This is a remarkably utilitarian approach to the Fourth Amendment, as the dissent notes. Essentially, it holds that the Fourth Amendment safeguards are not applicable to situations where the government has good reasons to want information and the intrusion on the person is not great. It makes no effort to distinguish between the searches of places or things, and searches of persons. As the two dissenters argue, "The majority's acceptance of dragnet blood and urine testing ensures that the first, and worst, casualty of the war on drugs will be the precious liberties of our citizens."[12] The dissent points out that the Fourth Amendment was designed to make governmental searches of citizens difficult, and that it is all too easy to balance away individual rights for the good of the state. However, that balancing was done by the Founders in favor of the individual. The dissenters agree that if the police were freed from the constraints of the Fourth Amendment, the resulting convictions would probably prevent thousands of fatalities. But "our refusal to tolerate this spectre reflects our shared beliefs that even beneficient governmental power—whether exercised to save money, save lives, or make the trains run on time—must always yield to a resolute loyalty to constitutional safeguards."[12]

The dissenters were unconvinced that there is any evidence that drug testing is a deterrent or provides useful evidence of the causes of accidents, and were even more concerned with the majority's standardless and shifting balancing of individual rights and state powers to invade those rights, and its "cavalier disregard" for the text of the Constitution: "There is no drug exception to the Constitution, any more than there is a Communist exception or an exception for other real or imagined sources of domestic unrest."[12] In continuing this argument, Justice Thurgood Marshall concluded:

In upholding the FRA's plan for blood and urine testing, the majority bends time-honored and textually-based principles of the Fourth Amendment—principles the Framers of the Bill of Rights designed to ensure that the Government has a strong and individualized justification when it seeks to invade an individual's privacy. I believe the Framers would be appalled by the vision of mass governmental intrusions upon the integrity of the human body that the majority allows to become reality. The immediate victims of the majority's constitutional timorousness will be those railroad workers whose bodily fluids the Government may now forcibly collect and analyze. But ultimately, today's decision will reduce the privacy all citizens may enjoy, for, as Justice Holmes understood, principles of law, once bent, do not snap back easily.[12]

The second case, *National Treasury Employees Union v. von Raab*,[14] concerned drug testing employees of the US Cus-

toms Services who apply for positions that meet one of three criteria: direct involvement in drug interdiction or enforcement of related laws, carrying a firearm, or access to classified material. An employee who applies for one of these positions is instructed that final selection is contingent upon successful completion of a drug screen. Therefore, unlike the railroad case, this is in essence an anti-drug loyalty test—there is no pretense of finding impairment. The goal is to keep drug users out of these positions. Anyone who tests positive for drugs is subject to dismissal although the results are not to be turned over to prosecutors.

In a 5 to 4 opinion, the court upheld this drug testing program. What is particularly remarkable here is that the interests that the Customs Service put forward as justifying the abridgement of its employee's Fourth Amendment rights are all theoretical. For example, the government argued that even off-duty drug use creates the risk of bribery and blackmail. Indeed, the Customs Service proved that several officials have been the target of bribery and others have accepted bribes. There was, however, no indication that any of these cases involved Customs officials who used drugs. It was argued that drug users might be unsympathetic to the mission of interdicting narcotics. It was argued that those who carry firearms need to be deterred from drug use which might impair their perception. Even the statistic that only five of the 3,600 employees who had already been tested were found to be positive for drugs had any force, since the Court pointed out that the program is designed to prevent drug use. In the absence of any proof of any real or substantial drug problem in the Customs Service, the Court upheld this drug testing program in order to ensure the "integrity" of the Customs Service.[14]*

Justice Antonin Scalia, one of the Court's conservatives, wrote a scathing dissent, noting "The Customs Service rules are a kind of immolation of privacy and human dignity in symbolic opposition to drug use." Justice Scalia believes that the justification set forth to uphold the testing scheme is not just speculation, but "not very plausible speculation." As he argues, the speculation that a drug user is more likely to be bribed by a drug smuggler, is no more likely than the chance of an employee who wears diamonds being bribed by a diamond smuggler. He asserts that police officers who speed in their private cars do not appear to be less sympathetic to enforcing speeding laws. Justice Scalia is not even impressed with the arguments dealing with gun-carrying agents—as he puts it, if they are not deterred by the knowledge that they "may be shot dead in unequal combat with unimpaired smugglers" it seems unlikely that drug testing would deter their drug use. Ultimately, Justice Scalia notes that since the justification for the Customs Service drug screening is so feeble, that its true rationale must be found elsewhere. He finds it in the Commissioner's memorandum announcing the program. The concluding sentence states, "Implementation of the drug screening program would set an important example in our country's struggle with this most serious threat to our national health and security." Scalia responds, "I think that this justification is unacceptable; that the impairment of individual liberties cannot be the means of making a point, that symbolism, even symbolism for so worthy a cause as the abolition of unlawful drugs, cannot invalidate an otherwise unreasonable search."[14]

What do these cases mean for the future right of individuals to be free of government intrusions? In some senses, these cases can be construed very narrowly. In Skinner,[12] it could be argued that we were dealing with a group of employees with a history of substance abuse who have caused substantial harm to life and property as a result of that abuse. In that circumstance, a serious accident could provide "reasonable suspicion" of substance use by those who may have caused the accident. Thus, it can be argued, that this case represents only a small expansion of the "reasonable suspicion" standard that has been used by courts in upholding the drug testing of other public safety employees. Even the Customs Service case can be construed narrowly. The Court of Appeals which upheld that the drug testing program did so in large part because of its limited scope—"Only employees seeking transfer to sensitive positions are required to take the test and only as a result of a process they choose to set in motion."[15] Viewed this way, the Customs Service testing program is largely "voluntary," and gives no support to mandatory testing.

Unfortunately, the majority opinions of the Supreme Court made no effort to limit their holdings to the narrow facts of the case before it. Whether or not they do so in the future is impossible to predict. It will take more cases before any defi-

*The Court did strike down part of the Customs' testing program. Included in the groups of employees who were deemed to have access to "sensitive information" were accountants, animal caretakers, all attorneys, mail clerks and electric equipment repairers. The Court felt that this categorization might be too broad and sent the case back to the lower courts to examine the issue.

nite answer about the constitutionality of any particular drug testing program can be confidently stated. However, particularly in the Customs Service case, five justices showed a strong propensity for upholding drug testing programs for speculative and symbolic reasons, and a willingness to ignore the protections of the Fourth Amendment.

The fear that these opinions have no principled boundaries was expressed by Justice Scalia when he pointed out that automobile drivers, construction equipment operators, and school crossing guards all have safety-sensitive jobs. Could they be drug tested based on the speculative injuries that they might cause if under the influence of drugs? Could states require physicians or nurses to be drug tested as a condition of licensure? There is more evidence of drug use by physicians and medical students than there was evidence of drug use by customs workers.[16] If the court is serious about upholding drug testing to ensure the integrity of a program and prevent the possibility of bribery, then certainly it is judges who should be tested, since they are the ultimate arbiters of imprisonment or freedom for accused drug dealers. One could go on indefinitely making lists of potential job categories that might be eligible for drug screening using the Court's rationale.

This is not idle speculation or liberal hysteria. The drug testing cases have already been used to expand the reach of government into the lives of individuals. For example, a licensed practical nurse was fired when he refused to submit to an HIV (human immunodeficiency virus) test, or to disclose the results of a test he had taken earlier.[17] His employer, a public hospital, had learned that his lover had recently died of AIDS (ac-

quired immunodeficiency syndrome), and wanted to know his HIV status in order to decide what duties he could perform. While the procedures he regularly performed could hardly be deemed invasive, this did not deter the hospital. One of the nurse's claims was that the hospital's demand violated his Fourth Amendment rights. Citing the hospital's desire to provide a "safe and efficient workplace," and pointing out that the nurse was in a "safety-sensitive" position, the court readily upheld the hospital's demand based on the appellate courts' decisions in the railroad workers and Customs Service cases. The result would seem to be supported by the Supreme Court's decisions.

In our well-intended desire to stop the flow of drugs into the country and reduce drug abuse, we are rapidly becoming a nation of suspects. Perfectly law abiding citizens who are under no suspicion of drug use are increasingly being called upon to prove their innocence. This activity extends the scope of those who are victims of the drug war. As Justice Scalia so eloquently put it:

> Those who lose because of the lack of understanding that begot the present exercise in symbolism are not just the Customs Service employees, whose dignity is thus offended, but all of us—who suffer a coarsening of our national manners that ultimately give the Fourth Amendment its content, and who become subject to the administration of federal officials whose respect for our privacy can hardly be greater than the small respect they have been taught to have for their own.[14]

### REFERENCES

1. Chambers M: Is mutilation and flogging the answer? National Law J. Feb 27, 1989, p. 13.

2. Alcohol and Drugs in the Workplace: Costs, Controls and Controversies—A BNA Special Report, Washington, DC: Bureau of National Affairs, 1986; 5.
3. Executive Order 12564. 51 Fed Reg 32889 (Sept 17, 1986).
4. Meese suggests drug steps by firms. Boston Globe, Nov 30, 1986, p. 8.
5. *Turner v. Fraternal Order of Police*, 500 A.2d 1005, 1011 (D.C. App. 1985) (Nebeker, concurring).
6. *Capua v. City of Plainfield*, 643 F.Supp 1507 (D.N.J. 1986).
7. *Shoemaker v. Handel*, 795 F.2d 1136 (3rd Cir. 1986).
8. *Marshall v. Barlow's*, 436 U.S. 307 (1978).
9. *Camara v. Municipal Court*, 387 U.S. 523 (1967).
10. *Horsemen's Benevolent Association v. State Racing Commission*, 403 Mass. 692 (1989).
11. *Lovvorn v. City of Chattanooga, Tenn.*, 846 F.2d 1539 (6th Cir. 1988).
12. 57 L.W. 4324 (March 21, 1989).
13. 839 F.2d 575, 588–9 (9th Cir. 1988).
14. 57 L.W. 4338 (March 21, 1989).
15. *National Treasury Employees Union v. von Rabb*, 816 F.2d 170, 177 (5th Cir. 1987).
16. McAuliffe W, *et al*: Psychoactive drug use among practicing physicians and medical students. N Engl J Med 1986; 315:805.
17. *Leckelt v. Board of Commissioners of Hospital District No. 1*, No. 86–4235, (E.D.La. March 15, 1989).

# NO

Robert L. DuPont

# MANDATORY RANDOM TESTING NEEDS TO BE UNDERTAKEN AT THE WORKSITE

## INTRODUCTION

In the late 1980s the workplace took center stage in the national drug abuse prevention effort with the focus being the drug test. No other aspect of the War on Drugs involved such a broad segment of the nation as the drug test at work. Urine tests for abused drugs had previously been limited to forensic, drug abuse treatment, and criminal justice settings (DuPont and Saylor, 1989). The drug test at work became the most controversial aspect of drug abuse prevention efforts.

Drug testing technology and practice evolved rapidly throughout the 1980s at the pinnacle of modern biotechnology, becoming effective, inexpensive, and reliable as a means of detecting recent use of specific drugs, including drugs that cause impairment in the workplace (Schottenfeld, 1989). The application of this technology in the workplace was justified by the rapid rise in the percentage of workers who used illicit drugs. In 1988, for example, the National Institute on Drug Abuse (NIDA) estimated that 12% of full-time employed Americans between the ages of 20 and 40 used an illicit drug in the previous month (National Institute on Drug Abuse, 1989). Among high school seniors entering the workforce, the levels of drug use were even higher; in 1988, 18% reported current use of marijuana and 3% use of cocaine. High school dropouts had even higher rates of illicit drug use (University of Michigan, 1989).

Drug use had many serious costs in the workplace, including the estimated $1,000 paid by each worker each year because of the effects of drug and alcohol abuse, whether or not that worker used drugs or alcohol. Included in this estimate are the costs of lost productivity, accidents, and health cost of drug- and alcohol-abusing workers. This involuntary Chemi-

From Robert L. DuPont, "Mandatory Random Testing Needs to Be Undertaken at the Worksite," in Ruth C. Engs, ed., *Controversies in the Addiction's Field, Volume One* (Kendall/Hunt, 1990). Copyright © 1990 by The American Council on Alcoholism, Inc. Reprinted by permission.

cal Dependence Tax has grave impacts on the nation's productivity and competitiveness (DuPont, 1989a). Cutting that tax by preventing drug problems is the goal of drug testing in the workplace with benefits in increased wages, improved health, lowered product costs, and improved product quality.

When the drug test came to the workplace there were intense controversies over any form of testing. For example, there were charges that the tests were inherently unreliable and that they identified as drug users people who were merely in the vicinity of someone using marijuana. It was also claimed by critics of testing at work that common over-the-counter and health food supplements would be misinterpreted as drug positive results (Hawks and Chaing, 1986). The publication of guidelines for workplace drug testing by the U.S. Department of Health and Human Services (1988), federal requirements for drug testing within the federal workforce and among many federally regulated workplaces, and a series of court cases all occurring between 1987 and 1989, shifted the controversy about drug testing away from the question of the reliability or legality of testing.

By 1990 most opponents of testing conceded that when done properly, drug tests were able to accurately and reliably identify recent drug use. The new battleground in workplace drug testing focused on two critical, unresolved areas. The first was whether testing was warranted for workers where there was no "safety or security" risk in their work. In the view of the critics of testing, drug tests at work might be justified for transportation or nuclear power workers, but not for most workers whose jobs were not safety-sensitive. The second battle-ground in the early 1990s about drug testing at work was whether testing should be required for workers on a "random" basis, that is, without individualized suspicion that the particular employee was impaired by drugs at the time the drug test was requested. This paper addresses the second of these two points, arguing that random, unindicated, drug testing at work is desirable.

## ABOUT THE AUTHOR

The reader of a chapter on so controversial and personal a subject as random drug testing in the workplace deserves to know something about the author. I am a medical doctor, a psychiatrist, who has worked for over two decades in drug abuse prevention and treatment.

The only drug users who have recovered from their addiction, in my experience, have recovered because someone else cared enough about them to insist that they become drug free. Surely the process of recovery requires that the former drug users ultimately adopt drug-free values and goals themselves, but the beginning of recovery is almost always the insistence of one or more people in the drug users' lives to end their drug use.

With reference to the specific topic of this chapter, I have seen hundreds of drug abusers who have recovered control of their lives because their employers put their employment on the line in what is called "job jeopardy." Bluntly, that means, "You work here, you don't use drugs; you use drugs, you don't work here." This new and, for most people, still unfamiliar approach has become known as Tough Love. It happens in the workplace just the way it does in families (DuPont, 1984). Even more personally, I have been drug tested at work for two decades. All staff members of the two organizations I work with are randomly tested for drugs. I am a "survivor" of random drug tests at work, and so are all the people with whom I work.

My views about drugs in the workplace, including my support for random drug tests at work, have been published in a variety of professional and general books, journals, and newspapers (DuPont, 1984, 1989a, 1989b, 1989c, 1989d, 1989e).

## "RANDOM" DRUG TESTING DEFINED

A drug test in the workplace today means a urine sample collected in a private, but secure, medical environment similar to routine urine collection at a doctor's office. The sample is tested to be sure it comes from the tested employee and has not been adulterated. Direct observation of the urine collection is not required in the workplace unless there is reason to believe the employee will falsify the drug test. The drug test is analyzed by a two-step process in a high-technology clinical laboratory. This drug test process includes careful collection, chain-of-custody, medical review, and retention of all positive samples for one year after collection. This total system, which is now standard in workplace drug testing, permits retest if an employee claims to have been falsely identified as a drug user. Using this system there are no false positives (U.S. Department of Health and Human Services, 1988; DuPont, 1989a, 1989b).

This system does not detect use of medicines, except for those that are on occasion abused by drug users. Thus, the workplace drug testing system does not identify use of birth control pills, heart medicines, or antidepressants. Workplace drug tests only detect use of "controlled substances," or drugs that are either purely illegal (such as marijuana and PCP), or drugs that can be used either medically or nonmedically (such as painkillers, antianxiety medicines, and sleeping pills). Medical use is separated from nonmedical use of these substances by a medical review officer, a trained physician who sees the drug tests before they are reported to the employer. Only urine drug tests taken at work that show recent use of potentially impaired drugs, for which there is no medical prescription for that employee, are reported to the employer as positive. Medical use of substances, such as Valium or codeine, are reported as "negative" tests.

"Random testing" needs to be contrasted to the other two common types of drug tests in the workplace. The first is "pre-employment" testing; that is, urine tests for recent drug use taken at the time a person applies for a new job. The second common form of drug test at work is "for-cause" testing. These are tests of a particular person because he or she shows some particular signs of possible drug use. Examples of causes for drug tests at work include appearing to be under the influence of a drug, being repeatedly late for work, or having an accident. Other causes justifying a drug test for a particular employee are a past history of treatment for drug abuse, and abnormal behavior at work (e.g., fighting or falling asleep). Neither pre-employment nor for-cause testing is now either particularly uncommon or controversial in the American workplace.

In contrast to pre-employment and for-cause testing, random testing remains controversial in nonmilitary workplaces in the United States. Random testing for drugs means that a particular worker is chosen at random to be tested at a particular time. Usually this selection is done by computer with a small percentage of workers being selected to be tested each day with only a few hours of notice. With random drug testing, every worker is subject to being drug tested every day the worker is at work regardless of how the worker is performing on that day.

## THE USES OF RANDOM DRUG TESTING IN THE WORKPLACE

If all drug users were obviously impaired at work, random testing would not be needed because supervisors could be trained to detect drug-caused impairment. They could, having identified a potentially impaired worker, request a for-cause drug test. Unfortunately, there is clear evidence that most illicit drug users do not appear to be impaired at work, even when drugs are having a profound effect on their performance. After 20 years working with drug abusers, I always insist on drug testing my patients simply because I cannot tell when they are using drugs, even when I spend 50 minutes talking with them in my office. If I cannot identify recent drug use, how can even the most highly trained supervisor?

Why should someone who has never used an illegal drug welcome a random drug test at work? Unless those non-using employees are tested, employees who do use illicit drugs will not be tested. The non-user of illicit drugs who is drug tested at work is in the same situation as those who have no intention of ever hijacking an airplane when they walk through metal detectors at airports;

if they do not submit to the slight inconvenience of going through the detector, then hijackers will not be deterred or, failing deterrence, detected.

Although most drug use does not produce easily detected symptoms, some drug use causes such flagrant symptoms of impairment that supervisor training is worth the investment. Supervisors, and co-workers, can identify the most outrageous examples of drug-caused impairment on the job. Even when signs of recent drug use are identified, such as irritable mood or the appearance of fatigue, these behaviors are often caused by other factors in the employees' lives. Thus, many for-cause tests for drugs will be negative. Supervisors are usually reluctant to ask for a drug test if there is any doubt that the abnormal behavior is caused by drug abuse. Employees are usually not pleased when a supervisor singles them out for a drug test. Supervisors are generally not pleased when the requested for-cause drug test comes back showing no recent drug use. Thus, when a company has a for-cause drug test program they typically do few drug tests, even when high percentages of their employees are using illicit drugs. This means that for-cause testing is a weak deterrent to drug use in the workplace because it is seldom used. Drug users in the workforce typically have a high level of confidence that their drug use will not be detected because they do not feel impaired and they do not believe they will be drug tested. All too often they are wrong in believing they are not impaired, but right in believing that they will not be tested.

One good reason to do random tests is that most drug-caused impairments are not identified when companies rely on for-cause tests. Another good reason is that such tests are routine and do not require a supervisor to confront an employee with the suspicion that he or she is using drugs. The military experience using random tests since 1982 and the smaller civilian experience with random testing over the last few years have established these two central points: Random testing is fair and it is effective. Random drug testing at work achieves its primary goal of preventing drug use and drug-caused problems, without demoralizing workers or forcing large numbers of workers either to leave their jobs or to enter treatment. It does this by making the drug-free workplace a reality. Random testing at work gives workers at all levels a strong, practical reason to stop using illicit drugs: If they do not stop using illicit drugs they will lose their jobs (National Institute on Drug Abuse, Office of Workplace Initiatives, 1989; Walsh and Gust, 1989).

Throughout this chapter I have focused on employees in safety and security positions, emphasizing that they are the most appropriate employees to be subjected to random drug testing. The same arguments that apply to these employees apply to all others: Random testing is the best, fairest, and most cost-effective way to prevent illicit drug use. Focusing on only those industries with safety-related jobs discriminates against all other employees. All workers stand to gain equally from random drug testing. The reason for beginning with safety and security roles is not because they are more important or because the employees in their other jobs are not equally benefited by random testing, it simply reflects the controversies over the use of random testing in the workplace today.

It is my strong belief that any employee subject to drug testing is helped by that testing. That randomly tested employee is not harmed by testing, whether or not that employee is in a safety-related job, and whether or not that employee uses illicit drugs. Anyone concerned for employee welfare should be arguing for random drug tests in the workplace today. Despite this belief, however, I recognize that many people are unfamiliar with random drug tests. These sometimes fearful people may even believe that such tests are a threat to them. Much of the media and many apologists for illicit drug use as well as many opponents of testing actively fuel these fears. Out of consideration for these fears, and the political and legal conflicts they support, I am respectful of the necessity of time passing before random drug testing is universally applied in the American workplace.

Random drug testing, still unfamiliar in the civilian workplace, is not for everyone. There are important contractual and financial issues in many workplace settings when it comes to random testing. There is an important educational requirement before beginning random testing to be sure everyone in the company understands the system and how it works. Particular concern needs to be shown to non-using employees who inappropriately but understandably may fear identification of their use of legitimate medicines. Concerns about the reliability of the entire drug testing system need to be dealt with fully.

## SOCIETAL IMPLICATIONS OF RANDOM DRUG TESTS AT WORK

After two decades of dealing with the drug abuse epidemic, it is becoming increasingly clear that the drug abuse epidemic will end only when the demand for drugs dries up. The recent calls for drug legalization again point out the terrible incentive provided for illicit drug traffickers by the huge demand of the 14.5 million Americans who now use illicit drugs on a regular basis. Seventy percent of these current American users of illicit drugs are employed (DuPont, 1989c; DuPont and Goldfarb, 1990). If this nation is to achieve the goal of drug abuse prevention and dry up the demand for drugs, the first and best place to act is in the workplace. We can give a clear signal to Americans of all ages, races, and social classes: Using illicit drugs is incompatible with work. Random drug testing in the workplace is the best way to make this point.

## REFERENCES

DuPont, R. L. (1984). *Getting Tough on Gateway Drugs: A Guide for the Family*. American Psychiatric Press: Washington, DC.

DuPont, R. L. (1989a). Drugs in the American workplace: Conflict and opportunity. Part I: Epidemiology of drugs at work. *Social Pharmacology,* **3** 133–146.

DuPont, R. L (1989b). Drugs in the American workplace: Conflict and opportunity. Part II: Controversies in workplace drug use prevention. *Social Pharmacology,* **3** 147–164.

DuPont, R. L. (1989c). Never trust anyone under 40: What employers should know about drugs in the workplace. *Policy Review,* Spring 1989, 52–57.

DuPont, R. L. (1989d). Workplace urine tests will cut drug use. *Newsday,* March 14, 1989.

DuPont, R. L. (1989e). A doctor's case for random drug tests. *The Washington Times,* March 27, 1989.

DuPont, R. L. and Goldfarb, R. L. (1990). Drug legalization: Asking for trouble. *The Washington Post,* January 26, 1990.

DuPont, R. L. and Saylor, K. E. (1989). *Urine Testing in Drug Treatment: Harnessing Technology to Promote Recovery.* Institute for Behavior & Health, Inc.: Rockville, MD. (unpublished).

Hawks, R. L. and Chaing, C. N. (1986). *Urine Testing for Drugs of Abuse.* Research Monograph #73. National Institute on Drug Abuse: Rockville, MD.

National Institute on Drug Abuse (1989). Highlights of the 1988 National Household Survey on Drug Abuse. *NIDA Capsules,* August 1989.

National Institute on Drug Abuse, Office of Workplace Initiatives. (1989). *Drugs in the Workplace: Research and Evaluation Data.* DHHS publication number (ADM)89-1612, NIDA Research Monograph 91. National Institute on Drug Abuse: Rockville, MD.

Schottenfeld, R. S. (1989). Drug and alcohol testing in the workplace—objectives, pitfalls, and guidelines. *Am J Drug Alcohol Abuse,* **15** 413–527.

University of Michigan. (1989). Teen drug use continues decline, according to U-M survey. Cocaine down for second straight year; crack begins decline in 1988. University of Michigan, News and Information Services, Institute for Social Research: Ann Arbor. February 24, 1989. (News release jointly with the Alcohol, Drug Abuse and Mental Health Administration and the National Institute on Drug Abuse.)

U.S. Department of Health and Human Services. (1988). Mandatory guidelines for federal workplace drug testing programs. *Federal Register,* April 11, 1988.

Walsh, J. M. and Gust, S. W. (Eds). (1989) *Workplace Drug Abuse Policy.* DHHS publication number (ADM)89-1610. National Institute on Drug Abuse, Office of Workplace Initiatives: Rockville, MD.

# POSTSCRIPT

## Does Drug Testing Violate Civil Rights?

As a follow-up to the discussion of whether or not to allow random drug testing, one needs to ask what should be done with people who test positive for drugs. Should they be fired or helped? Is the purpose of drug testing to eliminate workers who use drugs or to help workers who use drugs? Aside from the legal issues, how reliable are drug tests? What measures are being implemented to ensure confidentiality? Who has access to the results of drug tests? Far more accidents are attributed to alcohol than illegal drugs. Should drug tests apply to illegal drugs only?

Many questions surround the legalities of drug testing. Over the years, the courts have been divided over whether or not drug testing is reasonable and whether or not it constitutes a search under the Fourth Amendment. Most courts have concluded that a mandatory urine, blood, or breath test can be considered a search under the Fourth Amendment; the focus now is on the extent to which drug searches may be unreasonable. The extent to which a court feels that a drug test has been "demeaning, intrusive, or a violation of a person's general right to be free from governmental intrusions" is pertinent because it affects how the term *unreasonable* is defined.

Frequently, especially in the case of public employees whose Fourth Amendment rights are limited, the government declares "special needs" as a basis for drug testing. Special needs allows testing without a warrant and probable cause—two mandatory conditions under the Fourth Amendment. Some contend that too often the courts can make it easy to sacrifice individuals' rights for the needs of the government. When an individual is subjected to a blood or urine test without first giving any indication that he or she has used drugs, there is an infringement of this person's personal and civil liberties. Glantz believes mandatory drug testing at the workplace is an unjust government intrusion because it calls for all citizens to unduly stand trial and makes us all victims of the war on drugs.

One could argue that the ramifications of drug use have no boundaries and that everyone in one way or another is a victim. If this is true, should we not support federal and employee programs that identify and assist those individuals who use drugs so that we may all suffer fewer drug-related repercussions? Employee Assistance Programs help employees deal with and obtain treatment for drug problems that negatively affect their job performance as well as their personal lives. Without testing, many workers may never get the help they need; they may never admit to having a drug problem, and some drug users never appear to be impaired at work, even when drugs may be having a detrimental effect on job performance and adherence to safety standards. Mandatory drug testing would help identify such individuals.

Proponents of drug testing argue that anyone concerned with job welfare should be in favor of drug testing in the workplace. When the safety of the general public is at risk, which is often the case in certain safety and security jobs, succumbing to a random drug test at work may indeed be appropriate and warranted. Furthermore, nonusing employees should invite random drug testing because the only way those employees who are using drugs will get tested is if all employees are tested.

Advocates of random drug testing also argue that it is fair and effective. Testing at the workplace will help prevent illicit drug use and those problems associated with drug use. According to DuPont, when the government acts to protect all citizens from the problems of illicit drug use, as is the case in mandatory random testing, then drug testing is not a violation of our civil rights. But is drug testing always fair and effective? Drug tests are not always accurate, and they sometimes indicate drug use when there has been none. To avoid a positive result, some drug users submit another person's urine or put salt and detergent in their own samples, which affect the accuracy of the test. Views on both sides of the argument contend that more reliable tests are needed if drug testing is to be allowed.

Drug testing arouses other questions: How should drug test results be recorded at work? Should testing be implemented at the work site or on "neutral" ground? Who should be allowed access to employees' files regarding test results? How could employees be assured of their privacy? In addition, will job discrimination or employee stigmatization result? A larger question concerns what role employers have in regulating their employees' actions. If the government allows employers to mandate and control employees' actions with regard to personal habits, would this not carry over into other areas of their lives as well? These questions are not easily answered.

The merits of drug testing are discussed in Jonathan Harris's book *Drugged America* (Four Winds Press, 1991). An overview of drug testing procedures is given in "Drug Testing: The State of the Art," *American Scientist* (January–February 1989). The article "Costs and Benefits of Drug Screening for Job Applicants," *Journal of the American Medical Association* (January 1, 1992), by Craig Zwerling, James Ryan and John Orav, examines the relative costs and benefits of preemployment drug screening.

# ISSUE 4

## Should the Drinking Age Remain at 21?

**YES: Richard J. Goeman,** from "Why We Need a Minimum-Purchase Age of 21," in Ruth C. Engs, ed., *Controversies in the Addiction's Field, Volume One* (Kendall/Hunt, 1990)

**NO: David J. Hanson,** from "The Drinking Age Should Be Lowered," in Ruth C. Engs., ed., *Controversies in the Addiction's Field, Volume One* (Kendall/Hunt, 1990)

### ISSUE SUMMARY

**YES:** Research associate Richard J. Goeman points out that consumption of alcohol among adolescents and young adults accounts for a disproportionate number of automobile accidents, fatalities, and other alcohol-related problems. He argues that maintaining the current minimum drinking age is necessary to prevent further alcohol-related problems.

**NO:** David J. Hanson, a professor of sociology, argues that minimum-age drinking laws are unnecessary because they fail to prevent underage drinking and alcohol-related problems. He feels that a more realistic approach of socializing and educating youth in the direction of moderate alcohol consumption is needed.

In 1987, all U.S. states were required to mandate a legal minimum purchasing and drinking age of 21. The impetus for this legislation was provided by Congress in the previous year when it directed states to set 21 as the legal drinking age or lose federal highway funding. This legislation was prompted by (1) the drastic increase in drinking among youth and (2) the high incidence of alcohol-related motor vehicle accidents involving young people in the mid-1970s and 1980s.

According to the latest government study of high school seniors, over 90 percent have consumed alcohol. A more pertinent statistic is that almost one-third had five or more drinks in a row within two weeks of the survey. This fact is especially noteworthy when one realizes that teen drinking is responsible for a high proportion of all fatal automobile accidents. However, has raising the drinking age reduced the number of yearly motor vehicle accidents? To what extent has the change in the legal drinking age prevented adolescents and young adults from using and abusing alcohol?

A "gateway drug" is one of the first drugs young people use, and it often leads to the use of other drugs that are perceived to be more dangerous. Since alcohol is considered to be a gateway substance, many experts agree that delaying the age of initial alcohol use will minimize or defer potential problems associated with its use. Laws making it illegal for young people to purchase or consume alcoholic beverages appear to deter use and decrease problems related to alcohol. Yet, given that the rate of teen drinking remains steady, opinion is divided regarding how realistic the legal drinking age is and how well it discourages alcohol use among this age group.

Hard-liners against teenage drinking advocate stricter enforcement of the legal drinking age, harsher penalties for teens caught purchasing or consuming alcohol, and stronger antidrinking messages. This strident position reflects a belief that drinking among teens is fundamentally wrong. Many people feel that alcohol use among young people always results in unsafe and irresponsible behavior and that teenage drinking is intolerable. Statistics help illustrate why some people advocate stronger antialcohol laws and programs for teens. For example, the number one killer of youth in the United States is alcohol-related accidents. And in 1989, a young adult was killed every three hours in an alcohol-related car crash. Many people assert that when the legal drinking age is reduced to under 21 years, there is an increase in alcohol-related automobile accidents involving youth and other drinking-related problems. They feel that this justifies the need for a minimum drinking age of 21.

Others argue that laws do not reduce the number of teenage drinkers or drinking problems among teens and young adults. Moreover, having a prohibition law based on age sends out the wrong message to teens regarding what alcohol use means. Because alcohol is much a part of the adult social scene, many young people feel that drinking is a "rite of passage" into adulthood.

Some opponents of a legal drinking age call for a more effective and practical approach toward alcohol education that teaches young people responsible use of alcohol in controlled settings. In addition, more emphasis should be placed on moderate drinking practices. Many believe that to expect some people never to consume alcohol is unrealistic. Rather, the assumption should be that most young people *will* drink and that they should be educated and socialized in a manner that teaches them how to manage drinking at an early age if they should choose to do so.

In the following selections, Richard J. Goeman argues that lower legal drinking ages will increase teen drinking and drinking-related problems and that legislation is imperative to prevent further alcohol-related problems among young people. David J. Hanson maintains that legislation has virtually no impact on teen drinking and associated problems and that it will not prevent alcohol use among this or any other age group.

# YES
Richard J. Goeman

# WHY WE NEED A MINIMUM-PURCHASE AGE OF 21

With a current legal minimum-purchase age of 21 in the United States there has been, and continues to be, controversy. There are valid points concerning both sides of this issue, with either side offering fair grounds for debate. However, based on the literature, I have chosen to support the legal minimum-purchase age of 21. Available research appears to indicate this is the desired position and the current laws should remain unchanged. Although correct terminology states: "legal minimum-purchase age," for reasons of practicality, minimum age, minimum-drinking age, and legal age apply the same meaning. For this chapter these terms will be used interchangeably throughout.

For hundreds of years alcohol has been used for a variety of reasons. These include celebration, relaxation, and recreation (Wechsler, 1980). Also, before the practice of modern medicine alcohol was used incessantly as a medication to cure illness, as a vehicle for other drugs and potents, and for anesthesia.

Over the course of history beverage alcohol (i.e., beer, wine, and spirits) has been readily available and frequently misused, although it was rarely deemed hazardous. In fact, dating back as early as the eighteenth century some authorities considered alcohol wholesome and good for the soul. During this period of time, purchase and consumption of alcohol by young people were loosely governed. The majority of young persons drank while experiencing little opposition from authorities. Even during the temperance movement there were no restrictions placed solely on youth regarding their use of beverage alcohol. Instead, the entire population experienced restrictions through regulation of hours of sale, location of alcohol outlets, and high license fees (Wagenaar, 1983). Early in the twentieth century, laws were enacted to govern the sale of beverage alcohol to youth. This became one way in which the state could gain limited control over adolescent behavior. However, it was not until after the repeal of Prohibition in 1933 that strict minimum-age laws were implemented. At that time all fifty states passed laws concerning the legal minimum-purchase age; most states set the age at 21 (Wagenaar, 1983). Beyond that point little else took place for nearly four decades regarding the minimum-age law.

In 1970, the Twenty-Sixth Amendment to the United States Constitution was passed by Congress. This Amendment granted the right to vote in Federal elections to citizens between the ages of 18 and 21. Shortly thereafter, a movement began that would allow other rights and privileges to the new "citizens of legal age." Over the next five years (1970–1975) twenty-nine states lowered their legal minimum-purchase age (Engs and Hanson, 1988).

## EFFECTS OF THE REDUCED DRINKING-AGE LAW

With the reduction of these laws, controversy within the realms of academia, politics, law-enforcement, and industry quickly arose regarding the wisdom of such choices (Works, 1973; Distilled Spirits Council of the United States, 1973; Bowen and Kagay, 1973; Zylman, 1973). Some individuals in the political arena argued that huge increases in alcohol-related automobile accidents involving youth occurred immediately after lowering the minimum age. Other arguments surfacing during that time indicated these increases were due to changes in police-reporting techniques, increases in the number of young drivers, and long-term trends concerning alcohol consumption and the incidence of automobile accidents (Zylman, 1974). However, by the mid-1970s, controlled studies of the effects of reduced minimum-age laws were becoming available in the United States and Canada. Although the degree of magnitude varied among the states and provinces studied, the majority

of research concluded that lowering the minimum legal-purchase age led to significant increases in alcohol-related automobile accidents among young drivers (Wagenaar, 1983).

Research was accomplished concerning the rate of fatal automobile accidents among fifteen-to-seventeen-year-old and eighteen-to-twenty-year-old drivers in Michigan, Wisconsin, and Ontario where the minimum-drinking age had been lowered. The rate of fatal accidents in those states and province, for 36 months prior to and 12 months after the law change, was compared with the rate of fatal accidents in the bordering states of Indiana, Illinois, and Minnesota where the minimum-age law was not lowered. Significant increases in the number of fatal automobile accidents were found among all the ages previously listed in the states and province that chose to lower their minimum-drinking age. The rate was considerably higher for Michigan and Ontario than for Wisconsin. The lower rate in Wisconsin may have been due to a less drastic change in availability of alcohol. In Wisconsin, eighteen-to-twenty-year-olds had always been able to purchase beer and wine (Williams, Rich, Zador, and Robertson, 1974).

Studies conducted with the state of Massachusetts reported identical results. Research on automobile accidents using a "time series" method measured the rate of accident involvement of individuals aged fifteen-to-seventeen, eighteen-to-twenty, twenty-one-to-twenty-three, and twenty-four and over. After the minimum age was reduced, eighteen-to-twenty-year-old drivers experienced significant increases in total fatal automobile accidents, alcohol-related fatal automobile accidents, and alcohol-related property damage accidents. However, there were no significant changes for drivers aged twenty-one-to-twenty-three and twenty-four and over (Cucchiaro, Ferreira, and Sicherman, 1974). Monthly time series was also the method used to compare data collected from Maine, Michigan, and Vermont where the minimum age was lowered, with Louisiana, Pennsylvania, and Texas, where the minimum age remained constant over the study period. These results revealed a significant increase in the rate of involvement in alcohol-related automobile accidents among young drivers in Maine and Michigan. It was suggested that lack of significant change in rates of automobile accidents in Vermont was due to the eighteen-year-old drinking age in the bordering state of New York (Douglass, Filkins, and Clark, 1974).

Three years later, Douglass and Freedman (1977) replicated parts of the above study. Results produced from that effort showed that the alarming rate of automobile accidents involving alcohol and young drivers had persisted over the first four years after the minimum age was lowered (1972–1975). In yet a third study done in the state of Michigan, researchers using an entirely different analytical technique than Douglass were able to observe the same significant increase in alcohol-related automobile accidents among young drivers (Flora, Filkins, and Compton, 1978).

One of the most startling discoveries in opposition to reducing the legal age evolved from a study done in London, Ontario. Here, researchers examined the rates of automobile accidents in drivers aged sixteen-to-twenty and twenty-four years old for a six year period (1968 through 1973). Following a minimum-age reduction in Ontario, alcohol-related automobile accidents among drivers aged eighteen-to-twenty increased 150 to 300 percent. In the twenty-four-year-old age group, only a 20 percent increase in alcohol-related automobile accidents was noted (Whitehead et al., 1975). After an additional two years of examining accident data, Whitehead (1977) was able to show a permanently higher rate in this type of automobile accident among young drivers after reducing the minimum-drinking age.

In the province of Saskatchewan, researchers were able to document that after the legal age was lowered from twenty-one to nineteen in April 1970, drivers aged sixteen-to-twenty experienced a 20 to 50 percent increase in automobile accidents involving alcohol. After the legal age was again reduced, this time to eighteen, in June 1972, this same group of drivers experienced further increases in automobile accidents where alcohol was the major contributing factor (Shattuck and Whitehead, 1976).

Researchers studying the effect of allowing young people to drink alcohol in Alberta, Canada examined the rate of drivers with blood-alcohol concentrations of 0.08 percent or greater who had been fatally injured in automobile accidents. Alcohol related automobile accidents increased 118 percent among drivers aged fifteen-to-nineteen after the legal age was lowered (Bako, MacKenzie, and Smith, 1976).

## THE ECONOMIC AND OTHER COSTS TO SOCIETY

The cost to society regarding the effects of the minimum-age law and use of alcohol in general has been insurmountable. The author here is not opposed to drinking alcohol. However, the manner and degree to which it is consumed in this country indicates a serious dilemma.

In the span of time since the legal age was lowered, the United States has spent billions of dollars annually in health care, social services, property damage, and lost production (Berry and Boland, 1977; Schifrin, Hartsog, and Brand, 1980). Unfortunately, the trend continues.

During a subcommittee hearing of the U.S. House of Representatives in October 1983, a bill was introduced which favored prohibiting the sale of alcoholic beverages to persons under 21 years of age. It reads: "Each year, 25,000 people are killed by drunken drivers. In disproportionate numbers, these drivers appear to be young people. The twenty-year old age category is a particular problem. Each year, highway accidents involving alcohol create economic losses of over $20 billion, and incalculable losses in terms of human suffering, wasted potential, social dislocation, and death" (Florio, 1983).

A recent study done by the Insurance Institute for Highway Safety noted that when there was an increase in fatal automobile accidents for teenage drivers, especially accidents involving alcohol, a direct correlation existed between the legal minimum-drinking age and the incidence of these accidents.

In 1984, in New York State alone, the State Division of Alcoholism and Alcohol Abuse projected that a 21-year-old minimum-drinking age would save on an annual basis 60–70 lives, 1,200 serious injuries, and 75 million dollars in societal costs (Padavan, 1984). The organization, Mothers Against Drunk Driving (MADD, 1983) reported that 25 cents of every auto insurance premium dollar goes to pay for damage done by drunk drivers. These figures are astronomical when one considers a state such as Michigan, where only high-price "No-Fault" insurance is permitted. What our society pays in human suffering, wasted potential, and death is beyond anyone's comprehension.

## POSITIVE OUTCOME STUDIES

Contrasting all the studies reporting negative results, there are many that report positive after states and provinces raise the legal-age. For example, Maine experienced, between 1974 and 1979, a reduction from 14 to 20 percent in automobile accidents involving alcohol after raising their legal age (Klein, 1981). Research completed in the state of Illinois revealed a 9 percent decrease in nighttime single-vehicle accidents among nineteen-to-twenty-year-old drivers after raising their legal age from nineteen to twenty-one in January 1980 (Maxwell, 1981). One investigation examined fatal automobile accident involvement from 1975 to 1980 in nine states that chose to raise their minimum age. Bordering states were used in comparison which did not raise their minimum age. Eight of the nine states experienced decreases in young driver involvement in nighttime fatal automobile accidents after the minimum age was raised; accident reductions ranged from 6 to 75 percent. Averaging across the nine states studied, the researchers concluded that increasing the legal minimum-purchase age in any given state should result in a 28 percent reduction in nighttime fatal automobile accidents among the age group affected by the legal change (Williams, Zador, Harris, and Karpf, 1981). It should be noted here that Cook and Tauchen (1982) estimated the effect of allowing youth access to alcohol by reducing the drinking age, using nationwide United States data on the number of young people killed in automobile accidents. Results of the fatality data pooled across states and years revealed that a 7 percent increase in the number of youth killed in automobile accidents was correlated with reductions in the legal minimum-purchase age.

Other studies have shown that when minimum-age laws are lowered, there is an increase in alcohol-related problems other than driving while intoxicated. For example, Engs and Hanson (1986) report that in states with under 21 minimum-age laws, a higher percentage of students reported drinking an alcoholic beverage while driving, missing classes due to drinking, receiving lower grades due to drinking, and indicating they thought they had a drinking problem. In other research, it may be noted that among New England college students, 29 percent of the men and 11 percent of the women were classified as heavy drinkers (Wechsler and McFadden, 1979). Half of these students reported experiencing problems related to drinking, such as blackouts, fighting, and trouble with authorities (Wechsler and Rohman, 1981).

The apparent relationship between age and unsafe and irresponsible behavior while drinking or drunk driving is fairly easy to document. During adolescence and early adulthood (15 to 24), accidents, homicides, and suicides account for 75 percent of all fatalities. However, the activity generating the highest number of deaths in this age group is automobile accidents. Whatever the cause of death, alcohol is clearly implicated in at least 50 percent of the fatalities for this age population. During late adolescence and early adulthood, male and female alike have a higher risk of incurring some negative consequence(s) associated with use of alcohol than during any other point in their lifetime. Many individuals, professional or otherwise, acknowledge that a reduction in alcohol consumption by persons under the age of 21 is a necessary and effective means for reducing alcohol-related automobile accidents and other problems associated with the use of alcohol. These individuals cite data showing that when the legal minimum-purchase age is lowered, there is a significant increase in the rate of automobile accidents and cases in which young people operated a motor vehicle while intoxicated (Wechsler, 1980).

In summary, the information in review here indicates that the majority of studies concerning the impact of lower legal-drinking ages on involvement in automobile accidents and other alcohol-related problems continue to show significant increases. Persons most often involved with these increases are those who under the new law become eligible to purchase alcohol; usually eighteen-to-twenty-year-old individuals. Therefore, to prevent further drinking and other related problems among youth in our society, the current legal minimum-purchase age of 21 should continue.

## REFERENCES

Bako, G., MacKenzi, W. C., and Smith, E. S. O. (1976). "The Effect of Legislated Lowering of the Drinking Age on Total Highway Accidents Among Young Drivers in Alberta, 1970–1972." *Canadian Journal of Public Health*, 38 161–163.

Berry, R. E., Jr. and Boland, J. P. (1977). *The Economic Cost of Alcohol Abuse*, Free Press: New York.

Bowen, B. D. and Kagay, M. R. (1973). *Report to the White House Conference on Youth: The Impact of Lowering the Age of Majority to 18*. White House Conference on Youth: Washington, DC.

Cook, P. J. and Tauchen, G. (1982). *The Effect of Minimum Drinking Age Legislation on Youthful Auto Fatalities 1970–1977*. Unpublished manuscript.

Cucchiaro, S., Ferreira, Jr., and Sicherman, A. (1974). The Effect of the 18-year-old Drinking Age on Auto Accidents. Massachusetts Institute of Technology, Operations Research Center. Cambridge, MA.

Distilled Spirits Council of the United States. (1973). "Survey of Minimum Age Law Experience on Drinking/Driving." *DISCUS Newsletter*, 330.

Douglass, R. L., Filkins, L. D., and Clark, F. A. (1974). The Effect of Lower Legal Drinking Ages on Youth Crash Involvement. *The University of Michigan, Highway Safety Research Institute*. Ann Arbor, MI.

Douglass, R. L. and Freedman, J. A. (1977). Alcohol-related Casualties and Alcohol Beverage Market Response to Beverage Alcohol Availability Policies in Michigan. *The University of Michigan, Highway Safety Research Institute*. Ann Arbor, MI.

Engs, R. C. and Hanson, D. J. (1986). Age-Specific Alcohol Prohibition and College Students' Drinking Problems. *Psychological Reports*, **59** 979–984.

Engs, R. C. and Hanson, D. J. (1988). University Students' Drinking Patterns and Problems: Examining the Effects of Raising the Purchase Age. *Public Health Reports*, **103** (6) 667–673.

Flora, J. D., Filkins, L. D., and Compton, C. D. (1978). Alcohol Involvement in Michigan Fatal Accidents: 1968–1976. *The University of Michigan, Highway Safety Research Institute*. Ann Arbor, Michigan.

Florio, J. J. (1983). *Prohibit the Sale of Alcoholic Beverages to Persons Under 21 Years of Age*. H.R. 3870. U.S. House of Representatives, Committee on Energy and Commerce, Subcommittee on Commerce, Transportation, and Tourism. Washington, DC.

Klein, T. (1981). *The Effect of Raising the Minimum Legal Drinking Age on Traffic Accidents in the State of Maine*. U.S. National Highway Traffic Safety Administration. Washington, DC.

Maxwell, D. M. (1981). *Impact Analysis of the Raised Legal Age in Illinois*. U.S. National Traffic Safety Administration: Washington, DC.

Mothers Against Drunk Driving (MADD). (1983). *Striking Back at the Drunk Driver*, pp. 582–583.

Padavan, F. (1984). *"21"—It Makes Sense/Education, Prevention, Enforcement, Raising the Drinking Age*. New York, New York.

Schifrin, L. G., Hartsog, C. E., and Brand, D. H. (1980). "Costs of Alcoholism and Alcohol Abuse and Their Relation to Alcohol Research." In *Institute of Medicine, ed., Alcoholism, Alcohol Abuse and Related Problems: Opportunities for Research*, pp. 165–186. National Academy Press: Washington, DC.

Shattuck, D. and Whitehead, P. C. (1976). *Lowering the Drinking Age in Saskatchewan: The Effect on Collisions among Young Drivers*. Department of Health: Saskatchewan, Canada.

Wagenaar, A. C. (1983). *Alcohol, Young Drivers, and Traffic Accidents*. Lexington Books, Lexington, Massachusetts.

Wechsler, H. and McFadden, M. (1979). Drinking among College Students in New England. *Journal of Studies on Alcohol*, **40** 969–996.

Wechsler, H. and Rohman, M. (1981). Extensive Users of Alcohol among College Students. *Journal of Studies on Alcohol*, **42** 149–155.

Wechsler, H. (1980). *Minimum-Drinking-Age Laws*. Lexington Books: Lexington, MA.

Whitehead, P. C., Craig, J., Langford, N., MacArthur, C., Stanton, B., and Ferrence, R. G. (1975). "Collision Behavior of Young Drivers: Impact of the Change in the Age of Majority." *Journal of Studies on Alcohol*, **36** 1208–1223.

Whitehead, P. C. (1977) *Alcohol and Young Drivers: Impact and Implications of Lowering the Drinking Age*. Non-medical use of Drugs Directorate. Department of National Health and Welfare, Health Protection Branch, Research Bureau: Ottawa, Ontario.

Williams, A. F., Rich, R. F., Zador, P. L., and Robertson, L. S. (1974). The Legal Minimum Drinking Age and Fatal Motor Vehicle Crashes. *Insurance Institute for Highway Safety*: Washington, DC.

Williams, A. F., Zador, P. L., Harris, S. S., and Karpf, R. S. (1981). "The Effects of Raising the Legal Minimum Drinking Age on Fatal Crash Involvement." *Insurance Institute for Highway Safety*: Washington, DC.

Works, D. A. (1973). "Statement on 18-Year Old Drinking." *Journal of Alcohol and Drug Education*, **18** 14.

Zylman, R. (1974). "Drinking and Driving after It's Legal to Drink at 18: Is the Problem Real?" *Journal of Alcohol and Drug Education*, **20** 48–52.

Zylman, R. (1973). "When It is Legal to Drink at 18: What Should We Expect?" *Journal of Traffic Safety Education*, **20** 9–10.

# NO

David J. Hanson

# THE DRINKING AGE
# SHOULD BE LOWERED

There is extensive evidence that the consumption of alcoholic beverages has occurred in most societies throughout the world and has probably occurred since the Paleolithic Age and certainly since the Neolithic Age (Knupfer, 1960). The records of all ancient civilizations refer to the use of alcoholic beverages. Such accounts are found on Egyptian carvings, Hebrew script, and Babylonian tablets (Patrick, 1952). The Code of Hammurabi (cir 2225 B.C.) devoted several sections to problems created by the abuse of alcohol and in China, laws that forbade making wine were enacted and repealed forty-one times between 1100 B.C. and 1400 A.D. (Alcoholism and Drug Addiction Research Foundation of Ontario, 1961). These and other sources of evidence indicate that concern over alcohol use and abuse are not unique to present societies.

The place of alcohol in American society since the colonial period has clearly been ambivalent. "Drinking has been blessed and cursed, has been held the cause of economic catastrophe and the hope for prosperity, the major cause of crime, disease and military defeat, depravity and a sign of high prestige, mature personality, and a refined civilization" (Straus and Bacon, 1953). This ambivalence is reflected in the changing drinking age laws and drinking ethos as indicated in Table 1.

Organized efforts to limit drinking or the role of alcoholic beverages have existed in the United States since the early 1800s. However, alcohol has been the only substance whose proposed prohibition has provoked strong controversy and conflict. On one hand, the prohibition of narcotics has met little organized resistance while the prohibition of cigarette, coffee or cola beverages sales has not attracted significant political support. Gusfield (Gusfield, 1962; 1963) contends that alcohol has been a symbolic issue through which a struggle for primacy in social status has been fought between differing life styles—small town versus city, "old American" versus recent immigrant, the South and Midwest versus the Northeast. An alternate explanation is that while alcohol is clearly associated with numerous personal and social

*(continued on p. 80)*

*Table 1*

**A Schemata of Drinking Age Laws in the United States from 1700 to 1987 Relative to Drinking Ethos and Social Climate**

| Time | Age Law | Drinking ethos | Social climate |
|------|---------|----------------|----------------|
| 1700–1800 | No age laws except in a few locales very young. | Colonial North America thrives on drinking. Men, women and children all use alcohol. Moderation is a cultural norm. | Rural life in the colonies. Close family ties. Parents had absolute authority to define children's rights and restrictions. |
| 1800–1850 | Isolated state and local age laws began to evolve. The age varied, but usually was 16 or younger. | Drinking was beginning to change. Moderation was waning, and young (especially college youth) often drank heavily and sometimes engaged in delinquent behavior. | Industrial revolution. Temperance movement emerging. |
| 1850–1920 | Many local and state laws began to "protect youth" by age laws which varied from 16 to 20. | Temperance movement flourishing and is not a major political force. Heavy drinking also continued. | 16- to 20-year olds now being treated as preadolescents. Industrial development and job specialization put youth out of labor market. |
| 1920–1930 | Prohibition for all by constitutional amendment. | Drinking illegal, consumption moves underground. Mobster control of manufacture and distribution. Drinking continues in contempt of the law. | Nightlife flourishes in hidden bars and ballrooms. Unsettled period leading to economic depression. |
| 1934–1960 | Age 21 established for postprohibition alcohol use. | Drinking continuing with alcohol now legal. Underage drinking now "a problem" as teenagers drink outside adult sanction. | Recovery from economic depression. World War II and baby boom of postwar period. |
| 1960–1972 | Many states lower drinking age to 18. | Alcohol use flourishes along with use of marijuana and other drugs. | Youth participation in economy and society very evident. Issues made over 18 as age of majority with all rights expected. Vietnam. "Hippie movement." |
| 1972–1987 | States began moving drinking age back to 21. In 1986, Congress passes a law requiring all states to set 21 as legal age or lose highway funds. | Alcohol use flourishes with 75% of teenagers declaring that they use in national studies. | Negative reaction to high rate of youth involvement in drinking related auto accidents. Republican administration and conservative movement in U.S. society. |

(Lotterhos et al., 1988, pp. 631–632).

problems (thus motivating the prohibition impulse), its use is widespread and widely accepted (thus motivating its defense). In either case, the consequence is often intense emotion and struggle.

Following the repeal of the Eighteenth Amendment in 1933, prohibition efforts have largely been age-specific. In 1970, Congress passed the Twenty-Sixth Amendment, which grants the right to vote in Federal elections to citizens between the ages of 18 and 21. A movement then began to extend other rights and privileges of adulthood to those aged 18; between 1970 and 1975, 29 states reduced their minimum legal drinking age (Wagenaar, 1983). However, by the late 1970s controversy over mininum drinking age laws became widespread and this pattern was reversed. Much of the concern arose over the number of young people involved in automobile accidents, many of which were alcohol-related (Wechsler and Sands, 1980).

A common response to the need to "do something" about a perceived problem has been to seek a legal solution through legislation and it appears that laws in the United States are among the most stringent in the world (Mosher, 1980). Of course, raising the drinking age to reduce drunk driving is an indirect and incomplete way to attack the problem. "No doubt raising the drinking age to 25, 30 or even 50", as one house of the Mississippi legislature recently passed, "would also tend to reduce drunk driving. The youngest age group is being chosen as a symbolic gesture because of its political impotence and because . . . there are no major economic consequences. . . ." (Mosher, 1980, p. 31). A more direct and effective approach might be to address the problem of intoxicated drivers *regardless* of their age or social status.

Mosher has pointed out that

"these modern youthful-drinking laws and enforcement priorities contrast with trends in youthful-drinking patterns. In the abstract, one would predict that increasingly stringent controls on availability and emphasis on enforcement would lessen the actual amount of alcohol consumed. Indeed, for all the problems associated with national Prohibition, use did decline during that period. Such is not the case for youthful drinking. Statistics show that underaged persons increased their use of alcohol steadily from the 1930s to the 1960s, when legislation to curtail sales was most active. Ironically, a plateau was reached both in the prevalence of teenage drinking and in legislative action to restrict availability to teenagers at approximately the same time" (Mosher, 1980, p. 25).

Both up-dating and corroborating Mosher's observation is the fact that following the reduction of drinking age laws in the 1970s, the proportion of collegians who drink has trended downward (Engs and Hanson, 1988).

An unresolved issue underlying minimum drinking age laws is determining the age at which young people are mature enough to assume adult responsibilities. The lack of consensus regarding this issue in general is reflected in the diverse and changing minimum ages for other behaviors. These include age of consent for sexual intercourse, to purchase contraceptive devices, to marry without parental approval, to drive a car, to serve on a jury, and to buy and use tobacco (Wechsler and Sands, 1980).

Some studies (Perkins and Berkowitz, 1987; Engs and Hanson, 1986) have found little differences between drinking patterns of young people legally able and not legally able to drink. One reason for this lack of differentiation might be the pervasive informal supply networks and mechanisms whereby underage individuals generally experience little or no difficulty in obtaining alcohol. Another reason may be the ease with which many underage people were able to drive to neighboring states (or provinces) to purchase or consume alcohol. In any case, it would appear that legislation generally has had virtually no impact on alcohol behaviors and problems.

Drinking patterns are governed by the common fabric of values, symbols, and meanings shared by a group (Globetti, 1976). Legislation designed to prohibit customs embedded in a group risk failure, as did national prohibition in such countries as Iceland (1915–1922), Russia (1916–1917), Finland (1919–1932) and the United States (1920–1933) (Ewing and Rouse, 1976). National prohibition does not seem to be attainable except in those countries in which, by far, the large majority of inhabitants practice a religion prohibiting the use of alcohol (Tongue, 1976).

Underlying minimum age legislation are the assumptions of American prohibitionism: alcohol consumption is sinful and dangerous; it results in problem behavior; and drinking in any degree is equally undesirable because moderate social drinking is the forerunner of chronic inebriation (Sterne et al., 1967). Naturally, young people, if not everyone, should be protected from alcohol, according to this view.

Attempts to legislate behavior often lead to unintended and undesirable consequences. For example, Australian laws closing bars at six o'clock got the working men out of the establishments and possibly home to their families in time for dinner. However, they also produced the undesirable custom known as the six o'clock swill, which involves consuming as much beer as possible between the end of work and the six o'clock closing time (Room, 1976). Sterne and her colleagues (1967) concluded that minimum age laws not only fail in their intent but also produce very questionable consequences:

1. "The consumption of alcohol in automobiles is clearly undesirable, yet in denying the right of the older teenager to its public purchase and consumption, we unwittingly suggest this combination."

2. "The practice of patterned evasion of stringent liquor laws is a poor introduction of youth to adult civic responsibility, suggesting adult roles which incorporate neither respect for nor conformity to the law."

3. "As Prohibition amply demonstrated, liquor laws which do not meet with public acceptance provide illicit business opportunities. While taverns have not been found to be an important factor producing delinquency, a small minority of them capitalize on this opportunity for illicit business, catering to questionable entertainment and an outlet for drugs" (Sterne et al., 1967, pp. 58–59).

Alcohol legislation is often passed with less concern for the law's actual impact (or lack thereof) on drinking behavior than with its political value for the legislators; that is, with how their constituents will perceive their votes and how future opponents might be able to attack their voting records[1] (Room, 1976, p. 269). Furthermore, with over two-thirds of the adult American population being drinkers, rigorous enforcement of restrictive legislation is not viewed as a priority by the general population, by the police, or by the courts.

Even if enforcement of prohibitive legislation were vigorously pursued, there is little evidence that it would be successful. The widespread demand for alcohol and the ease with which a large variety of products can be converted into alcoholic beverages easily lead to "home brew" and other illicit manufacture. Ease of distribution gives natural rise to bootlegging and smuggling under such circumstances.

Not surprisingly, age-specific prohibition does not appear to be effective in reducing either the proportion of drinkers or their drinking problems. A study of a large sample of young people between the ages of 16 and 19 in Massachusetts and New York after Massachusetts raised its drinking age revealed that the average, self-reported daily alcohol consumption in Massachusetts did not decline in comparison with New York (Hingson et al., 1983). Comparison of college students attending schools in states that had maintained for a period of at least ten years a minimum drinking age of 21 with those in states that had similarly maintained minimum drinking ages below 21 revealed few differences in drinking problems (Engs and Hanson, 1986).

Comparison of drinking before and after the passage of raised minimum age legislation have generally revealed little impact upon behavior (Perkins and Berkowitz, 1985; Hanson and Hattauer, n.d.). For example, a study that examined college students' drinking behavior before and after an increase in the minimum legal drinking age from 18 to 19 in New York State found the law to have no impact on under-age students' consumption rates, intoxication, drinking attitudes, or drinking problems (Perkins and Berkowitz, 1985). These findings were corroborated by other researchers at a different college in the same state (Hanson and Hattauer, n.d.). A similar study at Texas A & M examined the impact of an increase of the minimum drinking age from 19 to 21. There was no increase in consumption or alcohol problems among under-age students. However, there was a significant increase among such students in attendance at events where alcohol was present. There were also significant increases in the frequency of their requests to legal-age students to provide alcohol and in their receipt of illicit alcohol from legal-age students (Mason et al., 1988).

A longitudinal study of the effect of a one-year increase of the drinking age in the province of Ontario found that it had a minimum effect on consumption among 18 and 19 year-old high school students and none among those who drank once a week or more (Vingilis and Smart, 1981). A similar study was conducted among college students in the State University System of Florida to examine their behavior before and after an increase in the drinking age from 19 to 21. While there was a general trend toward reduced consumption of alcohol after the change in law, alcohol-related problems increased significantly. Finally, an examination of East Carolina University students' intentions regarding their behavior following passage of a new 21-year age drinking law revealed that only 6% intended to stop drinking, 70% planned to change their drinking location, 21% expected to use a false or borrowed identification to obtain alcohol, and 22% intended to use other drugs. Anecdotal statements by students indicated the belief of some that it "might be easier to hide a little pot in my room than a six pack of beer" (Lotterhos et al., 1988, p. 644).

Over the past four decades it has been demonstrated that the proportion of collegiate drinkers increases with age (Straus and Bacon, 1953; Wechsler and McFadden,

1979; Perkins and Berkowitz, 1987). However, in July of 1987 the minimum purchase age became 21 in all states. Because drinking tends to be highly valued among collegians, because it is now illegal for those under 21 to purchase alcohol, Engs and Hanson (1989) hypothesized that reactance motivation (Brehm and Brehm, 1981) would be stimulated among such students, leading more of them to drink. Their data from 3,375 students at 56 colleges across the country revealed that, after the legislation, significantly more under-age students drank compared to those of legal age. Thus, the increase in purchase age appears to have been not only ineffective but actually counter-productive, at least in the short run.

There is extensive evidence that while an abstinence religious environment is associated with a lower proportion of people drinking, alcohol-related problems are much more common among those in such milieu who do drink (Hanson, 1972). This appears to result from several factors. First, such individuals have typically not learned how to drink. Thus, they have not learned how to use alcohol in moderation. Secondly, they are more likely to drink in a secretive manner or in environments free of moderating or restraining social control over their drinking. Thirdly, abstinence groups often portray the person who drinks as one who misuses alcohol. Thus, they inadvertently present a negative role model which can guide behavior of those who do drink (Globetti, 1976, p. 166). Fourthly, for young people, abstinence teaching may encourage rather than deter use by making alcohol use a symbol or tool of rebellion against authority. The nature of the rebellion can gain further strength and intensity from disapproval and repression (Globetti, 1976, p. 167).

Conversely, most Jews, Chinese, and Italians drink, yet those groups have low rates of drunkenness and other forms of problem drinking. In all three groups, children begin drinking at an early age in the home and they observe alcohol being used in an unemotional and controlled manner. They learn that alcohol is a natural and normal part of life, do not view its use as a sign or symbol of adulthood, nor associate it with intoxication. To the contrary, they learn that alcohol abuse is taboo. Importantly, they are provided with role models for the appropriate use of alcohol (Plaut, 1967; Wilkinson, 1970; Hanson, 1972).

It is clear that much formal alcohol education is unrealistic, alienates young people, and tends to be ineffective if not counterproductive (Hanson, 1982). Cisin has stated the problem very well:

"In our values as parents and educators, we have a responsibility for the socialization of our children, a responsibility for preparing them for life in the world. Part of our job is teaching children how to handle dangerous activities like driving, swimming, drinking, and sex. We behave toward our children as though there were really two different kinds of dangerous activities. Driving and swimming fall into the first type: we carefully teach our children that these are dangerous activities, and we deliberately set out to be sure that they know there is a right way and a wrong way to participate in these activities."

"On the other hand, when we look at the other kind of dangerous activities, exemplified by drinking and sex, we seem to know only one word: 'Don't.' We do not bother to say there is a right way and there is a wrong way; we just say 'Don't!' We do not really want to produce abstainers; we have the illusion that they will follow our advice and be abstainers (in the case of sex, until marriage; and in the case of alcohol, until maturity) until they reach the magic age at which they can handle these activities. But as to the rights and wrongs of handling it when the great day comes, we choose to keep them in the dark. Now this is sheer hypocrisy. We are slowly awakening to the fact that we owe our children sex education in the home and in the school—education not dominated by the antisex league. We should be brave enough to tell them the truth; that drinking is normal behavior in the society, that moderate drinking need not lead to abuse; that drinking can be done in an appropriate civilized way without shame and guilt. Perhaps greater socialization in the direction of moderate drinking is part of the program we need for prevention of alcohol problems in the future" (1978. p. 154).

In a major publication generated by the work of the Cooperative Commission on the Study of Alcoholism, Wilkinson (1970) proposed that the minimum age for the purchase or consumption of alcohol on commercial premises, or to have them in public possession, should be eighteen rather than twenty-one. However, with meals in bona fide restaurants serving alcohol, those under eighteen should be permitted to order alcoholic drinks, provided they are accompanied by their parents or guardians who approve. Unless a college has a specific ethos against drinking, it should provide supervised places enabling students to drink wine or beer with their meals. On the other hand, drinking at home should be free of any minimum legal age restriction (Wilkinson, 1970).

Clearly, the basic assumption underlying the above proposals is that most people who are going to drink as adults should learn to manage alcohol at an early age and with their families. Retrospective studies of the early drinking experiences of problem and non-problem drinkers support the hypothesis that early drinking experiences may influence subsequent drinking behavior. Problem drinkers appear to begin their drinking at a later age than others, to have their first drinking experience outside the home, to become intoxicated the first time they drink, and to drink as an act of rebellion (open or secret) against parental authority (Plaut, 1967).

It has been said that if there is one universal characteristic that pervades humanity, it may be the urge to manipulate and control the behavior of others (Cisin, 1978) and nowhere is this more apparent than in the effort to control drinking behavior through legislative edict. The minimum drinking age laws in the United States have undergone over 100 modifications since their introduction in the 1930s (Wechsler and Sands, 1980, p. 2). The most recent series of increases in the minimum age will be no more successful than were those of the past. What we need are not more laws but the wisdom and courage to move beyond such simplistic answers to a complex social problem.

## NOTE

1. For example, as governor of Massachusetts, Michael Dukakis vetoed two bills to lower the drinking age. His vetoes became a campaign issue that apparently contributed to an unexpected defeat in his bid for reelection in 1978 (Mosher, 1980).

## REFERENCES

Alcoholism and Drug Addiction Research Foundation of Ontario (1961). "It's best to know". Alcoholism and Drug Addiction Research Foundation of Ontario: Toronto, Ontario.

Brehm, S. and Brehm, J. W. (1981). Psychological reactance: A theory of freedom and control. Academic Press: New York.

Cisin, I. H. (1978). Formal and informal social controls over drinking. In Ewing, J. A. and Rouse, B. A. (Eds.). *Drinking: alcohol in American society—issues and current research.* Nelson-Hall: Chicago, IL.

Engs, R. C. and Hanson, D. J. (1986). Age-specific alcohol prohibition and college student drinking problems. *Psychological Reports,* 59 979–984.

Engs, R. C. and Hanson, D. J. (1988). University students' drinking patterns and problems: examining the effects of raising the purchase age, *Public Health Reports,* 103 667–673.

Engs, R. C. and Hanson, D. J. (1989). Reactance theory: a test with collegiate drinking. *Psychological Reports,* 64 1083–1086.

Ewing, J. A. and Rouse, B. A. (1976). Drinks, drinkers, and drinking. In Ewing, J. A. and Rouse, B. A. (Eds.). *Drinking: alcohol in American society—issues and current research.* Nelson-Hall: Chicago, IL.

Globetti, G. (1976). Prohibition norms and teenage drinking. In Ewing, J. A. and Rouse, B. A. (Eds.). *Drinking: alcohol in American society—issues and current research.* Nelson-Hall: Chicago, IL.

Gusfield, J. R. (1962). Status conflicts and the changing ideologies of the American temperance movement. In Pittman, D. J. and Snyder, C. R., (Eds.). *Society, culture and drinking patterns.* Wiley: New York.

Gusfield, J. R. (1963). *Symbolic Crusade: status politics and the American Temperance movement,* University of Illinois Press: Urbana, IL.

Hanson, D. J. (1972). *Norm qualities and deviant drinking behavior.* Syracuse University: Syracuse, NY, unpublished Ph.D. dissertation.

Hanson, D. J. (1982). The effectiveness of alcohol and drug education. *Journal of Alcohol and Drug Education,* 27 1–13.

Hanson, D. J. and Hattauer, E. (n.d.). Effects of legislated drinking norms on college students' behaviors. Potsdam College: Potsdam, New York, unpublished paper.

Hingson, R., Merrigan, D., and Heeren, T. (1985). Effects of Massachusetts Raising its Legal Drinking Age from 18 to 20 on Deaths from Teenage Homicide, Suicide and Nontraffic Accidents. *Pediatric Clinics of North America,* 32 221–233.

Knupfer, G. (1960). Use of alcoholic beverages by society and its cultural implications. *California's Health,* 18 17–21.

Lotterhos, J. F., Glover, E. D., Holbert, D. and Barnes, R. C. (1988). Intentionality of college students regarding North Carolina's 21-year-drinking age law. *International Journal of Addiction,* 23 629–647.

Mason, T., Myszka, M., and Winniford, J. (1988). Assessing the impact of the 21-year old drinking age: the Texas A & M study. Paper presented at annual meeting of New York State Sociological Association, Oswego, New York, October 7–8.

Mosher, J. F. (1980). The history of youthful-drinking laws: implications for current policy. In Wechsler, H. (Ed.). *Minimum-drinking-age laws.* Lexington Books: Lexington, MA.

Patrick, C. H. (1952). *Alcohol, Culture and Society.* Duke University Press: Durham, NC.

Perkins, H. W. and Berkowitz, A. D. (1985). College students' attitudinal and behavioral responses to a drinking-age law change: stability and contradiction in the campus setting. Paper presented at the Annual Meeting of the N.Y. State Sociological Association, Rochester, October 18–19.

Perkins, H. W. and Berkowitz, A. D. (1987). Stability and contradiction in college students' drinking following a drinking law change. Paper presented at the Joint Meeting of the American College Personnel Association and the National Association of Student Personnel Administration, Chicago, March 15–18.

Plaut, T. F. (1967). *Alcohol problems: a report to the Nation by the Cooperative Commission on the Study of Alcoholism.* Oxford University Press: New York.

Room, R. (1976). Evaluating the effect of drinking laws on drinking. In Ewing, J. A. and Rouse, B. A., (Eds.). *Drinking: alcohol in American society—issues and current research.* Nelson-Hall: Chicago, IL.

Sterne, M. W., Pittman, D. J. and Coe, T. (1967). Teenagers, drinking and the law: study of arrest trends for alcohol-related offenses. In Pittman, D. J. (Ed.). *Alcoholism.* Harper & Row: New York.

Straus, R. and Bacon, S. D. (1953). *Drinking in College.* Yale University Press: New Haven, CT.

Tongue, A. (1976). 5,000 years of drinking. In Ewing, J. A. and Rouse, B. A. (Eds.). *Drinking: alcohol in American society—issues and current research.* Nelson-Hall: Chicago, IL.

Vingilis, E. and Smart, R., (1981). Effects of raising the legal drinking age in Ontario. *British Journal of Addiction,* 76 415–424.

Wagenaar, A. C. (1983). *Alcohol, young drivers, and traffic accidents.* Lexington Books: Lexington, MA.

Wechsler, H. and McFadden, M. (1979). Drinking among college students in New England. *Journal of Studies on Alcohol,* 40 969–996.

Wechsler, H. And Sands, E. S. (1980). Minimum-age laws and youthful drinking: an introduction. In Wechsler, H. (Ed.). *Minimum-drinking-age laws.* Lexington Books: Lexington, MA.

Wilkinson, R. (1970). *The prevention of drinking problems: alcohol control and cultural influences.* Oxford University Press: New York.

# POSTSCRIPT

## Should the Drinking Age Remain at 21?

The popular consensus among high school students and underage college students who drink is that they have very easy access to alcohol. Also, they are generally unconcerned about the legal ramifications of drinking as a minor. Still, as the problems of alcohol use among teenagers continue, the debate on how to diminish the problems persists. Is abstinence an unrealistic goal, since young people will continue to drink alcohol regardless of the legal restrictions? Are teenagers irresponsible, or has society failed to teach young people how to act responsibly?

When European exchange students come to the United States to study at American colleges, they are often surprised to find that a minimum drinking age law exists. Alcohol consumption is legal for all ages in many European countries, and drinking is integrated into numerous rituals and customs. Children are raised with the understanding that alcohol consumption is a normal part of family life. Moderate drinking is culturally acceptable and viewed as a personal right, but there is also strong disapproval for excessive alcohol use. Consequently, there is less alcohol abuse and reckless drinking among European teens than among American teens. However, is the United States ready to adopt this European system? Also, would such a system work in America? More significantly, can the current U.S. economic, political, legal, and social systems afford the risks that come with abolishing the legal drinking age?

Goeman supports the legal prohibition of alcohol for those under 21, and he maintains that laws exist to protect youth and the rest of society from the dangers that are involved with teen drinking. Teenagers, he asserts, are not mature enough to handle the responsibilities that come with drinking alcohol. Hanson insists that educators and policymakers should incorporate "responsible use" messages into their alcohol prevention programs. They must not rely on legal recourse to prevent the problems that emanate from teen drinking because laws are not effective.

Research shows that simply providing information to teenagers does not decrease their alcohol usage. Many people advocate instead a combination of approaches to deter teens from using alcohol. A comprehensive program may include (1) information and knowledge about the effects of alcohol use, (2) self-concept and self-identity enhancement, (3) "responsible use" messages for those who are legally allowed to drink, and (4) discussions of legal matters.

In "The Primary Prevention of Alcohol Problems: A Critical Review of the Research Literature," *Journal of Studies on Alcohol* (January 1989), Joel Moskowitz concludes that raising the drinking age and strictly enforcing drunk driving laws are very effective means for reducing alcohol-related problems. In his book *An Ounce of Prevention: Strategies for Solving Tobacco, Alcohol, and Other Drug Problems* (Jossey-Bass, 1991), Don Cahalan describes several studies that found relationships between higher minimum drinking ages and lower rates of motor vehicle fatalities. Two essays in the Surgeon General's *Workshop on Drunk Driving* (Department of Health and Human Services, 1989) are especially pertinent to this debate. The first essay, "Mass Communication Effects on Drinking and Driving," is by Charles Atkin, and the second essay, "Youth Impaired Driving: Causes and Countermeasures," is by Michael Klitzner.

# ISSUE 5

# Is the War on Drugs Misdirected?

**YES: James F. Mosher and Karen L. Yanagisako,** from "Public Health, Not Social Warfare: A Public Health Approach to Illegal Drug Policy," *Journal of Public Health Policy* (Autumn 1991)

**NO: Office of National Drug Control Policy,** from *National Drug Control Strategy: A Nation Responds to Drug Use* (Government Printing Office, 1992)

## ISSUE SUMMARY

**YES:** Public health specialists James F. Mosher and Karen L. Yanagisako argue that drug problems should come under the province of public health and not the criminal justice system. They believe that too much emphasis is placed on controlling illegal drugs and not enough on legal drugs, like alcohol and tobacco.
**NO:** The Office of National Drug Control Policy, an executive agency that determines policies and objectives for the U.S. drug control program, feels that not only should drug users be prosecuted but that efforts should be directed toward disrupting and dismantling multinational criminal organizations.

Despite the marked decline in overall drug use in the United States throughout the 1980s, drug use remains prevalent. The following two selections look at the drug problem from vastly different perspectives. In the essay by James F. Mosher and Karen L. Yanagisako, the drug problem is viewed as a public health matter. They feel that the drug problem should be dealt with by implementing policies that would discourage drug use. Moreover, drug users should be treated, not jailed, and drug policies should be aimed at the political, social, and economic conditions that underlie drug problems. In the selection by the Office of National Drug Control Policy, drug use is described as a moral problem that is best handled through criminal channels. Accordingly, the deterrent for drug use would be to prosecute drug users, drug dealers, and drug traffickers and to halt the entry of drugs into the United States.

Many government officials believe that not only should drug users and sellers be prosecuted but that other countries should assist in stopping the flow of drugs across their borders. Reducing the demand for drugs and curtailing the supply of drugs by intercepting them before they reach the user are two methods that would help eliminate drug use. Critical elements in the lucrative drug trade are multinational crime syndicates. One premise is that if the drug production, transportation, distribution, and processing functions of these criminal organizations can be interrupted and eventually crippled, then the drug problem would diminish.

Before the drug supply can be significantly reduced, international cooperation is essential. In South American countries like Peru, Colombia, and Bolivia where coca—from which cocaine is processed—is prevalent, economic aid can be made available to help the governments of these countries fight the cocaine kingpins. One alleged problem is that a number of government officials in these countries are corrupt or fearful of the cocaine cartel leaders. One solution is to offer money to farmers to plant other crops, but how long could this type of program be afforded? In the mid-1970s the U.S. government gave money to farmers in Turkey to stop growing opium crops. After one year the program was discontinued due to the enormous expense, and opium crops were once again planted.

In the war on drugs, the *casual* user is the primary focus in deterring drug use; this is viewed by many people as a form of discrimination. Although most drug users escape arrest, the vast majority of drug users and sellers who are arrested and prosecuted are poor, members of minorities, homeless, unemployed, and/or disenfranchised. This is reminiscent of early drug laws in which certain drugs were made illegal after they were related to various minority groups.

How effective are drug laws at reducing use? In the early 1970s New York implemented the Rockefeller Laws, which stipulated that heroin sellers were to receive mandatory life sentences in prison. However, these laws had little effect on the availability of heroin. On the other hand, in states where marijuana has been decriminalized, there has been no increase in use.

Some critics contend that successful interdiction of one drug does not deter drug use because users simply turn to other drugs. Also, if drugs are in short supply, their costs go up, which makes the drug business more lucrative for sellers who do not get arrested. As profits increase, the violence that is connected to drugs escalates. Some question whether or not this is a valid reason to retreat from the drug problem. Others believe that drugs are sinister and morally corrupting to young people and that their use should be stopped regardless of costs. This is the approach that has been taken by the recent presidential administrations. Although more money has been allocated for drug treatment and education than in the past, the lion's share of the funds to fight the war on drugs has gone for enforcement.

The following selections address the problems associated with drug use and how the fight against drugs should be approached. Mosher and Yanagisako take the view that drug problems should be managed through public health measures. The Office of National Drug Control Policy attacks the problem of drugs through interdiction and enforcement.

# YES

James F. Mosher and
Karen L. Yanagisako

## PUBLIC HEALTH, NOT SOCIAL WARFARE: A PUBLIC HEALTH APPROACH TO ILLEGAL DRUG POLICY

### INTRODUCTION

This article makes three arguments: (1) **The "War on Drugs" is a misnomer.** The dominant thrust of current state and federal drug policy undercuts fundamental premises and values of public health. The War on Drugs, as defined by the primary architects of current drug policies, has framed the health consequences of illegal drug use as a moral issue requiring a moral and punitive response. At the same time, it has excluded alcohol and tobacco from the drug war, even though these legal drugs have far more devastating public health consequences than all illegal drug use combined. This framing leads to policies that exacerbate rather than reduce drug problems. The result is a war on the disenfranchised, people of color, the poor, the homeless and the unemployed. This scenario is familiar to drug policy historians. Misnamed drug wars that are in fact attacks on vulnerable and powerless populations and on principles and values of public health have become a familiar part of this nation's political culture.

(2) **Drug policy belongs in the realm of public health.** Drug problems are complex public health problems that need to be understood and responded to as such. Comprehensive policy initiatives are needed to address the multiplicity of causes of drug problems, particularly the social, economic, and political conditions that underlie them. Public health theory and practice provide the necessary grounding for developing such policy initiatives.

(3) **To take a leadership role in drug policy, the public health community must become more powerful, politically sophisticated and strategically oriented, and must build its grassroots support base.** The War on Drugs is premised on prejudice and fear. Its leaders have been successful in portray-

ing those who oppose its moralistic and punitive tone as insensitive to the public's legitimate concerns. Before policy reform can occur, the public health community will need to become effective in public forums, reshaping the terms and premises of the debate within the political and media arenas and activating new constituencies to support public health initiatives. . . .

## THE WAR ON DRUGS: MISDIRECTED SOCIAL POLICY

[A] two-tiered system regarding drugs, based on socioeconomic status, is a familiar pattern in public health and social welfare. Many other social and health problems are experienced most acutely among those with the least resources in society. Yet current drug policy hides and ignores this fundamental fact of drug use and problems, and is more accurately viewed as a form of social control rather than as a public health response to the problems posed.

### Assumptions and Priorities of the Current Drug War

The *National Drug Control Strategy*, submitted by the Bush Administration to Congress in 1989 and updated in 1990 and 1991 reports, provides a "comprehensive blueprint" for current national policy. The report, together with the followup reports and statements made by William Bennett, the chief architect of current drug policy, establishes these basic assumptions and priorities of the current drug war:

(1) **Illegal Drug Use is Fundamentally a Moral Problem.** This is stated flatly in the 1989 report, and provides the foundation for the report's analysis and recommendations. It treats illegal drug use

as a battle between good (those who do not use and those who support non-use) and evil (illegal drugs, their users, and those who question the non-use goal). Drug problems result from defects in individual character and therefore require moralistic and individualized responses. As stated in the report:

> [D]rug use degrades human character, and a purposeful, self-government society ignores its people's character at great peril. . . . [Using drugs is] a hollow, degrading, and deceptive pleasure . . . and pursuing it is an appalling self-destructive impulse.

Bennett has reinforced this view repeatedly in his personal remarks.

(2) **Illegal Drug Policy Should Focus on Deterring Use, not on Reducing Associated Problems.** This premise is repeated throughout the 1989 report and its 1990 and 1991 updates, and is based on the view that drug use is itself a moral problem. Policy should treat in an identical manner experimental first use, casual use, regular use and addiction. In fact, non-addicted users represent "a potential agent of infection" and are "highly contagious." Drug problems play a secondary role in establishing policy. As stated in the report:

> [W]e must come to terms with the drug problem in its essence: use itself. Worthy efforts to alleviate the symptoms of epidemic drug abuse—crime and disease, for example—must continue unabated. But a largely ad-hoc attack on the holes in our dike can have only an indirect and minimal effect on the flood itself.

Appendix A of the report lists nine quantifiable goals for federal illegal drug policy. Only one, the reduction of emergency room reports, involves problems. All of the other eight refer to reductions in use or availability.

(3) **All Illegal Drugs Should be Treated as the Same, and Legal Drugs are not Included.** The 1989 report states that cocaine and its derivative, crack, are the most dangerous and damaging of illegal drugs, but illegal drugs are equally dangerous because others are "gateway" drugs and should therefore evoke the same social response. Yet, the report and its 1990 and 1991 updates virtually ignore the two primary "gateway" drugs—alcohol and tobacco.

(4) **Punitive Measures to Stem Use and Supply Should Dominate Illegal Drug Policy.** Since drug use is the problem and since it is a moral problem, punishment is appropriate as the primary response. Punitive measures encompass a broad array of policy initiatives: increased penalties for use and distribution; increased law enforcement efforts to promote detection; drug testing; drug traffic interdiction; civil penalties, including loss of rights to public housing and forfeiture of property; limitations on civil rights. Enforcement is critical to deterring use and should focus on "casual" users because they create bad role models and because they are the ones who spread the "contagion."

The 1989 report views treatment with suspicion, and directly tied to threats of punishment. As stated by Bennett: "Many people in treatment would not be there had they not been arrested. Coercion is one of the most effective things we can use to get them into treatment." This suspicion has been tempered both in the 1990 and 1991 updates and in a White Paper published by the Office of National Drug Control Policy in June 1990, in part in response to Congressional pressure. The White Paper termed treatment a "major and necessary element in any adequate solution for the problems of addiction."

Despite this increased attention to treatment concerns, law enforcement and deterrence remains the dominant focus of national policy. Three factors demonstrate this overall emphasis. First, treatment funding has increased significantly in the last three years, but the increases are only now beginning to replace the severe budget cuts of the early 1980s. Treatment was significantly less available in 1987 (the most recent data available) than in 1976.

Second, funding for treatment is clearly available from the drug war, but it is being diverted to law enforcement and related activities. In 1988, approximately 75 percent ($3.1 billion) of the drug war budget (which totalled $4.1 billion) went to enforcement and related activities, with the remainder allocated for education and treatment. The total drug war budget increased to $6.3 billion in 1989 and $9.4 billion in 1990, but maintained the same 75–25 percent split. As a result, in 1990 enforcement and related activities received almost $4 billion more than in 1988, most of which went to prison construction, military and paramilitary operations overseas, and other Department of Justice activities.

Finally, drug treatment in the nation's inmate population is woefully inadequate. According to IOM [Institute of Medicine], there are approximately 320,000 inmates who need treatment in federal, state and local prisons. Yet NIDA [National Institute on Drug Abuse] reported in its NDATUS [National Drug and Alcohol Treatment Unit] survey that less than 7,000 actually received treatment in 1987, significantly less than the 9,100 inmates in treatment in 1977. The War on Drugs reports may argue that coercion is justified as a means to promote treatment, but treatment is a highly unlikely outcome for those being coerced.

## Flawed Assumptions, Misplaced Priorities

These four basic assumptions and priorities do not describe all federal activities funded by the current War on Drugs. Programs housed in the Department of Health and Human Services are most notable for their support of public health programs that question or ignore the Office of National Drug Control Policy ideology. Nevertheless, that ideology continues to dominate federal drug policy today, guiding overall strategic and funding priorities. The assumptions are reminiscent of past drug wars, and suffer from many of the same flaws.

**(1) Imposing Stricter Penalties and Increasing Law Enforcement Efforts Against Illegal Drug Users and Suppliers Will Have Only a Limited Effect on Drug Use.** Proponents of deterrent strategies argue that making drug use illegal and forcing availability into illegal channels will reduce overall consumption by making the drug less available and more expensive and by supporting a no-use social norm. The U.S. experience with Prohibition and its repeal suggest that this is the case, at least for drugs that are relatively easy to detect and difficult to conceal, such as beer. Increasing the severity and breadth of the illegality, however, will not necessarily increase this deterrent effect.

Research conducted on the impact of deterrent strategies on drug use has focused primarily on the efficacy of anti-drinking driving laws. Ross concludes that, for deterrence to be effective, threatened punishment must be perceived as certain and swift as well as severe. As the certainty and timeliness of the application of an effective sanction recedes, the effect of the sanction diminishes. Increasing the severity of punishment is not itself an effective prevention strategy.

Despite the rapidly growing arrest rates for illegal drug use, the likelihood of arrest remains miniscule. There are more than 155 million separate drug use violations in 1990 among monthly users of drugs alone. The total number of violations, including each drug episode among all users, is several times higher. Only 850,000 of these violations lead to arrests. Less than 2 percent of drug users and sellers are arrested each year. Drug use is far less likely to result in arrest than drinking-driving, which itself has a very low risk of arrest—too low for the possibility of arrest to be an effective deterrent. Nor is punishment swift—court cases involving illegal drug use and sales can take years to complete. Thus criminal actions against drug use and sales lack two of the three criteria for effective deterrent strategies.

Studies conducted following the enactment of the "Rockefeller Laws" against the heroin trade in New York in the early 1970s support this conclusion. Labelled the "nation's toughest drug law," it greatly increased penalties (a mandatory life sentence, with a minimum of 15 years before parole consideration for adults convicted of selling more than one ounce of narcotics).

Evaluations of the impact of the law showed no or little effect on the availability or use of heroin or other illegal drugs. A 1976 study found:

> The pattern of stable heroin use in New York City between 1973 and mid-1976 was not appreciably different from the

average pattern in other East Coast cities.

During the 1970s, penalties for possession of small amounts of marijuana were reduced to infractions (involving small fines instead of potential incarceration) in several states. Evaluations found that the reductions in penalties had no effect on marijuana use.

Of the various deterrent strategies proposed in the War on Drugs, only random drug testing appears to have the potential for meeting the criteria for effective deterrence. Remarkably, despite the increasing use of drug testing in government and business, there is little research documenting its impact on drug use and drug problems. Drug testing, moreover, raises serious policy and Constitutional issues. False positives are a real danger if tests are not properly conducted, and accurate testing is expensive, particularly when conducted in large populations. Illegal drug testing does not test impairment, and alcohol, the drug most likely to cause impairment, is usually not included. Finally, drug testing is a serious threat to the privacy and other Constitutional rights of those being tested. For these reasons, the American Public Health Association has passed a resolution opposing drug testing in all but a very limited number of circumstances and only in the context of an overall worker health and safety program.

**(2) Illegal Drug Interdiction Efforts Targeting Traffickers Will Have a Limited Effect on Illegal Drug Availability.** There is surprising agreement in the academic literature that drug interdiction (intercepting drugs between the place produced and the place used) has only limited effect on the availability of illegal drugs, particularly cocaine. Perhaps most persuasive is the RAND study, published in 1988, funded by the Department of Defense. RAND assumed current interdiction efforts against cocaine result in a seizure of 20 percent (a very optimistic assumption) of imports and analyzed the impact of increasing this figure to 50 percent, probably an impossible goal. Even this dramatic improvement, the report concluded, would increase cocaine prices by less than 3 percent. The authors conclude:

[G]reater efforts at interdiction are not going to have much of an effect on the nation's cocaine problem. A similar argument can be made with regard to much of the federal enforcement effort.

The study's conclusion is based on an analysis of the dynamics and structure of the cocaine trade. Importers can easily replace what is interdicted with cocaine from alternative, cheap sources, and the proportion of the retail ("street") price of illegal drugs accounted for by the import price is very small. In fact, cocaine prices have dropped and availability has increased dramatically during the last ten years, coinciding with the interdiction effort. The RAND study conclusion has been supported in numerous other studies.

**(3) Although Enforcement Efforts Are Supposed to Focus on the "Casual User," They in Fact Target Low Income Users.** The "casual" user is likely to be from any social class. Yet arrest and incarceration statistics demonstrate that current enforcement policies are targeting poor Black and Latino males. Other users have much lower arrest rates than would be anticipated based on their use rates. . . .

(4) **Drugs Cause Differing Levels of Social and Health Problems, and The Legal Drugs are by Far the Most Devastating. This is Particularly True When Problems Associated With Use Are Distinguished From Problems Associated With the Drug Trade.** Cocaine is singled out in the War on Drugs for special mention, but the strategies for waging that "war" do not differentiate among the illegal drugs and ignore by far the most devastating drug problems, alcohol and tobacco. The public health consequences of various illegal drugs vary greatly. Although marijuana is now much more potent than in earlier decades, its association with trauma and long-term health problems remains much lower than other drugs, legal and illegal alike.

(5) **Interdiction and Deterrence Strategies Have Serious Unanticipated Consequences That Adversely Affect Public Health.** What has received much less attention is the impact of interdiction and other deterrent strategies on the illegal trade itself, in part because studying an illegal business is so difficult. The few studies available suggest that interdiction and other deterrent efforts may have serious unintended consequences, even as they lessen the availability of a targeted drug. They may increase the availability of other, more dangerous drugs in a phenomenon termed "drug hardening." For example, "Operation Intercept" in the early 1970s curtailed marijuana importation. Smugglers turned to a more easily imported product—cocaine. At the same time, domestic growers developed a higher-potency marijuana strain. The criminalization of non-medical opiate use early this century caused increasing numbers of addicts to turn to what continues to be the most cost-effective and dangerous option—intravenous heroin

use. During alcohol Prohibition, smugglers and moonshiners concentrated on high-proof distilled spirits, which was easier to transport and conceal than beer and wine.

Interdiction and other deterrent strategies may also increase the profitability of smuggling and distribution, the violence associated with the illegal trade, and the likelihood of official corruption. As the illegal drug trade's profitability increases, so does its attractiveness to those outside the mainstream economy. . . .

Law enforcement efforts at the local level may have unintended consequences. One ethnographic study found that a police crackdown on crack houses in an inner city community resulted in dealers moving to more mobile locations on the street. Violence then increased because turf boundaries had become blurred. The police action ultimately did not reduce availability but did increase violence in the neighborhood.

Such unintended consequences can occur at the international level as well. Most eradication and interdiction efforts target economically-desperate peasant growers rather than large-scale smugglers, corrupt officials, and money launderers. Such efforts may exacerbate existing social, economic and political inequalities and increase the likelihood of corruption and violence.

Remarkably, there appears to be little government interest in assessing these unintended consequences, particularly as to their impact on illegal drug availability. Data collection and research studies are not available to assess the impact of increased enforcement and interdiction campaigns, and the documented lessons of past efforts, if they are not ignored, appear to have only a limited role in policy development. . . .

## Outlining the Public Health Agenda for Illegal Drugs

Viewing illegal drug problems from a public health perspective, we can now propose a broad-based, comprehensive approach for addressing those drug problems in the United States.

First, public health strategies should focus on both harm minimization (reducing the incidence and severity of illegal drug problems), as well as on the reduction of illegal drug use. Distinction should be made among drugs, examining each drug's environment and risks to health. Strategies to reduce the supply of drugs should be carefully planned in conjunction with broader, environmentally-based interventions, and the impact of those efforts on the drug trade should be carefully monitored.

Second, host strategies should focus on providing effective treatment and education programs, and should be planned in conjunction with agent and environmental strategies. . . . [T]he availability of treatment today is woefully inadequate, particularly for those populations most in need, who are more likely to face a punitive response. The public health system, not the criminal justice system, is the best place to treat health problems. The criminal justice system should focus primarily on deterring and preventing crimes of violence and insuring public safety.

Third, current priorities should be substantially redefined to target environmental risk factors rather than agent and non-health host factors. Interventions need to occur at all environmental levels—families, schools, workplaces, peer groups, etc.—and be planned in a comprehensive fashion.

Fourth, increased responsibility for program planning should be placed at the community level. Most environmental risk factors will vary by community, and each program will need to respond to a community's particular characteristics, culture, and historical experience. As discussed in the concluding section, the community level provides the best forum for empowering disenfranchised groups, providing them the opportunity to define and develop their own prevention responses. This will in turn build new political constituencies in support of public health activities.

Fifth, the public health field needs to address explicitly the social, political, and economic forces that put inner city and other low income communities at such high risk for illegal drug problems. Illegal drug prevention efforts should be directly tied to programs that address employment opportunities, adequate housing, community support systems, institutionalized racism, and other structural forces that marginalize these communities from the rest of society.

Finally, research priorities need to be substantially redefined to include study of environmental factors; their interaction with each other and with agent and host factors; the potential impact of comprehensive, community-based interventions; and the role of broader economic, political and social forces in illegal drug problems.

## CONCLUSION: TOWARD IMPLEMENTATION. . . .

### The Politics of Illegal Drug Policy

Perhaps the most remarkable aspect of the current War on Drugs is how effectively it has shaped the political landscape. Success in political races at all levels of government has appeared to hinge on which candidate is viewed as tougher on drugs and drug dealers. Even those who question the law enforcement emphasis of current policy have offered limited alternative options—usually focusing on education and treatment, without addressing broader environmental concerns. A public health analysis that focuses on political, social and economic conditions has, for the most part, not been a part of the political dialogue. When it is, it is almost invariably cast in terms of the legalization debate. . . .

The success of the War on Drugs spokespeople, in defining the terms of the debate, reflects their political power. The current drug war is backed by a powerful coalition that views the drug war as only one aspect of a broad social agenda. The drug war effectively redefines social problems as moral problems of individuals. This in turn helps justify continuing cuts in social programs, reductions in governmental services, continued redistribution of wealth in favor of the wealthy, curtailment of civil rights, and massive expenditures on social control, particularly increased law enforcement and prison construction.

Public health proponents will be able to challenge the War on Drugs coalition only when they become effective in the policy arena. Lessons from the alcohol and tobacco policy fields underscore this fundamental point. Research has established the public health risks of alcohol and tobacco consumption and the importance of addressing environmental risk factors. The research, however, had little effect on the politics of alcohol and tobacco until public health advocates became effective in changing policy at local, state and federal levels. This has meant confronting the powerful alcohol and tobacco industries—huge, highly con-

centrated conglomerates with effective and heavily financed political lobbies.

Three sets of skills, now recognized as an integral part of the alcohol and tobacco policy movements, are critical in the policy arena:

### Community Organizing

The public health field was ineffective in confronting the alcohol and tobacco lobbies until it organized the grassroots level, bringing new constituencies into the field that learned to be effective in the policy arena. The financial clout of these industries can only be matched with a strong grassroots network of activists and community organizations, relying on developing a true democracy based on our democratic traditions. Building a grassroots base is perhaps the single most important task for the alcohol field today.

Redefining the War on Drugs will require challenging the political coalition that supports current policy, perhaps a more imposing and certainly more amorphous force than the alcohol and tobacco lobbies. As in the alcohol and tobacco fields, this means building a grassroots movement. This is not an easy task. Those who have experienced the devastation of illegal drug problems most acutely tend to be the least powerful in our society, the most discouraged, and the least effective in the political arena. Yet they are a critical part of the coalition that needs to be built.

Community organizing skills and strategies provide a vehicle for the creation of grassroots movements. Community organizing has the issue of power at its core. It seeks to empower new constituencies, who, working together, define the nature of their problems and construct effective strategies for addressing them. It does not work in a service model, where professionals provide solutions developed in a process that does not involve those receiving the services.

Successful community organizing will change the power balance in a community. It will activate new voices, redefine problems, and develop new solutions. This will in turn change the nature of the political debate and the range of political options. A public health agenda regarding illegal drugs can become a part of the public dialogue as this power shift occurs.

Community organizing should be distinguished from those community programs (sometimes described as "community organization" or "community development" strategies) that work within the current community power structure, thereby reinforcing current power relationships. Programs which work within current community structures may provide a forum for changing some illegal drug environmental factors, but it does not provide a viable substitute for community organizing.

### Coalition Building and Political Advocacy Skills

Bridges across communities and between diverse groups within a community will be needed to address illegal drug problems and policies at all societal levels—local, regional, state and federal. Coalitions of diverse grassroots, service, community, professional, and other organizations need to work together to change public policy agendas. Coalition building complements community organizing, stimulating community involvement, building on the power of numbers and diversity in a community.

Coalition-building requires special skills. The diversity of the alcohol and illegal drug field will become its weakness if it is not turned into its strength. Potential coalition members are not used to working together and have difficulty communicating. Styles, interests, and language may be different. In many cases, power and authority are inequitably distributed among coalition members, causing resentment and lack of commitment. For the public health field to be effective in the political arena, advocates must learn to overcome these barriers, developing strong coalitions and alliances in support of public health agendas.

Political advocacy and policy analysis skills are also needed. To be effective, the coalition must learn how the system operates and how to influence its outcomes. This involves building good relationships with policy makers; providing good information that is presented concisely and powerfully to support the advocate's argument; developing proposals and responses to counter-proposals that help reframe the issue and that will garner political support; and learning a keen sense of political timing. Obviously, not everyone in a coalition needs these skills, but the coalition must develop a strategy for insuring that the group as a whole acts effectively in the political process.

### Media Advocacy Skills

The mass media has been a powerful force in shaping the political debate regarding illegal drug policy. It has reinforced the War on Drugs' underlying assumptions and priorities and given illegal drugs an enormous profile in the public mind, often at the expense of accuracy and full debate of policy options. According to Reinerman and Levine, increased public concern during the early 1980s about illegal drugs was attributable more to mass media coverage than to objective changes in the nature of illegal drug problems in society.

The media discussion of illegal drug problems needs to be reframed. Alcohol and tobacco policy advocates have faced a similar challenge. Media portrayals of alcohol and tobacco issues have been shaped in large measure by the alcohol and tobacco industries. They have enormous advertising and public relations budgets (totalling more than $5 billion annually), and use their vast financial resources to reach and influence editors, publishers and producers.

In response, the alcohol and tobacco fields have developed a new set of skills termed "media advocacy." Pertschuk et al. define media advocacy as "the strategic use of mass media as a resource for advancing a social or public policy initiative." Wallack expands on this, describing it as promoting "a range of strategies to stimulate broad-based media coverage in order to reframe public debate to increase public support for more effective policy level approaches to public health problems." Media advocates take a proactive stance vis-à-vis the media, capitalizing on media opportunities to focus news stories about alcohol and tobacco away from individual explanations and towards broader social factors, e.g. irresponsible industries, lax government regulators, inconsistent public policies and so on. Media advocates focus in particular on taking control of the mass media's agenda-setting function. The traditional public health reliance on free air-time for health promotion messages is complemented by aggressive efforts to make the news, to become the primary and most trusted source for health information. This kind of active approach to the media is badly needed to influence the media's portrayals of illegal drug issues.

# NO

## Office of National Drug Control Policy

# INTERNATIONAL INITIATIVES

Last September the National Drug Control Strategy established an international strategy designed to disrupt and dismantle the multinational criminal organizations that support the production, processing, transportation, and distribution of drugs to the United States and to other nations. The chief emphasis of that strategy is to attack the international drug trade by focusing on efforts aimed at the points of greatest value to the drug trafficking organizations and networks.

It is clear that the United States cannot assume the burden of combatting drugs by itself. A cornerstone of our international drug control strategy, therefore, is to work with and motivate other countries—those that are involved in production, transit or consumption, as well as those that have little or no drug problem as yet—to engage their own resources and efforts to defeat the drug trade. Only through a broad, cooperative international effort can we achieve the objectives of reducing the foreign supply of drugs while working with other countries to dismantle their own illicit drug operations, reduce the demand for drugs, and combat the worldwide drug trade.

## DRUG SOURCE AREAS

**Coca Producing and Distributing Areas.** A major component of our international efforts is a strategy aimed at supporting the principal cocaine source countries—Colombia, Peru and Bolivia—in their efforts to control and defeat the drug trade. U.S. strategy is to work with the host governments to disrupt and destroy the growing, processing and transportation of coca and coca products within these source countries, with the long-term goal of effecting a major reduction in the supply of cocaine from these countries to the United States, while also working to reduce the demand for drugs by users in the United States.

The national Strategy seeks to attain three near-term goals. The first of these is to strengthen the political will and institutional capability of

From Office of National Drug Control Policy, Executive Office of the President. *National Drug Control Strategy: A Nation Responds to Drug Use.* Washington, DC: Government Printing Office, 1992.

## Cocaine: Production to Sales

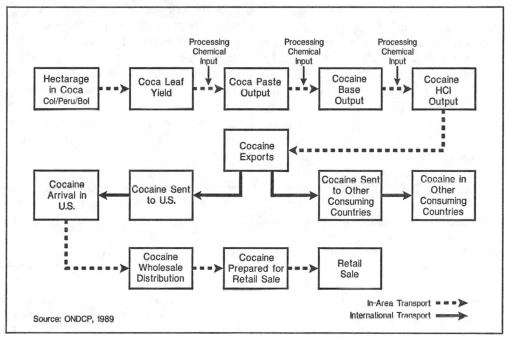

Source: ONDCP, 1989

Colombia, Peru and Bolivia, to enable them to take the needed steps to disrupt the activities of, and ultimately dismantle, the cocaine trafficking organizations. This involves supporting the commitment of the three host governments' political leadership against narcotics trafficking, by providing enhanced security training and equipment, and military assistance. The strategy also incorporates expanded economic assistance, beginning in Fiscal Year 1991 and conditioned on the drug control performance and the existence of sound economic policies of the host countries, to offset some of the economic dislocations associated with successful drug suppression efforts. It also includes assisting these countries to strengthen their ability to prosecute, extradite, and punish narcotics traffickers, illicit arms traffickers and drug money launderers, through the application of resources needed to reorganize and strengthen the laws and legal institutions now in place. Finally, it involves supporting the resolve of judges and other individuals within the legal system to prosecute and sentence traffickers.

The second short-term goal is to increase the effectiveness of law enforcement and military activities of the three countries against the cocaine trade. This involves assisting them in isolating key coca growing areas through measures aimed at controlling road, river and air access, and controlling their national airspace by providing real-time air targeting data through appropriate channels while helping them to develop a rapid response capability against air trafficking threats.

Attacking the cocaine trade involves blocking shipments of key precursor chemicals, by controlling their importation and distribution to, and interdicting the movement of chemicals already within, the region; destroying existing laboratories and processing centers; and controlling the importation and distribution of illicit munitions. And it means carrying out eradication programs on a case-by-case basis, with a view to their effect on total country production and their costs and benefits when compared to other drug control programs in the same country or areas. The likely political consequences of proposed eradication programs will be carefully weighed before such operations are pursued. As drug suppression efforts succeed, our strategy calls for U.S. economic assistance to help provide legal, self-sustaining, income-earning alternatives to growers and workers. Such assistance will be applied in coca producing areas and in contiguous regions which have been the source of permanent and seasonal migration to the coca-producing zones.

The third near-term goal is to inflict significant damage to the trafficking organizations which operate within the three countries, by working with the countries concerned to disrupt or dismantle trafficking operations and elements of greatest value. This involves focusing on trafficking leaders and their key lieutenants, to incapacitate them through arrests, prosecution and incarceration; impeding the transfer of drug-generated funds; and seizing the assets of traffickers within the United States and in other countries where they operate.

U.S. information and public awareness programs will explain and support the attainment of the three principal goals outlined above.

Recent events, including the interdiction of air trafficking by Colombia; the extradition of important traffickers and money launderers by Colombia, Bolivia and Uruguay; the effective Colombian operation against Rodriguez Gacha; and, most importantly, the steadfastness of Colombia's Barco Administration against the trafficking organizations, underscore the efficacy of cocaine source country strategy.

As pressure is brought to bear on the cartels that operate within the three principal coca-producing countries, drug production, processing, and trafficking are likely to continue expanding to other countries in the region, including Ecuador, Venezuela, Paraguay, Argentina, Chile, and Brazil. The law enforcement and air, water, and land interdiction programs of these six countries may need to be strengthened on an urgent basis, before the trafficking organizations become entrenched. The Department of State, in cooperation with the Office of National Drug Control Policy, will coordinate a review involving all concerned Federal agencies, focusing on those South American countries most vulnerable to the drug trade. The interagency review will place emphasis on determining how assistance requested in the President's Fiscal Year 1991 budget can best be utilized to provide to these countries law enforcement support, U.S. military training and materiel assistance, and intelligence to support both law enforcement programs and military anti-drug activities. It will also study the effectiveness of these forms of assistance, and what may be needed in later years. The review will also focus on the strengthening of current mutual legal assistance procedures, the development of assistance programs keyed to judicial institution-building to strengthen the likelihood that drug traffickers will be prosecuted and incarcerated in these countries, and the extradition of narcotics and arms traffickers under U.S. indictment.

**Heroin Producing and Distributing Areas.** While heroin currently ranks second to cocaine as the greatest foreign drug threat to the United States, it is the primary drug of use in Europe and Asia. Although there is no firm estimate of heroin availability or use in the United States, the drug is known to have found new markets through combination with other drugs, and smokeable varieties of heroin. The high volume of opium production, as well as heroin's great profitability and addictive properties, add urgency to cooperative efforts to suppress the international trade in heroin.

Yet heroin may prove even more difficult to control than cocaine, because much of the world's opium and heroin is produced in countries such as Afghanistan, Burma (Myanmar), Laos, and Iran, where U.S. government and Western influence is greatly limited, and political unrest makes it difficult for these countries to exercise control over production areas. Moreover, opium and heroin production, distribution and consumption patterns show an alarming persistence and resistance to control, as evidenced by the fact that poppy cultivation has moved across the Mexican border into Guatemala, while Pakistan, Iran and Thailand have become net *importers* of the drug to satisfy their burgeoning addict populations.

The Administration has accordingly undertaken a government-wide study of the threat which will form the basis for our future strategies. All major aspects of heroin suppression will be examined.

Following the pattern of our overall international strategy, our goals include strengthening the political will and institutional capability of cooperating opium- and heroin-producing countries to combat their drug trade; increasing the effectiveness of host country law enforcement and military organizations to detect, monitor, and apprehend traffickers and seize major shipments; and inflicting significant damage on the trafficking organizations that operate within the source countries and distribution areas. To these ends, particular attention will be given to how best to utilize funding included in the President's Fiscal Year 1991 budget, and possible needs in later years to improve intelligence collection and analysis of information on source country production; trafficking mechanisms and routes; transportation elements; money laundering topology used to bring heroin to the United States; and international drug syndicates and their key personnel. Other ways will also be examined to assist producer and transit countries to improve their laws and strengthen their legal institutions, and to provide military and law enforcement assistance, including security assistance, to help source and transit countries improve their interdiction capabilities against drug transporters and their means of shipment. We will continue to provide assistance for effective crop control measures, depending on the extent to which they support the principal goals outlined above and with the objective of effecting a net reduction in opium production in the country or area where they are applied.

The increasingly global nature of the heroin threat will require greater participation both by other developed countries and by the producer and trafficker countries. We expect to work closely with members of the European Community, Canada, Japan and Australia, as well as the Soviet Union, to develop effective approaches to opium-producing countries where the United States has limited access, and to share the burden of controlling the growth and production of opium and heroin. Increased emphasis will be given to strengthening joint measures, financial control mechanisms, and conspiracy laws to target money launderers, and to detect, seize and confiscate traffickers' assets. Attention will be given to the role of the United Nations and regional organizations in international heroin suppression. In addition, emphasis will be given to the ratification by other countries of the U.N. (Vienna) Convention, which calls for the criminalization of the production, cultivation, transportation and trafficking of heroin, as well as other drugs, and calls for the criminalization of money laundering, illegal arms and chemical precursor trafficking. We will encourage regional organizations to assume greater responsibility for playing an active role in this process. Finally, since a key to successful narcotics control is public awareness in producer, trafficking, and consumer countries, we will improve U.S. international and regional diplomacy and public awareness programs, focusing on all aspects of the opium and heroin problem as it affects consumers and producers alike.

**Marijuana Production.** Foreign marijuana control remains an important element of our international strategy. U.S. domestic marijuana control efforts support our foreign initiatives in this area because of the health threat posed by marijuana use, because international agreements obligate us to domestic control programs, and because the vigorous pursuit of our own marijuana reduction programs supports our efforts to convince other countries to engage in strong marijuana control programs of their own. As the Drug Enforcement Administration and other Federal agencies intensify their efforts to eradicate domestically-produced marijuana, therefore, we will continue to pursue *cannabis* eradication programs with other producing countries. At the same time, U.S. funding of foreign marijuana control programs will be weighed against the use of the same funds for programs to control other foreign drugs that have greater potential for damage. In certain countries where narcotics control programs are directed against the production and trafficking of coca or opium *and* marijuana, resources and priority attention will be given to efforts which can have the greatest impact in reducing the supply of the most dangerous illegal drugs entering the United States.

## TRANSIT AREAS

Drug transit countries present an array of problems and opportunities significantly different from countries that produce illegal drugs. On the one hand, drug trafficking and use have taken a serious toll within a number of these countries, which are therefore willing to work closely with the United States and other nations to the degree that their concerns about national sovereignty and their own resources permit. On the other hand, many transit countries have permissive drug laws and lax financial regulation; underfunded law enforcement, investigatory, prosecutory, and judicial systems; and undeveloped law enforcement intelligence capabilities. Several produce drugs, have their own powerful domestic drug trafficking groups, and are used as transshipment areas by multinational drug organizations. Transit areas of special concern include Mexico, Central America, and the Caribbean.

**Mexico.** Mexico is a principal source for drugs entering the United States, both as a producer of marijuana and opium, and as a major transit country for cocaine. Mexico cultivates sufficient *cannabis* to satisfy an estimated 25 percent of the U.S. marijuana demand, accounts for a significant amount of the heroin supplied to the U.S. market, and is a transshipment area for at least half of the cocaine that enters the United States. Since the inauguration of the Salinas Administration in 1988, the Mexican Government has embarked on a vigorous effort to diminish the supply of drugs to and within Mexico, and their transit to the United States. Several major Mexican figures connected to Colombian trafficking organizations have been arrested and their organizations have been disrupted. Mexico has also ratified the 1988 U.N. Convention and has negotiated numerous bilateral anti-drug agreements with other countries.

To reduce the flow of drugs from Mexico and to disrupt Mexican, Colombian, and other narcotics trafficking organizations, the Administration will continue to develop cooperative actions related both to drug supply reduction within and through Mexico, and drug demand reduction within Mexico. In cooperation with the Office of National Drug Control Policy and other concerned departments, the Department of State will be responsible for coordinating all U.S. plans and programs supporting U.S.–Mexican anti-drug efforts. In the area of law enforcement, the United States will pursue cooperative initiatives to identify and dismantle trafficking organizations, to improve tactical information sharing with appropriate Mexican Government authorities, and to help in the development of Mexico's interdiction programs aimed at smuggler aircraft crossing Mexican airspace or landing in Mexico. Eradication will be supported in conjunction with interdiction efforts, where it is effective and can contribute to a net reduction of Mexican drug crop production.

In addition, we will seek to strengthen Mexico's ability to track illegal money and firearms flows and the diversion of essential and precursor chemicals. We will propose the establishment of procedures for increased cooperation on investigations in these areas, and will examine with the Mexican Government the possibility of integrating its financial investigations, munitions control, and essential and precursor chemical diversion programs with related U.S. programs. We will also enhance law enforcement investigative lead sharing building on, among other foundations, the recently ratified U.S.–Mexican Mutual Legal Assistance Treaty; assist Mexico in identifying clandestine labs, landing strips, cache sites, and smuggling routes; continue to provide specific logistic assistance to Mexican law enforcement units on a case-by-case basis; continue the development of effective mechanisms to ensure that drug traffickers are either fully prosecuted or successfully extradited; and initiate a seized asset sharing program between the U.S. and Mexico. Public awareness and demand reduction programs will be pursued through the media, expert visits, and assistance with community and school education and drug abuse programs.

**Central America.** Central America has gained in importance as a transit area for cocaine shipments to the United States. One country, Guatemala, now produces a significant quantity of opium. The Department of State, working with other Federal agencies, will increase U.S. and joint U.S.–host country intelligence efforts to identify and track drug traffickers by air and land through Central America to Mexico, by expediting the installation of the Joint Information Collection Center (JICC) system.

**The Caribbean.** The broad objectives of U.S. drug control strategy in the Caribbean are to deny safe havens to drug traffickers, and to prevent drug production, storage and transit operations, and drug-related activities such as money laundering. Much has been done to deter traffickers' free use of Caribbean airspace and waters through the application of U.S. interdiction programs, but special attention will also be given to initiatives focused on the Caribbean countries and their territorial waters and airspace. With respect to these initiatives, the Administration will seek ways to improve local intelligence and law enforcement capabilities, strengthen Caribbean banking laws and financial regulations, and increase national criminal asset seizures. It will also seek to improve access to the territorial waters and airspace of producer and transit countries. In the area of law enforcement information sharing, the Administration will work cooperatively to strengthen the current JICC system and assist Caribbean countries to establish appropriate new JICCs that can become the basis for a broad network of linked centers for the exchange of drug law enforcement intelligence and tactical data throughout the region. The Office of National Drug Control Policy, through the Supply Reduction Working Group, will develop and coordinate U.S. initia-

tives to enable Federal agencies to disseminate tactical air data to countries identified as primary originators or receivers of drug trafficking flights.

# POSTSCRIPT

## Is the War on Drugs Misdirected?

The drug trade spawns violence; people die from using drugs or by dealing with people in the drug trade; families are ruined by drugs; prisons are filled with people who were and probably still are involved with illegal drugs; and drugs can devastate careers. The adverse consequences of drugs can be seen everywhere in society. Yet, should the government debate whether drugs are good or bad, or should it determine the best course of action to follow in remedying the negative effects of drugs?

Two paths that are traditionally followed involve either reducing the supply or the demand for drugs. Four major agencies involved in the fight against drugs in the United States—the Drug Enforcement Administration, the Federal Bureau of Investigation, the U.S. Customs Service, and the U.S. Coast Guard—seized almost 500,000 pounds of marijuana, 250,000 pounds of cocaine, and over 2,000 pounds of heroin in 1990, according to the U.S. Department of Justice. Also, worldwide estimates of opium production declined between 1989 to 1991. Drug interdiction and international initiatives appear to be reducing the availability of drugs. However, what effect does drug availability have on drug use?

Annual surveys of high school seniors indicate that availability is not a major factor in determining drug use. The number of high school seniors who smoked marijuana in 1979 was twice as great as in 1991. Likewise, cocaine use in 1991 was less than half of what it was in 1986. These declines occurred even though the availability of marijuana and cocaine was the same as in previous years. This has been attributed to the perceived harm of these drugs: As these drugs are increasingly seen as harmful, usage decreases. How much of the government's antidrug campaign contributes to the perception of drugs as harmful cannot be easily determined.

Efforts to prevent drug use may prove fruitless if people have a natural desire to alter their consciousnesses. In his 1989 book *Intoxication: Life in the Pursuit of Artificial Paradise* (E. P. Dutton), Ronald Siegel contends that the urge to alter consciousness is as basic and universal as the craving for food and sex. Joseph Treaster, in "Costly and Scarce, Marijuana is a High More Are Rejecting," *The New York Times* (October 29, 1991), discusses how the perception of marijuana and law enforcement efforts have affected marijuana use. In his article "Let Our Police Take on the Drug Dealers," *Reader's Digest* (January 1990), Charles Brandt argues that drug enforcement is the way to go and that drug enforcement officials need better support. "The Failure of Crop Substitution," by Julius Glys and Mark Heil, in *New Frontiers in Drug Policy* (The Drug Policy Foundation, 1991), speaks against the international initiatives of the federal government.

# ISSUE 6

## Should Needle Exchange Programs Be Promoted?

**YES: Merrill Singer, Ray Irizarry, and Jean J. Schensul,** from "Needle Access as an AIDS Prevention Strategy for IV Drug Users: A Research Perspective," *Human Organization* (vol. 50, 1991)

**NO: Office of National Drug Control Policy,** from "Needle Exchange Programs: Are They Effective?" *ONDCP Bulletin No. 7* (July 1992)

### ISSUE SUMMARY

**YES:** Professors Merrill Singer and Jean J. Schensul and drug treatment specialist Ray Irizarry believe that the tremendous rise in the incidence of AIDS necessitates exploring needle exchange programs for intravenous drug users as a prevention strategy.

**NO:** The Office of National Drug Control Policy, an executive agency that determines policies and objectives for the U.S. drug control program, sees needle exchange programs as an admission of defeat and a retreat from the ongoing battle against drug use, and it argues that compassion and treatment are needed, not needles.

Both articles presented here refer to intravenous drug use as a factor in the escalating incidence of AIDS (acquired immunodeficiency syndrome). One point needs to be clarified: Any type of drug injection, whether it is intravenous (mainlining), intramuscular, or just below the surface of the skin (skin popping), can result in the transmission of AIDS. Technically, what is transmitted is not AIDS but the human immunodeficiency virus (HIV), which ultimately leads to the development of AIDS.

Until a cure for AIDS is found or a vaccine against HIV is developed, the relationship between AIDS and injecting drugs will remain a cause of great concern. The second leading cause of AIDS in the United States is drug injection. Between 1981 and 1990, the federal government estimated that almost 39,000 intravenous drug users developed AIDS. This figure does not take into account the number of intravenous drug users who infected their sexual partners. Also, over one-half of pediatric AIDS cases are related to drug injection.

No one disagrees that the spread of AIDS is a problem and that the number of people who inject drugs is a problem. The issue that needs to be addressed is what is the best course of action to take to reduce drug injection and the transmission of AIDS. Is it better to set up more drug treatment facilities, as the Office of National Drug Control Policy (ONDCP) suggests, or to allow people who inject drugs access to clean needles?

One concern of needle exchange opponents is that endorsement of these programs conveys the wrong message concerning drug use. Instead of discouraging drug use, they feel that such programs merely teach people how to use drugs or encourage drug use. Needle exchange advocates point to studies showing that these programs have not resulted in an increase of intravenous drug users. Other studies indicate that many drug users involved in needle exchange programs drop out and that drug users who remain in the programs were not as likely to share needles in the first place.

Proponents of needle exchange programs argue that HIV is easily transmitted when needles are shared and that something needs to be done to stem the practice. Opponents argue that whether or not needle exchange programs are available, needles will be shared. Three reasons cited by drug users for sharing needles are (1) they do not have access to clean needles, (2) they do not own their own needles, or (3) they cannot afford to buy needles. If clean needles were readily available, would drug addicts necessarily use them? Some studies show that people who inject drugs are concerned about contracting AIDS and will alter their drug-taking behavior.

Although needle exchange programs may result in the use of clean needles and encourage people to obtain treatment, they do not get at the root cause of drug addiction. Drug abuse and many of its concomitant problems stem from inadequate or nonexistent employment opportunities, unsafe neighborhoods, underfunded schools, and insufficient health care. Some argue that until these underlying causes of drug abuse are addressed, stopgap measures like needle exchange programs should be implemented. However, needle exchange programs may forestall the implementation of other programs that could prove to be more helpful.

Needle exchange programs generate a number of legal and social questions. Since heroin and cocaine are illegal, giving needles to people for the purpose of injecting these drugs contributes to illegal behavior. Should people who are addicted to drugs be seen as criminals or as victims who need compassion? Should drug users, especially drug addicts, be incarcerated or treated? The majority of drug users involved with needle exchange programs are members of minorities. Could it be that needle exchange programs promote the continuation of drug use and, hence, the enslavement of minorities rather than a turn to healthier alternatives?

In the following selections, Merrill Singer, Ray Irizarry, and Jean J. Schensul address the benefits of needle exchange programs and respond to some of the criticisms of these programs. The ONDCP points out the inadequacies of previous research regarding needle exchange programs and argues that these programs exacerbate drug abuse problems by facilitating drug use.

# YES

Merrill Singer, Ray Irizarry, and Jean J. Schensul

## NEEDLE ACCESS AS AN AIDS PREVENTION STRATEGY FOR IV DRUG USERS: A RESEARCH PERSPECTIVE

Needle exchange and needle distribution as AIDS prevention strategies have attracted considerable attention over the last five years. Consideration of these approaches was especially emphasized at the Fifth International Conference on AIDS in Montreal (Des Jarlais et al. 1989; Hagan, Des Jarlais et al. 1989; Hagan, Reid et al. 1989; Hartgers et al. 1989; Purchase et al. 1989). In the absence of an effective treatment or preventive vaccine for HIV infection, and in response to an alarming rise in the rate of AIDS cases among IV drug users (CDC 1989), prevention workers have been forced to consider options that they recognize are emotionally loaded and highly controversial. Consideration of needle access emerges from the realization that our ability to slow the AIDS epidemic "lies in breaking the link between substance abuse and HIV infection" (Joseph and Des Jarlais 1989: 5). Interest in needle access has been especially sharp in Australia, the United Kingdom, the US and in Scandinavia. Private companies in both Norway and the Netherlands have produced and are field testing syringe exchange vending machines (Buning et al. 1989, Stimson 1989, Stimson et al. 1990). In assessing the appropriateness of making clean syringes and needles available to IV drug users (IVDUs) as a means of preventing the transmission of HIV infection, several questions emerge:

1. How common is needle sharing among IVDUs?
2. If needle access existed in any given city, would IVDUs make use of it?
3. What is the attitude of the wider non-IV drug user community: is needle access a socially acceptable AIDS prevention strategy?
4. Will needle access contribute to the recruitment of new IVDUs or increased IV injection among current users?
5. Will needle access contribute to a drop in needle sharing and HIV incidence among IVDUs?

All of these are *research questions*, and should be answered through accepted procedures of scientific inquiry. It is in light of the findings of such research that we can develop informed opinions about needle access. Separate from such research, however, we have only a variety of conflicting uninformed attitudes, necessarily limited personal experiences, ideologically rooted biases, and personal preferences. Given the gravity of the AIDS situation in this country, especially among IVDUs, their sexual partners and children, the time has come to move the issue of needle exchange out of the realm of emotionalism and into the realm of empiricism. We will do so on the basis of our own research in Hartford, as well as through a review of other studies by drug and AIDS researchers. . . .

## AIDS RESEARCH IN HARTFORD

. . . The largest social scientific AIDS research effort in Hartford is a community demonstration initiative entitled Project COPE. This project is a consortium effort that includes the Institute for Community Research, the Hispanic Health Council, Latino/as Contra SIDA, the Urban League, the Hartford Dispensary, and the City Health Department. Project COPE is designed to study rates of HIV infection, AIDS risk, AIDS knowledge, and culturally appropriate risk reduction for IVDUs and their sexual partners citywide. . . .

## NEEDLE SHARING PATTERNS AMONG IV DRUG USERS

It is clear to all observers of the contemporary drug scene that needle sharing is a common behavior among IVDUs (Battjes and Pickens 1988); however, it is equally certain that some types of individuals are much more likely to share than others, some social contexts promote needle sharing more than others, and the users of some drugs administered intravenously are more likely to share than the users of other types of drugs. Among the first 200 participants in Project COPE, we found that men are more likely to report needle sharing than women (76% and 48% respectively), while women are more likely to engage in needle cleaning (41% and 28% respectively). Research by Selwyn and co-workers found that the most common reason (46% of persistent needle-sharers) given by IVDUs for continued needle sharing, despite awareness of the inherent AIDS risk, was "the need to inject drugs, with no clean needle available" (Selwyn 1988: 102). Similarly, Magura et al. (1989), in a study of methadone patients who reported current IV drug use, found that the variables directly associated with needle sharing included inability to afford new needles and not owning a set of "works" (syringes and related paraphernalia), in addition to attitudes conducive to sharing (e.g., tolerance of withdrawal symptoms, concern about insulting friends, fatalistic beliefs). In the National Institute on Drug Abuse sponsored national AIDS demonstration outreach projects (NADR), of 10,174 IVDUs interviewed as of September 30, 1989, 40% indicated that they had shared a needle with a sex partner in the last 6 months, 54% had shared needles with a close friend, and 24% had shared needles with a stranger (NOVA 1989). In this study, use of unclean needles is equally common among white, African American, and Latino IVDUs.

This last finding is significant because higher rates of HIV prevalence among African American and Latino IVDUs compared to white addicts has led to the assumption that minority IVDUs are more involved in needle sharing. According to the Centers for Disease Control (1989), approximately 78% of known AIDS cases among heterosexual IVDUs are Black or Latino. Studies that have examined needle sharing patterns across ethnic and racial groups have produced conflicting results, with some studies suggesting greater concern with using clean needles among white IVDUs and other studies finding that whites have higher rates of needle sharing than African American and Latino "shooters" (Schilling et al. 1989). Based on their research in Texas, Dolan et al. (1987) concluded that compared to IVDUs who do not share needles, those who do: 1) tend to combine multiple drugs, such as heroin and cocaine, or amphetamine and methamphetamine in a single injection; 2) are more likely to shoot up in a shooting gallery; and 3) are more deeply involved in drug use. However, needle sharing was found to be: 1) not peculiar to a particular racial or ethnic group; 2) not associated with a user's level of education; and 3) not characteristic of a particular personality profile (Dolan et al. 1987). Chaisson et al. (1987: 93) conclude that "While needle-sharing is no more prevalent among blacks and Latinos than among whites, the risk of infection is clearly greater for individuals who share needles with minority group members due to the higher prevalence of infection in this group." Moreover, it may be that while needle sharing and use of unclean needles occurs among a large percentage of street IVDUs regardless of race or ethnicity, African Americans and Latinos may be forced more frequently to adopt these behaviors. As Rogers and Williams (1987:91) suggest, "Sterile needles may be more available to whites, and whites may be more able to afford them."

Dolan's finding of a relationship between shooting galleries and needle sharing is of special pertinence to the assessment of needle exchange (also see Des Jarlais, Friedman, and Strug 1986, Marmor et al. 1987). Shooting galleries or "get off houses" as they are known in some regions have become a cottage industry in the drug subculture, not only because they provide a comparatively safe place to inject drugs and, if necessary, access to needles and syringes, but because they offer an arena for socialization among fellow users and a degree of protection in case of a drug overdose. Still, most IVDUs avoid galleries if they can because "no user likes to part with the fee" (Walters 1985:43) charged by the owner. About 40% of the IVDUs in the national NIDA sample, nonetheless, reported using shooting galleries at least some of the time. The character of needle sharing behavior in shooting galleries is seen in the following account by the former operator of a gallery interviewed by the lead author in Hartford in 1988.

> Everyday people would come to my house. They would cop [buy drugs] and do their drugs right there in my house. If they stay in my house to get high, they would have to give me some. A lot of people would come to my house. . . . Sometimes I'd go for four days without sleeping. Word got around that it was a place you could get high. I would charge them. Some guys would give me $10 for using works, plus they got to give me a high. I'd buy a bundle of works from people who were diabetic. . . . We shared works. If one would clog up, someone would use another works to clean it out without washing it. We didn't care, we only cared about the high. . . . Usually ten to twelve people would come to the house everyday, twenty-four hours a day. . . . I had two bedrooms that I

would use to rent to guys who did drugs. Some guy might go in their with a girlfriend to get laid. I'd rent him the room for the money and the drugs. . . .

A study of shooting gallery behavior among 125 IVDUs by Friedman and co-workers (Friedman et al. 1989a) in New York found that IV cocaine users are less likely than IV heroin users to share needles in shooting galleries . . . because cocaine users "shoot up" much more frequently and thus like to hang on to their own needles. Friedman also suggests that cocaine tends to engender a greater sense of mistrust which also interferes with needle sharing. Friedman and co-workers (Friedman, Des Jarlais et al. 1989b) moreover found that increased use of crack and the inhalation of heroin (a practice called "chasing the dragon") have not led to any measurable decrease in intravenous drug use. Since awareness of AIDS and its routes of transmission are now widespread among IVDUs in New York, it does not appear that this population is switching to alternative means of drug consumption to avoid the risk of HIV infection.

In a street ethnography project in New York, Hopkins (1988) reports the following findings: 1) illicit needle sellers make profits of 50 to 100% from the sale or rental of needles; 2) needles are commonly purchased with forged prescriptions, stolen from hospital emergency rooms, and purchased from diabetics with prescriptions; and 3) about half of illicit needle sellers report repackaging and reselling used unsterilized needles. These findings indicate there is a strong demand among IVDUs for clean needles, and this demand produces behaviors that put users at risk for both infection and arrest.

Finally, over 30,000 IVDUs in the US already have been diagnosed with AIDS

(CDC 1990). Among active street IVDUs in Hartford, Project COPE (Flores et al. 1989, Singer, Owens, and Reyes 1989) found an HIV positivity rate in the first 900 program participants of about 40%. In New Jersey, IVDUs now account for 54% of reported AIDS cases (CDC 1989), while in Puerto Rico they comprise 60% of AIDS cases among men (ARS 1990). A study of IVDUs in methadone treatment in New York by Selwyn et al. (1989) found a threefold increase in deaths due to AIDS, with mortality related to AIDS growing from 3.6 per 1000 in 1984 to 13.6 per 1000 in 1987. Needless to say, this is a disturbing rate of increase. Moreover, HIV infection is not equally distributed among IVDUs. Crosstabulations of data from the first 200 participants in Project COPE showed that individuals who reported always "shooting up" at home were significantly more likely to be HIV negative (i.e., uninfected) than individuals who never or only sometimes shoot up at home ($p = 0.026$). Conversely, IVDUs who have injected drugs in a shooting gallery were significantly more likely to be infected than those who reported never using galleries ($p = 0.035$). Also respondents who reported that they at least sometimes gave their needle to a friend immediately after injecting drugs (i.e., needle sharers) were significantly more likely to be infected than those who never gave their equipment to friends to use ($p = 0.031$). . . .

## DRUG USER RESPONSE TO THE AIDS EPIDEMIC

The standard conception of an IV drug user (a view, by the way, that is shared by some active and some ex-users) is that of an individual who is so preoccupied with shooting up and avoiding "getting sick" (undergoing drug withdrawal) that s/he couldn't care less about viral infection. As Becker and Joseph (1988:403) note, "There is a general impression that IVDUs are incapable of (or disinterested in) changing their behavior, while IVDUs view public health authorities with suspicion and distrust." If one embraces this view of the IVDU, then needle exchange by definition is a dead end approach because it is assumed that IVDUs will not go to the trouble of getting clean needles from a distribution program. There are problems with this understanding of the IVDU, however, as there is consistent evidence showing that IVDUs can and do change their behavior in response to the threat of HIV infection. Over half of IVDUs interviewed in New York in several different studies report behavioral changes to reduce the risk of infection (Selwyn et al. 1986, Des Jarlais et al. 1988). The two most commonly reported changes in this regard are: 1) increased use of (illicitly acquired) sterile needles and 2) reduction in the number of partners with whom an individual shares needles. The demand for sterile needles has already been felt among illicit needle suppliers in New York (Des Jarlais et al. 1985). Research in San Francisco has shown that an IVDU street education program that included the distribution of bottles of 2.5% bleach solution produced a marked increase in needle cleaning behavior among addicts. In 1985, only 6% of needle sharers interviewed in San Francisco reported that they usually or always sterilized their needles with bleach; by 1987, this figure had jumped to 47%, while the percentage of individuals who maintained that they never used bleach dropped from 76% to 36% (Chaisson et al. 1987). In the national

NIDA study mentioned above, of the first 570 individuals who were exposed to AIDS education and counseling as part of the study, 22% had not "shot up" again six months after their first interview; among the remaining individuals who were still using drugs intravenously: 28% decreased the number of individuals they shared needles with, 20% increased the number of individuals they shared needles with, and 52% reported no change in needle sharing behavior (Sowder 1989). Among the active "shooters," 15% reported that they had stopped renting or borrowing needles, 13% started renting or borrowing needles, and 73% reported no change in this behavior. Finally, 28% reported switching to safer needle practices such as using new or bleach-cleaned needles, 11% changed to less safe needle practices, and 61% reported no changes in needle practices. A New York study by Kleinman and colleagues (cited in Friedman, Des Jarlais et al. 1989) found that 16% of IVDUs who had been injecting for under two years, 29% of individuals who had been injecting for 3–5 years, and 33% of individuals who had been injecting from six to ten years reported taking deliberate steps to reduce exposure to the human immunodeficiency virus. These changing attitudes and patterns are reflected in the following comments of a respondent in Project COPE,

> Very few people are going to stop using drugs. I don't do as much. If I became a 1st and 16th of the month junkie, that's an improvement. I have bleach signs up in my house. . . . You have to assume that everyone has [the virus].

What these data suggest is that some IV drug users, especially those who have longer drug injection histories, are changing their behaviors to prevent HIV infection. This finding supports the needle exchange strategy in two ways: 1) some IVDUs would decide to make use of needle exchange as an AIDS prevention strategy because they are open to behavioral change; and 2) existing prevention strategies for IVDUs that do not include a needle exchange component are insufficient to prevent exposure to viral infection.

A final piece of evidence that should be mentioned in this regard is the view of IVDUs toward the needle exchange concept. The generally shared attitude of IVDUs who participated in the Northeast Hispanic AIDS Consortium focus groups was that the illegality of needle possession in Hartford contributed to needle sharing because of the legal risk to individuals of carrying their own injection equipment. One ex-addict described in some detail the conditions IVDUs are willing to put up with at shooting galleries to avoid the threat of arrest for the possession of drug paraphernalia:

> If you don't have any works, they come out with a bag of the most disgusting, vile looking tools [syringes] you ever saw. They're so old the numbers are worn off them, the needles are so dull it feels like you're poking through leather to get a hit, but that's what people use. I've seen people use needles that were ready to bust in half. I know plenty of people that have had them bust off in their arm. The reasons that people went to shooting galleries is because people didn't like to carry works on them. You got caught with works, you were busted.

Another ex-addict with AIDS affirmed, "to stop the spread of AIDS, the main thing is education and loosening up the legal restrictions on works." These attitudes are not unique. Beginning in November, 1988, during their first follow-up interview, IVDUs in Project COPE were asked whether they would participate in a needle exchange program if it was available in Hartford. Of the first 54 respondents interviewed, 87% indicated that they would participate in the program. The primary reasons given by these individuals for supporting an NEP program were: 1) reducing risk of infection; 2) gaining access to free needles; and 3) increasing the convenience of getting needles when needed.

## COMMUNITY ATTITUDES CONCERNING NEEDLE EXCHANGE

There is also the issue of community attitudes. For example, Congressman Charles B. Rangel, chairman of the House Select Committee on Narcotics Abuse and Control, a number of police agencies, and several prominent ministers have complained either that needle access will promote drug use or that it will be used as a cheap substitute for the effective drug treatment programs that are so sorely needed in inner city areas. Needle exchange is seen by opponents as "sending the wrong message" to current IVDUs and others at risk for drug involvement and it is viewed as cruel abandonment of these individuals to the tortures of drug addiction. As a staff member of Project COPE in Hartford stated, "I refuse to give my brother a needle to stick in his arm."

Moreover, there is a concern in African American and Latino communities that needle access reflects a racist disregard for the heavy toll drugs and drug-related behavior take on people of color in this country. Consequently, needle exchange has been seen as genocidal by some of its opponents. In the words of Rev. Reginald Williams of the Addicts Rehabilitation Center in East Harlem,

> ... there will never be a needle-exchange program here. I think the communities and neighborhoods will rise up in opposition. .... Why must we again be the guinea pigs in this genocidal mentality? (quoted in Marriott 1988:8)

Additionally, in the view of some individuals from minority communities, drug use only became a national concern when white, middle class youth began to show up in the drug statistics. Further, the idea exists that the ready availability of drugs in many African American and Latino communities is not an accident, but rather part of a governmental plan for the exploitation and social control of minorities. As a participant in the Heroin Lifestyles Study asserted:

> A Black man has no control what goes down in this world. Not in America. There's no heroin where the White boys hang out at. They don't let it up in their neighborhoods. They send it down to where the poor Black boys hang out at. ... No Black man could have brought that kind of shit (heroin) into this country, they just don't allow that, they don't allow that (Beschner and Brower 1985:19–20).

In an insightful summation of African American response to the AIDS epidemic, Dalton (1989:219) asks of needle exchange advocates:

> You say that making drug use safer (by giving away bleach or distributing clean needles) won't make it more attractive to our children or our neighbor's children. But what if you are wrong? What if as a result we have even more addicts to contend with? Will you be around to help us then, especially if the link between addiction and AIDS has been severed? Why do you offer addicts free

needles but not free health care? Why do you show them how to clean their works but not how to clean up their lives?

In fact, none of these concerns can be dismissed out-of-hand. While heroin use became widespread among African American and Latino youth in the 1950s, it was not until 1970, *after the emergence of a middle class youth drug subculture*, that the Nixon administration began to implement a federal treatment program (Chein et al. 1964, Hanson et al. 1985). In his study of the governmental response to the drug problem, Epstein (1977) demonstrates the exclusive role of political as opposed to public health considerations in directing federal efforts. For example, the Harrison Narcotic Act of 1914 that outlawed the use of heroin and related drugs, and insured, thereby, the creation of an underground drug use and needle sharing subculture, was not motivated by public health concerns but rather by a Congressional interest in "restricting British dominance of the opium trade to China" (Partridge 1978:356–357). Also we do not know yet if needle exchange, if it proved effective in preventing the spread of HIV infection, would come to be seen as a low budget, cost cutting approach for keeping AIDS out of the white heterosexual population. Financial considerations rather than research and treatment needs certainly dominated federal response to the AIDS crisis during the Reagan administration (Shilts 1987). And, there have been various reports that intelligence branches of the federal government have been involved with groups active in drug smuggling both during the Vietnam War and more recently in Afghanistan and Central America (McCoy 1972). What is clear is that community concerns about needle exchange, and the meaning such programs have for oppressed communities, must be taken into consideration in the needle exchange debate. Community resistance to needle access could doom such programs, even if they proved to be effective in AIDS prevention (e.g., Podelfsky 1985).

To help assess community attitudes, the AIDS Community Research Group studies in Hartford included data collection on the "cultural feasibility" (van Willigen 1986) of needle exchange. In the first study, 41% of the respondents stated that they supported government sponsored NEPs for IV drug users as an AIDS prevention approach. Support was highest among African American respondents, with 49% saying needle exchange should be initiated, while the lowest percentage of supporters was found among Latino respondents, with only 37% supporting this strategy (ACRG 1988). In the second study, 67% of the respondents supported needle exchange, with 67% of African Americans, 63% of Latinos, and 72% of whites supporting this strategy (ACRG 1989). In both studies, it should be noted, community support was higher for distribution of condoms and bleach for needle cleaning than for distribution of sterile needles. And in both studies, Latinos were the least enthusiastic about needle exchange. Nonetheless, these data suggest that while there is considerable community concern about NEPs, a perhaps growing percentage of people of all major ethnic backgrounds in Hartford would support the initiation of a government sponsored NEP. This interpretation rests on the assumption that the differences in the findings between the two studies reflect a mounting receptivity to the idea of needle exchange in Hartford, perhaps as a result of growing public awareness and understanding of AIDS.

This interpretation is supported by the fact that participants in the second study were better informed about the disease and its prevention than were participants in the first study. Moreover, there has been increasing mass media attention to the issue of needle exchange so that the initial unfamiliarity and discomfort with the practice may be waning. The possibility also exists that different attitudes toward needle access exist in different parts of the city and that neighborhood demographics or experience rather than the passage of time between the two studies explains the ACRG findings.

## THE IMPACT OF NEEDLE EXCHANGE ON IV DRUG USE

There also is serious concern that NEPs will lead to increased drug use while not effectively promoting decreased needle sharing. Existing evidence, however, suggests these concerns are not warranted. One of the most publicized NEPs has been going on in the Netherlands since 1984. By 1987, 700,000 needles had been distributed through existing social agencies and treatment facilities and needle exchange is now ongoing in 40 municipalities in the Netherlands. In a recently reported longitudinal study of the Amsterdam program, van den Hoek and co-workers (1989:1359) report that they found "no evidence that the non-intravenous drug users in [their] study started intravenous use in spite of the availability of clean needles and syringes." This finding is supported by a parallel study in the southern part of the Netherlands (Buning et al. 1989, Buning 1990). Also of note is a NEP in Liverpool, England, run by the municipal drug dependency clinic. During the initial months of this program, addicts returned 2,949 needles in exchange for a sterile replacement, indicating that IVDUs will bring in used needles if clean needles are made available. Users of the Liverpool needle exchange are also supplied condoms (Marks and Parry 1987).

There are over half a dozen public or underground NEPs going on in the US. The Tacoma Syringe Exchange, with support from the Tacoma–Pierce County Board of Health, is distributing 1,400 needles per week. The AIDS Prevention Project needle exchange in Seattle is giving out about 4,000 syringes a month. The Prevention Point, an underground program in San Francisco, has recorded a rate of 450 exchanges each evening since it began in November, 1988. The ACEs program, an underground effort in New Haven, CT, distributes 200 needles and bleach kits each week. The Project Exchange in Boulder, CO, run by the county health department, also has recently begun distributing needles. Until it was discontinued by the mayor, there was, in addition, the Pilot Needle Exchange in New York City (AIDS Community Educators 1989, Buning et al. 1989, McGough 1989, New York City Department of Health 1989, Prevention Point 1989, Strickland 1989). Finally, in its 1990 legislative session, the Connecticut State Legislature became the first state government in the nation to approve a NEP pilot program (for New Haven), followed shortly thereafter by Hawaii. Organizers of many of these programs came together in 1989 at a public forum sponsored by the San Francisco AIDS Foundation. As Buning et al. (1989:11) point out, the overriding conclusion of forum participants was that "such programs did not increase drug use. . . ." In the view of Samuel Friedman of the

Narcotic and Drug Research, Inc., who participated in the San Francisco forum (Des Jarlais et al. 1988:171);

> Barring a dramatic breakthrough with respect to increased use of proper sterilization techniques, IV drug users must have access to noncontaminated injection equipment if the spread of HIV among continuing IV drug users . . . is to be contained. . . . Based on current data from . . . face-to-face education programs, there appears to be no contradiction between teaching IV drug users how to sterilize drug injection equipment and reducing IV drug use. . . . [N]onjudgemental programs for AIDS risk reduction—programs that do not tell an IV drug user that he or she must stop injecting drugs—appear to be "discouraging" rather than "encouraging" IV drug use.

These conclusions were affirmed by participants at the first North American Syringe Exchange Convention held in Tacoma in October, 1990.

## NEEDLE EXCHANGE AND NEEDLE SHARING

But do needle exchange programs produce less needle sharing among active IVDUs? An examination of several of the existing programs suggests that they do. The Seattle program, for example, began in March 1989 as a project of the local branch of Act Up, a grassroots activist organization that has been highly critical of government foot dragging in response to the AIDS crisis. In April of 1989, at the urging of AIDS Prevention Project staff, the Seattle–King County Board of Health approved needle exchange. The AIDS Prevention Project subsequently began to staff the exchange program, while Act Up members continued to provide volunteer support. Needles are exchanged in a section of town known for its high rate of drug trafficking as well as police surveillance. Nonetheless, 40 syringes are exchanged each hour, two to four hours a day, six days a week. New syringes are marked for identification and are counted upon return. Participants in the program can exchange up to ten needles at a time and they are not required to provided I.D. About 70% of the needles turned in to the program in exchange for new ones bear the project's identifying mark. In other words, a yet to be determined number of IVDUs in Seattle are making regular and repeated use of the exchange program for the purpose of AIDS prevention. In addition to sterile needles, the project also provides participants with bleach, condoms, AIDS educational materials, and referral for drug treatment, health, and social needs. Plans are underway for a well designed evaluation of the project (McGough 1989).

In September and October 1988, a pilot survey was conducted of the Tacoma needle exchange program begun by David Purchase (Hagan, Des Jarlais et al. 1989; Hagan, Reid et al. 1989). During the survey, every third individual who brought in a needle for exchange was approached about participating in an interview concerning needle use practices before and after first use of the exchange program. Sixty-six of the 75 individuals who were approached agreed to participate in the study. Of these, 57% were male, their mean age was 32.4 years, and the largest percentage (49%) were white, with 21% being African American and 15% being Latino. The majority (66%) of the respondents reported that they had been injecting drugs for more than five years, while 54% had not been in drug treatment during the last year. Most (67%) were "speedballers" (combiners of heroin and cocaine). Participants averaged 150 IV injects per month, or about five per day, prior to and following their involvement with the NEP. In other words, the program is serving established IVDUs rather than users attracted to IV drug use by the existence of the NEP. Seventy-one percent reported engaging in needle sharing prior to visiting the needle exchange program, while 37% shared needles after visiting the program. Bleach was used for needle cleaning by 51% of those who shared needles before visiting the program compared to 75% of those who engaged in needle sharing afterward (Hagan, Des Jarlais et al. 1989; Hagan, Reid et al. 1989). Ninety percent of the respondents reported that after visiting the program they either did not share needles or else shared them but almost always used bleach or boiling for sterilization, compared to 66% prior to exchanging needles. All of the respondents who had been to the needle exchange 6 or more times reported these safer needle practices. . . .

Studies of needle exchange programs have been criticized on two grounds. Most of the studies have been based on the self-report of IVDUs and control groups generally have not been built into the study design. Needless to say, the special circumstances under which needle exchange takes place does not lend itself easily to sophisticated research designs. Further, designs that are too intrusive on program users may tend to discourage participation (Joseph and Des Jarlais 1989, Stimson et al. 1989). Nonetheless, in response to criticisms, exchange programs are attempting to improve their evaluation methodology. The pilot needle exchange study in New York, for example, specifically was developed to address the control group problem. In the study, a sample of IVDUs received sterile syringes in exchange for used injection equipment, as well as drug conseling and intensive AIDS education. A control group, recruited from the IV drug using patients at a private medical practice in the South Bronx, received counseling and AIDS education but did not participate in the exchange component. Both groups were recruited for drug treatment. The purposes of the study were: 1) to test whether needle exchange helps to keep IVDUs on often protracted waiting lists for drug treatment; and 2) to see if needle exchange programs create an environment that fosters effective AIDS risk reduction (New York City Department of Health 1988). The Portland NEP, run by the Outside Inn, an agency that provides health services for low income populations, also is maintaining a control group of IVDUs who receive AIDS prevention education but not needle exchange. To avoid providing needles to individuals who are not currently IVDUs, participants in the Portland program are required to show visual evidence of "tracks" (scarification of veins due to intravenous drug injection). In addition to sterile needles, participants are provided a safety kit that includes AIDS prevention information, bleach, condoms, a clean "cooker" (bottle cap for "cooking down" or dissolving drugs), and a fresh cotton ball (used to filter drugs to avoid clogging the needle). These last two items are offered to participants because of the risk of HIV transmission through shared cookers and cotton, a type of infection risk that is not addressed through either bleach or syringe distribution. In the Boulder Exchange, participants may receive five needles for the first needle they bring in,

but must exchange on a one-for-one basis thereafter. In this program, needles are packaged with a label that indicates they are sterile needles for AIDS prevention. Labels are designed so that they come off when removed from the package, so that the needles cannot be used and repacked for sale with the sterile needle label. In Boulder, sterile needles can be obtained 24 hours a day through a drug detoxification program. . . .

Beyond critiques of the research efforts intended to evaluate their effectiveness, exchange programs face difficulty on a number of other fronts as well. The Tacoma program, for example, is threatened with closure because the city attorney decided in July 1989 that needle exchange is illegal. This decision is being tested in the courts by the county health department and may well lead to a ruling that could have ramifications on all exchange programs now in existence as well as those being considered by local health officials. Other projects, like the Portland NEP, have encountered difficulties with liability insurance, although in this instance, financial aid from the county health department helped to overcome the problem. In Glasgow, England, local residents picketed the local program for six months (Stimson et al. 1989). Lack of support outside the health department cost the New York NEP its community based sites, making access to the program difficult for participants (Eaton 1989).

Due to community opposition a mayoral mandate precluded any site for needle exchange located within 1000 feet of a school. The only available site was a former X-ray clinic on the first floor of . . . the central office of the Department of Health. This setting, surrounded by criminal justice facilities and personnel, and far from the residential neighborhoods where addicts live, was not the user-friendly site that had been planned (New York City Department of Health 1989:7).

A problem reported for exchange programs in both the UK and in New York is a high turnover of clients. In his evaluation of British NEPs, Stimson (1989) found that only 33% returned for as many as five exchanges. Similarly, in New York, the number of revisits during the first ten months ranged between one and 15 with a mean of 2.2 (New York City Department of Health 1989). There are a number of reasons, positive and negative, for the high turnover rate, including entrance into drug treatment, cessation of IV drug use, a decision not to participate following counseling, imprisonment, and death. Finally, a number of programs have not been particularly successful in attracting younger IVDUs and women (Stimson 1989). However, in the New York program, one-third of the participants were women. The mean age of participants in New York was 33.4 years, which compares with a mean age of 40.7 for IV drug users recruited for the comparison group (New York City Department of Health 1989). Despite the problems they encounter, new NEPs continue to appear. For example, approval has been granted recently for programs in Victoria and Vancouver, BC.

## CONCLUSION

Ten years before the first AIDS patient was diagnosed, Edward Brecher (1972: 524) prophetically warned that the criminalization of the sale or possession of hypodermic needles without a prescription "leads to the use of nonsterile needles, to the sharing of needles, and to epidemics of hepatitis and other crippling, sometimes fatal, needle-borne diseases." Failure to heed this warning has contributed to the contemporary AIDS crisis. The dimension and toll of the AIDS epidemic demand a reconceptualization of societal response to intravenous drug users. Needle exchange is one of a number of controversial strategies that have appeared in recent years (widespread street distribution of condoms and bleach for needle cleaning are others) in an effort to halt the spread of AIDS to the drug using sector of the population.

The stance taken by individuals and institutions with regard to needle exchange often has been influenced by emotional, political, or other factors, in the absence of a serious consideration of existing research. For example, Louis Sullivan, Secretary of Health and Human Services, stated in March 1989 that he would be very supportive of experimental needle exchange trials. However, following President Bush's July 1989 statement that he opposed needle exchange "under any circumstance" (Ginzburg 1989:1351), Sullivan denounced clean-needle programs as inconsistent with administration policy (Strickland 1989).

The existing research, however suggests that needle exchange should not be ruled out as an AIDS prevention strategy. There is no evidence to suggest that needle exchange leads to the production of new IV drug users or more IV drug use, while there is evidence indicating that at least some IVDUs do change their behaviors to avoid HIV infection, do make use of existing needle distribution programs, do decrease their needle sharing behaviors when provided access to a ready supply of clean needles, and will use needle exchange as a gateway to drug treatment if it is available. Needle exchange programs also provide a mechanism for the safe disposal of potentially contaminated needles, reducing thereby the risk of accidental exposure through contact with a discarded needle. In other words, in a narrowly defined cost/benefit analysis, with increased drug use being the potential cost and prevention of AIDS transmission being the potential benefit, needle exchange, especially when combined with AIDS counseling/education and implemented as a gateway to drug treatment, appears to have merit (Joseph and Des Jarlais 1989, Stimson 1989, Stimson et al. 1988).

But human affairs, including health promotion and disease prevention efforts, are never decided in such restricted terms. Issues of social relationship and power as well as community understandings and interpretation always influence the development of health policy, the implementation of health programs, and community response to both. In Partridge's (1978:371) apt phrase, the "formation of policy is a political process. . . ." Thus Partridge points to Willner's (1973:550) caution that

> Politicians and the policy makers they appoint are not likely to be influenced by knowledge unless it is politically convenient or personally congenial. And politically convenient information can always be found to buttress political decisions.

A notable example of this pattern was the impact of the "culture of poverty" notion on public policy. In Valentine's (1971:193) estimation, "Few ideas put forward by social scientists in recent years have been so widely accepted or so influential in practical affairs as the "culture of poverty" concept propounded by

Oscar Lewis." The appeal of this concept is not hard to find. As Hicks and Handler (1978: 322) note,

> The massive War on Poverty mounted by the federal government in the 1960s was based, according to Gladwin, "upon a definition of poverty as a way of life" (Gladwin 1967:26). The entire series of programs—VISTA, Job Corps, Head Start, and so on—aimed at changing attitudes, beliefs, and values, rather than on redistributing wealth and power.

Policies based on political convenience have produced cynicism and distrust in minority communities. These attitudes are magnified by community awareness of past abuses in the health field, including the use of Puerto Rico for clinical trials of oral contraceptives during the 1950s and 1960s (Vaughan 1972) and the withholding of medical treatment from 600 African American syphilis patients for 40 years in the Tuskegee Study of the long term biological effects of venereal disease (Heller 1972). As Benjamin Ward, New York City's Police Commissioner stated on a television call-in program, "As a black person [I] have a particular sensitivity to doctors conducting experiments, and they too frequently seem to be conducted against blacks" (quoted in Marriott 1988:8). At present there are very strong and very understandable concerns in minority communities about the ultimate purposes and effects of needle exchange programs.

However, continued research findings like those reported in this paper might help to create a broad public consensus for federally or state funded needle exchange trials. As noted, our research in Hartford suggests the possibility that community resistance to needle exchange may lessen as AIDS knowledge increases. Community based organizations working in AIDS prevention can play an important role in this regard. In San Francisco, for example, a number of minority organizations, including the Black Coalition on AIDS, the Latino AIDS Coalition, and the Third World AIDS Advisory Task Force, have come out in support of needle exchange (Buning et al. 1989). In Connecticut in 1989, the Hispanic Leadership Council passed a resolution that called for a legalization of needle sales and possession, initiation of a pilot needle exchange program, and increased availability of drug treatment in the state. The needle exchange concept was also endorsed by the board of directors of the Hispanic Health Council in Hartford. NEPs that are implemented by or in collaboration with community based organizations and consortiums, especially programs that have the support of experienced community AIDS prevention workers, have the greatest chance of winning community support. Further, as most organizers of NEPs maintain, needle exchange must be accompanied by and connected to other interventions, including AIDS education and counseling, active referral for drug treatment and social services, and advocacy on behalf of the health, treatment, job training and related needs of IV drug users and their families.

It is now estimated that between one and one and a half million individuals in the US are infected with the virus that causes AIDS. Approximately 50 individuals die of AIDS each day in the US. African American and Latino populations, groups that already suffer from disproportionate rates of poverty and related health and social problems, comprise about 40% of known AIDS cases although they constitute only about 18% of the total US population. IV drug use has become a dominant source of new infection, especially in ethnic minority communities (Singer, Flores et al. 1990). While needle exchange will continue to have vocal opponents in high places, especially among those who fear it represents a trial balloon for the decriminalization of drug use, already the AIDS crisis has produced several heretofore unexpected changes in government health policy (e.g., the early release of experimental AIDS drugs), clinical interest in previously unthinkable treatment options (e.g., the payment of IVDUs to enter and remain in treatment), and public acceptance of formerly unmentionable topics (e.g. condom use, sexual practices). Clearly existing approaches to both the drug problem and the spread of HIV infection among IVDUs have not led to significant improvements. For example, failure of . . . Reagan's 1982 War on Drugs (primarily cocaine), did not lead to any notable innovations in Bush's War on Drugs. Similarly, the last three governors of New York have launched aggressive though ineffective campaigns to stop drug use by catching and punishing suppliers (Peele 1985). Perhaps the time has come for radical alternatives.

# NO

# Office of National Drug Control Policy

## NEEDLE EXCHANGE PROGRAMS: ARE THEY EFFECTIVE?

When President Bush took office, most Americans regarded the use of illegal drugs as the most serious problem confronting the Nation. Since that time, the Nation has made substantial progress in reducing drug use. But now, in response to the AIDS epidemic, there are those who are ready to sound a retreat in the war against drugs by distributing clean needles to intravenous drug users in the hope that this will slow the spread of AIDS. I believe this would be a serious mistake. We must not lose sight of the fact that illegal drugs still pose a serious threat to our Nation. Nor can we allow our concern for AIDS to undermine our determination to win the war on drugs.

In 1988, 14.5 million Americans and nearly two million young people, aged 12–17, were using drugs. In response to the devastation caused by drug use, the President boldly announced the first National Drug Control Strategy in a televised address to the Nation in 1989. That Strategy was a landmark document. Not only did it establish a coherent, coordinated policy for the national effort against drugs, but it committed unprecedented new resources for fighting drug use.

The Strategy is working; the use of illegal drugs by Americans is declining. Between 1988 and 1991, almost two million fewer Americans were using drugs, a drop of almost 13 percent. And by 1991, about half a million fewer young people were current users of drugs, a drop of 27 percent. Since 1985, the number of Americans using drugs has fallen by over 10 million.

Key to the success of the Strategy has been increasing Americans' intolerance of illicit drugs. But, for those already caught in the deadly web of addiction, we must act with compassion. The Administration therefore vigorously supports efforts to provide effective drug treatment to those who want it and can benefit from it, and has increased finding for drug treatment from $1.1 billion in 1989 to a proposed $2.1 billion for 1993.

Our gains against drug use have been hard-won, and this is no time to jeopardize them by instituting needle exchange programs. Despite all the

From Office of National Drug Control Policy, Executive Office of the President, "Needle Exchange Programs: Are They Effective?" *ONDCP Bulletin No. 7* (July 1992). Some notes omitted.

arguments made by proponents of needle exchange, there is no getting around the fact that distributing needles facilitates drug use and undercuts the credibility of society's message that using drugs is illegal and morally wrong. And just as important, there is no conclusive evidence that exchange programs reduce the spread of AIDS.

The Administration's concerns about needle exchange are widely shared. Recently, for example, the Congress extended a prohibition on the use of most Federal drug treatment funds to support needle exchange programs. And in June 1992, the National Association of State Alcohol and Drug Abuse Directors informed every member of Congress of its support for continuing this prohibition. Also, in February 1992, the National District Attorneys Association passed an official policy position condemning needle exchange.

The Administration will continue to work with the Congress, and with State and local officials to support alternatives to needle exchange, including expanded and improved drug treatment and aggressive outreach programs. These efforts will provide addicts with something that needle exchange programs cannot: hope and a chance for real recovery from drug addiction.

## NEEDLE EXCHANGE PROGRAMS IN THE UNITED STATES

**Intravenous Drug Use and HIV/AIDS.**[1] Intravenous drug users in the United States are one of the groups most at risk for contracting AIDS. AIDS prevention and education programs, which have had a measurable effect on the behavior of other high-risk groups, have not been so successful with intravenous drug users. In fact, the Centers for Disease Control estimates that about 32 percent of the diagnosed AIDS cases in this country, involving nearly 70,000 individuals, resulted from intravenous drug use or sexual contact with intravenous drug users. In addition, intravenous drug use is responsible for half of the AIDS cases among women.

AIDS is spread among intravenous drug users primarily through the sharing of hypodermic syringes, or "needles," and other drug-using paraphernalia (e.g., cotton and water) that have been contaminated with the AIDS virus, and secondarily by high-risk sexual behavior. Thus, intravenous drug users pose a threat not only to themselves, but to their sexual partners and offspring as well. In fact, 58 percent of all reported pediatric AIDS cases are associated with intravenous drug use.

Faced with the growing link between intravenous drug use and AIDS, some cities and communities have instituted or are contemplating programs to provide clean needles to addicts in the hope that this will help reduce the sharing of needles, and hence, the spread of the HIV virus.

**Needle Exchange Programs.** Needle exchange programs provide free, clean needles to intravenous drug users in an attempt to reduce the likelihood that they will share needles with other users. Some programs operate from fixed locations such as city government offices or pharmacies. Others are mobile, using outreach workers in vans, on foot, and at temporary sites. Some programs provide a new needle only in exchange for an old one, while others provide at least one "starter" needle. Most programs limit the number of needles that can be exchanged at any one time. Some programs provide needles to persons only if they have a verifiable history of drug injection, and most have age limits. Most programs are privately funded; others are supported with State or municipal government funds.[2]

Needle exchange programs also differ in scope. Some only exchange needles, while others are more comprehensive and provide counseling, referral to testing and drug treatment, bleach to clean needles, and safer sex information.

**Needle Exchange and the Law.** In 39 States and the District of Columbia, sterile needles can be purchased inexpensively without a prescription in many pharmacies.[3] In most of the remaining 11 States, a prescription is required. However, four of the 11 are considering legislation that would broaden access to needles. Only one State, Alabama, is considering legislation that would restrict accessibility by making it a criminal offense for those other than licensed pharmacists or practitioners to sell needles.

Forty-nine States, the District of Columbia, and numerous local jurisdictions have laws to prohibit the sale and distribution of drug paraphernalia. The majority of these laws conform with the Model Drug Paraphernalia Act, which was released by the Drug Enforcement Administration in August 1979. The Model Drug Paraphernalia Act would make it a crime to possess, deliver, or manufacture needles with the intent to violate antidrug laws. Therefore, operating needle exchange programs may be a violation of the law in many States and local jurisdictions. Furthermore, operating such programs may subject municipalities to civil liability in some jurisdictions.

**What the Research Shows.** Several studies on the efficacy of needle exchange programs have been conducted in the United States and abroad. Some of these studies have been cited by proponents of needle exchange as evidence that such programs work. However, all of the needle exchange programs studied have yielded either ambiguous or discouraging results. Moreover, the methodology used to conduct these studies has been flawed. For example:

• Many studies make long-term projections of addict behavior based on short-term results;

• Many use a small or insufficient sample size and then project results to larger populations;

• Despite claims that needle sharing was reduced, none of the studies conducted objective tests (e.g., analysis of blood types on returned needles) to determine whether needles were shared;

• Most do not use valid comparison or control groups; and

• Most have program staff, rather than independent evaluators, conduct client interviews on which the findings of the studies are based.

There are four other significant problems with the research. First, needle exchange programs are plagued by high levels of attrition. Programs may have initial contact with intravenous drug users who are at the highest risk of sharing needles and contracting AIDS, but only as few as 20 percent may return for a second or third visit.

Second, needle exchange programs tend to attract and retain a self-selecting group of older, long-term intravenous drug users who are less likely to share needles than less experienced, more promiscuous users. Therefore, positive reports on the effectiveness of exchange programs may be due *more* to the behavior of this less risky subset of the intravenous drug using population and *less* to the availability of clean needles.

Third, programs offering needle exchange often provide bleach for cleaning needles, referrals to testing and treatment, and other services. However, the research conducted to date has not isolated the specific impact that exchanging needles has had on reducing the transmission of AIDS compared with these other factors. Most researchers have simply attributed positive results to needle exchange.

The fourth weakness with the research relates to the dynamics of addiction. No matter what addicts promise when they are not on drugs, they may still share needles when they shoot up heroin or cocaine. In many cases it is simply part of the ritual of taking drugs. More often, a drug-induced state overwhelms rational thinking. Many addicts know that they can get AIDS from dirty needles. Yet hazards to their health—even deadly ones—do not weigh heavily on their minds. Rather, they are primarily concerned with the instant gratification of drugs.

To expect an individual locked in the grip of drug addiction to act responsibly by not sharing needles is unrealistic. Such a change in behavior requires self-discipline and a willingness to postpone gratification and plan for the future—all of which are contrary to the drug-using lifestyle. The fact that addicts can purchase clean needles cheaply, without prescription, in many pharmacies in most States, but often fail to do so, is evidence of their irresponsible behavior.[4] In fact, the only proven way to change an addict's behavior is through structured interventions, such as drug treatment.

**The New Haven Study.** A 1991 interim study of a needle exchange program in New Haven, Connecticut, is cited by many needle exchange advocates as evidence of the benefits of needle exchange. The study asserts numerous positive findings, most of which are not supported by the data.

The study states that retention rates stabilized after a high attrition rate early in the program. But, of the 720 addicts who initially contacted the New Haven program over an eight-month period, only 288 (40 percent) returned at least once to exchange a used needle (Figure 1). The New Haven study defines the 288 returning intravenous drug users as "program participants," but does not distinguish between those who exchanged needles once and those who exchanged needles more frequently.[6] The loose definition of "program participation" exaggerates the program's reported retention rate and calls into question the claim that participation in the program stabilized. In addition, the study does not provide information on the 288 individuals who remained in the program and whether they shared needles before the program

*Figure 1*

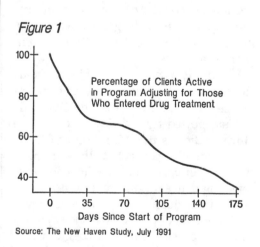

Percentage of Clients Active in Program Adjusting for Those Who Entered Drug Treatment

Days Since Start of Program

Source: The New Haven Study, July 1991

started. In fact, the study reports that of the 720 addicts who contacted the program, 436 (61 percent) reported never sharing needles before the program began (Figure 2).

The study also states that about half of the 10,180 needles distributed by the program between November 1990 and June 1991 were returned, and that an additional 4,236 "street" or nonprogram needles were brought in for exchange. However, the study fails to account for the 4,917 needles—50 percent of those given out—that were not returned. Based on this information, the study claims that the circulation time for needles was reduced and that fewer contaminated needles were appearing in public places. However, no data are presented to directly support such conclusions.

The authors also report that 107 intravenous drug users (about 15 percent of those who contacted the program) entered treatment over an eight-month period through contact with the New Haven program, but there are no data on how many of these individuals were "program participants" (e.g., had exchanged needles more than once). Therefore, the study does not present any basis for correlating the *exchange* of needles to entry into drug treatment. Also, no data on treatment retention or completion are presented.

The study also claims that intravenous drug use in the community did not increase. Although this may be true, it is not supported by convincing data. The study indicates that 92 percent of those who initially contacted the program were experienced users who had been injecting drugs for one year or more. The study uses this statistic to demonstrate that the availability of free needles did not entice individuals to begin using

*Figure 2*

**Extent of Needle Sharing Reported at Initial Contact With Program**

How Often Shared Works

| | | |
|---|---|---|
| Always (100%) | 16 | ( 2%) |
| Almost Always (67–99%) | 16 | ( 2%) |
| Half the Time (34–66%) | 43 | ( 6%) |
| Sometimes (1–33%) | 196 | (27%) |
| Never (0%) | 436 | (61%) |
| (Missing) | 13 | ( 2%) |

Source: The New Haven Study, July 1991.

intravenous drugs. However, there is no evidence to verify that experienced users did not use needles distributed by the program to initiate new users. The study also cites an unchanged rate in drug arrests as evidence that no increase in intravenous drug use occurred due to the program. However, the New Haven program had only been in operation for two months and had been contacted by fewer than 200 addicts at the time statistics on drug arrests were recorded. Therefore, it is unlikely that the program could have had any impact on the rate of drug arrests.

The most striking finding of the New Haven study—that the incidence of new HIV infections was reduced by one-third among those participating in the program—is based on tenuous data. The study indicates that 789 needles—581 from the program, 160 from the street, and 48 from a local "shooting gallery"[7]—were tested for the presence of HIV.[8] The tests found that program needles were much less likely to be HIV positive than street or gallery needles. The tests also indicated that "dedicated" program needles (e.g., those returned by the original recipient) were much less likely to be HIV positive than other program needles. Based on this information, the study concludes that "dedicated" needles were not shared, *although no tests were conducted to determine if different blood types appeared on the needles or the blood type on the needle matched that of the program participant.* Without conducting such tests, accurate conclusions as to whether needles were shared cannot be drawn, and a reduction in the spread of HIV cannot be attributed to needle exchange.

Finally, the study projects that expanding the availability of clean needles to New Haven's entire intravenous drug using population would also reduce the incidence of new HIV infections by one-third. The projection is based on a highly complex mathematical model involving eight different factors that are supported by numerous assumptions, estimates, probabilities, and rates. While the model may be valid, its projections are based on the tenuous assumption that the 288 intravenous drug users "participating" in the New Haven program are representative of the general intravenous drug using population. However, the high attrition rate of the New Haven program demonstrates that such an assumption cannot be made.

## FOREIGN NEEDLE EXCHANGE PROGRAMS

In recent years, other countries—most notably the Netherlands and the United Kingdom—have established needle exchange programs. Studies of these programs have also produced mixed results. Most reflect the problems noted in existing research on needle exchange. Many report anecdotal or other unquantified information. Furthermore, some base "success" on the number of needles distributed.

In Amsterdam, a program started in 1984 reported that the number of partici-

pants grew more than tenfold in four years. The program also reported that during the first four years participants shared fewer needles, the HIV prevalence rate among intravenous drug users stabilized, and instances of Hepatitis B decreased.

In England, about 120 exchange programs distribute approximately four million needles annually. These programs reportedly reach users who have not been in contact with drug treatment services, decrease needle sharing, and increase contact with other social services by participants.

Sweden's three needle exchange sites reported after three years that no project participant had become infected with HIV, that needle sharing had declined, and that many users not previously in contact with drug treatment had been attracted to the program.

Although generally positive, the reports on these programs are scientifically weak and present very few objective indicators of success. All claim that needle exchange reduced the number of needles shared, but none of the programs conducted the tests (e.g., blood-type tests) necessary to make that determination.

In addition, the attrition rates in foreign programs are extremely high. A 1989 study of 15 needle exchange programs in England and Scotland reported that only 33 percent of intravenous drug users who initially contacted the programs returned up to five times. As in the United States, needle exchange programs in other countries are more likely to attract and retain intravenous drug users who are already predisposed not to share needles, and who therefore are at lower risk of contracting AIDS than other, less cautious, users.

## ALTERNATIVES TO NEEDLE EXCHANGE

The challenges to society presented by drug use and HIV/AIDS require the steady development of scientific understanding and the promotion of effective interventions. Requested Federal funding for AIDS prevention, treatment, research, and income maintenance in 1993 is $4.9 billion—a 69 percent increase since 1990 (Figure 3). The President's National Drug Control Strategy supports using a portion of these funds for research, experiments, and demonstrations to seek out high-risk drug users; to encourage and support their entry into drug treatment; and to provide them with information on the destructiveness of their behavior and ways to change it. The Strategy also supports efforts to expand the capacity and effectiveness of drug treatment for intravenous drug users.

**Outreach Programs.** The most effective method of reducing the spread of AIDS among intravenous drug users is to treat successfully their drug addiction. However, Federal studies estimate that more than 40 percent of intravenous drug users have never been in treatment, even though many have used drugs intravenously for more than 10 years. Therefore, it is essential to continue efforts to aggressively recruit intravenous drug users into treatment.

Since 1987, the Department of Health and Human Service's National Institute on Drug Abuse has funded projects in more than 40 cities to help identify intravenous drug users and persuade them to enter treatment. In these cities, squads of outreach workers contact addicts and encourage them to avoid sharing nee-

*Figure 3*

**Federal Funding for HIV/AIDS, 1990–1993**

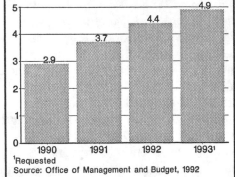

¹Requested
Source: Office of Management and Budget, 1992

dles and other risky behaviors and to enter treatment. Outreach workers also provide addicts with information on the threat of AIDS and dispense materials (e.g., bleach and condoms) to reduce the risk of HIV infection.

Between 1987 and 1992, outreach workers contacted approximately 150,000 intravenous drug users. Of these, 45,000 addicts (54 percent of whom reported regularly sharing needles) and 9,500 sexual partners were provided with information on treatment, counseling and methods for reducing the risk of infection. Program participants were assigned to standard and enhanced interventions. Follow-up surveys were conducted six months after the assignments were made, and the results of those surveys indicated that:

- 31 percent of the intravenous drug users had enrolled in formal drug treatment programs;
- 38 percent were sharing needles less frequently;
- 44 percent had begun to always clean their needles, always use a new

needle, or had stopped injecting completely; and

• 47 percent had stopped injecting or reduced their frequency of injection.

The success of this effort demonstrates that outreach programs are highly effective in persuading intravenous drug users to avoid sharing needles and to seek treatment. By comparison, only 15 percent of those who contacted the New Haven program entered treatment. The Federal government will continue to support outreach programs by awarding approximately 60 grants in 1992 and 1993.

The Centers for Disease Control also administers an extensive outreach program for preventing the spread of the HIV virus among intravenous drug users. This program, which is operated through State departments of health and community-based organizations, offers intravenous drug users counseling, testing, and referral to treatment. An evaluation of the program will be completed in about two years.

**Expanding Treatment Capacity.** The Federal government continues to support expanded treatment capacity for intravenous drug users, primarily through the Alcohol, Drug Abuse and Mental Health Services Block Grant program, which requires States to use at least 50 percent of their drug allotment for outreach and treatment of these drug users. Also, the Capacity Expansion Program, which was created by the Bush Administration in Fiscal Year 1992, will increase the number of drug treatment slots for areas and populations in the greatest need of treatment, including intravenous drug users. If Congress fully funds this program in Fiscal Year 1993 (the Administration has requested $86 million), an additional 38,000 addicts—many of whom will be intravenous drug users—will be provided with drug treatment.

**Medications Development.** The Federal government is continuing its efforts to develop medications to treat heroin addiction. New pharmacological therapies, such as LAAM (a longer-acting alternative to methadone), depot naltrexone, and buprenorphine, are showing considerable promise in treating heroin addiction and should be available within the next few years.[9] In addition, performance standards and clinical protocols are being developed for methadone treatment programs to enhance their safety and effectiveness in treating heroin addiction.[10]

## CONCLUSION

The rapid spread of AIDS has prompted officials of some of America's cities to institute programs that distribute clean needles to intravenous drug users. Such programs are questionable public policy, however, because they facilitate addicts' continued use of drugs and undercut the credibility of society's message that drug use is illegal and morally wrong. Further, there is no compelling research that needle exchange programs are effective in preventing intravenous drug users from sharing needles, reducing the spread of AIDS, or encouraging addicts to seek drug treatment.

Research does show, however, that aggressive outreach efforts are an effective way to get intravenous drug users to end their high-risk behavior and seek treatment. Therefore, the National Drug Control Strategy will continue *to* support such outreach programs. It also will continue to support expanded treatment capacity for high-risk populations, including intravenous drug users; the development of medications for treating heroin addiction; and the exploration of other options that may offer intravenous drug users a real chance for recovery.

toms and craving for heroin for 24 hours. Methadone is only administered as part of a supervised treatment program.

## NOTES

1. Human Immunodeficiency Virus/Acquired Immunodeficiency Syndrome.

2. Federal law prohibits the use of Alcohol, Drug Abuse, and Mental Health Services Block Grant funds—the major source of Federal support for drug treatment—to pay for needle exchange programs.

3. In some States, such as California, needles may be sold without prescription for the administration of insulin or adrenaline if the pharmacist can identify the purchaser and records the purchase.

4. Syringes cost about $.30 each. For example, in a recent study of pharmacies in St. Louis, Compton et al found the cost of a package of 10, 28-gauge, 100-unit insulin syringes to range from $1.92 to $4.28.

See Compton, W., et al. "Legal Needle Buying in St. Louis," American Journal of Public Health, April 1992, Vol. 82, No. 4.

5. In Fiscal Year 1992, the National Institute on Drug Abuse awarded a grant to Yale University to conduct a rigorous evaluation of the New Haven program over a three-year period. Results of the evaluation will be available in 1995.

6. Researchers estimate that intravenous heroin users on average inject two or more times a day, heavy users four to six times a day. Intravenous cocaine users invariably inject more frequently. There is very little data yet available on the number of injections an average user gets from a needle before it is discarded, although a 1989 California survey of 257 users found a mean of 22.5 uses (with 27 reporting one use and 15 reporting over 100).

7. A "shooting gallery" is a communal injection site notorious for inadequate sterilization of injection equipment.

8. The study does not specify the method used to select program and street needles or whether they are considered random or representative samples.

9. LAAM is a longer-acting alternative to methadone, depot naltrexone is a long-acting heroin blocker, and buprenorphine is being investigated for treating individuals addicted to both heroin and cocaine.

10. Methadone is a synthetic medication used to treat heroin addicts by relieving withdrawal symp-

# POSTSCRIPT

## Should Needle Exchange Programs Be Promoted?

Whether or not needle exchange programs will help slow the spread of AIDS is extremely relevant since people who inject drugs are the primary sources for heterosexual transmission of AIDS to sexual partners. Individuals who inject cocaine are more likely to infect their sexual partners than are heroin users since cocaine heightens perceptions of sexual arousal. Also, the immune systems of drug addicts are impaired not only by their addictions but by their typically poor environment as well. With a weakened immune system, one can contract HIV more easily.

One potential advantage of needle exchange programs is that needles may be safely discarded after they have been used. Unsafely discarded needles may accidentally prick someone and lead to HIV transmission. A second potential benefit is that when people come to needle exchange sites, they can be encouraged to enter drug treatment programs. It is not always easy to locate the drug-injecting population; one place to reach these individuals is where they exchange needles.

Despite the difficulties of studying people who inject drugs, long-term studies are needed to determine the impact of needle exchange programs on (1) the incidence of AIDS, (2) the continuation or reduction of drug use, (3) whether or not these programs attract new users to the drug culture, (4) the likelihood of program participants entering drug treatment programs, and (5) the impact on other high-risk behaviors. Preliminary studies into the effectiveness of needle exchange programs are contradictory. When one such program was introduced in Tacoma, Washington, needle sharing declined 30 percent. However, nearly two-thirds of the people who inject drugs in Louisville, Kentucky, continued sharing needles after an exchange program was introduced. In Louisville, however, needles are obtained through a prescription, which may have a different effect than does receiving needles through an exchange program.

Two articles in *New Frontiers in Drug Policy*, edited by Arnold Trebach and Kevin Zeese (Drug Policy Foundation, 1991), discuss different aspects of needle exchange programs: "Time to Medicalize IV Drug Use," by Mostafa Nagi, and "Forcing Needle Exchange Through the Courts," by Joey Tranchina. In "Getting the Point in New Haven," *Time* (May 25, 1992), Dick Thompson discusses the effects of New Haven's needle exchange program. The politics of needle exchange programs are examined in Warwick Anderson's article "The New York Needle Trial: The Politics of Public Health in the Age of AIDS," *American Journal of Public Health* (November 1991).

# ISSUE 7

## Should Drug Use by Pregnant Women Be Considered Child Abuse?

**YES: Paul A. Logli,** from "Drugs in the Womb: The Newest Battlefield in the War on Drugs," *Criminal Justice Ethics* (Winter/Spring 1990)

**NO: Alida V. Merlo,** from "Prosecuting Pregnant Drug Users," in Arnold S. Trebach and Kevin B. Zeese, eds., *New Frontiers in Drug Policy* (Drug Policy Foundation, 1991)

### ISSUE SUMMARY

**YES:** Paul A. Logli, a prosecuting attorney, argues that it is the government's duty to enforce children's right to begin life with healthy, drug-free minds and bodies. Logli believes that pregnant women who use drugs should be prosecuted because they risk harming their unborn children.

**NO:** Professor of criminal justice Alida V. Merlo asserts that the prosecution of pregnant drug users is unfair and discriminatory because such prosecution primarily affects poor, minority women who lack access to quality prenatal care and drug treatment facilities.

The effects of drugs on a fetus can be mild and temporary or severe and permanent, depending on the frequency of drug use by the mother, the type of substance used, and the stage of fetal development at the time the drug crosses the placental barrier and enters the bloodstream of the fetus. In recent years, there has been a drastic increase in the number of drug-exposed babies born in the United States, and medical experts are now beginning to understand the health consequences that these children face. Both illegal and legal drugs, like cocaine, crack, marijuana, alcohol, and nicotine, are increasingly found to be responsible for incidents of premature birth, congenital abnormalities, fetal alcohol syndrome, mental retardation, and serious birth defects. The exposure of the fetus to these substances and the long-term involuntary physical, emotional, and intellectual effects are disturbing. In addition, the social, medical, and economic costs to treat and care for babies who are exposed to or become addicted to drugs while in utero (in the uterus) warrant serious concern.

Much of what is argued in regard to prosecuting pregnant drug users is whether this is a legal problem or a medical problem. In recent years, attempts have been made to establish laws that would allow the incarceration of drug-using pregnant women on the basis of "fetal abuse." Some cases have been successfully prosecuted. Mothers have been denied custody of their infants until they entered appropriate treatment programs, and criminal charges have been brought against mothers whose children were born with drug-related complications. The underlying presumption is that the unborn fetus should be afforded protection against the harmful actions of another person, specifically the use of harmful drugs by the mother.

Those who profess that prosecuting pregnant women who use drugs is necessary insist that the welfare of the unborn child is the highest priority. They contend that the possibility that these women will avoid obtaining health care for themselves or their babies because they fear punishment does not absolve the state from the responsibility of protecting the babies. They argue that criminalizing these acts is imperative to protect fetuses or newborns who cannot protect themselves. It is the role of the legal system to deter pregnant women from engaging in future criminal drug use and to protect the best interests of the infant.

Others maintain that drug use and dependency by pregnant women is a medical problem, not a criminal one. Many pregnant women do seek treatment but are faced with limited or unavailable rehabilitation programs. Shortages of openings in chemical dependency programs may keep a prospective client waiting for months, during which she will most likely continue to use the drugs to which she is addicted and prolong the fetus's drug exposure. Also, most women who use illegal drugs are poor, uneducated, and often unmarried. For these women, drug treatment and adequate prenatal care are impossible due to financial constraints. Finally, women who fear criminal prosecution because of their drug use may simply avoid prenatal care altogether.

Some suggest that medical intervention, drug prevention, and education is needed for pregnant drug users instead of prosecution. Others respond that prosecuting pregnant women who use drugs will help identify those who need attention, at which point adequate medical as well as social welfare services can be provided to treat and protect the mother and child.

In the following selections, Paul A. Logli argues for the prosecution of pregnant drug users, contending that it is the state's responsibility to protect the unborn and the newborn because they are least able to protect themselves. He charges that it is a prosecutor's responsibility to deter future criminal drug use by mothers who he feels violate the right of the potential newborn to have an opportunity for a healthy and normal life.

Alida V. Merlo insists that prosecuting pregnant drug users defeats the purpose of helping the mother and child because it advocates criminalization and punishment instead of treatment and concern. She feels that it is necessary to emphasize treatment, prevention, and education rather than incarceration because often it is not the woman's fault that she receives inadequate medical attention and prenatal care.

# YES

Paul A. Logli

# DRUGS IN THE WOMB: THE NEWEST BATTLEFIELD IN THE WAR ON DRUGS

## INTRODUCTION

The reported incidence of drug-related births has risen dramatically over the last several years. The legal system and, in particular, local prosecutors have attempted to properly respond to the suffering, death, and economic costs which result from a pregnant woman's use of drugs. The ensuing debate has raised serious constitutional and practical issues which are far from resolution.

Prosecutors have achieved mixed results in using current criminal and juvenile statutes as a basis for legal action intended to prosecute mothers and protect children. As a result, state and federal legislators have begun the difficult task of drafting appopriate laws to deal with the problem, while at the same time acknowledging the concerns of medical authorities, child protection groups, and advocates for individual rights.

## THE PROBLEM

The plight of "cocaine babies," children addicted at birth to narcotic substances or otherwise affected by maternal drug use during pregnancy, has prompted prosecutors in some jurisdications to bring criminal charges against drug-abusing mothers. Not only have these prosecutions generated heated debates both inside and outside of the nation's courtrooms, but they have also expanded the war on drugs to a controversial new battlefield—the mother's womb.

A 1988 survey of hospitals conducted by Dr. Ira Chasnoff, Associate Professor of Northwestern University Medical School and President of the National Association for Perinatal Addiction Research and Education (NAPARE) indicated that as many as 375,000 infants may be affected by maternal cocaine use during pregnancy each year. Chasnoff's survey in-

From Paul A. Logli, "Drugs in the Womb: The Newest Battlefield in the War on Drugs," *Criminal Justice Ethics*, vol. 9, no. 1 (Winter/Spring 1990), pp. 23–39. Copyright © 1990 by *Criminal Justice Ethics*. Reprinted by permission of The Institute for Criminal Justice Ethics, 899 Tenth Avenue, New York, NY 10019. Notes omitted.

cluded 36 hospitals across the country and showed incidence rates ranging from 1 percent to 27 percent. It also indicated that the problem was not restricted to urban populations or particular racial or socio-economic groups. More recently a study at Hutzel Hospital in Detroit's inner city found that 42.7 percent of its newborn babies were exposed to drugs while in their mothers' wombs.

The effects of maternal use of cocaine and other drugs during pregnancy on the mother and her newborn child have by now been well-documented and will not be repeated here. The effects are severe and can cause numerous threats to the short-term health of the child. In a few cases it can even result in death.

Medical authorities have just begun to evaluate the long-term effects of cocaine exposure on children as they grow older. Early findings show that many of these infants show serious difficulties in relating and reacting to adults and environments, as well as in organizing creative play, and they appear similar to mildly autistic or personality-disordered children.

The human costs related to the pain, suffering, and deaths resulting from maternal cocaine use during pregnancy are simply incalculable. In economic terms, the typical intensive-care costs for treating babies exposed to drugs range from $7,500 to $31,000. In some cases medical bills go as high as $150,000.

The costs grow enormously as more and more hospitals encounter the problem of "boarder babies"—those children literally abandoned at the hospital by an addicted mother, and left to be cared for by the nursing staff. Future costs to society for simply educating a generation of drug-affected children can only be the object of speculation. It is clear, however,

that besides pain, suffering, and death the economic costs to society of drug use by pregnant women is presently enormous and is certainly growing larger.

## THE PROSECUTOR'S RESPONSE

It is against this backdrop and fueled by the evergrowing emphasis on an aggressively waged war on drugs that prosecutors have begun a number of actions against women who have given birth to drug-affected children. A review of at least two cases will illustrate the potential success or failure of attempts to use existing statutes.

*People v. Melanie Green* On February 4, 1989, at a Rockford, Illinois hospital, two-day old Bianca Green lost her brief struggle for life. At the time of Bianca's birth both she and her mother, twenty-four-year-old Melanie Green, tested positive for the presence of cocaine in their systems.

Pathologists in Rockford and Madison, Wisconsin, indicated that the death of the baby was the result of a prenatal injury related to cocaine used by the mother during the pregnancy. They asserted that maternal cocaine use had caused the placenta to prematurely rupture, which deprived the fetus of oxygen before and during delivery. As a result of oxygen deprivation, the child's brain began to swell and she eventually died.

After an investigation by the Rockford Police Department and the State of Illinois Department of Children and Family Services, prosecutors allowed a criminal complaint to be filed on May 9, 1989, charging Melanie Green with the offenses of Involuntary Manslaughter and Delivery of a Controlled Substance.

On May 25, 1989, testimony was presented to the Winnebago County Grand

Jury by prosecutors seeking a formal indictment. The Grand Jury, however, declined to indict Green on either charge. Since Grand Jury proceedings in the State of Illinois are secret, as are the jurors' deliberations and votes, the reason for the decision of the Grand Jury in this case is determined more by conjecture than any direct knowledge. Prosecutors involved in the presentation observed that the jurors exhibited a certain amount of sympathy for the young woman who had been brought before the Grand Jury at the jurors' request. It is also likely that the jurors were uncomfortable with the use of statutes that were not intended to be used in these circumstances.

It would also be difficult to disregard the fact that, after the criminal complaints were announced on May 9th and prior to the Grand Jury deliberations of May 25th, a national debate had ensued revolving around the charges brought in Rockford, Illinois, and their implications for the ever-increasing problem of women who use drugs during pregnancy.

*People v. Jennifer Clarise Johnson* On July 13, 1989, a Seminole County, Florida judge found Jennifer Johnson guilty of delivery of a controlled substance to a child. The judge found that delivery, for purposes of the statute, occurred through the umbilical cord after the birth of the child and before the cord was severed. Jeff Deen, the Assistant State's Attorney who prosecuted the case, has since pointed out that Johnson, age 23, had previously given birth to three other cocaine-affected babies, and in this case was arrested at a crack house. "We needed to make sure this woman does not give birth to another cocaine baby."

Johnson was sentenced to fifteen years of probation including strict supervision, drug treatment, random drug testing, educational and vocational training, and an intensive prenatal care program if she ever became pregnant again.

## SUPPORT FOR THE PROSECUTION OF MATERNAL DRUG ABUSE

Both cases reported above relied on a single important fact as a basis for the prosecution of the drug-abusing mother: that the child was born alive and exhibited the consequences of prenatal injury.

In the Melanie Green case, Illinois prosecutors relied on the "born alive" rule set out earlier in *People v. Bolar.* In *Bolar* the defendant was convicted of the offense of reckless homicide. The case involved an accident between a car driven by the defendant, who was found to be drunk, and another automobile containing a pregnant woman. As a result, the woman delivered her baby by emergency caesarean section within hours of the collision. Although the newborn child exhibited only a few heart beats and lived for approximately two minutes, the court found that the child was born alive and was therefore a person for purposes of the criminal statutes of the State of Illinois.

The Florida prosecution relied on a live birth in an entirely different fashion. The prosecutor argued in that case that the delivery of the controlled substance occurred after the live birth via the umbilical cord and prior to the cutting of the cord. Thus, it was argued, that the delivery of the controlled substance occurred not to a fetus but to a person who enjoyed the protection of the criminal code of the State of Florida.

Further support for the State's role in protecting the health of newborns even against prenatal injury is found in the statutes which provide protection for the fetus. These statutes proscribe actions by a person, usually other than the mother, which either intentionally or recklessly harm or kill a fetus. In other words, even in the absence of a live birth, most states afford protection to the unborn fetus against the harmful actions of another person. Arguably, the same protection should be afforded the infant against intentional harmful actions by a drug-abusing mother.

The state also receives support for a position in favor of the protection of the health of a newborn from a number of non-criminal cases. A line of civil cases in several states would appear to stand for the principle that a child has a right to begin life with a sound mind and body, and a person who interferes with that right may be subject to civil liability. In two cases decided within months of each other, the Supreme Court of Michigan upheld two actions for recovery of damages that were caused by the infliction of prenatal injury. In *Womack v. Buckhorn* the court upheld an action on behalf of an eight-year-old surviving child for prenatal brain injuries apparently suffered during the fourth month of the pregnancy in an automobile accident. The court adopted with approval the reasoning of a New Jersey Supreme Court decision and "recognized that a child has a legal right to begin life with a sound mind and body." Similarly, in *O'Neill v. Morse* the court found that a cause of action was allowed for prenatal injuries that caused the death of an eight-month-old viable fetus.

Illinois courts have allowed civil recovery on behalf of an infant for a negligently administered blood transfusion given to the mother prior to conception which resulted in damage to the child at birth. However, the same Illinois court would not extend a similar cause of action for prebirth injuries as between a child and its own mother. The court, however, went on to say that a right to such a cause of action could be statutorily enacted by the Legislature.

Additional support for the state's role in protecting the health of newborns is found in the principles annunciated in recent decisions of the United States Supreme Court. The often cited case of *Roe v. Wade* set out that although a woman's right of privacy is broad enough to cover the abortion decision, the right is not absolute and is subject to limitations, "and that at some point the state's interest as to protection of health, medical standards and prenatal life, becomes dominant."

More recently, in the case of *Webster v. Reproductive Health Services*, the court expanded the state's interest in protecting potential human life by setting aside viability as a rigid line that had previously allowed state regulation only after viability had been shown but prohibited it before viability. The court goes on to say that the "fundamental right" to abortion as described in *Roe* is now accorded the lesser status of a "liberty interest." Such language surely supports a prosecutor's argument that the state's compelling interest in potential human life would allow the criminalization of acts which if committed by a pregnant woman can damage not just a viable fetus by eventually a born-alive infant. It follows that, once a pregnant woman has abandoned her right to abort and has decided to carry the fetus to term, society can well impose a duty on the mother to insure that the fetus is born as healthy as possible.

A further argument in support of the state's interest in prosecuting women who engage in conduct which is damaging to the health of a newborn child is especially compelling in regard to maternal drug use during pregnancy. Simply put, there is no fundamental right or even a liberty interest in the use of psycho-active drugs. A perceived right of privacy has never formed an absolute barrier against state prosecutions of those who use or possess narcotics. Certainly no exception can be made simply because the person using drugs happens to be pregnant.

Critics of the prosecutor's role argue that any statute that would punish mothers who create a substantial risk of harm to their fetus will run afoul of constitutional requirements, including prohibitions on vagueness, guarantees of liberty and privacy, and rights of due process and equal protection. . . .

In spite of such criticism, the state's role in protecting those citizens who are least able to protect themselves, namely the newborn, mandates an aggressive posture. Much of the criticism of prosecutorial efforts is based on speculation as to the consequences of prosecution and ignores the basic tenet of criminal law that prosecutions deter the prosecuted and others from committing additional crimes. To assume that it will only drive persons further underground is to somehow argue that certain prosecutions of crime will only force perpetrators to make even more aggressive efforts to escape apprehension, thus making arrest and prosecution unadvisable. Neither could this be accepted as an argument justifying even the weakening of criminal sanctions. . . .

The concern that pregnant addicts will avoid obtaining health care for themselves or their infants because of the fear of prosecution cannot justify the absence of state action to protect the newborn. If the state were to accept such reasoning, then existing child abuse laws would have to be reconsidered since they might deter parents from obtaining medical care for physically or sexually abused children. That argument has not been accepted as a valid reason for abolishing child abuse laws or for not prosecuting child abusers. . . .

The far better policy is for the state to acknowledge its responsibility not only to provide a deterrant to criminal and destructive behavior by pregnant addicts but also to provide adequate opportunities for those who might seek help to discontinue their addiction. Prosecution has a role in its ability to deter future criminal behavior and to protect the best interests of the child. The medical and social welfare establishment must assume an even greater responsibility to encourage legislators to provide adequate funding and facilities so that no pregnant woman who is addicted to drugs will be denied the opportunity to seek appropriate prenatal care and treatment for her addiction.

## ONE STATE'S RESPONSE

The Legislature of the State of Illinois at the urging of local prosecutors moved quickly to amend its juvenile court act in order to provide protection to those children born drug-affected. Previously, Illinois law provided that a court could assume jurisdiction over addicted minors or a minor who is generally declared neglected or abused.

Effective January 1, 1990, the juvenile court act was amended to expand the definition of a neglected or abused minor. . . .

> those who are neglected include . . . any newborn infant whose blood or urine contains any amount of a controlled substance. . . .

The purpose of the new statute is to make it easier for the court to assert jurisdiction over a newborn infant born drug-affected. The state is not required to show either the addiction of the child or harmful effects on the child in order to remove the child from a drug abusing mother. Used in this context, prosecutors can work with the mother in a rather coercive atmosphere to encourage her to enter into drug rehabilitation and, upon the successful completion of the program, be reunited with her child.

Additional legislation before the Illinois Legislature is House Bill 2835 sponsored by Representatives John Hallock (R-Rockford) and Edolo "Zeke" Giorgi (D-Rockford). This bill represents the first attempt to specifically address the prosecution of drug abusing pregnant women. . . .

The statute provides for a class 4 felony disposition upon conviction. A class 4 felony is a probationable felony which can also result in a term of imprisonment from one to three years.

Subsequent paragraphs set out certain defenses available to the accused.

> It shall not be a violation of this section if a woman knowingly or intentionally uses a narcotic or dangerous drug in the first twelve weeks of pregnancy and: 1. She has no knowledge that she is pregnant; or 2. Subsequently, within the first twelve weeks of pregnancy, undergoes medical treatment for substance abuse or treatment or rehabilitation in a program or facility approved by the Illinois Department of Alcoholism and Substance Abuse, and thereafter discontinues any further use of drugs or narcotics as previously set forth.

. . . A woman, under this statute, could not be prosecuted for self-reporting her addiction in the early stages of the pregnancy. Nor could she be prosecuted under this statute if, even during the subsequent stages of the pregnancy, she discontinued her drug use to the extent that no drugs were present in her system or the baby's system at the time of birth. The statute, as drafted, is clearly intended to allow prosecutors to invoke the criminal statutes in the most serious of cases.

## CONCLUSION

Local prosecutors have a legitimate role in responding to the increasing problem of drug abusing pregnant women and their drug-affected children. Eliminating the pain, suffering and death resulting from drug exposure in newborns must be a prosecutor's priority. However, the use of existing statutes to address the problem may meet with limited success since they are burdened with numerous constitutional problems dealing with original intent, notice, vagueness, and due process.

The juvenile courts may offer perhaps the best initial response in working to protect the interests of a surviving child. However, in order to address more serious cases, legislative efforts may be required to provide new statutes that will specifically address the problem and hopefully deter future criminal conduct which deprives children of their important right to a healthy and normal birth.

The long-term solution does not rest with the prosecutor alone. Society, including the medical and social welfare establishment, must be more responsive in providing readily accessible prenatal care and treatment alternatives for pregnant addicts. In the short term however, prosecutors must be prepared to play a vital role in protecting children and deterring women from engaging in conduct which will harm the newborn child. If prosecutors fail to respond, then they are simply closing the doors of the criminal justice system to those persons, the newborn, who are least able to open the doors for themselves.

# NO

Alida V. Merlo

# PROSECUTING PREGNANT DRUG USERS

In recent years, Americans have become more cognizant of and sensitive to drugs. Our attention has focused increasingly on illicit drugs like heroin and cocaine and, to a lesser extent, on tobacco and alcohol. While there is some debate whether drug use is increasing or decreasing in America, attention is now being focused on a specific user—the pregnant woman. Recently, there has been some impetus for greater involvement in the lives of pregnant substance users. Specifically, women who use crack or cocaine during pregnancy are subject to closer scrutiny and in some instances, harsh treatment. This paper will examine the various types of intervention in the lives of pregnant women that have occurred thus far, their implications, and some alternative approaches to deal with the problem.

Part of the rationale for identifying the pregnant substance user as a public health concern is based upon the large number of babies who are born addicted to or who have been exposed to cocaine or crack in utero. For example, in their analysis of New York City data, Habel, et al., document the dramatic increase in the number of infants exposed to drug abusing mothers. Although the number remained relatively constant between 1978 and 1981, it has surged from 730 or 6.7 per 1000 births in 1981 to 2586 or 20.3 per 1000 live births in 1987.[1]

Although no one can ascertain precisely the extent and the number of drug-exposed infants born each day in the United Stats, the estimates are staggering. Every year over 350,000 infants are exposed prenatally to some form of illicit drug.[2,3] Two of these illicit drugs, crack and cocaine, are estimated to affect approximately 10,000 to 100,000 babies born each year.[4] In his analysis, Besharov contends that the national total of crack babies is probably closer to 1 or 2 percent of all live births or 30,000 to 50,000 per year. While there have been claims that these estimates are exaggerated, certainly

From Alida V. Merlo, "Prosecuting Pregnant Drug Users," in Arnold S. Trebach and Kevin B. Zeese, eds., *New Frontiers in Drug Policy* (Drug Policy Foundation, 1991). Copyright © 1991 by The Drug Policy Foundation, 4455 Connecticut Ave., NW, Suite B500, Washington, DC 20008. Reprinted by permission.

the numbers are large enough to warrant public concern.[5]

In addition to the social and medical costs related to fetuses exposed to drugs in utero, there are serious economic considerations. California spends $178 million per year to provide care for these infants. The foster care and medical treatment for 9,000 drug-exposed babies who were born in 1989 are estimated to cost $500 million for the first five years of their lives.[6]

The long term effects of crack on children are not yet fully known; but they appear to be serious. The first group of children who were exposed to crack prenatally entered kindergarten in September of 1990. Teachers report considerable difficulty in dealing with these children who manifest verbal, developmental, and emotional problems. Some officials in New York attribute the dramatic increase in the number of five year old children referred to special education classes to their contact with crack.[7]

Exposure to crack and cocaine are not the only illegal drugs to affect the fetus. Marijuana use in pregnancy has been linked to problems from premature births and low birth-weight to congenital abnormalities and perinatal problems.[8]

Legal substances can also impact the fetus. Nolan reports that 6,000 to 8,000 infants are born with fetal alcohol syndrome each year.[9] There is also some evidence that alcohol can be related to retardation and serious birth defects.[10] Researchers are just now beginning to understand and explore the relationship between maternal contact with other dangerous substances like carbon monoxide and lead.[11] The exposure of the fetus to these substances and the long term costs to society and the involuntarily affected children are troublesome.

Although no one doubts the harmful effects of exposing fetuses to toxic substances, there is some fear that, if current trends persist, increased attention to this problem will lead to more interference and intervention in the lives of pregnant women. Government officials and public sentiment suggest that society is willing to exercise more control over women's reproductive decision making. Several recent cases where regulation of women's rights to reproductive freedom have occurred may help to illustrate. During its most recent term, in *Rust v. Sullivan*, No. 89–1391, the United States Supreme Court upheld the regulations imposed during the Reagan Administration which prohibit employees in family planning clinics that receive federal funds from discussing abortion with their patients.[12] The regulations require the staff members to read a government scripted statement to patients who inquire about terminating their pregnancies. The patient is to be informed that, " . . . the project does not consider abortion an appropriate method of family planning."[13]

Judges have also included birth control requirements as part of the sentences in at least two cases where women were the defendants. In November of 1990, in Florida, a 17 year old girl who admitted smothering her newborn daughter in the hospital was sentenced to two years in prison and then ordered to use birth control for 10 years after her release.[14] In January, a California judge sentenced Darlene Johnson, after she plead guilty to child abuse, to one year in jail and three years of probation.[15] As a condition of probation, Ms. Johnson is to have a birth control device implanted in her arm. The judge asserted that " . . . the state had a compelling interest in protecting any children Ms. Johnson had not yet conceived."[16] This case has sparked considerable debate among medical ethicists and civil rights activists.[17]

Women's rights to abortion have also been examined and subjected to more restrictions. Recently, the Governor of Utah signed one of the strictest anti-abortion laws in the country, prohibiting almost all elective abortions.[18] According to Pollitt, only 16 states now pay for poor women's abortions.[19] There is also some evidence that women who identified themselves as HIV-positive were refused abortions by more than half the centers in New York.[20]

Not only have these official actions impacted women, but there is widespread belief that women who are pregnant may be subject to special sanctions by the public. For example, two cocktail servers in a Seattle restaurant were fired after they refused to serve a strawberry daiquiri to a woman who was pregnant. Instead, they repeatedly asked her if she wanted the drink and then peeled off an alcoholic beverage warning label from a bottle and brought it to her table. When the restaurant patron complained, both servers were dismissed.[21] Their actions have been viewed as heroic.[22]

Similarly, a pregnant woman, Mary Dunn, was forced out of a fitness-center hot tub by staff who insisted that she needed written permission from her doctor in order to utilize the tub. Although Ms. Dunn assured them that she had the physician's verbal authorization, that was insufficient.[23] These reports suggest that pregnant women who engage in a variety of legal behaviors from smoking to exercising can expect increased public scrutiny and interference in their daily lives.

## OFFICIAL RESPONSE TO DRUG USE DURING PREGNANCY

The government has dealt with the problem of drug use during pregnancy through the utilization of a variety of legal actions: narcotics laws, criminalization laws, and informant laws.[24] When the state has resorted to applying narcotics laws, women have been charged under previously established drug statutes for offenses like drug distribution. This approach has not been entirely successful. Some states have convicted women using these statutes, while others have decided not to indict or judges have dismissed the charges.[25,26]

Those states that opt for the second approach, criminalization laws, enact legislation which defines behavior like fetal endangerment or fetal abuse.[27] These statutes are intended to address specific maternal conduct like ingestion of illegal drugs.[28] They are employed in lieu of narcotics laws.

Of the three legal approaches, informant laws are the most commonly utilized. They require legislatures to revise or interpret existing child abuse legislation to apply to the transmission of drugs to the fetus in utero. The identification and reporting of maternal drug use (aided by toxicological screens) are the responsibility of hospital staff in the delivery room or other health care professionals who provide services to the woman during her pregnancy.[29] When it has been determined that the woman used drugs during her pregnancy, some child welfare agencies can take temporary custody of the infant. Custody is not returned until the mother has successfully completed a treatment program and/or proven to the child welfare authorities that she can assume her parental responsibilities capably.[30,31]

## ARGUMENTS OPPOSING CURRENT APPROACHES

All three of these legal approaches, narcotics laws, criminalization laws and informant laws, that states have currently chosen are inappropriate and should be avoided on legal and moral grounds. They are legally untenable because they are discriminatory. Women and men are treated unequally. Women can be prosecuted while men are not responsible for any damage they may cause. They are unjust because they target poor minority women who are the most likely to go to public hospitals and to be reported. The laws are also morally wrong because they prosecute women for drug use while failing to provide treatment for pregnant women or prenatal care for low income women. They also do not require any conclusive evidence that it is solely the mother's ingestion of a substance that is to blame for any problems the child may have. Focusing attention on the activities and behavior of the pregnant woman exclusively, suggests that she alone is responsible for every bad birth outcome.[32]

Recent evidence suggests that the father's conduct and activities can affect the fetus. For example, in their research Little and Sing compared the alcohol consumption by the father during the month of conception to that of the mother. They found that a stronger relationship existed between the father's drinking and low-birth weight than the mother's. [33] Previous research has found traces of alcohol in the seminal fluid and changes in the reproductive organs of men who drink. In order to fully understand the effects of alcohol on the fetus, Little recommends including data on the father in future research.[34]

Researchers have also found an increased incidence of brain cancer, acute lymphocytic leukemia, and lymphoma in the children of fathers who smoke.[35] Smoking is speculated to have affected the father's sperm.[36,37] Failing to factor the drug, alcohol and tobacco use of the father while simultaneously holding the mother responsible appears to be discriminatory.[38] If women are to be legally sanctioned for exposing the fetus to toxic substances, men should be treated equally.

Prosecuting women for drug use during pregnancy also demonstrates the unequal application of the law. Most of the women who have been charged are poor members of racial minorities.[39] The disproportionate representation of blacks and Hispanics has been attributed, in part, to the fact that they are more likely to use cocaine while white middle-class women use marijuana. They are also more often admitted to public hospitals to deliver their infants; and public hospitals are more likely to conduct toxicological screens and to report the results to the authorities than private hospitals.[40,41]

Another injustice of drug use prosecutions of pregnant women is that they fail to acknowledge that other factors could have been responsible for the birth outcomes.[42] Part of the difficulty in assessing the damage caused by maternal ingestion of substances like cocaine is the lack of data on the father. However, the mother's cocaine use is exacerbated by a number of variables which range from polydrug use to little or no prenatal care and poor maternal nutrition during pregnancy.[43] Habel, et al., examined data obtained from New York City infant birth and death certificates between 1976 and 1986 to explore maternal drug use during pregnancy.[44] They found that only 56 percent of drug-abusing mothers were reported to have had prenatal care compared to 87 percent of all mothers throughout the city.[45] A closer analysis of the drug-abusing sample data found that 61 percent of methadone-maintained pregnant addicts received prenatal care, compared to only 49 percent of the women who were cocaine abusers and 48 percent of the heroin abusers. Marijuana-only users' involvement in prenatal care was similar to that among all mothers, 82 percent.[46]

The fact that prenatal care is not widely available makes the prosecution of these women morally untenable. Chasnoff contends that the developmental risks posed by cocaine use are preventable.[47] In order to deal with them, the public and professional sectors must be educated. Unfortunately, even the primary care physicians do not fully recognize the risks that cocaine use has on the mother and her child.[48] Until such time as drug education and prevention become priorities, it is likely that the number of cocaine-using pregnant women will continue to increase.[49]

Prosecutions of pregnant women are also unfair because they have occurred despite the fact that very little research has been conducted on the effects of drugs on women during pregnancy. Most of our data on drugs which have been gathered on human subjects are from studies conducted on young, adult, healthy males. Not only have very few studies which utilize women subjects been undertaken, but there is an even smaller number conducted on women subjects during various stages like pregnancy and lactation. These studies are expensive and time-consuming; they require researchers to monitor women throughout their pregnancy and then to continue gathering data on their children for many years.[50,51]

Furthermore, women who use cocaine during pregnancy frequently contend with a host of other problems. Chasnoff suggests that women from substance-abusing backgrounds do not have a proper model for parenting.[52] It is insufficient to examine the effects of cocaine without exploring:

> ... the interactive effects of polydrug use, the dynamics of maternal/infant interaction in a substance abusing mother and the environmental factors that place these infants at high risk for future medical and developmental disabilities.[53]

## SANCTIONS IMPOSED ON PREGNANT SUBSTANCE USERS

The sanctions that women who use drugs during pregnancy can be subjected to are too harsh. One case in Washington, involved a pregnant woman who was apprehended for forging $800 in checks. The defendant, Brenda Vaughan, would have normally been placed on probation. However, because she tested positive for cocaine at the time of her arrest, the judge sentenced her to jail for four months in order to protect the fetus from additional exposure.[54]

Not only are these kinds of punishments too harsh, but jail will not do the fetus any good. Inmates have sued women's prisons and jails for the lack of prenatal care they provide pregnant offenders.[55] Women who use drugs frequently enter prison with high risk pregnancies. They need to be carefully monitored; and they require special medical services.[56] Probably, the quality of care that pregnant drug-exposed women receive in custody could be duplicated and significantly improved at substantial savings if provided in the community.

Another example of a harsh sanction occurred in the case of Jennifer Clarise Johnson. Ms. Johnson was convicted in Florida through a unique application of the narcotics laws, in this case delivering a controlled substance to a minor. For Ms. Johnson, delivery took place through the umbilical cord in the minutes after the baby was born. She was sentenced to 15 years probation with a number of special restrictions which included strict supervision, random drug testing and a thorough prenatal care program if she became pregnant.[57]

The sanctions imposed in the Vaughan and Johnson cases are not nearly as common as the removal of the child from the custody of the mother at birth. Prosecuting the mother under narcotics or criminalization laws does not preclude the state from also taking temporary custody of the child.[58] Informant laws are somewhat different, because the sanctions are imposed by the family court as opposed to the criminal court; and it is the infant's dependency or neglect that are at issue as opposed to the mother's criminal conduct. In those instances, a toxicological screen is administered to the infant or mother by the hospital staff.[59] Not surprisingly, those women who are most often tested are the ones who deliver their babies in public hospitals. As previously stated, they tend to be disproportionately poor and minority women.[60]

The fact that it is the family court taking the custody of a newborn away from the mother does not lessen the severity of the sanction. The separation can be harmful for both the mother and the baby. Removing the infant from the mother precludes the mother from bonding with her child, and it subjects the infant to foster care which may be especially disruptive. Besharov reports that 56 percent of the infants who went from hospitals to foster care in a three-year period in New York City had been placed in two or more foster homes, while 20 percent had been placed in three or more homes.[61]

These separations can last for years. A chronology of the steps taken by one New York mother, Michelle Rogers, to convince the authorities she was drug free and able to regain custody of her children was detailed in a recent press account. After Ms. Rogers lost custody of her infant daughter and her other children, she had to prove to the authorities that she was no longer drug dependent and then obtain appropriate housing. Although the judge had decided to return the children to their mother in July of 1990, she did not have an apartment. At a cost of $19,000 per year, the children stayed in foster homes for two years.[62] It was not until January of 1991 that Ms. Rogers was able to persuade an apartment owner to rent to a mother on public assistance. The judge then determined that she was able to be reunited with her children. At the hearing, the Judge, noting the high cost of foster care, commented that the system should be doing more to help mothers like Ms. Rogers.[63]

## LIMITED EFFECTIVENESS OF THE SANCTIONS

The removal of the custody of infants from women substance users is especially severe if one realizes that, even for those women who want to get treatment for their drug use, there are few such programs available. In her survey of drug treatment programs in New York City, Chavkin found that 54 percent would not accept pregnant women and 67 percent refused women whose costs were being paid by Medicaid.[64] Most programs are concerned with the liability of treating women who are pregnant.

Those drug treatment programs that are available frequently fail to provide integrated services for pregnant women. For example, when Habel, et al., reported that 61 percent of the methadone-maintained women obtained prenatal care, they found no explanation for the other 39 percent of methadone-maintained women who did not obtain prenatal care. They suggest that their data demonstrate a lack of coordination between drug treatment and prenatal services.[65]

Informant laws are only as effective as the health care professionals who choose to cooperate and do so on a consistent and fair basis. Frequently, the laws are premised on physicians or other health care professionals acting as deputies in investigating cases of suspected maternal drug use and then contacting the authorities. Such procedures may result in women avoiding prenatal care for fear of apprehension.[66]

Additionally, health care professionals rely on their patients to give them detailed background information in order to be able to most effectively treat them. This information is especially critical if the mother is using cocaine.[67] Forcing the women who most need closely monitored prenatal care underground cannot serve to protect the fetus or society's interests.

Before resorting to legal intervention, states could pursue some alternative approaches. For example, states should provide educational materials, counseling services, parenting training and support groups in each community.[68] In order to facilitate the participation of at risk parents and prospective parents, day care services and a convenient and accessible location are critical. If prospective parents are made aware of the dangers of their behavior and offered assistance, the incidence of drug-exposed infants could be reduced.

One of the most serious consequences of this increased focus on the welfare of those fetuses that are exposed to drugs is that it diverts attention away from the staggering incidence of infant mortality in America. The infant mortality rate in the United States is reprehensible. According to 1987 data, the United States ranks twentieth in infant mortality when compared to other industrialized countries.[69] For every 1,000 live births in 1987, the overall infant mortality rate was 10.1. For blacks, the rate was 17.9; and for whites it was 8.6.[70] For one of the wealthiest countries in the world to rank twentieth in infant mortality cannot be justified.

To understand infant mortality it is necessary to examine a number of factors that are related to it. First, good quality prenatal care is not available for all expectant mothers. For example, in 1985 one third of all the women who gave birth did not have adequate prenatal care.[71] The fact that pregnant women do not receive such care can result in poor nutrition and diet, lack of appropriate history taking and fetal monitoring, high risk deliveries, and low birth weight infants. Until such time as the government is prepared to commit the necessary resources for prenatal care for all women, it will continue to have to bear the cost for infant mortality, premature and high risk births, and drug dependent or drug-exposed infants who may require long term hospital stays.

At least part of the problem can be attributed to the lack of health insurance. Paltrow reports that 25 percent of all women in America have no coverage for prenatal care or delivery.[72] Medicaid cannot compensate for the increasing number of women who do not have private insurance because it provides coverage to only 40 percent of the women living below the poverty line, more and more obstetricians are opting not to participate in the program, and the bureaucratic paper work and late payment to providers discourage both patients and doctors from involvement.[73]

Finally, prosecuting pregnant women for drug use is an illusory way of dealing with the drug problem in America. Such actions convey the message that the public is concerned enough about drugs to penalize pregnant women for drug use. Unfortunately, while these ill-advised prosecutions appeal to the public as a "get tough" approach to the problem, they only serve to deter the development of more effective methods of prevention.[74]

## CONCLUSION

Rather than prosecute women who use drugs during pregnancy, the government should opt for a more comprehensive approach to the problem. The number of drug prevention and drug education programs needs to be substantially increased. For too long, the focus of governmental efforts to deal with the drug problem have been oriented toward control rather than prevention.

The government should take immediate action to commit its resources to a nationwide program designed to reduce the appalling rate of infant mortality in the United States. The fact that good prenatal care is unavailable to many women is a tragedy. Any action that can extend such care to poor women and facilitate their involvement in programs should be pursued. For example, the state of Ohio has recently expedited the administrative process for poor women to get prenatal care. Officials there prepared a single four-page application to enroll pregnant women for extra benefits like supplemental food and care. The previous application was 36 pages and the women frequently cited its length and the cumbersome procedures as impediments to participating.[75]

There is some evidence that such intervention can ameliorate the effects of drug exposure. A study conducted by the National Association of Perinatal Addiction Research and Education followed 300 children from the beginning of their mothers' pregnancy. Not only were the mothers provided with prenatal care and a balanced diet, but they were also monitored after the births and offered assistance with their children. The preliminary results indicate that 60 to 70 percent of the drug-exposed infants showed no perceptible problems at age 3 or 4.[76]

The government needs to increase the number of drug treatment programs for both men and women. Not only are more programs necessary, but the government also should revise the policies which discourage poor and minority women from securing treatment. Currently, Medicaid rules preclude payment for residential drug treatment because substance abuse is classified as a form of mental illness. Congress should enact legislation that would eliminate such policies.[77]

Communities ought to provide more services for prospective and new parents. In addition to prenatal and postnatal care, these services should include parenting classes, nutrition classes, and child care services. Such programs would assist parents in coping with their new babies and might also help to identify infants who need special services.

During the last 10 years we have begun to realize that there are no quick and easy solutions to the drug problem in America. These proposals represent a long-term approach to dealing with drugs. As indicated by preliminary results from the National Association of Perinatal Addiction Research and Education study, sustained intervention early in the pregnancy of drug users and after the children are born reduces the harmful effects of exposure. Surely, the lives of children are worth the investment.

## NOTES

1. Habel, Leo, Kaye, Katherine, and Lee, Jean, "Trends in Reporting of Maternal Drug Abuse and Infant Mortality Among Drug-Exposed Infants in New York City," *Women & Health*, 1990, 16:45.

2. Nolan, Kathleen, "Protecting Fetuses from Prenatal Hazards: Whose Crimes? What Punishments?" *Criminal Justice Ethics*, 1990, 9, Winter/Spring:14.

3. Logli, Paul A., "Drugs in the Womb: The Newest Battlefield in the War on Drugs" *Criminal Justice Ethics*, 1990, Winter/Spring, p. 23–29.

4. Nolan, 1990, p. 14.

5. Besharov, Douglas J, "The Children of Crack: Will We Protect them?" *Public Welfare*, 1989, 47:7.

6. Editorial, "How to Protect Babies from Crack," *New York Times*, March 11, 1991, A14.

7. Daley, Suzanne, "Born on Crack, and Coping with Kindergarten," *New York Times*, Feb. 7, 1991, A1–13.

8. Ibid.

9. Nolan, 1990.

10. Anderson, Sandra C. and Grant, James Fraser, "Pregnant Women and Alcohol: Implications for Social Work," *Social Casework*, January, 1984.

11. Nolan, 1990.

12. Greenhouse, Linda, "5 Justices Uphold U.S. Rule Curbing Abortion Advice," *New York Times*, May 24, 1991, p. 1.

13. Ibid.

14. Lewin, Tamar, "Implanted Birth Control Device Renews Debate Over Forced Contraception," *New York Times*, January 10, 1991, A13.

15. Ibid. See also Lev, Michael, "Judge Firm on Forced Contraception," *New York Times*, January 11, 1991, A12.

16. Lev, 1991.

17. Ibid.

18. Lewin, Tamar, "Strict Anti-Abortion Law Signed in Utah," *New York Times*, January 26, 1991, 10.

19. Pollitt, Katha, "Tyranny of the Foetus," *New Statesman & Society*, March 30, 1990, 28–30.

20. Rosenthal, Elisabeth, "AIDS Infection Often Blocks Abortion Access, Study Says," *New York Times*, Oct. 23, 1990, A1, B2.

21. London, Robb "2 Dismissed in Warning on Alcohol and Pregnancy," *New York Times*, March 30, 1991, 5.

22. Kantrowitz, Barbara; Quade, Vicki; Fisher, Binnie; Hill, James; and Beachy, Lucille, "The Pregnancy Police," *Newsweek*, Vol. CXVII, April 29, 1991, 52.

23. Ibid.

24. Merlo, Alida V, "Pregnant Women Substance Abusers: The New Female Offender," Paper presented at the Annual Meeting of the American Society of Criminology, November 10, 1990. Baltimore, Maryland.

25. Ibid.

26. Pollock-Byrne, Jocelyn M. and Merlo, Alida V, "Against Compulsory Treatment: No 'Quick Fix' for Pregnant Substance Users," 1991. Under review for publication.

27. Merlo, 1990.

28. Curriden, Mark, "Holding Mom Accountable," *American Bar Association Journal*, 1990, March 1990, 50–53.

29. Robin-Vergeer, Bonnie I., "The Problem of the Drug-Exposed New Born: A Return to Principled Intervention," *Stanford Law Review*, 1990, 42:745–809.

30. Chavkin, Wendy, "Drug Addiction and Pregnancy: Policy Crossroads," *American Journal of Public Health*, 1990, 80:483–487.

31. Spitzer, Brian C, "A Response to 'Cocaine Babies'—Amendment of Florida's Child Abuse and Neglect Laws to Encompass Infants Born Drug Dependent," *Florida State University Law Review*, 1987, 15:865–884.

32. Blumberg, Lisa, "Why Fetal Rights Must Be Opposed," *Social Policy*, 18, Fall 1990, 40–41.

33. Robinson, Rita, "High-Proof Paternity," *Health*, June 20, 1988.

34. Ibid.

35. John, Esther M., Savitz, David A., and Sandler, Dale P, "Prenatal Exposure to Parents' Smoking

and Childhood Cancer," *American Journal of Epidemiology*, 133, January 1991, 123–132.

36. Ibid.

37. "Greater Risk of Cancer is Reported in Children of Fathers Who Smoke," *New York Times*, Jan. 24, 1991, A11.

38. McNulty, Molly, "Pregnancy Police: The Health Policy and Legal Implications of Punishing Pregnant Women for Harm to Their Fetuses," *Review of Law & Social Change*, 1987–1988, XVI:277–319.

39. Kolata, Gina, "Racial Bias Seen on Pregnant Addicts," *New York Times*, July 20, 1990, A13.

40. Ibid.

41. Robin-Vergeer, 1990.

42. Mariner, Wendy K., Glantz, Leonard H., and Annas, George J, "Pregnancy, Drugs, and the Perils of Prosecution," *Criminal Justice Ethics*, Winter/Spring, 1990, 30–41.

43. "Behavior Varies in Babies Exposed to Cocaine," *New York Times*, January 22, 1991, B6.

44. Habel, et al., 1990.

45. Ibid., p. 49.

46. Ibid., p. 54.

47. Chasnoff, Ira J, "Cocaine, Pregnancy, and the Neonate," *Women & Health*, 1989, 15:23–35.

48. Ibid., p. 34.

49. Ibid.

50. Berlin, Cheston M, "Women's Health: Pregnancy and Childbirth. The Use of Drugs During Pregnancy and Lactation," *Public Health Reports*, 102, July/August, 1987:54.

51. Pollock-Byrne and Merlo, 1991.

52. Chasnoff, 1989.

53. Ibid., p. 34.

54. Johnsen, Dawn, "From Driving to Drugs: Government Regulation of Pregnant Women's Lives After Webster," *University of Pennsylvania Law Review*, 1989, 138:179–215.

55. Stein, Loren and Mistiaen, Veronique, "Pregnant in Prison," *The Progressive*, 52, February 1988: 18–21.

56. Ibid.

57. Logli, 1990, p. 25.

58. Merlo, 1990.

59. Robin-Vergeer, 1990.

60. Kolata, 1990.

61. Besharov, 1990, p. 16.

62. Rimer, Sara, "Snapping Red Tape to Regain Children," *New York Times*, January 25, 1991, A16.

63. Ibid.

64. Chavkin, 1990, p. 485.

65. Habel, et al., 1990, p. 56.

66. McNulty, 1987–1988. See also Thompson, Elizabeth L. Note: "The Criminalization of Maternal Conduct During Pregnancy: A Decisionmaking Model for Lawmakers," *Indiana Law Journal*, 1989, 64:357–374; Note: "Maternal Rights and Fetal Wrongs: The Case Against the Criminalization of 'Fetal Abuse'," *Harvard Law Review*, 1988, 101, March:994–1012; and Chavkin, 1990.

67. Chasnoff, 1989.

68. Kahn, Judith, "Of Women's First Disobedience: Forsaking A Duty of Care to Her Fetus—Is This A Mother's Crime?" *Brooklyn Law Review*, 1987, 53:807–843.

69. Friend, Tim, "Infant Mortality Could Soar," *USA Today*, March 11, 1990, A1.

70. Pear, Robert, "Study Says U.S. Needs to Battle Infant Mortality," *New York Times*, Aug. 6, 1990, A1 and B9.

71. Johnsen, 1989, p. 210.

72. Paltrow, Lynn M., " 'Fetal Abuse' Should We Recognize It As A Crime? No," *American Bar Association Journal*, 1989, 75, August: 39.

73. McNulty, 1987–1988, p. 318.

74. Thompson, 1989, p. 374.

75. Frankel, Bruce, "Ohio Tackles Growing Rate of Infant Mortality," *USA Today*, March 28, 1991, 5A.

76. Daley, 1991, p. A13.

77. Editorial, 1991, p. A14.

*An earlier version of this paper was presented at the Annual Meeting of the Academy of Criminal Justice Sciences on March 6, 1991, in Nashville, Tennessee.

# POSTSCRIPT

## Should Drug Use by Pregnant Women Be Considered Child Abuse?

Recently the need for medical intervention and specialized treatment programs to serve pregnant women who have drug problems has been recognized. The groundwork has been set for funding and developing such programs. The Office of Substance Abuse Prevention is funding chemical dependency programs specifically for pregnant women in several states.

Merlo argues that federal and state programs are being created on the premise that drug use by pregnant women is a medical problem and needs medical, not criminal, attention. She supports the notion that pregnant drug users and their drug-exposed infants are victims of the disease called "chemical dependency." She also feels that these women lack proper medical care because they are poor. However, as drug treatment programs for pregnant women are developed, so is further legislation intended to punish the mother.

Logli argues that "eliminating the pain, suffering and death resulting from drug exposure in newborns must be a prosecutor's priority." He insists that the criminal justice system should protect newborns and, if legal cause does exist for prosecution, then statutes should provide protection for the fetus. However, will prosecution result in more protection or less protection for the fetus?

If women can be prosecuted for using illegal drugs like cocaine and narcotics during pregnancy because they harm the fetus, then should women who smoke cigarettes and drink alcohol during pregnancy also be prosecuted? The evidence is clear that tobacco and alcohol place the fetus at great risk; however, most discussions of prosecuting pregnant drug users overlook women who use these drugs. Also, the harm caused by secondhand smoke is well documented. Should people be prosecuted if they smoke around pregnant women?

Two recent studies throw doubt on the harmful effects of drugs. In "The Problem of Prenatal Cocaine Exposure: A Rush to Judgment," *Journal of the American Medical Association* (January 15, 1992), Linda Mayes and her colleagues report that the adverse effects that are often seen in babies born to mothers who use cocaine may result from their environment. Ernest Abel and Robert Sokol, in "A Revised Conservative Estimate of the Incidence of FAS and its Economic Impact," *Alcoholism: Clinical and Experimental Research* (June 1991), indicate that the extent of fetal alcohol syndrome is overestimated. The position of the American Bar Association is spelled out in its 1990 publication *Drug Exposed Infants and Their Families: Coordinating Responses of the Legal, Medical and Child Protection System.*

# PART 2

## Researching Tobacco, Caffeine, and Alcohol

*Debates about drugs often center on the use of illegal drugs. Yet, the drugs most frequently used in society are legal drugs. Because of their prevalence, the adverse effects of tobacco, alcohol, and caffeine are minimized or discounted. Although caffeine use is not fatal, tobacco and alcohol are directly or indirectly responsible for far more deaths and disabilities than all illegal drugs combined.*

*The following debates do not question the harmful effects of tobacco smoking and alcohol consumption but the dangers of passive smoking and the causes of alcoholism. The role of caffeine in the development of heart disease and other health conditions is also debated in this section.*

Is Passive Smoking Harmful to Nonsmokers?

Can Caffeine Be Bad for Your Health?

Is Alcoholism Hereditary?

# ISSUE 8

## Is Passive Smoking Harmful to Nonsmokers?

**YES: Richard G. Schlaadt,** from *Tobacco and Health* (The Dushkin Publishing Group, 1992)

**NO: Gary L. Huber, Robert E. Brockie, and Vijay K. Mahajan,** from "Passive Smoking: How Great a Hazard?" *Consumers' Research* (July 1991)

### ISSUE SUMMARY

**YES:** Based on his review of numerous studies, Richard G. Schlaadt, director of the University of Oregon Substance Abuse Program, concludes that the evidence regarding passive smoking shows that it poses a great risk to nonsmokers.

**NO:** Physicians Gary L. Huber, Robert E. Brockie, and Vijay K. Mahajan contend that claims about the adverse effects of passive smoking are not based on scientific fact because the level of exposure to secondhand smoke and the dose retained by nonsmokers cannot be measured.

The movement to restrict passive smoking is growing. Smoking has been banned on all commercial airplane flights within the continental United States. Canada and Australia have similar bans. Railroads restrict smoking to certain passenger cars. Smoking is prohibited or restricted in all federal public areas and workplaces. The right to smoke in public places is quickly being eliminated. Is this fair, considering tobacco's hold over smokers? Former surgeon general C. Everett Koop called smoking an addiction that is as difficult to overcome as addiction to cocaine and heroin. Should a person be penalized for having a nicotine addiction?

Articles about passive smoking can be confusing because several terms are frequently used to describe passive smoking. *Passive smoking* has been referred to as *involuntary smoking,* and the smoke itself has been identified as both *secondhand smoke* and *environmental tobacco smoke,* or *ETS.* Secondhand smoke is further broken down into *mainstream smoke* and *sidestream smoke.* Mainstream smoke is the smoke that the smoker exhales. Sidestream smoke is the smoke that comes off the end of the tobacco product as it burns. Ironically, sidestream smoke has higher concentrations of carbon monoxide and other gases than mainstream smoke. Scientists also believe that sidestream smoke contains more carcinogens than mainstream smoke.

The issue of passive smoking is extremely divisive. On one side of the debate are nonsmokers, who strongly believe that their rights to clean air are being violated by smokers. Their objections are based on more than aesthetics; it is not simply a matter of smoke being unsightly or noxious. Nonsmokers are more concerned about the health effects of smoke. Groups of nonsmokers and numerous health professionals have initiated a massive campaign to educate the public on the array of health-related problems associated with inhaling the smoke that is generated by those who smoke tobacco products.

On the other side are smokers, who believe that they should have the right to smoke. This group is backed by the tobacco industry, which has allocated much money to conduct research on the effects of secondhand smoke. Based on the results of these studies, smoking rights groups claim that the health concerns related to secondhand smoke are based on emotion, not scientific evidence. They argue that there are too many variables involved to determine the exact impact of secondhand smoke. For example, to what extent does a polluted atmosphere or a poorly ventilated house contribute to the health problems that are attributed to secondhand smoke? Also, some smokers and tobacco companies contend that what the nonsmokers call an educational campaign is in reality a program of indoctrination. Additionally, they argue that there are already enough laws in place that restrict smokers.

Even smokers who acknowledge that smoke may have adverse effects on health argue that their freedoms should not be limited. They feel that they should have the right to engage in behaviors, even if those behaviors are unhealthy. These smokers reason that if smoking behavior is regulated, perhaps other behaviors, such as eating, will also become regulated. They fight against the regulation of smoking because they believe that behavior regulation is a harmful trend.

If tobacco smoking is restricted, many people employed by the tobacco industry may lose their jobs. What may be seen as a health benefit to some people will be detrimental to the economic health of others. Are those people who want to restrict smoking and who will consequently affect the financial prosperity of others be willing to help these affected individuals?

In the following selections, the authors look at the research data and arrive at different conclusions. Richard G. Schlaadt argues that there is now substantial evidence that exposure to even low doses of secondhand smoke is harmful, especially to young children and fetuses. Gary L. Huber, Robert E. Brockie, and Vijay K. Mahajan claim that much of the information about the health hazards of passive smoking has been distorted by a "social movement" and has been accepted as fact without adequate critical questioning.

# YES

Richard G. Schlaadt

# THE INNOCENT VICTIMS

Any argument that supports a person's right to engage in something potentially dangerous relies strongly on the notion that the chosen activity—whether it's race car driving, fire swallowing, or walking a tightrope—will harm only the participant and not innocent passersby. For many years, advocates of smokers' rights applied this theory in good faith, believing that only smokers themselves could suffer lung cancer, bronchitis, or any of the other diseases caused by cigarettes. There was, they stressed, no documented proof to the contrary, but in late 1986 two reports delivered a stunning blow to these advocates. In their respective reports, both the National Research Council and the U.S. Surgeon General found that environmental smoke—that is, sidestream smoke from a cigarette—could threaten the health of nonsmokers who are exposed to it. In the meantime, scientists were gathering increasing evidence linking smoking during pregnancy to such birth defects as low birth weight. By the end of 1986, the message was clear: Smoking is dangerous not only to those who smoke, but to nonsmokers and unborn children as well.

## SOME STARTLING RESULTS

The two 1986 reports were both based on comprehensive studies and reached very similar conclusions. For the sake of simplicity, [we] will focus mostly on the first of the two studies to be released, that of the National Research Council. This report examined the amount of chemicals passive smokers inhale and found that nonsmokers exposed to sidestream smoke (also called environmental tobacco smoke, or ETS) had significantly higher levels of nicotine in their blood, urine, and saliva than those who were not exposed.[1]

Next the report looked at how passive smoking among pregnant women affected the growth of their newborns. Later on . . . we will take a look at the damages pregnant women who smoke cause their unborn children. Husbands who smoke and expose their pregnant wives who do not smoke to

ETS may also cause damage. One study, first done in 1966 and confirmed in 1971, found that babies of mothers exposed to ETS from a smoking father suffer almost as high an incidence of low birth weight as do the babies of actively smoking mothers.[2] Furthermore, the study found that the low birth weight babies of actively smoking mothers were in fact healthier than those of actively smoking fathers (and, therefore, passively smoking mothers).[3] Another study of 5,000 children done in 1973 showed that babies whose fathers smoked more than 10 cigarettes a day had a higher incidence of prenatal death than did the babies of nonsmoking parents.[4] Finally, the most recent study, conducted in 1986 among 500 newborn babies, found that smoking among fathers during the first trimester of the mothers' pregnancy reduced the weight of their newborn babies 12 grams (about half an ounce) per 10 cigarettes smoked per day.[5] In other words, if the husband of a pregnant woman smokes a pack each day—and his wife is exposed to the sidestream smoke of each cigarette—that baby's weight will be reduced by one ounce each day.

The dangers of passive smoking do not end for a child once he or she is born. One study found that children exposed to ETS at home on a regular basis had a lower rate of growth than did children of nonsmoking parents; more specifically, the children studied lost .03 cms a day from their normal rate of growth for every 20 cigarettes smoked each day in their home.[6] Three surveys of the children over the age of 5 who had smoking mothers (including those whose mothers did not smoke during pregnancy) found that the exposure to sidestream smoke curtailed the development of the children's lung capacity. That is, the growth of each child's lung capacity was much slower and less complete than that of the children of nonsmoking mothers.

Possibly related to this finding are the studies citing the rate of lung irritation suffered by children of smoking parents. Six studies in the report found that this group suffered a significantly higher incidence of minor lung infections, such as wheezing and coughing, than do the children of nonsmoking parents. One such study, which surveyed 5,000 British students who live at home, found that while 16 percent of children with nonsmoking parents had a cough, 18 percent of children with one smoking parent had a cough, and 23.5 percent of children with two smoking parents suffered this irritation.[7] Other studies showed that bronchitis and pneumonia occurred more frequently in children with one or more smoking parents than in those whose parents did not smoke. Yet another study found a direct relationship between the amount of maternal smoking and the rate of lung infection during the first year of life.[8] This relationship lessened significantly during the second year of life and disappeared altogether during the third.

Just as shocking as the statistics concerning children were the report's findings involving the link between passive smoking and lung cancer. The findings published in the report concerned nonsmokers married to smokers. According to these findings, exposure to sidestream smoke increases the lung cancer risk of a person married to a smoker by 25 percent.[9] The same studies reported that nonsmokers who are not married to smokers but who may come in regular contact with ETS in the workplace or in a restaurant have an 8 percent increased risk of getting the disease compared to those who are not exposed at all. All in all, the National Academy of Sciences reports that passive smoking may be responsible for as many as 24,000 deaths from lung cancer every year.[10] The report's final conclusion is that passive smokers receive about 3/4 of 1 percent of the elements active smokers inhale, and that for every 100,000 people exposed to ETS, 390 will suffer lung cancer.

Published a month after the first report, the 1986 Surgeon General's Report reached the same conclusions: Passive smoking can cause disease in non-smokers, and children of parents who smoke have a greater risk of suffering respiratory infections such as bronchitis and pneumonia than do children of non-smoking parents.[11] Furthermore, the report stressed that the risk of passive smoking would not be eliminated by separating nonsmokers and smokers within the same air space.

## NONSMOKERS VS. SMOKERS

The excitement and passionate responses the publication of the two reports generated was not limited to nonsmokers. Representatives from the tobacco companies protested the studies' conclusions, claiming that the findings were not conclusive. This may be true to a certain extent. It is very difficult to establish beyond a shadow of a doubt the biological process by which sidestream smoke causes cancer. Nevertheless, studies have continued to accumulate information linking the likelihood of smoking-related diseases to the noxious chemicals found in sidestream smoke. Studies done in late 1989 and in 1990 have not only confirmed the conclusions the two 1986 reports reached, but have gone on to find further possible links.

One study of 674 women done in Utah in 1989, for example, found that women who were exposed to sidestream smoke on a regular basis were more likely to suffer cervical cancer than were those not exposed.[12] (The National Academy of Science report did not find a significant association between passive smoking and any cancers other than lung cancer.) Although clinical evidence suggests that cervical cancer results from a virus, researchers involved in the Utah study claim that passive smoking may make the cervix more vulnerable to viral infection. The study remains controversial and for the most part inconclusive. Skeptics claim that active and passive smokers may be more likely to have multiple sex partners than those who are not exposed to smoke, and that this is what increases one's likelihood of getting cervical cancer.

Although some studies remain inconclusive, the possibilities they present are frightening and have raised the ire of people who work or eat in the same restaurants as smokers. Lawmakers have concurred with this view. Within two years of the publication of the two reports, virtually every airline banned smoking on domestic airline flights shorter than two hours (this regulation has since been extended to cover all domestic flights). Many state-government-run and private companies posted stringent antismoking laws, limiting smoking only to designated areas, such as smoking lounges and private offices, and sometimes outlawing it altogether on company premises. Restaurants split their seating areas into nonsmoking and smoking sections and came under public pressure to eliminate smoking areas completely. Anti-smokers urging this say, and have hard evidence supporting them, that sharing air space with smokers—even if they are in separate areas—is a major health hazard. . . .

## TOBACCO AND PREGNANCY

Passive smokers are innocent victims of cigarette smoke and its potential health dangers. Without engaging in the habit themselves, they are, often involuntarily, exposed to ETS. But passive smokers can do some things to protect themselves. They can often walk away from a smoker. They can request a friend to extinguish his or her cigarette. They can petition for more stringent antismoking laws. Unborn babies who come in contact with cigarette smoke can do none of these things. Instead, protecting an unborn child is left solely to the mother's discretion. If a pregnant woman chooses to smoke, she is placing her unborn child in grave danger of serious physical or mental damage.

### Low Birth Weight

Cigarette smoking during pregnancy can cause premature birth, low birth weight, shorter body length, breathing difficulties at birth, behavioral and learning problems, and hyperactivity. The most frequent of these defects is low birth weight. This occurs when the fetus's growth and development within the mother's uterus is slowed or retarded, a condition known as intrauterine growth retardation (IUGR). IUGR results when the flow of oxygen and nutrients to the fetus is cut off or interfered with. Hundreds of scientific surveys have studied the link between cigarette smoking and low birth weight. One of these reports surveyed 127,000 American women who became mothers between 1979 and 1985 and found that babies of women who

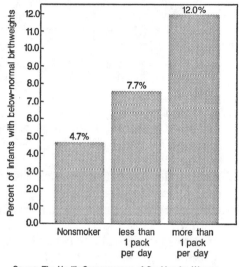

**Low Birth Weight and Smoking**

Source: *The Health Consequences of Smoking for Women,* Department of Health and Human Services, 1981.

Infants whose mothers smoke more than one pack of cigarettes per day are more than twice as likely to be underweight at birth as infants born to nonsmoking mothers.

smoked more than a pack of cigarettes a day during pregnancy were an average of 11.7 ounces lighter than the children of women who did not smoke. Five studies concerning 113,000 births in the United States, Canada, and Wales found that mothers who smoke lightly to moderately were 50 percent more likely—and those who smoke heavily twice as likely—to have babies weighing less than 5 pounds.[13]

Low birth weight can also cause a host of other problems. For example, it can increase the child's risk of suffering physical and mental defects, illnesses, learning disabilities, and behavioral problems. It can also lower the child's survival rate: the lower the child's weight at birth, the lower his or her chances of survival. The average weight of a newborn is between 7 and 9 pounds. Babies

## INFERTILITY AND SMOKING

We know that a pregnant woman's smoking can harm her unborn baby, and that the smoke inhaled from parental cigarettes can impair an infant's health. Can the habit also hurt a couple's chance of conceiving a child in the first place?

While it has not been proved that smoking leads to infertility, a relationship has long been suspected, and several studies have strongly suggested a cause-and-effect relationship.

In one recently reported study, a team from the National Institute of Environmental Health Sciences investigated the time required for 678 women to become pregnant after they had stopped using birth control because they wanted to conceive.

The results: during the first menstrual cycle, 38 percent of the nonsmokers conceived, but only 28 percent of the smokers did so. And the smokers were 3.4 times more likely to take more than a year to become pregnant. The researchers estimated that smokers were only 72 percent as fertile as nonsmokers and that those who smoked more than a pack a day had only 57 percent of the fertility of nonsmokers.

Their conclusion: "Reduced fertility should be added to the growing list of reproductive hazards of cigarette smoking."

Does the hazard persist? Or does an ex-smoker regain a nonsmoker's chances of conceiving? Among the women studied, 31 had stopped smoking within the year before attempting to become pregnant. These women did not experience reduced fertility. The investigators cautioned, however, that the number was too small to interpret definitively.

Source: Dodi Schultz, *Priorities* (Winter 1989), p. 5.

who weigh less than 5.8 pounds have a significant risk of dying. Those weighing 3.5 pounds or less are in very grave danger indeed.

### Premature Birth

Smoking increases the likelihood of vaginal bleeding during pregnancy, which can in turn lead to premature birth. Even if bleeding does not occur, studies show that premature birth occurs 10 percent more frequently among moderate smokers and 20 percent more frequently among heavy smokers than among nonsmokers.[14] Premature babies not only are underweight but can suffer a host of problems, such as underdevelopment of the respiratory tract, nervous system, muscles, and other organs. Cigarettes also increase a woman's risk of suffering a miscarriage or stillbirth or of the child dying during his or her first weeks of life. According to studies, smokers have a 30 to 70 percent greater chance of suffering a miscarriage than nonsmokers, depending in part on the number of cigarettes smoked each day. One study found that smoking a pack a day or more virtually doubled the risk of miscarriage.[15] Smoking also increases the rate of stillbirths, particularly among women who are receiving poor prenatal care because of socioeconomic factors, such as poverty or lack of education.[16]

## Respiratory Infections and Other Illnesses

Children of smokers are especially susceptible to certain health ailments. Earlier we saw that passive smoking increases a child's susceptibility to respiratory infection. The same holds true for the children of mothers who smoked during pregnancy even if they have quit since giving birth. Several studies have shown that these babies have more illnesses before the age of 5 than do the children of nonsmokers. They have a significantly higher frequency of colds, for example, which can in turn lead to more serious problems, such as lung and ear infections.[17] Researchers have also found that the babies of smokers suffer a higher rate of bronchitis and pneumonia during their first year of life.

The risk of illness is not limited to the respiratory system. There is evidence that the babies of mothers who smoked during pregnancy are as much as 50 percent more likely to suffer childhood cancers such as leukemia than the children of nonsmoking mothers. Many studies have found that these babies have an increased likelihood of suffering behavioral problems, such as hyperactivity. This disorder is characterized by excitability, concentration problems, and overactivity.

## Congenital Deformities

It has not been definitively proven that cigarette smoking during pregnancy can cause congenital deformities, but some studies have found that children of mothers who smoke may have a higher frequency of heart malformations, abnormally small jaws and mouths, and upturned noses than those of nonsmokers. Several studies have found that smoking mothers who also take tranquilizers have a decidedly higher risk of bearing a deformed child than do mothers who do not take any drugs. Scientists are continuing to conduct surveys of smoking mothers to determine more conclusively if there is a link between smoking and congenital malformations.

## Chemicals That Cross the Placenta

Scientists have studied not only the ways cigarette smoking can damage an unborn child, but the reasons these problems occur.... [C]igarette smoke ... is comprised of nearly 4,000 different compounds, such as nicotine and carbon monoxide. It also contains some heavy metals, such as cadmium and lead.

These two elements enter the blood every time a cigarette smoker inhales, and they can cause grave damage to the placenta. In animal studies, even low doses of cadmium resulted in low birth weights. In these same animal studies, at high concentrations cadmium caused miscarriages, stillbirths, and malformed offspring. Lead can interfere with the fetus's enzyme systems; studies show that babies born to smoking mothers have a significantly reduced enzyme activity compared to those of nonsmokers.

Cyanide from cigarette smoke also travels to the bloodstream. The body's metabolic process quickly converts this chemical to thiocyanate, a substance that is normally present in the human body in minute quantities from the foods we eat. But cyanide and thiocyanate are both toxic compounds and at higher levels can reduce the ability of cells to use oxygen, interfere with the body's ability to process vitamin $B_{12}$, and damage brain cells. Many scientists believe that thiocyanate is a significant cause of low birth weight babies among smokers.

## Perinatal Mortality and Smoking

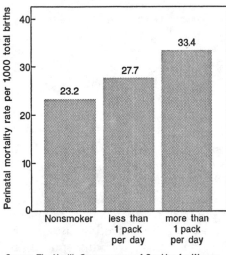

Source: *The Health Consequences of Smoking for Women*, Department of Health and Human Services, 1981.

Women who smoke one or more packs of cigarettes a day have approximately a 50 percent greater chance of losing their child during or prior to birth.

## NOTES

1. *Environmental Tobacco Smoke: Measuring Exposures and Assessing Health Effects* (Washington, DC: National Research Council, 1986), 144.
2. *Environmental Tobacco Smoke*, p. 269.
3. *Environmental Tobacco Smoke*, p. 270.
4. *Environmental Tobacco Smoke*, p. 271.
5. *Environmental Tobacco Smoke*, p. 271.
6. *Environmental Tobacco Smoke*, p. 268.
7. *Environmental Tobacco Smoke*, p. 191.
8. *Environmental Tobacco Smoke*, p. 205.
9. *Environmental Tobacco Smoke*, p. 245.
10. "Involuntary Risk," *Time*, 29 December 1986, 64.
11. "Passive Smoking: Beliefs, Attitudes, and Exposures," *Journal of the American Medical Association* (20 May 1988): 1986.
12. K. A. Fackelman, "More Cervical Cancer in Passive Smokers," *Science News* (18 March 1989): 166.
13. Patrick Young, *Drugs and Pregnancy* (New York: Chelsea House Publishers, 1987), 55.
14. Dodi Schultz, "Born Under a Cloud," *Priorities*, Winter 1989, 6.
15. Young, p. 56.
16. Young, p. 56.
17. Schultz, p. 7.

Nicotine and carbon monoxide are the two most studied chemicals in cigarette smoke. Both cross the placenta. Nicotine causes blood vessels to narrow, including those that carry blood through the placenta. As a result, blood flow to the placenta is reduced, lessening the organ's ability to supply nutrients to the unborn child. . . . [C]arboxyhemoglobin forms when carbon monoxide bonds to hemoglobin. The blood of a smoker contains 4 to 5 times the amount of this compound as does that of a nonsmoker, and the level of carboxyhemoglobin in the fetus runs 10 percent to 20 percent higher than in its mother. The presence of carboxyhemoglobin interferes with the flow of oxygen and nutrients to the fetus, which we know is a major cause of IUGR and low birth weight.

It is easy to conclude from the studies done on passive smokers and the children of smoking mothers that nobody should smoke cigarettes, period.

# NO

## Gary L. Huber, Robert E. Brockie, and Vijay K. Mahajan

## PASSIVE SMOKING: HOW GREAT A HAZARD?

About 50 million or so Americans are active smokers, consuming well over 500 billion tobacco cigarettes each year. The "secondhand" smoke—usually called "environmental tobacco smoke," or more simply "ETS"—that is generated is released into their surroundings, where it potentially is inhaled passively and retained by nonsmokers. Or is it?

Literally thousands of ETS-related statements now have appeared in the lay press or in the scientific literature. Many of these have been published, and accepted as fact, without adequate critical questioning. Based on the belief that these publications are accurate, numerous public policies, regulations, and laws have been implemented to segregate or restrict active smokers, on the assertion that ETS is a health hazard to those who do not smoke.

What *quantity* of smoke really is released into the environment of the nonsmoker? What is the chemical and physical *quality*, or nature, of ETS remnants in our environment? Is there a health risk to the nonsmoker? In concentrations as low as one part in a billion or even in a trillion parts of clean air, some of the highly-diluted constituents in ETS are irritating to the membranes of the eyes and nose of the nonsmoker. Cigarette smoking is offensive to many nonsmokers and some of these highly-diluted constituents can trigger adverse emotional responses, but do these levels of exposure really represent a legitimate health hazard?

Clear answers to these questions are difficult to find. The generation, interpretation, and use of scientific and medical information about ETS has been influenced, and probably distorted, by a "social movement" to shift the emphasis on the adverse health effects of smoking in the active smoker to an implied health risk for the nonsmoker. The focus of this movement, initiated by Sir George Godber of the World Health Organization 15 years ago, was and is to emphasize that active cigarette smokers injure those around them,

From Gary L. Huber, Robert E. Brockie, and Vijay K. Mahajan, "Passive Smoking: How Great a Hazard?" *Consumers' Research* (July 1991). Copyright © 1991 by Consumers' Research, Inc., 800 Maryland Ave., NE, Washington, DC 20002. Reprinted by permission.

including their families and, especially, any infants that might be exposed involuntarily to ETS.

By fostering the perception that secondhand smoke is unhealthy for nonsmokers, active smoking has become an undesirable and an antisocial behavior. The cigarette smoker has become ever more segregated and isolated. This ETS social movement has been successful in reducing tobacco cigarette consumption, perhaps more than other measures, including mandatory health warnings, advertising bans on radio and television, and innumerable other efforts instituted by public health and medical professional organizations. But, has the ETS social movement been based on scientific truth and on reproducible data and sound scientific principles?

At times, not surprisingly, the ETS social movement and scientific objectivity have been in conflict. To start with, much of the research on ETS has been shoddy and poorly conceived. Editorial boards of scientific journals have selectively accepted or excluded contributions not always on the basis of inherent scientific merit but, in part, because of these social pressures and that, in turn, has affected and biased the data that are available for further analyses by professional organizations and governmental agencies. In addition, "negative" studies, even if valid, usually are not published, especially if they involve tobacco smoke, and thus they do not become part of the whole body of literature ultimately available for analysis. Negative results on ETS and health can be found in the scientific literature, but only with great difficulty in that they are mentioned in passing as a secondary variable in a "positive" study reporting some other finding unrelated to ETS.

To evaluate critically any potential adverse health effects of ETS, it must first be appreciated that not all tobacco smoke is the same, and thus the risk for exposure to the different kinds of tobacco smoke must be considered independently.[1]

## WHAT IS ETS?

The three most important forms of tobacco smoke are depicted in Figure 1. *Mainstream smoke* is the tobacco smoke that is drawn through the butt end of a cigarette during active smoking; this is the tobacco smoke that the active smoker inhales into his or her lungs. . . . *Sidestream* smoke is the tobacco smoke that is released in the surrounding environment of the burning cigarette from its smoldering tip between active puffs. Many publications have treated sidestream smoke and ETS as if they were one and the same, but sidestream smoke and ETS are clearly not the same thing. Sidestream smoke and ETS have different physical properties and they have different chemical properties. *Environmental tobacco smoke* is usually defined as a combination of highly diluted sidestream smoke plus a smaller amount of that residual mainstream smoke that is exhaled and not retained by the active smoker. What *really* is ETS? In comparison to mainstream smoke and sidestream smoke, ETS is so highly diluted that it is not even appropriate to call it smoke, in the conventional sense. Indeed, the term "environmental tobacco smoke" is a misnomer.

Why is ETS a misnomer? Several reports on smoking and health from the Surgeon General's Office, a National Research Council review of ETS in 1986, the more recent Environmental Protection

*Figure 1*
**Particulate Phase and Gas Phase of Tobacco Smoke\***

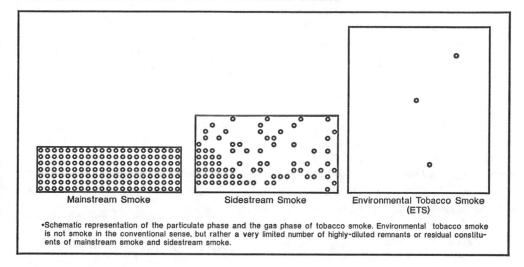

Mainstream Smoke    Sidestream Smoke    Environmental Tobacco Smoke (ETS)

\*Schematic representation of the particulate phase and the gas phase of tobacco smoke. Environmental tobacco smoke is not smoke in the conventional sense, but rather a very limited number of highly-diluted remnants or residual constituents of mainstream smoke and sidestream smoke.

Agency's risk assessment of ETS, and several review articles all have provided a long list of chemical constituents derived from analyses of mainstream smoke and sidestream smoke, with the implication that because they are demonstrable in mainstream smoke and sidestream smoke these same constituents must, by inference, also be present in ETS. No one really knows if they are present or not. In fact, most are not so present or, if they are, they are present only in very dilute concentrations that are well below the level of detection by conventional technologies available today.

Only 14 of the 50 biologically active "probable constituents" of ETS listed by the Surgeon General, for instance, *actually* have been measured or demonstrated at any level in ETS. The others are there essentially by inference, not by actual detection or measurement. Thus, there are 36 constituents in these lists that are inferred to be present in ETS, but their presence has not been confirmed by actual detection or measurement. In this

sense, then, ETS is really not smoke in the conventional sense of its definition, but rather consists of only a limited number of "remnants" or *residual constituents* present in highly dilute concentrations.

Because the levels of ETS cannot be quantified accurately as such in the environment, some investigators have attempted to measure one or more constituent parts of ETS as a "substitute marker" for ETS as a whole. The most frequently employed such "marker" has been nicotine or its first metabolically stable breakdown product, cotinine. Nicotine was considered an "ideal marker" because it is more or less unique to tobacco, although small amounts can be found in some tomatoes and in other food sources. In the mainstream tobacco smoke that is inhaled by the active smoker, nicotine starts out almost exclusively in the tiny liquid droplets of the particulate phase of the smoke. Because the smoke particles of ETS become so quickly and so highly diluted, however, nicotine very rapidly vaporizes from the liquid suspended particulates and enters the surrounding gas. In technical terms, the process by which nicotine leaves the suspended aerosol particle to enter the surrounding gas phase is called "denudation."

As a vapor or gas, nicotine reacts with or adsorbs onto almost everything in the environment with which it comes into contact. Thus, nicotine is not a representative or even a good surrogate marker for the particulate phase, or even the gas-vapor phase, of ETS. In fact, there are no reliable or established markers for ETS. The remnant or residual constituents of ETS each have their own chemical and physical behavior characteristics in the environment and none is present in a concentration in our environment that reaches an established threshold for toxicity.[2]

## MEASURING HEALTH RISKS

Because the level of exposure to ETS or the dose of ETS retained cannot be quantified under every-day, real-life conditions, the health effects following exposure to residual constituents of ETS have been impossible to evaluate directly. In broad terms, two different approaches have been employed in an attempt to assess indirectly the health risks for exposure of the nonsmoker to the environmental remnants of ETS. The first of these involves a theoretical concept that is called "linear risk extrapolation." Linear risk extrapolation has been employed extensively in attempts to determine the risk for lung cancer in nonsmokers exposed to ETS.[3]

This concept of linear risk assumes that if there is a definable health risk for the active smoker, then there also must

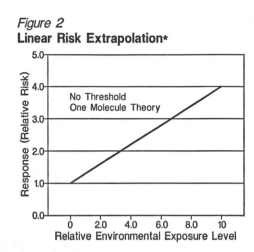

Figure 2
**Linear Risk Extrapolation***

No Threshold
One Molecule Theory

*The concept of linear risk extrapolation. In this theory, the health response (expressed as a relative risk) is directly or linearly related to the relative environmental exposure level. This theory suggests that there is no "safe" threshold below which there is no response, and that exposure to as little as one molecule of the environmental substance can cause an adverse response.

be a projected lower health risk for the nonsmoker exposed to ETS. This is represented schematically in Figure 2. The risk has been presumed to be linear from the active smoker to the nonsmoker exposed to ETS, based proportionately on the relative exposure levels and retained doses of smoke; it thus requires some measurement of tobacco smoke exposure for both groups. This is fairly easy to achieve in the active smoker, in part because mainstream smoke has been so well-characterized and it is delivered directly from the butt-end of the cigarette into the smoker. Such is obviously not the case, however for the nonsmoker exposed to ETS.

Most projections of linear risk for ETS-exposure have been based on the use of nicotine as a representative marker of exposure. A few projections have been based on carbon monoxide levels or amounts of respirable suspended particulates in the environment, but these approaches are fraught with even greater error. Since nicotine initially is in the particulate phase of the mainstream smoke inhaled by the active smoker and it is present primarily as a highly diluted gas-phase remnant or residual vapor-phase constituent in the nonsmoker's environment, the concept of a linear health risk from the active smoker to the nonsmoker is based on rather shaky sci-entific-reasoning.

That is to say, it is not valid to estimate a health risk for exposure to the particu-late phase in the active smoker and then compare it with the health risk for expo-sures to the gas phase in the ETS-exposed nonsmoker. Simply stated, "like" is not being compared to "like." Main-stream smoke and the residual constitu-ents of ETS represent very different exposure conditions. Whether present in mainstream smoke or in ETS, particulate phase and gas phase constituents have very different biological properties, as well as different physical and chemical characteristics, and any associated health risks are also very different. The concept of linear risk extrapolation for ETS is based on a theory that when applied to ETS incorporates unsound assumptions that are not valid. There is no way, as yet, to evaluate or compare the levels of ex-posure in active smokers and nonsmokers exposed to ETS.

The second approach used to evaluate health risks for nonsmokers exposed to ETS has employed epidemiologic studies. Epidemiology is a branch of medical sci-ence that studies the distribution of dis-ease in human populations and the factors determining that distribution, chiefly by the use of statistics. The chief function of epidemiology is the identi-fication of populations at high risk for a given disease, so that the cause may be identified and preventative measures implemented.

Epidemiologic studies are most effec-tive when they can assess a well-defined risk. Because ETS-exposure levels cannot be measured or in any other way quan-tified directly, even by representative markers, epidemiologists have had to use indirect estimates, or surrogates, of ETS exposure. For nonsmoking adults, the number of active smokers that are present in the household has been used as a surrogate for ETS exposure. Usually the active smoking household member has been the nonsmoker's spouse. With a few limited exceptions, disease rates in nonsmokers exposed to a spouse who smokes have been the basis for all epi-demiologic assessments.

Almost all of these studies have evalu-ated nonsmoking females married to a husband who smokes. For children, the surrogate for ETS exposure has been the number of parents in the household who smoke. Estimates of ETS exposure based on spousal or parental surrogates have been derived by various questionnaires; no study employs any direct quantifica-tion of ETS or of ETS remnant constitu-ents in the actual environment of the nonsmoker. Questionnaires of smoking habits are notoriously limited and often inaccurate, in part because of the "social taboo" that smoking has become and, in part, for other reasons related to the ETS social movement. Nevertheless, data from questionnaires about smoking behavior in spouses or in parents are the only esti-mates of ETS exposure available. Rates for three diseases in nonsmokers ex-posed (via surrogates) to ETS have been assessed: lung cancer, coronary heart disease, and respiratory illness in infants and small children. Only lung cancer will be discussed in this article.

## ETS AND LUNG CANCER

What is the state of evidence on ETS and lung cancer? Almost all of the epidemiologic studies that are available to answer that question are based on the concept of some measurement of relative risk. None of the studies actually has measured exposure to ETS or to any of its residual constituents directly. Relative risk is a relationship of the rate of the development of a disease (such as lung cancer) within a group of individuals exposed to some variable in the population studied (such as ETS) divided by the rate of the same disease in those not exposed to this variable.

Relative risk is most frequently expressed as a "risk ratio," which is a calculated comparison of the rate of the disease studied in the exposed population divided by the rate of that disease in some control population not exposed to the variable studied. The terms "risk ratio" and "relative risk" are often used synonymously. Thus, the relative risk in all epidemiologic ETS studies on lung cancer is expressed as the rate of lung cancer in the ETS-exposed group (individuals married to a household smoker) divided by the rate of lung cancer where there was no ETS exposure (no household smokers). If the disease rates were exactly the same in these two groups, the risk ratio would be 1.0.

There have been 30 epidemiologic studies on spousal smoking and lung cancer published in the scientific literature. Twenty-seven of these epidemiological studies were case control studies, where the effect of exposure to spousal smoking was evaluated retrospectively on data that had already been available for review. The "cases" in these case-control studies were nonsmoking individuals with lung cancer married to smokers. The rate of lung cancer in these "cases" was compared, by the derived risk ratio, to the rate of lung cancer in "control" or nonsmoking individuals who were married to nonsmokers.

Three of the studies followed cohort populations of individuals exposed to spousal smoking prospectively over the course of time. A "cohort" is any designated group of people. A "cohort study" identifies a group of people that will be exposed to a risk and a group that will not be exposed to that risk, and then follows these groups over time to compare the rate of disease development as a function of exposure or no exposure.

The first studies were published in 1982 and the last studies were published in 1990. The studies originate broadly from different parts of the world and, for the most part, involve evaluations of lung cancer in nonsmoking females married to a smoking male partner; eight of the studies have limited data on nonsmoking males married to smoking females. Some of the studies are quite small, listing fewer than 20 subjects; others are based on larger populations, with four studies reporting between 129 and 189 cancer cases. Of the 30 studies, six reported a statistically significant association (identified by a positive relative risk ratio in the spousally-exposed to the non-exposed population) and 24 of the studies reported no statistically significant effect. The average estimated relative risk ratio for each study and each sex is listed in Table 1, as are the confidence intervals reported by the authors or, where not reported, calculated by others in published review articles.[4]

Some of the negative studies—that is, some of the 24 studies that did not show

(continued on p. 172)

*Table 1*

## Studies of ETS and Lung Cancer in Nonsmokers

| Study | Sex | Number of Cases | Relative Risk* | 95% Confidence Interval |
|---|---|---|---|---|
| **Case Control Studies** | | | | |
| Chan and Fung, 1982 | F | 34 | 0.75 | (0.43, 1.30) |
| Trichopoulos et al., 1983 | F | 38 | 2.13** | (1.18, 3.83) |
| Correa et al., 1983 | F | 14 | 2.07 | (0.81, 5.26) |
| | M | 2 | 1.97 | (0.38, 10.29) |
| Kabat and Wynder, 1984 | F | 13 | 0.79 | (0.25, 2.45) |
| | M | 5 | 1.00 | (0.20, 5.07) |
| Buffler et al., 1984 | F | 33 | 0.80 | (0.34, 1.81) |
| | M | 5 | 0.51 | (0.15, 1.74) |
| Garfinkel et al., 1985 | F | 92 | 1.12 | (0.94, 1.60) |
| Wu et al., 1985 | F | 29 | 1.20 | (0.50, 3.30) |
| Akiba et al., 1986 | F | 73 | 1.52 | (1.00, 2.5) |
| | M | 3 | 2.10 | (0.5, 5.6) |
| Lee et al., 1986 | F | 22 | 1.03 | (0.37, 2.71) |
| | M | 8 | 1.31 | (0.38, 4.59) |
| Brownson et al., 1987 | F | 19 | 1.68 | (0.39, 2.97) |
| Gao et al., 1987 | F | 189 | 1.19 | (0.6, 1.4) |
| Humble et al., 1987 | F | 14 | 1.78 | (0.6, 5.4) |
| Koo et al., 1987 | F | 51 | 1.55 | (0.87, 3.09) |
| Lam et al., 1987 | F | 115 | 1.65** | (1.16, 2.35) |
| Pershagen et al., 1987 | F | 33 | 1.20 | (0.70, 2.10) |
| Geng et al., 1988 | F | 34 | 2.16** | (1.03, 4.53) |
| Inoue and Hirayama, 1988 | F | 18 | 2.55 | (0.91, 7.10) |
| Katada et al., 1988 | F | 17 | — | (NS; p = 0.23) |
| Lam and Cheng, 1988 | F | 37 | 2.01** | (1.12, 1.83) |
| Shimizu et al., 1988 | F | 90 | 1.10 | N/A |
| He, 1990 | F | 45 | 0.74 | (0.32, 1.68) |
| Janerich et al., 1990 | F | 129 | 0.93 | (0.55, 1.57) |
| Kabat, 1990 | M | 13 | 1.20 | (0.54, 2.68) |
| | F | 35 | 0.90 | (0.46, 1.76) |
| Kalandidi et al., 1990 | F | 91 | 2.11 | (1.09, 4.08) |
| Sobue et al., 1990 | F | 64 | 0.94 | (0.62, 1.40) |
| Svensson, 1990 | F | 17 | 1.20 | (0.40, 2.90) |
| Wu-Williams et al., 1990 | F | 205 | 0.7 | (0.6, 0.9) |
| **Cohort Studies** | | | | |
| Garfinkel, 1981 | F | 88 | 1.17 | (0.85, 1.89) |
| | | | | (0.77, 1.61) |
| Gillis et al., 1984 | F | 6 | 1.00 | (0.59, 17.85) |
| | M | 4 | 3.25 | |
| Hirayama, 1984b | F | 163 | 1.45 | (1.04, 2.02) |
| 1984a | | 7 | 2.28** | (1.19, 4.22) |

*Weak relative risks have risk ratios of between 1 and 3, or so. Any risk ratio below 1 represents a negative relationship. Note that none of the studies show a strong relative risk.

**Statistically significant at the 5% level.

a statistically significant association between the development of lung cancer and exposure to spousal smoking—contained data that suggested to the authors or to other reviewers a "positive trend." In most of science, "trends" do *not* count; data stand as either statistically significant or not statistically significant, with significance determined by specific accepted rules of biostatistics. New rules should not be "made to fit" an otherwise unproved hypotheses, just because the subject is tobacco and the observed results do not support the hypothesis investigated.

## ETS RISK WEAK

A relative risk is called strong or it is called weak, depending on the degree of association, or the magnitude of the risk ratio. A strong relative risk would be reflected by a risk ratio of 5 to 20 or greater. Weak relative risks, by conventional definition, have risk ratios in the range of 1 to 3 or so. Within the 30 epidemiologic studies on ETS and lung cancer, there are 37 different total reported sets of risk ratios for male or female nonsmokers. None of the studies reports a strong relative risk.

Nine of the studies report risk ratios of *less* than 1.0. Thus, the results from all epidemiologic studies consistently reveal only weak lung cancer risks for nonsmokers exposed to spousal smoking, with only six of the studies reaching statistical significance; 24 epidemiologic studies report no statistically significant effect for ETS exposure.

Weak relative risks, however, do not exclude causal relationships. When the relative risks are weak it is very difficult to determine if the effect is artifactual or if it is real. Weak associations are close in magnitude to a level of risk that is sometimes called "background noise," and at this level of risk there are variables other than the one studied that can influence the statistical association.

When a series of epidemiologic studies reveals consistently weak associations that sometimes individually reach statistical significance and sometimes do not, all of the data can be pooled into a more comprehensive assessment to enhance the confidence of the assessment. This is called a "meta-analysis." There are specific rules, however, for combining data and not every published study lends itself to this kind of assessment. The National Research Council concluded, in 1986, that 13 of the then available studies met criteria that would permit a combined meta-analysis risk assessment. When the data from these 13 studies were combined, the net relative risk from all available studies was represented by a risk ratio of 1.34. The risk ratios as the result of other adjusted meta-analyses available for review vary from 1.08 to 1.42, with generally lower values derived from population studies in the United States and with somewhat higher levels or risk derived on populations outside of the United States.

No matter how the data from all of the epidemiological studies are manipulated, recalculated, "cooked," or "massaged," the risk from exposure to spousal smoking and lung cancer remains weak. It may be 1.08 or it may be 1.34 or it may be 1.42, but all of those still represent a weak relative risk. No matter how these data are analyzed, no one has reported a strong risk relationship for exposure to spousal smoking and lung cancer. Combining all the data from all epidemiological studies does not result in an enhancement of the relative risk—the risk for lung cancer with exposure to spousal smoking is weak.

In addressing this problem, Ernst Wynder, of the American Health Foundation, stated that when an assessment of relative risk is weak (that is, when the odds risk ratios are in the range of 2 to 1 or less) the possibility exists that the finding is artificial and a consequence of problems in the case control selection or is due to the presence of confounders (or confounding variables) and interpretation biases which need to be carefully considered. Confounding variables must be controlled in order to obtain an undistorted estimate of the effect of a study factor, such as spousal smoking, on risk. This is especially true when the studied risk factor has a weak association.

At least 20 confounding factors have been identified as important to the development of lung cancer. These include nutrition and dietary prevention, exposure to occupational carcinogens, exposure to various air pollution contaminants, genetic predisposition and family prevalence, circulating beta-carotene levels (as well as vitamin E and vitamin A levels), history of alcohol consumption, exposure to alpha omitting radiation (such as radon daughters), geographical residence and country of origin, presence or absence of selenium and other trace metals, healthy versus unhealthy lifestyles, age, gender, housing conditions, race, marital status, ethnicity, socio-economic status, diagnostic criteria, and perhaps most importantly of all, an enhanced clustering of risk factors. Thus, a large number of confounding variables are important to any consideration of spousal smoking and lung cancer, and no reported study comes anywhere close to controlling, or even mentioning, half of these.

## IS ETS A HEALTH HAZARD?

Does exposure to the remnants or residual constituents of ETS represent a legitimate health hazard to the nonsmoker? In considering spousal smoking, lung cancer, and the confounding factors, Linda Koo, at the University of Hong Kong, cautioned that it may not be the hazards of tobacco smoke that are being evaluated, but a whole range of behaviors that result from having a smoking husband, which may, in turn, increase the risk for certain diseases among the wives and children. Indeed, confounding variables are always present and they are so numerous and so complex that they may make it impossible ever to know the true risk for lung cancer in nonsmokers exposed to spousal smoking.

Are the studies on the projections of levels of ETS residual constituents in our environment, and the studies on the spousal smoking and lung cancer, a reflection of "bad science?" Not necessarily, for they are the best science that is available today. Sir Bradford Hill of Oxford University cautioned years ago that it is important to remember that all science is subject to being reinterpreted or to being changed and modified by advancing knowledge. As newer technologies are applied to the assessment of environmental tobacco smoke, clearer understandings will evolve.

Has there been a "misrepresentation of science" in the common perception of ETS today? Active tobacco smoking and environmental tobacco smoke are controversial, very emotional, and highly politicized subjects. In the quagmire of ETS forces operative in politics, emotion, and science, it has been difficult to sort out scientific fact from unsound conjecture. Unfortunately, scientific data have not always been utilized objectively by governmental agencies or regulatory bodies that have their own inherent public health or political agenda. Good science ultimately must rest on established proven scientific methods, and the full results generated by these scientific methods. When these methods are compromised, scientific integrity is lost and society pays the price. Interpretations and judgements may vary, as a function of an investigator's bias or to expedite one or another political, social or emotional objective.

Richard Lindzen, of the Massachusetts Institute of Technology, has emphasized that problems will arise where we will need to depend on scientific judgement, and by ruining our credibility now we leave society with a resource of some importance diminished. The implementation of public policies must be based on good science, to the degree that it is available, and not on emotion or on political needs. Those who develop such policies must not stray from sound scientific investigations, based only on accepted scientific methodologies. Such has not always been the case with environmental tobacco smoke.

## NOTES

1. A burning cigarette has been described as "a miniature chemical factory," producing numerous new components from its raw materials. When a cigarette is smoked, the burning cone has a temperature of about 860 to 900°C during active puffing, and smolders at 500 to 600°C between puffs. When tobacco burns at these temperatures, the products of pyrolyzation are all vapors. As the vapors cool in passage away from the burning cone, they condense into minute liquid droplets, initially about two ten-millionths of a meter in size. Generally, then, all forms of smoke are micro-aerosols of very small liquid droplets of particulate matter suspended in their surrounding vapors of gases. Thus, all smoke has a "particulate phase" and a "gas phase."

2. A *threshold limit value* (usually expressed as milligrams of a substance per cubic meter of air or as parts of a substance present per million parts of respirable clean air) is the recommended concentration of a substance as the maximal level that should not be exceeded to prevent occupational disease through exposure in the workplace. Threshold limit values have not been established for our general, every-day environment outside of industrial exposure. Threshold limit values are determined by toxicologists, epidemiologists, and hygienists through their interpretation of literature, and usually are sanctioned by the American Conference of Governmental Industrial Hygienists. No constituent of ETS has been measured in our every-day environment at levels that exceed the threshold limit values permitted in the workplace.

3. The concept is based on a theoretical extrapolation of the risk for lung cancer in the active smoker to the risk for lung cancer in the passive smoker on the basis of a "representative marker" for both smoke exposures. This "linear risk extrapolation" from one to the other is a model that is based on mathematical theory and on several assumptions. The theory assumes that the risk applies to all exposure levels, even if they are very low. Some advocates of the model even assume a "one molecule, one hit" mechanism, where exposures so low that they cannot be detected or measured can still cause disease if only a single molecule reaches a vulnerable body tissue. The linear risk theory also assumes that the risk for accumulative exposure remains constant and, thus, that the exposed individual has no capacity to adapt or develop tolerance mechanisms for the exposure. Since active smokers readily and rapidly develop tolerance through a variety of defense mechanisms, it seems illogical to assume those repeatedly exposed to ETS would not do the same. The linear risk model assumes that the risk for exposure to ETS is independent of any confounding factors. Finally, for this theory to be valid, it must be assumed that the risk is linear for duration of exposure and that it is linear for concentration of exposure. None of these assumptions holds true on scientific testing for comparative projections of mainstream smoke to ETS.

4. A confidence interval is a range of values that has a specified probability of including the true value (as opposed to the estimated average value) within that range. In the data presented in Table 1, the confidence intervals are set such that there is a 95% probability that the true value will fall within the range of values listed.

# POSTSCRIPT

## Is Passive Smoking Harmful to Nonsmokers?

In today's health-conscious society, people seem to be more aware of what they eat, whether or not they get enough exercise, and how much stress they experience. Thus, it is only logical that people are also concerned about possible environmental threats such as passive smoking.

Huber, Brockie, and Mahajan make a poignant statement about the isolation of smokers in society. Smokers are now almost pictured as social outcasts. There is increasing contempt and disdain shown toward smokers. Currently, more than 40 states and 300 municipalities restrict smoking—thereby restricting smokers—in restaurants and other public places. Huber and his colleagues refer to the emotionalism that "clouds the issue." The emotionality of this issue is unfortunate because smokers are often put on the defensive. This confrontational stance is not conducive to constructively addressing the issue of smokers' rights versus nonsmokers' rights.

A report released by the Environmental Protection Agency (EPA) in January 1993 links environmental tobacco smoke to lung cancer in nonsmokers and to respiratory infections in children. The report states that passive smoking is responsible for an estimated 3,000 lung cancer deaths annually in adults and as many as 300,000 cases of bronchitis and pneumonia in children. In addition, the EPA declared that secondhand cigarette smoke is a Group A cancer-causing agent as dangerous as benzene, arsenic, and radon. The Tobacco Institute contends that the EPA report is not conclusive, that the statistics are flawed, and that the EPA's studies ignored studies that indicate environmental smoke is less of a threat than the agency suggested.

In the article "The Teflon Coating of Cigarette Companies," *Priorities* (Spring 1990), Larry White discusses how tobacco companies deflect some of the criticism directed at their industry. *The United States Office on Smoking and Health Fact Book* (Government Printing Office, 1989) describes the effects of passive smoking, especially on young people. A regular publication that lobbies for smoking restrictions is *Smoking and Health Review,* published by Action on Smoking and Health. And an overview of health and legal matters as they relate to passive smoking is presented in "Passive Smoking: A Review of Medical and Legal Issues," *American Journal of Public Health* (February 1989), by James Byrd, Robin Shapiro, and David Scheidermayer.

# ISSUE 9

## Can Caffeine Be Bad for Your Health?

**YES: Janis A. Work,** from "Are Java Junkies Poor Sports?" *The Physician and Sportsmedicine* (January 1991)

**NO: Diederick E. Grobbee, Eric B. Rimm, Edward Giovannucci, Graham Colditz, Meir Stampfer, and Walter Willett,** from "Coffee, Caffeine, and Cardiovascular Disease in Men," *The New England Journal of Medicine* (October 11, 1990)

### ISSUE SUMMARY

**YES:** Free-lance writer Janis A. Work argues that the consumption of caffeine, even at low levels, can have adverse physical effects, and she contends that drinking caffeinated beverages is not conducive to a healthy life-style.

**NO:** Dr. Diederick E. Grobbee and associates from the Department of Epidemiology and Nutrition at Harvard University's School of Public Health report that, in a study of more than 45,000 men, caffeine use did not increase the risk for cardiovascular disease.

Caffeine is one of the most widely consumed legal drugs in the world. In the United States, more than 9 out of every 10 people drink some type of caffeinated beverage, mostly for its stimulating effects. Caffeine elevates mood, reduces fatigue, increases work capacity, and stimulates respiration. Caffeine often provides the lift people need to start the day. Although many people associate caffeine primarily with coffee, caffeine is also found in numerous soft drinks, over-the-counter medications, chocolate, and tea. Since caffeinated drinks are so common in society and there are very few legal controls regarding the use of caffeine, caffeine's physical and psychological effects are frequently overlooked, ignored, or minimized.

One notable change in recent years is that coffee consumption has declined; however, the amount of caffeine being consumed has not declined appreciably because of the increase in (caffeinated) soft drink consumption. To reduce their levels of caffeine intake, many people have switched to decaffeinated soft drinks and coffee. Although this results in less caffeine intake, decaffeinated coffee still contains small amounts of caffeine.

Research studies evaluating the effects of caffeine consumption on personal health date back to the 1960s. In particular, the medical community has conducted numerous studies to determine whether or not there is a relationship between caffeine consumption and cardiovascular disease, since heart disease is the leading cause of death in many countries, including the United States. In spite of the many studies on this subject, a clear relationship between heart disease and caffeine is not yet apparent. Studies have yielded conflicting results. Rather than clarifying the debate regarding the consequences of caffeine, the research only adds to the confusion. As a result, studies suggesting that there is a connection between caffeine consumption and adverse physical and psychological effects have come under scrutiny by both the general public and health professionals.

A serious limitation of previous research indicating that caffeine does have deleterious effects is that the research focused primarily on coffee use. There may be other ingredients in coffee besides caffeine that produce harmful effects. Moreover, an increasing percentage of the caffeine being consumed comes from other sources, such as soft drinks, tea, chocolate, antihistamines, and diet pills. Therefore, studies involving caffeine are not truly representative of the amount of caffeine that people ingest.

Another important criticism of caffeine research, especially studies linking caffeine use and heart disease, is gender bias. Until recently, research has focused solely on the caffeine consumption of men. This situation is slowly being rectified. The potential cardiovascular consequences of caffeine use for women are currently being researched. The bias in medical research is not limited to caffeine studies; men have traditionally been the primary group studied regarding many facets of health.

People who believe that drinking caffeine in moderation does not pose a significant health threat are critical of previous and present studies. This is particularly true of those studies that demonstrate a relationship between caffeine and heart disease. If there are adverse effects linked to caffeine, a fundamental question would be, How much caffeine is too much? It is unclear as to what is a safe level of caffeine. Also, critics contend that it is difficult to establish a definitive relationship between caffeine and heart disease due to a myriad of confounding factors. Cardiovascular disease has already been linked to family history, a sedentary lifestyle, cigarette smoking, obesity, fat intake, and stress. Many individuals who consume large amounts of coffee also smoke cigarettes, drink alcohol, and are hard-driven. Several factors also affect caffeine's excretion from the body. Cigarette smoking increases caffeine metabolization, while the use of oral contraceptives and pregnancy slow down metabolization. Therefore, determining the extent to which caffeine use causes heart disease while adjusting for the influence of these other factors is difficult.

In the following selections, Janis A. Work cautions readers about the use of caffeine, even in moderate amounts. In contrast, Diederick E. Grobbee and colleagues argue that small amounts of caffeine intake may not be significantly harmful to one's cardiovascular health.

# YES                                   Janis A. Work

# ARE JAVA JUNKIES POOR SPORTS?

Most of us are aware of the presence of caffeine in regular coffee and tea. But it is present in many other beverages as well. Several brands of soda pop contain caffeine. Decaffeinated coffee and tea also retain some trace amounts of caffeine, which, for the heavy decaf drinker, can add up. Chocolate contains caffeine, as do some medications. Unless we read the fine print, we may not even be aware that caffeine is contained in a particular product we regularly consume.

Caffeine has a notable physical and psychological impact on most people. It makes some people more alert and more energetic, while it makes others feel nervous and shaky. But regardless of how people consciously *feel* when they ingest caffeine, the drug makes its effects known on various systems of the body. The question is: Are those effects *good*?

Some people use caffeine to achieve a specific performance objective. Athletes, for example, have sometimes been known to use caffeine to enhance their endurance performance, according to Robert K. Conlee, PhD, professor of physical education at Brigham Young University in Provo, Utah. But he says that while there is some evidence to support the use of caffeine to improve endurance, there is other evidence that suggests it has no effect on endurance performance.[1] Likewise, he says, there is little evidence to support the use of caffeine to improve strength.[1]

## PERFORMANCE EFFECTS

In light of research findings reported in the literature, Conlee believes that the benefit of caffeine as an ergogenic aid is questionable and he says he would therefore discourage individuals from using it as such. "And if a naive user ingests it, there is no way of predicting what the results would be," Conlee adds. "It could actually hurt that person's performance by causing irritability and nervousness."

Some athletes who take caffeine prior to performance do so for the psychological effect, says Melvin H. Williams, PhD, director of the Human

Performance Laboratory at Old Dominion University in Norfolk, Virginia. And it seems there is no prohibition against competitive athletes doing so if the amount of caffeine is moderate. "Although the US Olympic Committee drug policy regarding other drugs is strict, the current ruling on caffeine use actually is fairly liberal," Williams says. "An athlete would need to ingest the equivalent of 5 or 6 cups of coffee in a 2-hour period prior to competition to be banned," he says.

Nevertheless, Conlee says he would never want to encourage individuals to use caffeine or other stimulants in any amount to improve their performance. To do so, he says, would be an endorsement of the use of drugs, which would be both inappropriate and unethical.

In addition to enhancing performance, caffeine also is thought to affect the cardiovascular system in several ways. Thomas G. Allison, PhD, an exercise physiologist in the Cardiovascular Health Clinic at Mayo Clinic in Rochester, Minnesota, says caffeine can increase blood pressure, but the increase usually is only in the range of 5 to 10 mm Hg.[2] "The mechanism seems to be peripheral vasoconstriction rather than an increase in central cardiac output," says Allison. "Not only will resting blood pressure be up slightly, blood pressure during exercise will rise slightly as well." From an intuitive standpoint, even that amount of elevation in a patient with hypertension might have adverse consequences, Allison says. "We simply don't know whether a small, transient elevation would be significant for long-term health."

For those who ingest caffeine *and* smoke cigarettes, Allison says, there is a still greater increase in blood pressure. "We do know that the combination of coffee ingestion and smoking raises the blood pressure of hypertensive patients about 15/13 mm Hg for as long as 2 hours," he says.[3] Coincidentally, caffeine is known to cause constriction of cerebral arteries, so it can actually be useful for treating hypertensive headaches.[4]

## IS IT HARD ON THE HEART?

As for caffeine's effect during acute exercise, Allison says at least one study showed neither a comparative increase nor a decrease in heart rate.[2] However, in one study of subjects with angina, caffeine before exercise actually raised their angina threshold, so they were able to exercise longer on the treadmill before experiencing chest pain.[5]

The effects of caffeine on arrhythmias are disputed. According to Allison, evidence suggests that ingesting 2 to 3 cups of coffee increases the frequency of premature ventricular contractions (PVCs), but does *not* increase the frequency of more serious arrhythmias either in healthy subjects[6] or in cardiac patients.[7]

Says Allison, "We should avoid overreacting, because the studies do *not* show that caffeine induces ventricular tachycardia, fibrillation, or any kind of serious arrhythmias, except in the case of an overdose."

Although studies are inconclusive, some professionals continue to advise people to avoid caffeine. Conlee says that even though there may not be *dramatic* effects with caffeine use, he thinks more concern over caffeine may be in order. "Caffeine is considered the most abused drug in the world," says Conlee, adding that he sees caffeine use as being somewhat contrary to the principles of fitness and good health. "I would personally recommend that no one use caffeine," he says.

"The problem is that most people who use it do not think of it as a drug, I suppose because of its common presence in what we drink and eat."

And even though some evidence suggests that caffeine temporarily decreases fatigue and improves alertness, Conlee still doesn't see anything to recommend its use. "If a person who has never used caffeine before ingests some prior to exercise, the physiologic effects would be unpredictable," says Conlee. "The effects could certainly be more dramatic than with a seasoned caffeine user."

Gerald Gau, MD, director of the Cardiovascular Health Clinic at the Mayo Clinic, suggests that heart patients be especially cautious. "I always advise patients with any kind of heart problem to refrain from using caffeine," he says. "But for others, I would say that used in moderation, it shouldn't present a problem."

However, Gau acknowledges that chronic caffeine users can develop both physical and psychological dependence on the drug and that they may experience withdrawal symptoms when they abstain. "These symptoms are not life-threatening, but they can be uncomfortable, with the primary symptom being a headache," says Gau. "Some people may also feel fatigued and have general aching."

## CAFFEINE AND RESPIRATION

Data on possible links between cholesterol levels or cardiovascular mortality and caffeine consumption tend to be confounded by other variables, according to Allison. "People who drink a lot of coffee also tend to have other cardiovascular risk factors, such as a sedentary life-style, a high-fat diet, or a smoking habit," Allison says. "So it is difficult to determine what effects are actually related to caffeine use."[8,9]

But caffeine is known to have some effect on respiration. The respiratory center of the medulla is stimulated by caffeine, although a relatively large dose is needed to produce a noticeable increase in respiration rate. Caffeine has been shown to be effective in dilating bronchial passages in asthmatic patients, but as with a fatal dose, the therapeutic dose must be so large (10 mg/kg) that it produces unpleasant side effects in most patients before they would get to the point of relief from the asthma.[10]

A number of studies have demonstrated that caffeine increases gastric secretion. Increased secretions of stomach acids may lead to or aggravate ulcers, hiatus hernias, and heartburn. Caffeine also acts on the smooth muscle of the gastrointestinal tract, tending to suppress motility in the stomach and small intestine, but to relax the muscles of the large intestine. An endurance athlete might therefore want to think twice about ingesting caffeine before a marathon race, during which even a minor case of diarrhea could be a major inconvenience.

Another physiologic effect of caffeine is well known to any coffee, tea, or cola drinker—it is an effective diuretic and can increase urination by as much as 30% for up to 3 hours after consumption.[10] It may result in reduced body fluids, which would also be of special concern to an endurance athlete. But casual exercisers, who may not even realize they are becoming dehydrated until their symptoms are severe, should recognize this as well.

Other than the diuretic effect, the connection between weight loss and caffeine is unclear, although caffeine is a common
(continued on p. 182)

## WHAT IS CAFFEINE?

Humans have had a long, affectionate relationship with caffeine and have been eating or chewing caffeine-containing beans, leaves, bark, and nuts for generations.[4] But despite the widespread use of caffeine and the fact that people know its effects on them, few people know exactly what caffeine is, where it comes from, or what physiologic effects it has.

Caffeine is an alkaloid found in a variety of plants, such as the cocoa plant and the coffee bean, which grow in many parts of the world. Like amphetamines, caffeine acts as a stimulant to the sympathetic nervous system, although its effects are milder. It can make people feel more alert, alleviate fatigue, promote more rapid thought, and increase motor activity and muscle capacity. The source of the caffeine doesn't seem to make much difference physiologically, and because the substance is readily absorbed by the body, the effects are usually felt within minutes.

Though people may not know much about the origin of caffeine, most know that it is considered a drug. And, as with many drugs, large doses can be fatal. But for caffeine, a fatal dose would have to be extremely large—for an adult, at least 5,000 mg, or 40 cups of *strong* coffee over a short period of time. Consumption for the average person never approaches that level: For example, in 1982, the average 20-year-old American was reported to consume about 130 mg of caffeine a day from coffee and soft drinks combined.[10] But detectable subjective effects can be produced in some people at much lower doses—about the amount contained in an average chocolate bar (20 mg).[13] An average cup of regular coffee, by comparison, contains about 85 mg.

### Short Road to Addiction

Caffeine is known to be addictive. Longtime coffee drinkers often report feeling out of sorts if they don't have their morning dose. And if they stop using caffeine completely, they experience withdrawal symptoms, says Gerald Gau, MD, director of the Cardiovascular Health Clinic at the Mayo Clinic in Rochester, Minnesota. "When caffeine withdrawal occurs, severity of symptoms can range from mild to incapacitating," according to Roland R. Griffiths, PhD, professor in the departments of psychiatry and neuroscience at Johns Hopkins University School of Medicine in Baltimore. "The withdrawal syndrome has an onset of 12 to 24 hours, peaks at 20 to 48 hours, and has a total duration of up to 1 week," Griffiths says. "The most common symptoms are headache and fatigue, but a wide variety of other symptoms may be experienced, including nausea and impaired psychomotor performance."

Griffiths emphasizes that large amounts of coffee are not necessary to produce addiction. "A person can get hooked with a relatively small amount of caffeine consumption if it's on a fairly regular basis," he says. "Even 3 to 4 cups of regular coffee per day may be sufficient to induce withdrawal symptoms upon abrupt abstinence."[14]

constituent of many nonprescription diet medications. According to Williams, caffeine will increase the metabolic rate by 8% to 16%,[11] which may provide an explanation for its inclusion.

Both exercise and caffeine increase the release of free fatty acids, which could be an alternate substrate to glucose. However, Williams says his study[12] failed to show that caffeine improved the exercise performance of moderately trained women.

## WHY TAKE THE RISK?

Overall, it appears that moderate use of caffeine will not cause problems for most people. "I don't think we can identify a health risk in minimal to moderate caffeine consumption," Allison says. "But people who are susceptible to its effects, such as those who respond with arrhythmias, may want to avoid using caffeine." Gau agrees, adding that limiting coffee consumption may not go far enough. "If you have an arrhythmia, why drink it at all?" says Gau. "Switch to a noncaffeinated beverage instead."

## REFERENCES

1. Wadler GI, Hainline B: Drugs and the Athlete. Philadelphia, FA Davis Co, 1989, pp. 107–113.
2. Sung BH, Lovallo WR, Pincomb GA et al: Effects of caffeine on blood pressure response during exercise in normotensive healthy young men. Am J Cardiol 1990; 65 (13): 909–913.
3. Freestone S, Ramsay LE: Effect of coffee and cigarette smoking on the blood pressure of untreated and diuretic-treated hypertensive patients. Am J Med 1982; 73(3): 348–353.
4. Gilman A, Goodman LS, (eds): The Pharmacological Basis of Therapeutics, ed 5. New York, Macmillan Publishing Co, Inc., 1975.
5. Piters KM, Colombo A, Olson HG, et al: Effect of coffee on exercise-induced angina pectoris due to coronary artery disease in habitual coffee drinkers. Am J Cardiol 1985; 55(4): 277–280.
6. Newcombe PF, Renton KW, Rautaharju PM, et al: High-dose caffeine and cardiac rate and rhythm in normal subjects. Chest 1988; 94(1): 90–94.
7. Myers MG, Harris L, Leenen FH, et al: Caffeine as a possible cause of ventricular arrhythmias during the healing phase of acute myocardial infarction. Am J. Cardiol 1987: 59(12): 1024–1028.
8. Jacobsen BK, Thelle DS: The Trømso Heart Study: is coffee drinking an indicator of a life style with high risk for ischemic heart disease? Acta Med Scand 1987; 222(3): 215–221.
9. Thelle DS, Arnesen E, Førde OH: The Trømso heart study. Does coffee raise serum cholesterol? N Engl J Med 1983; 308(24): 1454–1457.
10. Gilbert RJ: Caffeine: The Most Popular Stimulant. New York, Chelsea House Publishers, 1986.
11. Toehlman E: Influences of caffeine as the resting metabolic rate of exercise-trained and inactive subjects. Med Sci Sports Exerc 1985; 17: 689–694.
12. Perkins R, Williams MH: Effects of caffeine upon maximum muscular endurance of females. Med. Sci Sports 1975; 7: 221–224.
13. Griffiths RR, Evans SM, Heishman SJ, et al. Low-dose caffeine discrimination in humans. J Pharmacol Exp Ther 1990; 252(3): 970–978.
14. Griffiths RR, Woodson PP: Caffeine Physical Dependence: A review of human and laboratory animal studies. J Psychopharmacology 1989; 94: 437–451.

# NO

Diederick E. Grobbee,
Eric B. Rimm, Edward Giovannucci,
Graham Colditz, Meir Stampfer,
and Walter Willett

## COFFEE, CAFFEINE, AND CARDIOVASCULAR DISEASE IN MEN

For many years, an association has been suspected between coffee drinking and cardiovascular disease, in particular coronary heart disease.[1-22] Studies have been inconsistent, however, fueling a debate about the hazards of coffee drinking.[23] Although findings in several case-control studies support an elevated risk of myocardial infarction among men and women with high coffee intakes,[2,3,9,18-20] others do not,[4,7,11] and reports of prospective studies show similarly conflicting results.[5,6,8-10,12-17,21,22] It has been suggested that some negative findings may be due to the relatively small size of most of the studies or the long time between the assessment of coffee intake and the occurrence of cardiovascular events.[9,11,14,24-27] In a study by LaCroix and coworkers,[14] of 1130 male medical students followed for up to 35 years, those who drank five or more cups of coffee daily were reported to have a 2.5-fold risk of coronary heart disease as compared with nondrinkers. This risk was greatest for coffee use reported within a few years before the event, and the authors speculated that the absence of a positive association in some other studies was due to an excessively long period between the assessment of coffee intake and the occurrence of cardiovascular events.[14]

Studies addressing the mechanisms by which coffee consumption increases cardiovascular disease also offer conflicting results. Coffee may raise serum cholesterol levels, although this effect is probably influenced by the brewing method.[28,29] In a preliminary report of a randomized trial, decaffeinated coffee increased levels of low-density lipoprotein cholesterol, and findings in a second double-blind study did not support an effect of caffeine.[30,31] Coffee may also raise blood pressure[32-34] and induce cardiac arrhythmias.[35] The best-known pharmacologically active substance in coffee is caffeine, but effects may be mediated by a variety of other substances.[34]

Excerpted by Raymond Goldberg from Diederick E. Grobbee, Eric B. Rimm, Edward Giovannucci, Graham Colditz, Meir Stampfer, and Walter Willett, "Coffee, Caffeine, and Cardiovascular Disease in Men," *The New England Journal of Medicine*, vol. 323, no. 13 (October 11, 1990), pp. 1026–1032. Copyright © 1990 by The Massachusetts Medical Society. Reprinted by permission.

In this paper we examine the relation of coffee, caffeine, and tea intake with the incidence of coronary heart disease and cerebrovascular disease in a large cohort of U.S. men participating in the Health Professionals Follow-up Study.

## RESULTS

Among the 45,589 men free of diagnosed coronary heart disease and cerebrovascular diseases at the start of the study, 181 participants experienced a nonfatal myocardial infarction, 136 underwent coronary-artery surgery or angioplasty, and 54 had a stroke during two years of follow-up. In addition, 40 men died of myocardial infarction or sudden death.... Of the participants, 83 percent drank coffee, and 69 percent reported the use of caffeinated coffee. Those who did not drink coffee were slightly younger and leaner than coffee consumers. Coffee consumers were more than twice as likely to smoke as those who did not drink coffee, but the proportion of smokers in the group as a whole was only 10 percent. Other characteristics were similar among the groups.

Total coffee consumption (caffeinated plus decaffeinated) was not associated with an increased risk of nonfatal myocardial infarction and fatal coronary heart disease, total coronary heart disease, stroke, or total cardiovascular disease.... As compared with the men who consumed no coffee, the age-adjusted relative risk of total cardiovascular disease among those who drank four or more cups per day was 1.04 (95 percent confidence interval, 0.74 to 1.46). Some suggestion of a trend for an increasing risk of having coronary-artery bypass grafting and coronary angioplasty with increasing consumption of coffee was observed; however, this was limited to an association with decaffeinated coffee (see next paragraph). After adjustment for present and past smoking habits, diabetes mellitus, alcohol use, dietary intake of cholesterol and saturated, monounsaturated, and polyunsaturated fat, family history of coronary heart disease, and profession, the relative risk of total cardiovascular disease among those consuming four or more cups of coffee per day was 0.90 (95 percent confidence interval, 0.67 to 1.22). Those with a total consumption of six or more cups of coffee per day had a relative risk of total cardiovascular disease of 0.65 (95 percent confidence interval, 0.31 to 1.35).

Men drinking caffeinated coffee had no increases in the risk of cardiovascular disease with higher intakes.... Rather, the estimates of relative risk were below 1.0 for total coronary heart disease and total cardiovascular disease in those drinking four or more cups of caffeinated coffee per day. There was a positive trend, however, toward an association between a higher consumption of decaffeinated coffee and coronary-artery bypass grafting and coronary angioplasty, and there was a slight and marginally significant increase in the risk of coronary heart disease and total cardiovascular disease with increased consumption.... Because fewer participants drank decaffeinated than caffeinated coffee, the confidence intervals for the estimates for decaffeinated coffee were wider. Multivariate analysis changed the risk estimates only slightly. No apparent association was observed between the consumption of tea and the risk of any cardiovascular end point ... however, only 664 men drank four or more cups of tea per day.

Although histories of hypercholesterolemia and hypertension were associated with an increased risk of cardiovascular disease, they were not related to coffee or caffeine intake; thus, the inclusion of these variables in the multivariate model did not change the risk estimates for coffee or caffeine intake. Similarly, including categories of physical activity assessed on the baseline questionnaire did not alter associations with coffee consumption. The findings were also essentially the same when we limited the analyses to definite end points (relative risk of any coronary heart disease among those drinking four or more cups of caffeinated coffee per day, 0.89; 95 percent confidence interval, 0.57 to 1.40). The associations were not materially altered when events occurring before January 1, 1987, were disregarded: the relative risks of any coronary heart disease were 0.81 among those drinking four or more cups of caffeinated coffee per day (95 percent confidence interval, 0.48 to 1.36) and 1.71 among men drinking four or more cups of decaffeinated coffee per day (95 percent confidence interval., 0.95 to 3.06).

We also examined total caffeine intake and observed no pattern of higher risk across categories of increasing intake from all sources. . . . [T]he relation of total coffee use to the incidence of total cardiovascular disease was not modified appreciably by age.

## DISCUSSION

Our findings among 45,589 men 40 to 75 years of age, with more than 70,000 person-years of follow-up, indicate that the use of caffeinated coffee and the total intake of caffeine do not appreciably increase the risk of coronary heart disease or stroke. By contrast, a high consumption of decaffeinated coffee was associated with a moderate and marginally significant increase in risk of coronary heart disease.

Several previous reports suggesting an association between coffee consumption and coronary heart disease stem from studies among hospitalized patients and control subjects.[2,3,9,18-20] In these studies, it is difficult to exclude the possibility that reported coffee use before hospitalization is subject to recall and selection bias. The prospective design of the present study greatly reduced the possibility of biased reporting of coffee use or other characteristics because this information was collected before the diagnosis of cardiovascular disease. Most other prospective studies have not observed coffee intake to be associated with the risk of fatal coronary heart disease.[4,6,8,9,12,13,15,16,21] Our data confirm these reports for total coffee consumption and extend the findings to nonfatal coronary heart disease and cerebrovascular disease.

In our analysis, drinking four or more cups of decaffeinated coffee per day was associated with a moderate elevation in the risk of all cardiovascular end points (multivariate relative risk, 1.58). This finding was unexpected and requires further study. In a recent randomized trial,[30] the consumption of three to six cups of decaffeinated coffee per day did raise the levels of low-density lipoprotein cholesterol. For the time being there seems to be little merit in switching from caffeinated coffee to decaffeinated coffee as a means of reducing the risks of cardiovascular disease.

A possible limitation of our data is the relatively short follow-up period and the fact that the data on coffee use refer to the patterns of consumption within one to three years of the symptoms of coronary heart disease or stroke. Several authors, however, have suggested that the adverse effects of coffee on the cardiovascular system may be particularly evident within the four-year period before a cardiovascular event.[9,11,14,24-27] This hypothesis of a short-term effect derives from the relatively consistent absence of coffee-induced effects on cardiovascular disease in studies in which the intake was assessed long before the coronary events, and from the elevated risks reported in several case-control studies. In a prospective study, recent coffee-drinking habits appeared to be associated with a 2.5-fold increased risk of combined nonfatal and fatal coronary heart disease; however, the study included only 51 cases of coronary heart disease and only 21 cases of myocardial infarction, and thus the confidence intervals around the estimates of relative risk were wide.[14] All subjects in our study who reported previous cardiovascular disease at the start of the follow-up period were excluded from the analysis. We further limited the possibility of an effect of existing subclinical disease on coffee use by ignoring cardiovascular events that occurred in the first year of follow-up; this analysis yielded results that were essentially unchanged.

Confounding may have been a problem in the analysis of some previous prospective studies. Coffee drinkers are more likely to smoke than those who do not drink coffee,[36] and they may have higher intakes of total and saturated fat and cholesterol.[37] Adjustments for the intake of fat and cholesterol did not materially change our findings, however. Most cohorts of men studied thus far included large proportions of smokers. Since the rates of smoking among men have decreased markedly over the past decades, a measure of smoking status at the start of a follow-up period a decade or more long may not provide adequate control for smoking as a confounding factor. In our study, only 10.1 percent of the members of the cohort were current smokers . . . and the data on both smoking habits and coffee use refer to a period less than three years before the event. As discussed by Rosenberg et al., another concern is the possibility that risk estimates in some of the previous reports have been overadjusted when variables that may influence the effect of the coffee on cardiovascular disease, such as blood pressure and serum lipid levels, were included in the multivariate models.[19] In our study, we analyzed the data both with and without the inclusion of these variables, with no appreciable change in the results.

The present study provides data from a very large cohort. The findings indicate that a substantial adverse effect of coffee use on the incidence of cardiovascular disease is unlikely. There remains the possibility of a threshold effect of coffee for its effect on the heart and the vessels; a very high coffee consumption may increase individual risk.[2,3,17,20] In the Western Electric Company Study, mortality from coronary heart disease was increased in those drinking more than six cups per day when compared with all others.[17] In the Western Electric cohort, however, coffee-drinking habits appear to have been somewhat atypical, since only 68 participants (3.5 percent) reported no intake of coffee. In a recent report from a Scandinavian study of middle-aged men, drinking nine cups of coffee per day or more was associated with a risk of myocardial infarction 2.2 times that of drinking less than one cup.[23] Only 2.9 percent of the men in the

Health Professionals Follow-up Study drank six or more cups of coffee per day. Even for this group, however, the relative risk of cardiovascular disease was not increased. A second restriction of our data is that no women were included in the cohort. Although there is little previous evidence to suggest a different association between coffee and cardiovascular risk among women as compared with men, the findings may not apply to women. In a recent case-control study in women, a nonsignificant increase in the risk of nonfatal myocardial infarction (relative risk, 1.72; confidence interval, 0.92 to 3.23) was noted in women who drank more than three cups of coffee per day relative to women who never drank coffee.[20] As indicated by the low prevalence of cigarette smoking and relatively low intake of dietary cholesterol, the population of health professionals in our study is not strictly representative of men as a whole in the United States. However, we have no reason to believe that the effect of coffee consumption on the incidence of cardiovascular disease would be substantially different in this relatively low risk population.

In summary, our data support the conclusion that caffeinated coffee as it is currently consumed by men in the United States causes no substantial increase in the risk of coronary heart disease or stroke.

## REFERENCES

1. Paul O, Lepper MH, Phelan WH, et al. A longitudinal study of coronary heart disease. Circulation 1963; 28:20–31.

2. Coffee drinking and acute myocardial infarction: report from the Boston Collaborative Drug Surveillance Program. Lancet 1972; 2:1278–81.

3. Jick H, Miettinen OS, Neff RK, Shapiro S, Heinonen OP, Slone D. Coffee and myocardial infarction. N Engl J Med 1973; 289: 63–7.

4. Klatsky AL, Friedman GD, Siegelaub AB. Coffee drinking prior to myocardial infarction: results from the Kaiser-Permanente Epidemiologic Study of Myocardial Infarction. JAMA 1973; 226: 540–3.

5. Hrubec Z. Coffee Drinking and ischaemic heart-disease. Lancet 1973; 1:548.

6. Dawber TR, Kannel WB, Gordon T. Coffee and cardiovascular disease: observations from the Framingham Study. N Engl J Med 1974; 291: 871–4.

7. Hennekens CH, Drolette ME, Jesse MJ, Davies JE, Hutchison GB. Coffee drinking and death due to coronary heart disease. N Engl J med 1976; 294: 633–6.

8. Yano K, Rhoads GG, Kagan A. Coffee, alcohol and risk of coronary heart disease among Japanese men living in Hawaii. N Engl J M 1977; 297: 405–9.

9. Wilhelmsen L, Tibblin G, Elmfeldt D, Wedel H, Werkö L. Coffee consumption and coronary disease in middle-aged Swedish men. Acta Med Scand 1977; 201: 547–52.

10. Heyden S, Tyroler HA, Heiss G, Hames CG, Bartel A. Coffee consumption and mortality: total mortality, stroke mortality, and coronary heart disease mortality. Arch Intern Med 1978; 138: 1472–5.

11. Rosenberg L, Slone D, Shapiro S, Kaufman DW, Stolley PD, Miettinen OS. Coffee drinking and myocardial infarction in young women. Am J Epidemiol 1980; 111: 675–81.

12. Murray SS, Bjelke E, Gibson RW, Schuman LM. Coffee consumption and mortality from ischemic heart disease and other causes: results from the Lutheran Brotherhood Study, 1966–1978. Am J Epidemiol 1981; 113: 661–7.

13. Welin L, Svärdsudd K, Tibblin G, Wilhelmsen L. Coffee, traditional risk factors, coronary heart disease, and mortality. In: McMahon B, Sugimura T, eds. Coffee and health. Banbury report 17. Cold Spring Harbor, N.Y.: Cold Spring Harbor Laboratory, 1984: 219–29.

14. LaCroix AZ, Mead LA, Liang K-Y, Thomas CB, Pearson TA. Coffee consumption and the incidence of coronary heart disease. N Engl J. Med 1986; 315: 977–82.

15. Jacobsen BK, Bjelke E, Kvale G, Heuch I. Coffee drinking, mortality and cancer incidence: results from a Norwegian prospective study. J Natl Cancer Inst 1986; 76: 823–31.

16. Yano K, Reed DM, MacLean CJ. Coffee consumption and the incidence of coronary heart disease. N Engl J. Med 1987; 316–946.

17. LeGrady D, Dyer AR, Shekelle RB, et al. Coffee consumption and mortality in the Chicago Western Electric Company Study. Am J Epidemiol 1987; 126: 803–12.

18. Rosenberg L, Werler MM, Kaufman DW, Shapiro S. Coffee drinking and myocardial infarc-

tion in young women: an update. Am J Epidemiol 1987; 126: 147–9.

19. Rosenberg L, Palmer JR, Kelly JP, Kaufman DW, Shapiro S. Coffee drinking and nonfatal myocardial infarction in men under 55 years of age. Am J Epidemiol 1988: 128: 570–8.

20. La Vecchia C, Gentile A, Negri E, Parazzini F, Franceschi S. Coffee consumption and myocardial infarction in women. Am J Epidemiol 1989; 130: 481–5.

21. Wilson PW, Garrison RJ, Kannel WB, McGee DL, Castelli, WP. Is coffee consumption a contributor to cardiovascular disease? Insights from the Framingham Study. Arch Intern Med 1989; 149: 1169–72.

22. Tverdal, A, Stensvold I, Solvoll K, Foss OP, Lund-Larsen P, Bjartveit K. Coffee consumption and death from coronary heart disease in middle aged Norwegian men and women. BMJ 1990; 300: 566–9.

23. Lehman BA. A tempest in a coffee pot. Boston Globe. November 27, 1989: 25.

24. Sawicki P, Berger M. Coffee consumption and the incidence of coronary heart disease. N Engl J Med 1987; 316: 946.

25. Robertson D, Frölich JC, Carr RK, et al. Effects of caffeine on plasma renin activity, catecholamines and blood pressure. N Engl J Med 1978; 298: 181–6.

26. Rotenberg FA, DeFeo JJ. The effects of caffeine on cardiac irritability. Fed Proc 1976; 35:384. abstract.

27. Greenland S. Quantitative methods in the review of epidemiologic literature. Epidemiol Rev 1987; 9: 1–30.

28. Thelle DS, Heyden S, Fodor JG. Coffee and cholesterol in epidemiological and experimental studies. Atherosclerosis 1987; 67: 97–103.

29. Bak AAA, Grobbee DE. The effect on serum cholesterol levels of coffee brewed by filtering or boiling. N Engl J Med 1989; 321: 1432–7.

30. Superko HR, Bortz W, Albers JJ, Wood PD. Lipoprotein and apolipoprotein changes during a controlled trial of caffeinated and decaffeinated coffee drinking in men. Circulation 1989; 80: Suppl II:II–86. abstract.

31. Bak AAA, Grobbee DE. Effects of caffeine on blood pressure and serum lipids: results from a double blind study. Am J Clin Nutr (in press).

32. Lang T, Degoulet P, Aime F, et al. Relation between coffee drinking and blood pressure: analysis of 6,321 subjects in the Paris region. Am J Cardiol 1983; 52: 1238–42.

33. Bak AA, Grobbee DE. A randomized study on coffee and blood pressure. J Hum Hypertens 1990; 4:259–64.

34. Whitsett TL, Manion CV, Christensen HD. Cardiovascular effects of coffee and caffeine. Am J Cardiol 1984; 53: 918–22.

35. Prineas RJ, Jacobs DR Jr, Crow RS, Blackburn H. Coffee, tea and VPB. J Chronic Dis 1980; 33:67–72.

36. Jacobsen BK, Thelle DS. The Trømso Heart Study: is coffee drinking an indicator of a life style with high risk for ischemic heart disease? Acta Med Scand 1987; 222: 215–21.

37. Haffner SM, Knapp JA, Stern MP, Hazuda HP, Rosenthal M, Franco LJ. Coffee consumption diet, and lipids. Am J. Epidemiol 1985; 122: 1–12.

# POSTSCRIPT

## Can Caffeine Be Bad for Your Health?

Although caffeine is commonly consumed by millions of people without much regard to its physical and psychological effects, many studies have questioned its safety. However, others have found few hazards. For example, Grobbee et al. did not find a link between total coffee consumption and an increased risk of coronary heart disease or stroke, but they did find that higher levels of decaffeinated coffee were associated with a moderate and marginally significant increased risk of coronary heart disease.

Whether certain foods or beverages promote disease or are healthy can be very disturbing. Many people become frustrated because many of the things they eat or drink are suspected of being unhealthy. Various reports indicate that the fat in beef is unhealthy, that we should consume less salt and sugar, that processed foods should be avoided, and that whole milk, butter, and margarine should be reduced or eliminated from our diets. If people paid attention to every report about the harmful effects of the foods and beverages they consumed, then they would not be able to eat much food.

A legitimate question is whether or not such studies are worth the effort, since so many of those products that are reportedly bad are enjoyed by millions of people. Caffeine is simply one more example in which a product that is commonly consumed is now suspect. In addition, although the research is vast, it is inconclusive and contradictory. One study linked caffeine to pancreatic cancer, only to find later on that the culprit was not caffeine but cigarette smoking. Research on caffeine's effect on cancers of the bladder, urinary tract, and kidney have also proven to be inconsistent and inconclusive. If professional researchers cannot agree as to whether something is safe or harmful, how can the average person know what to believe?

In their study, Grobbee et al. indicate that there may be a connection between different brewing methods and serum cholesterol levels. Another article that addresses this topic is Annette Bak and Diederick E. Grobbee's "The Effect on Serum Cholesterol Levels of Coffee Brewed by Filtering or Boiling," *The New England Journal of Medicine* (November 23, 1989). Much of Work's article examines the abuse of caffeine as a stimulant drug in modern society. More discussion on caffeine addiction is found in "Caffeine Physical Dependence: A Review of Human and Laboratory Animal Studies," *Journal of Psychopharmocology* (April 1988), by Ronald Griffith and Phillip Woodson.

Another article that reviews research into caffeine's harmfulness is Corby Kummer's "Is Coffee Harmful?" *The Atlantic* (July 1990). And the impact of caffeine on athletic ability is discussed in Gary Wadler and Brian Hainline's *Drugs and the Athlete* (F. A. Davis, 1989).

# ISSUE 10

# Is Alcoholism Hereditary?

**YES: Secretary of Health and Human Services,** from *Seventh Special Report to the U.S. Congress on Alcohol and Health*, U.S. Department of Health and Human Services (January 1990)

**NO: Stanton Peele and Archie Brodsky,** from *The Truth About Addiction and Recovery: The Life Process Program for Outgrowing Destructive Habits* (Simon & Schuster, 1991)

## ISSUE SUMMARY

**YES:** The U.S. Department of Health and Human Services maintains that heredity is the major risk factor contributing to alcoholism and that evidence remains inconclusive as to whether or not environmental influences contribute to alcoholism.
**NO:** Social and clinical psychologist Stanton Peele and health care activist Archie Brodsky argue that research studies claiming a genetic basis for alcoholism are scientifically unpersuasive and that they ignore the critical links between personal values, environmental factors, and self-destructive or antisocial behavior.

Alcoholism is a serious health problem in many countries throughout the world. The number of people with an addiction to alcohol surpasses the number of addicts of any other drug. The National Institute on Alcohol Abuse and Alcoholism reports that there are approximately 10 million alcoholics in the United States and millions more that are problem drinkers. Yet, it is not fully understood what determines a person's disposition to alcoholism. For years, scientists have been reporting that there is a genetic tendency toward alcoholism. Research shows that there may exist specific biochemical and behavioral differences in the way sons and daughters of alcoholics respond to alcohol that may be a key as to why these children are more prone to becoming addicted to or abusive of the drug.

Children of alcoholics have been consistently shown to have high rates of alcoholism. In fact, these offspring are two to four times more likely to become alcoholic than children of nonalcoholic parents, according to the National Council on Alcoholism. Thus, alcoholism has been called a "family disease" because it tends to run in families.

The degree to which hereditary and biological risk factors make some individuals more likely candidates for addiction once they begin drinking is unknown. Psychological forces and environmental influences may also play major roles in predisposing one to alcoholism. Certainly, there is agreement among experts that a combination and interplay of all three of these factors—biological, psychological, and environmental—are responsible for alcoholic behaviors. Still, evidence for a genetic basis is increasing, and researchers are working to discover if specific genetic elements that may biologically make a person prone to alcoholism exist.

In one of the largest studies ever conducted on females and alcoholism, the *Journal of the American Medical Association* reports that heredity plays a major role in determining whether or not a woman becomes an alcoholic. Researchers found that genes do not automatically cause alcoholism, but they do account for 50 to 61 percent of a woman's risk of becoming an alcoholic. The report mirrors the results for men. Another research group found that college-aged sons of alcoholics tend to have a lower hormonal response to alcohol and feel less drunk when they drink too much when compared to young men whose parents are not alcoholic. And many adoption and twin studies indicate a genetic predisposition to alcoholism among children of alcoholic parents, lending further support to a biological possibility.

Although many scientists and psychologists believe that there is a genetic component for many people, genetic theories are still inconclusive. Researchers have not identified a single gene that creates a predisposition to alcohol abuse. Some argue that risk factors for alcoholism cannot be translated directly into genetic and biological terms and that factors such as personality traits, values, individual needs, attitudes, family upbringing, peers, and other sociocultural influences in a person's life affects one's use or abuse of alcohol.

Studies of family members show (1) common causal factors that are shared among relatives and (2) risk factors that are unique to an individual family member's life experiences and environment. In addition to sharing genes, many family members share similar environments, customs, culture, diet, and patterns of behavior. The interaction of these factors may be the foundation for a pattern of alcoholism in the family or an individual family member. Thus, the conclusion that the sole cause of alcoholism is genetics is viewed skeptically because there are too many other psychological and environmental factors that may play key roles in the onset of alcoholism.

In the following report, the U.S. Department of Health and Human Services argues that the major risk factor for developing alcoholism is being the close relative of an alcoholic. The report maintains that the research conclusively demonstrates a shared genetic vulnerability to alcoholism among family members. Stanton Peele and Archie Brodsky, in opposition, contend that addictive drinking is not written in the genes and that a variety of environmental and psychological factors and personal choices determine one's potential for alcohol abuse and addiction.

Secretary of Health
and Human Services

# GENETICS AND ENVIRONMENT

## INTRODUCTION

The observation that alcoholism tends to run in families has been confirmed by numerous reports in the modern scientific literature. For example, Cotton (1979), in a frequently cited review, analyzed 39 familial alcoholism studies published over a 10-year period. She found substantial agreement among the studies that an alcoholic is much more likely than a nonalcoholic to have a parent or other relative who is also alcoholic; two-thirds of the studies found that at least 25 percent of the alcoholics had alcoholic fathers. Based on her review, Cotton estimated that, on average, one-third of any sample of alcoholics will have at least one parent who is also alcoholic. Although most of the studies found high rates of alcoholism among the parents of alcoholics, several also found high rates among siblings. Fathers and brothers of alcoholics were more likely to have alcohol problems than the mothers and sisters of alcoholics, a fact that probably reflects the greater incidence of alcoholism among males. Thus many studies indicate that a major risk factor for developing alcoholism is being the close relative of an alcoholic.

As in the case of alcoholism, a number of common pathologies have been found to occur more frequently in some families than in others, including cardiovascular, neoplastic, emotional, and endocrine disorders (Williams 1988). One cannot, however, interpret such findings in exclusively genetic terms, since genetic factors in some diseases do not negate the contribution that environmental factors can make to the risk of developing such diseases (Williams 1988).

Traits that are familial may be passed from generation to generation by genetic factors or environmental factors. Research has produced evidence that both genetic and environmental factors contribute to alcoholism, and the interaction of genetic and environmental factors is emerging as a fundamentally important issue in the etiology of alcohol problems. As yet,

From Secretary of Health and Human Services, U.S. Department of Health and Human Services. *Seventh Special Report to the U.S. Congress on Alcohol and Health*. Rockville, MD: National Institute on Alcohol Abuse and Alcoholism, January 1990. References omitted.

the specific gene or genes involved have not been identified and the mechanisms by which genetic transmission occurs have yet to be defined. Likewise, the specific environmental risk factors are not known, although research does suggest possible childhood antecedents of alcoholism as well as potential psychological and social mechanisms related to drinking behavior and to the process of becoming dependent.

It is most plausible that the relative contribution of genetics or environment to the expression of alcohol problems in any given individual will vary depending on a number of factors including the subtype of alcoholism (Cloninger et al. 1981). For example, one form of alcoholism appears to be highly dependent on genetic factors, another form appears to require both specific genetic and environmental factors, and there are also cases of alcoholism without any obvious genetic factors (Cloninger et al. 1981).

The discussion begins with a review of recent studies involving . . . humans . . . that collectively point to the influence of heredity in the establishment of drinking patterns and in susceptibility to alcoholism. This review is followed by a discussion of research on psychological and social factors that influence drinking behavior. The chapter includes a discussion of possible heredity-environment interactions in the development of alcoholism, an area that seems likely to receive much more attention in the future.

## TWIN AND ADOPTION STUDIES

Numerous studies have demonstrated that alcoholism tends to run in families and that the pattern is consistent with genetically transmitted susceptibility. Other explanations, however, are possible, because the social environment shared by members of the same family could also predispose to alcoholism. For this reason, studies assessing the role of genetics in alcoholism must minimize or control for environmental variables. Several different approaches are possible, including the study of twins and adoptees. . . .

Twin studies are based on the principle that if a trait (for example, alcohol dependence) has genetic determinants, then persons who are genetically identical (identical twin pairs) should tend to develop more similar drinking patterns and problems than those who are genetically no more alike than ordinary siblings (fraternal twin pairs). Adoption studies are based on the principle that children born to alcoholics but adopted at an early age and raised by others, even in a nonalcoholic environment, may have a greater tendency to abuse alcohol or become alcohol dependent if they have inherited genes that make them vulnerable.

### Twin Studies

One of the earliest studies of alcoholism in twins was by Kaij (1960), who found 74 percent concordance of alcoholism between identical twins. That is, if one member of a pair of genetically identical twins was alcoholic, the probability of the other member's also being alcoholic was 74 percent. In contrast, concordance of alcoholism between fraternal twins was only 32 percent. A higher concordance rate among identical than among fraternal twins was also found by Hrubec and Omenn (1981), who reported 26-percent concordance of alcoholism in identical twins and only 13 percent in fraternal twins.

The higher concordance of alcohol dependence rates among identical twins compared to fraternal twins suggests that genetic factors are involved in predisposition to alcoholism. Identical twins have identical genetic makeup because they developed from the same fertilized ovum. Because alcohol dependence more frequently affects both members of identical twin pairs than both members of fraternal twin pairs, a plausible explanation is that it arises from shared genetic vulnerability.

An environmental explanation is also possible. For example, Partanen et al. (1966) suggested that part of the concordance of alcohol abuse patterns between twins arises from their tendency to be socially closer than nontwin siblings and, therefore, presumably more imitative. Other studies (Kaprio et al. 1979; Kaprio et al. 1978) have found that the frequency of social contact is especially high between identical twins; a study of twin brothers in the United Kingdom (Clifford et al. 1981) found evidence suggesting that at least 20 percent of the variance in alcohol consumption could be attributed to shared family experiences.

The issue of the confounding effects of social contact between twins was addressed in a recent Finnish study (Kaprio et al. 1987) of concordance of alcohol use patterns in adult twin brothers between the ages of 24 and 49. This study, involving virtually the entire population of twins in that age group in Finland (more than 2,800 pairs, nearly one-third of whom were identical twins), is the largest to date on the concordance of drinking patterns among twins.

Subjects were given a questionnaire to determine frequency and quantity of drinking, drinking "density" (regularity of drinking at particular times, such as weekends), frequency of passing out from drinking, and frequency of social contact

between twins, including cohabitation. Analysis of the data showed that cohabitation or frequent social contact between twins was indeed correlated with concordance in their drinking patterns, that identical twins had more social contact with each other during adulthood than fraternal twins, and that concordance of drinking patterns was greater between identical twins. However, greater social interaction did not fully explain the strongly similar drinking habits of identical twins, and analytical methods that adjusted for the contribution of cohabitation and social contact variables revealed a significant genetic contribution to the concordance.

For measures of frequency, quantity, and density of drinking episodes, genetic factors were significant, with heritability estimates ranging from 36 percent to 40 percent (Kaprio et al. 1987). Genetics was found to play no role in the frequency of drinking to unconsciousness. The investigators concluded that the greater similarity in drinking patterns reported by identical twin brothers cannot be fully explained by their greater social contact with each other, and that genetic factors play a significant role in the similarity of their drinking patterns.

One of the most recent twin studies (Heath et al. 1989) was also quite large, obtaining drinking information from a population of more than 1,200 identical and more than 750 fraternal female twin pairs located through the Australian National Twin Register. These sample sizes were large enough to permit a detailed analysis of the interaction of genetic and environmental factors in determining alcohol consumption levels.

In addition to questions about alcohol consumption, the respondents, whose average age was about 35, were asked for information about their marital status (which turned out to be a very influential environmental variable) and the amount of social contact between twins.

Unlike the study of Finnish male twins (Kaprio et al. 1987), analysis of the Heath et al. (1989) data gave no evidence that concordance of drinking habits in these female twin pairs was influenced in any way by either their frequency of social contact with each other or by their cohabitation. This finding might reflect gender differences in social influences on drinking habits or cultural differences between Finland and Australia.

The most significant finding, however, was a significant interaction between genetics and environment in relation to marital status, which was found to be a major modifier of genetically influenced drinking habits. (For purposes of statistical analysis, living together with a man was considered the equivalent of marriage.) In the younger cohorts (age 30 and under), genetic differences accounted for 60 percent of the variance in drinking habits in twins who were not married, but for only 31 percent of the variance in married twins. Likewise, in the older cohorts (age 31 and older), genetic factors accounted for 76 to 77 percent of the variance in drinking habits in the unmarried women, but for only 46 to 59 percent of that variance in married respondents. In other words, in both cohorts, being married or having a marriagelike relationship modified the magnitude of the impact of inherited factors that affect drinking behavior.

Another recent twin study investigated factors associated with adolescent alcohol use. Heath and Martin (1988) surveyed adult twin pairs (aged 20–30) from the Australian National Twin Register concerning their current and teen-age alcohol use in a study of genetic and social determinants of adolescent drinking. When genetic and shared environmental effects were pooled, the resulting measure of familial influences was substantially important in explaining age of drinking onset during adolescence, accounting for 51 percent of the variance in males and 58 percent in females. Gender differences were found to exist, however, in the relative importance of genetic and shared environmental factors. Among males, age of initiation of drinking was uninfluenced by genetic factors but strongly influenced by shared environment; among females, moderate genetic influence and little shared environmental effect were found. In contrast, current alcohol consumption among adult twins was strongly influenced in both sexes by genetic factors, which accounted for 58 percent of the variance in consumption in females and 45 percent in males, while 0 and 21 percent respectively was accounted for by shared environment.

Martin et al. (1985a) found genetic influences in psychomotor performance and pulse rate among twins following alcohol ingestion. Alcohol administered acutely to 206 twin pairs (42 percent of them identical) elicited great differences in psychomotor and psychological responses in individuals that had not been apparent during sobriety. About half the total variance in body sway immediately after alcohol ingestion was found to be due to genetic differences. Significant genetic contributions were also found in the variance of alcohol-elicited effects on hand steadiness, arithmetic ability, and pulse rate. These variations were significantly correlated with measures of blood alcohol concentration (BAC), previous drinking experience, and extraversion in the subjects. However, analysis led to the conclusion that very little of the genetic variation could be explained by these correlated factors, and that most of it was due to genetic factors.

## Adoption Studies

The *Sixth Special Report to the U.S. Congress on Alcohol and Health* (USDHHS 1987) gave considerable attention to adoption studies which had shown that children born to alcoholic parents but adopted during infancy and raised by others were at greater risk for alcoholism than adopted children who were born to nonalcoholics (Cloninger et al. 1981; Goodwin et al. 1973).

Adoption studies are important because they allow genetic and environmental factors to be assessed independently. Thus the effects of environmental factors can be estimated by comparing individuals with different genetic backgrounds who were raised in the same home (adoptees and their nongenetic siblings), and genetic influences can be assessed by comparing genetically related individuals who were raised in different environments (adoptees and their nonadopted genetic siblings).

The *Sixth Special Report* summarized adoption studies conducted in Sweden (Bohman et al. 1981; Cloninger et al. 1981). These studies, which examined the backgrounds of both adoptive and biological parents in relation to the existence and extent of alcohol abuse and alcohol dependence in the adopted offspring, led to the recognition of two types of alcoholism having different patterns of inheritance: type 1, milieu-limited; and type 2, male-limited. (These typologies are discussed more fully later in this chapter.) As with earlier studies in Denmark by Goodwin et al. (1973), the Swedish studies found no correlation of alcohol dependence between adoptive parents and adoptees.

It must be noted that some authors have found previous twin and adoption studies unconvincing (Peele 1986; Murray et al. 1983; Fillmore 1988a,b; Searles 1988). Criticisms involve possible biases introduced by adoption agency practices that match adoptees and adoptive parents and by the effects of use of subject cohorts spanning several decades. In addition, generalizability concerns were expressed based on both the use of nonstandard definitions of alcoholism and on possible differences between persons who place their children for adoption and persons who do not. Whether procedural imperfections in twin and adoption studies would be sufficient seriously to weaken their major conclusions is a question that can be settled only by further research. . . .

## LONGITUDINAL STUDIES

The association of parental alcoholism with adverse effects in children is well documented. In reviews of the literature on the impact of parental alcoholism on offspring (e.g., El-Guebaly and Offord 1977, 1979) numerous authors have cited evidence of negative effects at every age level from prenatal life (the fetal alcohol syndrome and other alcohol-related birth defects) to adulthood. Longitudinal studies of the children of alcoholics have explored childhood factors and their relationship to the development of alcoholism in adulthood.

One such study of children (Werner 1986) focused on factors that allow some offspring of alcoholics to go through childhood and adolescence without developing any serious problems. Asian and Polynesian natives of Hawaii having at least one alcoholic parent and having experienced alcohol-related family problems as children were selected for study; control subjects were from the same cohort of native Hawaiians. Serious problems at home, school, work, or in the community had developed by age 18 in 41 percent of the children of alcoholic parents, and 30 percent had records of repeated or serious delinquency. A striking contrast was found with respect to contacts with social services and mental health agencies; 37 percent of the children of alcoholics had made such contacts during their teens, compared with only 7 percent of the children without alcoholic parents.

The frequency of adjustment problems associated with parental alcoholism was significant in this study. Nevertheless, nearly 60 percent of the offspring of alcoholics had not developed such problems by age 18. Interviews and community records indicated that the members of the resilient group did well in school, at work, and in social life and that they had realistic goals and expectations for the future (Werner 1986). Further evaluation of the resilient and nonresilient children of alcoholics indicated differences in the two groups in temperament, communication skills, and locus of control (i.e., the belief as to whether one's life is controlled by oneself or by external factors). Characteristics differentiating the problem-free offspring of alcoholics from others included relative intelligence, achievement orientation, early social skills, responsible and caring attitude, positive self-concept, and belief in their own effectiveness. One of the factors that most strongly influenced outcome in the children was the presence or absence of alcoholism in the mother; 25 percent of the nonresilient offspring had an alco-

holic mother, compared with only 3.5 percent of resilient offspring.

A study in Stockholm (Rydelius 1981) followed for a 20-year period the health and social adjustment in children of alcoholic fathers and control children, all of whom were from families of lower socioeconomic status. A high frequency of health, learning, and social problems was found in the children of alcoholic fathers when they were first studied (at 4 to 12 years of age) and 20 years later. At the time of followup, male children of alcoholics had greater frequency of alcoholism, drug abuse, mental health problems, and antisocial behavior than females.

McCord (1988) reevaluated men who, during their youth, had been interviewed as part of a treatment program to prevent delinquency in a high-risk population. Of the men whose fathers were alcoholic, 47 percent had become alcoholic by middle age, compared with 25 percent of those whose fathers were not alcoholic. Three major factors that differentiated alcoholic from nonalcoholic sons were found: Alcoholic sons tended to come from families in which the father was alcoholic, the mother nevertheless held the father in high esteem, and the son's behavior was beyond the mother's control. The rate of alcoholism in men whose mothers expressed high regard for their alcoholic husbands was nearly double the rate in men whose mothers did not express this high regard. McCord noted, however, that other social and biological factors must be considered in understanding the development of alcoholism.

A longitudinal study by Drake and Vaillant (1988) sought to identify predictors of alcoholism and personality disorders in the children of alcoholics. The study population consisted of males who had been evaluated more than three decades earlier as nondelinquent control subjects in a study of juvenile delinquency (Glueck and Glueck 1950, 1968). At that time, the subjects were adolescents living in high-crime areas of Boston. A review of data gathered when the subjects were adolescents revealed clear differences between the sons of alcoholics and the sons of nonalcoholics. The sons of alcoholics had a greater number of other relatives who were also alcoholic (24 percent versus 13 percent); were more often of non-Mediterranean background (54 percent versus 33 percent); were more likely to have had poor relationships with their mothers (34 percent versus 24 percent) as well as with their alcoholic fathers (58 percent versus 24 percent); and on a variety of measures were more likely to have had poor adjustment, emotional problems, low competence in skills appropriate to their age, and poor physical health. The adolescent adjustment problems were most strongly related to a single variable: a poor relationship with the mother.

At the followup, alcohol dependence, diagnosed by standard clinical criteria, was more than twice as high in the children of alcoholics (28 percent versus 12 percent). Analysis revealed that predictors of eventual alcoholism in the children of alcoholics included the number of alcoholic relatives, ethnicity, and socioeconomic status. School truancy and behavior problems during adolescence were predictive in very few cases (Drake and Vaillant 1988): The investigators reported that their measures of environmental disruption and adolescent adjustment were "remarkably unrelated to subsequent alcoholic drinking" (p. 803). Except for the few subjects who had displayed behavior problems in school, no significant correlations were found between adjustment difficulties in early adolescence and alcoholism in adulthood. Vaillant and his colleagues concluded from their longitudinal studies of these subjects (Vaillant and Milofsky 1982) that behavioral traits and symptoms associated with alcoholism, including antisocial behavior in childhood, are not causes of alcoholism, and that genetic factors probably contribute far more to children's later risk of alcoholism than psycho-social factors associated with their growing up in an alcoholic home.

Zucker and Gomberg (1986) reexamined data reported by Vaillant and Milofsky (1982) and came to different conclusions. Zucker and Gomberg argued that the data of Vaillant and his colleagues, when analyzed by a different statistical technique, revealed a substantial relationship between disturbed adolescence and adult alcohol problems: Children who became alcohol dependent as adults had more behavioral and truancy problems in school, including childhood antisocial behavior, and were more likely to have dropped out of high school. A poor environmental support system and a distant relationship with the father were more common among children who later developed alcohol problems. Zucker and Gomberg also cited several cross-sectional and longitudinal studies that found childhood antisocial behavior to be a significant antecedent of alcoholism (Gomberg 1982; Jessor and Jessor 1977; Zucker and Fillmore 1968).

Zucker and Gomberg (1986) observed, however, that temporal associations among characteristics identified in longitudinal studies do not define causal factors. Nearly all such studies, they noted, have compared individuals at only two points in time, an approach that cannot yield the kind of information needed to trace causal pathways or compare the merits of alternative causal explanations.

Steinglass (1983) discussed methodological problems in family environment studies: In addition to the problem of one-point followup, lack of control groups has been a major deficiency. Jacob and Seilhamer (1987) noted methodological problems in the literature on the impact of parental alcoholism on the psychosocial and psychiatric status of offspring as including overrepresentation of subjects with multiple problems from nonintact families of lower socioeconomic status and over-reliance on self-report data. In addition to limiting the ability to generalize findings, design limitations create uncertainty about the developmental patterns involved in adverse outcomes, as well as about the nature of family and nonfamily influences that protect many children of alcoholics from such outcomes (Jacob and Seilhamer 1987).

In summary, many studies have found associations between adult alcohol dependence and circumstances of childhood and adolescence. Yet research to date has been inconclusive about the specific environmental influences involved, and causal roles for any particular family environmental factor in the development of alcoholism remain hypothetical. Nevertheless, some promising areas of inquiry have been identified. These include the question of developmental continuity between social, adjustment, and learning problems in youth and adult alcoholism; issues of parenting; and factors that may protect those at risk from developing alcoholism.

# NO

**Stanton Peele and
Archie Brodsky**

# ARE PEOPLE BORN ALCOHOLICS?

## "BUT ISN'T IT GENETIC?"

The straightforward, human view of alcoholism we have described—one that emphasizes social groups and personal responsibility—runs counter to the fashionable belief that alcoholism is an "inherited disease." For example, a front-page article in *The Wall Street Journal* in 1989 erroneously announced:

> Researchers have identified single genes as well as combinations of genes that are sometimes passed from alcoholics to their offspring that they believe create a predisposition toward alcoholism, much like blue eyes or nearsightedness.

It is essential that we firmly refute this science fiction, which creates needless fears and concerns both about our own ability to overcome drinking problems and about our children's susceptibility to alcohol abuse.

Here, in highlight form, is what scientific research has shown about the inheritance of alcoholism . . . :

- It is true that children of alcoholics are perhaps two to three times more likely than others to become alcoholics themselves.
- How much of this inheritance is due to genetic factors is open to dispute, and important studies and reviews of the research suggest the genetic component is negligible.
- No genetic marker or set of genes for alcoholism has been identified.
- Even those researchers who believe they have shown alcoholism may be inherited largely restrict their claims to a small group of extreme male alcoholics.
- *No* research disputes that alcoholism takes a good deal of time to develop, and that all sorts of environmental and psychological factors—and personal choices—bring about the ultimate outcome. In other words, no one is guaranteed to become, or to remain, an alcoholic.

- A *majority* of the offspring of alcoholics do not become alcoholic, and many make sure to drink moderately *because of* their parents' negative examples.

Popular books that insist that alcoholism is purely a "genetic disease" appeal to an understandable desire we all may feel for simple answers about painful subjects, but they do not have a sound scientific foundation. Those who actually do research on the genetic inheritance of alcoholism speak far more cautiously, often downplaying the inheritance of alcoholism:

- Robert Cloninger, psychiatrist and genetic researcher, Washington University: "The demonstration of the critical importance of sociocultural influences in most alcoholics suggests that major changes in social attitudes about drinking styles can change dramatically the prevalence of alcohol abuse regardless of genetic predisposition."

- George Vaillant, psychiatrist and alcoholism researcher (paraphrased in *Time*): "Vaillant thinks that finding a genetic marker for alcoholism would be as unlikely as finding one for basketball playing. . . . The high number of children of alcoholics who become addicted, Vaillant believes, is due less to biological factors than to poor role models."

- David Lester, a leading biological researcher at the Rutgers Center of Alcohol Studies, after reviewing several surveys of genetic research on alcoholism, concluded "that genetic involvement in the etiology of alcoholism, however structured, is weak at best."

Research on the inheritance of alcoholism has exploded since the 1970s. The first, and still the best-known, research of this kind was conducted by Donald Goodwin and his associates with Danish adoptees. They found that 18 percent of male adoptees with biological parents who were alcoholic became alcoholic themselves, compared with only 5 percent of male adoptees whose biological parents were not alcoholic. Taken at face value, this is probably the strongest evidence of the genetic inheritance of alcoholism in all the research on the subject. Yet it shows that the great majority (82 percent) of men with alcoholic fathers do not become alcoholic solely by biological inheritance—that is, when they are not directly exposed to their fathers' influence.

This research shows that whatever genetic inheritance predisposes a man to alcoholism has only a weak link with the actual behavior that we call alcoholism. But the Goodwin research has an even more surprising message for daughters of alcoholics. Daughters who were raised away from alcoholic parents did *not* become alcoholic more often than female adoptees who did not have alcoholic parents. To accept the Goodwin research, the research that established in many people's minds that there is a genetic source for alcoholism, is to *reject* the idea that women can inherit alcoholism! Other research confirms that alcoholism in women is hard to trace to genetic origins. But this raises an important question—if alcoholism is supposedly inherited, why is it only typed to one sex?

Quite a bit of additional evidence about genetic transmission of alcoholism has appeared since Goodwin's research was first published in the early 1970s. Yet, despite extravagant claims about our knowledge of the genetics of alcoholism, hardly any two researchers agree on what the inherited mechanism is that causes alcoholism. Rarely do two researchers report the same findings about the brain waves or cognitive impairments or alcohol metabolizing that each suggests is a major source for alcoholism. Other researchers have conducted large-scale studies that have not found *any* differences between offspring of alcoholics and those who did not have an alcoholic parent in terms of alcohol metabolism, sensitivity to alcohol, tolerance for alcohol, and mood.

Not only is there contradictory evidence about when, how, and by whom alcoholism is inherited, but other research casts doubt altogether on the increased risk for inheritance of alcoholism by biological relatives of alcoholics. Robin Murray, dean of the Institute of Psychiatry at Maudsley Hospital in Britain, compared alcoholism rates for a group of identical and fraternal twins. Identical twins have the same genetic makeup, whereas fraternal twins are no more alike genetically than any brothers or sisters are. Therefore, if alcoholism were transmitted genetically, an identical twin of an alcoholic would more likely be alcoholic than would a fraternal twin of an alcoholic. Not so, Murray found. Nonidentical twins of alcoholics in his research were just as likely to be alcoholic as identical twins of alcoholics. We do not hear about Murray's research from popularizers of science in the United States. Murray has commented: "Students of alcoholism must continually beware lest they fall victim to the extravagant swings of intellectual fashion that so bedevil the field, and nowhere is such vigilance more necessary than in considering the possible etiological role of heredity."

Research *does* generally find that alcoholics differ in having somewhat reduced cognitive capacity. But here is the problem. Alcoholics, as we have seen, are usually in worse socioeconomic circumstances

and more often come from disturbed and abusive families. It is frequently very hard to separate these factors from any signs of impairment that offspring of alcoholics show. This may be why Marc Schuckit, a psychiatrist who has investigated college students and staff with alcoholic parents, did *not* find significant cognitive or neurological problems. In other words, the few alcoholics who come from the middle- or upper-middle-class families that send people to college don't inherit the traits that supposedly characterize all alcoholics.

As a result of his research, Schuckit, though arguing that alcoholism is inherited, disputes the neurological mechanisms many researchers claim to be at the heart of the inheritance of alcoholism. Instead, Schuckit proposes that the susceptibility to alcoholism is inherited in the form of a *lessened sensitivity* to alcohol. In other words, the children of alcoholics have an inbred tolerance for alcohol that means they feel fewer effects when they drink heavily (although this description sounds very different from the stories told by A.A. [Alcoholics Anonymous] members, who typically describe getting drunk the first time they drank). The person may then drink excessively without realizing it for a long enough time to become fully dependent on alcohol. In this theory, even the alcoholically predisposed individual has to drink a great deal over a long period to become alcoholic.

Another of the best-known genetic researchers, psychiatrist Robert Cloninger, maintains that inherited alcoholism is present in a minority of male alcoholics, for whom it is transmitted through paternal genes via the same route as criminality. The research Cloninger and his associates have conducted in Sweden suggests that what puts children at risk for alcoholism has little to do with bio-chemical reactions. These researchers identified personality as the main source of alcoholism for the high-risk group of men who either drink excessively or become criminals. Children's personalities were rated at age eleven and their alcohol use assessed at age twenty-seven. The children most likely to become alcohol abusers were relatively fearless, novelty-seeking, and indifferent to others' opinions of them. Indeed, 97 percent of the boys who ranked very high in novelty-seeking and very low in avoiding harm later abused alcohol, while only 1 percent of those very low in novelty-seeking and *average* in avoiding harm did so—a difference so enormous as to dwarf any supposed biological markers of alcoholism claimed by one or another researcher! At the other end of the scale, boys who were very harm-avoidant or very sensitive to others' opinions of them also ran a fairly high risk of alcohol abuse.

Are these personality traits inherited or environmentally caused, or do they represent some combination? Whichever, they take us far away from alcohol metabolism as a prime risk factor for alcoholism. Instead, they describe *types of people* who become alcoholics. Few people accept that personalities, such as the "criminal personality," are wholly formed at birth. To do so, for example, would mean that we believe that the extremely high rate of crime among blacks is genetically caused, or that the visibility of Italians in organized crime is a biological phenomenon! Furthermore, to accept Cloninger's theory is to believe that offspring of alcoholics are as genetically predisposed to become criminals as they are to become alcoholics.

## PERSONALITY AND VALUES IN ALCOHOLISM

Cloninger is not the first researcher to note the heavy overlap between criminal traits and alcoholism. Researchers have consistently found that the personality profile most closely associated with alcoholism involves an antisocial disposition, aggressiveness, and lack of inhibition and impulse control. Several studies, indeed, have measured these traits in college and high-school men and then successfully predicted which young people were more likely to become alcoholics, without even examining how much they drank! One psychologist, Craig Mac-Andrew, has established a scale that has regularly shown that alcoholics have "an assertive, aggressive, pleasure-seeking character" which closely resembles that found for criminals and delinquents. Women alcoholics as well as men often show this proclivity for excitement-seeking and criminality.

There is a second, smaller group of alcoholics who express a great deal of emotional pain which they drink to relieve. A higher percentage of women alcoholics fall into this group. But whether a person is antisocial or not hardly seems like an inbred trait that is unaffected by environment and upbringing. Nor, on the other hand, is it likely that, just *because* a person has a painful sense of the world, he or she will become an alcoholic in response to these feelings. The role of personality in alcoholism suggests that a range of factors goes into producing alcoholism, even among those who find that drinking alleviates negative feelings. In addition to a predisposing personal orientation, a person must have *values* that set up and perpetuate the behavior we call alcoholism.

As we saw in the last section, psychiatrist Marc Schuckit finds that children of alcoholics inherit a lessened sensitivity to alcohol. Thus, they may drink more for longer periods without being fully aware of the effects. Why, however, don't such negative signs as hangovers, criticism from family and loved ones, legal and work problems, and so on discourage their continued heavy drinking? Psychiatrist George Vaillant's results from examining drinkers over forty years of their lives likewise demonstrated that alcoholism is the result of a long history of problem drinking. Vaillant found "no credence to the common belief that some individuals become alcoholics after the first drink. The progression from alcohol use to abuse takes years." Whether or not you have some special sensitivity—or insensitivity—to alcohol, you must persist in problem drinking for years, oblivious to all the negative feedback your behavior elicits, before you develop a full-blown addiction. Whatever your biochemical reaction to alcohol, you have to have *reasons* to drink regularly and excessively over such a long period.

If, on the other hand, you have reasons not to continue destructive drinking—such as conflicting priorities, values, and social pressures—it wouldn't seem that you would continue on this path. You would heed the many warnings to change your behavior that you receive over a drinking career. The idea that many people avoid drinking too much because they don't like the consequences of overdrinking, regardless of how their genes prime them to react to alcohol, is straightforward and logical. We all know people who say things like, "After more than a drink or two I'm really out of it, so I rarely drink that much—maybe at a wedding." In fact, studies reveal that even young people develop strategies to control their drinking. Researchers sent nearly twenty-five hundred students at nine universities a questionnaire asking how important various reasons were in their decision to limit their drinking. The students' answers grouped themselves into four overall motivations (listed here with a few examples of each):

1. *Preference for self-control*
"I've seen the negative effects of someone else's drinking."
"Drinking heavily is a sign of personal weakness."
"It's bad for my health."
"I'm concerned about what people might think."

2. *Influence of upbringing and respect for authority*
"I was brought up not to drink."
"My religion discourages or is against drinking."
"I'm part of a group that doesn't drink much."

3. *Attempts at self-reform*
"I've become concerned with how much I've been drinking."
"Someone suggested that I drink less."
"I was embarrassed by something I said or did when drinking."

4. *Performance aspirations*
"Drinking reduces my performance in sports."
"Drinking interferes with my studies."
"I wouldn't want to disappoint my parents."

Here we see young people taking in feedback from the outside world, making value judgments, and adjusting their habits with a view toward health, responsibility, personal satisfaction, and social appropriateness. There's nothing medical or mystical about it.

## CHILDREN CAN AND DO REJECT THEIR PARENTS' ALCOHOLISM

Even though an alcoholic is more likely to have alcoholic offspring than is the average person, nowhere near a majority of children of alcoholics become alcoholics themselves. That is, most people don't imitate their parents' problem drinking—at least they don't do so over the long haul. Often, they even learn to avoid problem drinking *because* of their parents' negative examples. Epidemiologists at the University of Michigan followed the drinking patterns of residents of Tecumseh, Michigan, for seventeen years, beginning in 1960. Their findings can only be called good news for those who worry that children of alcoholics, when they drink, are destined to progress to alcoholism. The researchers found that the children of moderate drinkers were much more likely to imitate their parents' drinking habits than were those whose parents were at the high or low extremes of alcohol consumption. "That is, whereas most offspring of moderate drinkers drink moderately, most children of heaviest drinkers also drink moderately and there are more abstainers' offspring who drink than who abstain."

They conclude, based on their evidence and a review of the literature, that

> even alcoholic parental drinking only weakly invites imitation by offspring. Thus, despite the presence of familial alcoholism, the review of evidence indicates that parental heavy drinking (usually associated with interpersonal or social conflict) may not be followed closely by offspring and, in fact, that the majority of offspring seem to follow a less troublesome drinking style.

Many children actually learn from seeing and feeling the consequences of a parent's alcoholism to avoid drinking destructively themselves. Children in the Tecumseh study who were of the opposite sex from the heavy-drinking parent were especially unlikely to imitate the parent's heavy drinking. Moreover, when a heavy-drinking parent had an evident drinking problem, this made offspring *less* likely to imitate them. In such cases, it seems, it became easier for children to form an independent perspective on drinking and to reject their parents' model.

The more often the parent has drinking problems, the *less* likely the child is to follow the same path. This finding flies in the face of the notion of alcoholism as an inherited disease. But it is entirely understandable if we just think about what people really are like. A child may well be more likely to emulate a parent who is a quiet heavy drinker than one whose drinking has visibly unpleasant manifestations. The bigger fools the parents make of themselves, the less the child will want to imitate them. Consider, in this regard, Ronald Reagan's vivid recollections of how his mother picked his father up off the lawn after the father returned from a round of drinking, and how he himself resolved never to cause his mother this kind of unhappiness. That did not stop him, however, from drinking occasionally and moderately.

Not only are children of alcoholics *not* doomed to be alcoholics themselves, but several studies have shown that children of alcoholics who *have* developed a drinking problem do better at moderating their drinking (when that is the goal of treatment) than other problem drinkers. It seems as if some childhood problems can strengthen a person's resilience and independence. Yet today we undermine such resilience by telling the person that those problems are permanently disabling. As one woman, a moderate drinker, remarked when she received some literature about children of alcoholics, "It would have been helpful for me as a child to know that my father's behavior when he was drinking wasn't normal. It *wouldn't* have helped me to hear that I was likely to become an alcoholic myself."

It is in families and groups with the greatest social dysfunction—where crime and open alcoholism are most rampant and positive social values most lacking—that alcoholism is likely to be passed on from parent to child. Alcoholism is most frequently transmitted in ghetto and economically disadvantaged households and those disrupted by divorce and child abuse, where children have the fewest opportunities to escape the social and economic pressures that dominate their parents' lives. Most people who join Adult Children of Alcoholics (ACoA) groups, on the other hand, lead stable lives themselves and may have had a parent who was a "functioning" alcoholic. This family structure less often produces alcoholic children. Indeed, the gigantic growth of the "Children of Alcoholics" movement—most of whose members are women with alcoholic or heavy-drinking fathers who are not alcoholics themselves—is testimony to just how many people refuse to become alcoholics merely because their parents were.

# POSTSCRIPT

## Is Alcoholism Hereditary?

Is there a significant, substantiated relationship between heredity and alcoholism? The U.S. Department of Health and Human Services alleges that numerous studies demonstrate a high probability of biological vulnerability to alcohol addiction. Peele and Brodsky argue that critical environmental and psychological influences as risk factors for alcoholism cannot be overlooked. In the final analysis, this issue comes down to which research one chooses to accept.

Some experts have expressed concern for certain people who feel that alcoholism is a family legacy. An individual who believes that he or she is destined to become an alcoholic because his or her mother, father, aunt, uncle, or grandparent has suffered from alcoholism may become alcoholic to satisfy a self-fulfilling prophecy. Some psychologists believe that this may have lamentable consequences for such individuals who feel that alcoholism is their destiny anyway.

Some medical experts contend that this fear of people convincing themselves that they will become alcoholics is unfounded for two reasons. First, if a genetic predisposition to alcoholism were conclusively proven, then medical therapies could be designed to help those who had the hereditary risk. Second, if a person were diagnosed as having a genetic predisposition, then he or she could adopt behaviors that would help avoid problem drinking. That is, they would become aware of the hereditary factor and adjust their attitudes and actions accordingly.

Because of the lack of conclusive evidence identifying heredity as the primary cause of alcoholism, it may be wise to err on the side of caution with regard to consigning children of alcoholics to a fate of alcoholism. On the other hand, research that consistently finds higher rates of alcoholism and alcohol abuse among children of alcoholics cannot be dismissed. This link alone provides ample support for additional funding of research studies that may delineate the exact nature of and risk factors of alcoholism.

An interesting article that provides a different look at the genetic basis of alcoholism is C. Robert Cloninger's "D2 Dopamine Receptor Gene Is Associated but Not Linked With Alcoholism," *Journal of the American Medical Association* (October 2, 1991). The implications of heredity as a cause of alcoholism are examined in Newlin and Thomson's "Alcohol Challenges With Sons of Alcoholics: A Critical Review and Analysis," *Psychological Bulletin* (November 1990). In "The Role of Genetics in the Pathogenesis of Alcoholism," *Journal of Abnormal Psychology* (May 1988), John Searles supports heredity as a cause of alcoholism. An excellent book that studies a group of alcoholics over a 40-year period is George E. Vaillant's *The Natural History of Alcoholism* (Harvard University Press, 1983).

Pledge to th...

I pledge allegianc...
of the United States...
and to the Republic for...
one Nation under G...
with lib...
and justi...

# PART 3
## Drug Prevention and Treatment

*In spite of their legal consequences and the government's interdiction efforts, drugs are widely available and used. Two common ways of dealing with drug abuse is to incarcerate drug users and to intercept drugs. However, many drug experts believe that more energy should be put into preventing and treating drug abuse. An important step toward prevention and treatment is to find out what contributes to drug abuse and how to nullify these factors.*

*By educating young people about the potential hazards of drugs and by developing an awareness of social influences that contribute to drug use, many drug-related problems may be averted. The debates in this section focus on different prevention and treatment issues and the value of related policies and programs.*

Do Drug Education Programs Prevent Drug Abuse?

Should Tobacco Advertising Be Prohibited?

Is the "Disease" of Alcoholism a Myth?

Should Alcohol Advertising Be Limited?

Are Drug Addicts Always in Control of Their Addiction?

Do Alcoholics Have to Maintain a Lifetime of Abstinence?

Are the Dangers of Steroids Exaggerated?

# ISSUE 11

## Do Drug Education Programs Prevent Drug Abuse?

**YES: Falcon Baker,** from *Saving Our Kids from Delinquency, Drugs, and Despair* (Cornelia & Michael Bessie Books, 1991)

**NO: Harry H. Avis,** from *Drugs and Life* (Wm. C. Brown, 1990)

### ISSUE SUMMARY

**YES:** Despite the ineffectiveness of many early drug education programs, Falcon Baker, a director of delinquency programs, argues that drug education is a viable avenue for dealing with drug problems. He describes two drug education programs that have been successful.
**NO:** Professor of psychology Harry H. Avis highlights many of the inadequacies of drug education and argues that schools are unfairly being asked to address problems that exist in all of society.

Drug education is arguably one of the most logical ways of dealing with the problems of drugs in society. Drug-taking behavior has not been significantly affected by reducing the demand for drugs, and drug prohibition, as in the case of alcohol, has also failed. One remaining option to explore is drug education. Society often looks for quick cures for its problems. However, drug education is not an overnight panacea for eliminating drug problems. Rates of cigarette smoking have declined dramatically, but it took 25 years of public health efforts to achieve this. If drug education is to prove ultimately successful, it, too, will take years.

Many early drug education programs were misguided. One emphasis was on "scare tactics." Experts erroneously believed that if young people saw the horrible consequences of drug use, then they would certainly abstain from drugs. Another faulty assumption was that drug use would be affected by knowledge about drugs, but it is obvious that knowledge is not enough. Over 400,000 people die each year from tobacco use, but 30 percent of Americans continue to smoke, even though almost all smokers know the grim statistics about tobacco. Young people have a hard time relating to potential problems like lung cancer and cirrhosis of the liver, since these problems take years to show up if they show up at all. If drug education is going to be effective, it will need to deal with the immediate consequences of drugs, not the long-term consequences. Another major problem with early drug education programs was that much of the information that teachers relayed concerning drugs was either incorrect or exaggerated. Teachers were therefore not seen as credible.

Whether or not drug education is effective or shows promise of being effective is a debatable topic. There is also a lack of consensus as to what a drug education program should encompass. However, there is general agreement among drug prevention experts that "drug awareness" programs are counterproductive. Many schools conduct drug awareness programs, in which, over the course of a week, former drug abusers talk to students about how their personal lives and families were ruined by drugs, pharmacologists demonstrate the physical effects of drugs, and films are shown that depict the horrors of drugs. These sensationalized programs stimulate curiosity, and it is not unusual for drug use to increase after one of these special presentations.

Many drug prevention programs in the 1970s focused on self-esteem and values clarification. If low self-esteem is a factor in drug use, as many believed, then it would make sense to improve self-esteem to reduce drug use. However, self-esteem is not always a good indicator of drug use. Many young people who have good feelings about themselves use drugs. An important distinction is drug use versus drug abuse: Someone who abuses drugs is more likely to have low self-esteem. In addition to the erroneous belief that an increase in self-worth would decrease the likelihood of drug use, many believed that if students clarified their values, they would see the folly of using drugs. However, sometimes overlooked was the fact that some students value using drugs. Young people may value using drugs because they are more accepted by their peers, because drugs are forbidden, or simply because they enjoy the high that comes from drug use. The values clarification approach has been discarded by most drug educators.

The current emphasis in drug education is on primary prevention. It is easier to have young people not use drugs in the first place than to get them to stop after they have already started using drugs. This approach affects which students receive drug education. It is logical to put more energy into teaching elementary students about drugs than high school students, since the latter are more likely to have already begun using drugs. The drugs that are most likely to be discussed are tobacco, alcohol, and marijuana. These are considered to be "gateway drugs," which means that students who use other drugs are most likely to have used these first. The longer students delay using tobacco, alcohol, and marijuana, the less likely they are to use other drugs.

In the following selections, Falcon Baker discusses the reasons why drug education must be pursued and addresses what schools need to do to improve the quality of drug education. Harry H. Avis describes the limitations of drug education and points out that too much is expected from schools with regard to drug prevention.

# YES

Falcon Baker

# TOWARD A WINNABLE WAR ON DRUGS

### THE PROMISE OF DRUG EDUCATION

Juveniles (and adults) use drugs for two highly different reasons. The two are usually confused. One, *recreational use,* is relatively innocuous; the other, *escapism,* is devastatingly destructive to both the individual and society.

Recreational use—for pleasure and sociability—is by far the most common reason that drugs (including alcohol) are used. In the case of marijuana, this is usually self-limiting, both in frequency and amount, and also in the number of years that it is used. Young people generally begin to phase it out in their early twenties, and most have entirely stopped by the time they are thirty. This recreational use is, at worst, only a very minor social problem.

Likewise, most other drugs are not serious problems as long as they are used to facilitate socialization or relaxation and not as an aid to psychologically drop out of life. This does not imply that efforts to reduce, or stop, the recreational use of drugs should be abandoned. Definitely not! America knows all too well the tragic results of the recreational use of alcohol and tobacco.

But how are we to slow the recreational use of drugs?

Trying to reduce supply has been ineffective. Legal prohibition has been a fiasco. What remains is education . . . education to help young people decide on their own to reject drugs.

While education will not be the overnight miracle that many seek, there is considerable proof that it will work, albeit slowly. The twenty-five-year public health campaign on the dangers of tobacco has brought a dramatic reduction in smoking. It has been accomplished without passing laws, or putting people in jail, or requiring urine tests, or spraying fields of tobacco with dangerous herbicides. Ironically, the campaign has been least successful among the one group for whom cigarettes are illegal—juveniles. The health messages have not been youth-oriented and have been made largely in media not seen by most teenagers.

## The "How-not-to" Drug Education

Drug education got off to a disastrous start back in the 1970s when President Nixon made drug prevention money available to schools. An avalanche of hastily prepared materials was produced by greedy publishers out to make a fast buck. Most were based on two faulty assumptions: that young people lack sufficient information about drugs to make intelligent decisions, and that they can be scared away from experimentation by horror stories. Some of the educational "facts" came straight from the "killer weed" tales concocted by [Henry J.] Anslinger. Teachers lost credibility when they repeated these facts to youngsters who personally knew they were false.

The results? The "education" in the early seventies caused a rapid escalation of use among students. Films and pamphlets designed from an adult point of view to show the evils of drugs merely succeeded in introducing the youngsters to an exotic new world to be explored. Students figured they must be missing out on something pretty hot if adults were all that uptight.

Nearly twenty years ago Louie Nunn, while governor of Kentucky, unwittingly became the commonwealth's most successful drug pusher. To show the state's young people the dangers of drugs (at the time principally marijuana, pep pills, and LSD), he organized a statewide alert. A large exhibition hall in Louisville was filled with booths showing different stages of the evil weed from growth to a rolled joint, bottles of colorful prescription-only pills, exotic paraphernalia used with various drugs, and movies depicting wild hallucinogenic trips in which objects whirled madly about the room in psychedelic colors. Horrifying to adults, electrifying to juveniles.

To this drug carnival thousands of students from every corner of the state were bused in each day. They stared goggle-eyed at all the wonders. One streetwise city youth told me, "Them country dudes keep asking me, 'Hey, where can I get some of that stuff?' "

Teenage drug use in the state skyrocketed.

## Prevention Through Drug Education

Fortunately, educators learned from those counterproductive beginnings. A more honest approach to drug education has begun to get the message across. Program planners have learned that efforts must begin at the earliest elementary levels before the start of experimentation, which occurs at an ever younger age, even in the second and third grades. And the education must be continued all through school.

Adolescents are now-oriented, not future-oriented. This is an important key. In successful junior-high antismoking programs, the emphasis has been on immediate effects such as bad breath, discolored teeth, and reduced athletic ability, even sexual prowess. This has been more effective than the warnings about death from lung cancer or heart disease that have reached adults. For ten- and twelve-year-olds such things are too far in the future to be frightening. Many have not even internalized the concept of death.

A few schools are zeroing in on the reason most young people start using drugs: peer pressure. They are attempting to turn the tables and use it to prevent drug use. Discussions center on ways to avoid going along with the crowd without becoming an outcast. Effective lessons concentrate on providing accurate information about alcohol and drug dangers, teaching students decision-making skills, and giving them ideas for alternatives to drug use. Innovative approaches are being used. "Super Teams," for example, is a peer counseling program made possibly by the National Football Players Association and other professional athletes. Featuring visits by athletic luminaries, the program promotes self-respect and personal discipline.

D.A.R.E. (Drug Abuse Resistance Education), sponsored nationwide by Kentucky Fried Chicken, now has more than two thousand chapters in forty-nine states. It is expected that in 1991 nearly 5 million children in elementary school exit grades will hear a semester-long program designed to give them facts about drug abuse and to "inoculate" them against peer pressure. While a few critics question the use of uniformed policemen as teachers, preliminary evaluations indicate that the program is reducing the incidence of drug abuse, truancy, and vandalism.

One unsung hero of the drug war is Sheila Tate, who was the former First Lady's press secretary at the time Nancy Reagan's public image was that of a shallow and aloof ex-movie star, obsessed with designer clothes and a lavish life-style. Tate persuaded Mrs. Reagan to embark on her "Just Say No" campaign in an effort to create a new image.

While "Just Say No" itself is far too simplistic, it does head in the right direction—persuasion instead of force. There are indications that it has had more effect than have the billions Mrs. Reagan's husband used to fight supply. With encouragement from concerned parents and educators, voluntary youth programs sprang up. State networks were established in Mississippi, Texas, Flor-

ida, and Ohio. In May 1986, the nearly ten thousand "Just Say No" clubs sponsored a nationwide drug alert day in which it was claimed 5 million young people in six hundred communities participated.

Other groups with similar agendas, such as World Youth Against Drug Abuse and REACH (Responsible Adolescents Can Help), have been formed. Memberships range from fourth- and fifth-graders on up to college students. At the moment these groups exist primarily on the fringes of the in-group youth culture and probably fail to reach those at greatest risk for drug abuse. But their growth is evidence that peer pressure can be used as a positive force.

Along with these student programs other parts of a multidiscipline, multimedia effort have already begun. The Media Advertising Partnership for a Drug-Free America campaign has demonstrated that social attitudes toward drugs can be changed, although not as dramatically as some have hoped, and possibly least effectively with teenagers. TV and radio commercials and printed advertisements worth over $300 million in space and time have been donated in the past two years. In addition, the Advertising Council, the industry's non-profit public service arm, has aimed much of its annual half-billion dollars' worth of free advertising to the drug abuse problem.

The findings of a two-year study by the Harvard School of Public Health, published in the summer 1990 issue of *Health Affairs*, are critical of these media efforts. Among recommendations to make mass media campaigns more effective:

• Resist the use of scare tactics such as showing an egg in a frying pan which the commentator identifies as "your brain on drugs." As has been discovered in drug education in the classroom, viewers tune out scare tactics by denying that the message is relevant to them. Instead, the ads should be geared toward adopting healthy life-styles and obtaining love and acceptance.

• Persuade the advertising industry to utilize the same marketing techniques used in successful commercial campaigns. Instead of the scattergun approach, for example, ads should be targeted to specific segments of the population based on age and demographic characteristics (as is now done by the cigarette industry).

Ads also should be market-tested for effectiveness before being used on a large scale.

• In a similar manner, persuade managers of TV and radio stations and publishers of printed media fillers to schedule these ads with programs attracting the targeted audiences, particularly teenagers, instead of using them at odd periods as fillers.

• Persuade independent television producers to insert dialogue with an antidrug message into prime-time network shows. The report points to the 1988 success of the Harvard Center for Health Communications in persuading fifteen producers to include in their shows favorable mention of the designated driver program to prevent drunk driving accidents. When combined with prime-time commercials on all three major networks, a Gallup poll found a 15 percent increase in persons reporting the use of a designated driver.

Too easily ignored in most drug education plans is the number-one drug abuse—alcohol. Despite the many pompous pronouncements about marijuana, *alcohol* is the gateway drug that introduces virtually all youths to the euphoria and mood-altering excitement to be found by taking chemicals into the body. If recreational drug use is to be slowed, a tremendous educational effort in the schools is required to counter the effects of the annual $1.4 billion spent on media advertising to promote beer, wine, and hard liquor. Much of this, particularly the $800-million advertising budget for beer, only thinly disguises its appeal to the youth of America.

The Workshop on Drunk Driving assembled by former U.S. Surgeon General C. Everett Koop reported that a two-year-old will have seen 100,000 beer commercials by the age of eighteen. Many of these will have been in connection with sports events such as baseball and football games, and others will have included youth-oriented celebrities. Special promotions at Florida's ritualistic spring break, at rock concerts, and on college campuses are brazenly addressed to audiences where the majority is too young to drink legally. Is it any wonder that two-thirds of America's high school seniors report they are currently consumers of alcohol? Virtually all underage! And with this introduction to mind-altering substances, many have gone on to illegal drugs.

Just as efforts to reduce cigarette consumption made it necessary to require tobacco companies to modify their advertising, so it is necessary if drug education is to be successful that the alcohol industry be forced to modify its advertising and promotions so as not to be so blatantly targeted to youth. To head off legislative restrictions, brewers have been offering public service ads promoting "safe" drinking.

The slogan "Know when to say when" is a compelling public relations gimmick, but few youngsters approaching the dangerous level of intoxication are in sufficient control either to know or to say when. However, the slogan succeeds in conveying to teenagers a false sense of confidence that they can always be in control. So it is safe to guzzle beer. If youngsters really were able to say when, beer would not be the number-one cause of drinking-and-driving accidents. One hopes such public relations ploys will not silence demands that advertising be prevented from imprinting on juvenile minds the excitement to be found in this gateway drug.

### The Big Three

Antidrug education in the schools should be targeted at three drugs, two legal, one currently illegal—alcohol, tobacco, and marijuana. Efforts should begin in the early elementary levels. If young people could be steered away from these three, problems with drug abuse would be 98 percent eliminated.

The June 1989 issue of the *Journal of the American Medical Association* reports a comprehensive community program involving 22,500 sixth- and seventh-graders in forty-two schools in Kansas City, Missouri, and Kansas City, Kansas. For evaluation the schools were randomly assigned to the experimental program or to a control group being given the regular drug education curriculum. Efforts were aimed primarily at the same big three—alcohol, tobacco, and marijuana. Students were taught the dangers of using drugs and ways to avoid peer pressure. Parents were involved in parent-child discussions, rule setting, and role-playing. Newspaper articles along with TV and radio spots were coordinated with the school activities.

At the end of the year results of this coordinated school, home, and community program were dramatic. In the control schools 13.1 percent of the students reported having smoked cigarettes in the previous month compared to 3.4 percent of those in the program. With alcohol the comparison was 9.4 percent to 4.2 percent, and with marijuana 7.1 percent to 3.4 percent. Even more encouraging, follow-up data three years later indicated that not only had the program effects been maintained, in some cases they had increased.

Report of the project, headed by Mary Ann Pentz of the University of California, is indeed good news in an arena sadly lacking in good news. It indicates that school-based drug education can be successful.

# NO

**Harry H. Avis**

# DRUG EDUCATION AND
# DRUG PREVENTION

Virtually everyone knows that cigarette smoking is harmful, and a similarly high percentage believe the same about marijuana, cocaine, and heroin. Why then do we continue to spend billions of dollars to buy and use these drugs? Surely a drug education program could be developed that would reduce or eliminate the use of harmful chemical substances. In spite of the billions of dollars that have already been spent for that purpose, drug use continues to increase. This leads us to conclude that current programs do not seem to be working. Is there anything that can be done? We can best begin by examining the kinds of programs that already exist.

Drug education and drug abuse prevention programs can be divided into three groups: those that try to prevent drug use from occurring in the first place (primary prevention), those geared for early intervention (secondary prevention), and those aimed at helping the drug abuser after abuse is established (tertiary prevention). Each of these programs is geared to specific tactics, and each has had its "day in the sun," with millions of dollars being poured into the prevention pipeline. Rarely has there been an attempt to come up with an integrated approach, incorporating all three kinds of programs.

## PRIMARY PREVENTION

Primary prevention would seem to be the ideal—the goal being to get to the potential user/abuser *before* he or she has an opportunity to begin using drugs. Programs with this approach have to start very early, since recreational use of licit and illicit drugs is beginning at an earlier and earlier age. Many programs begin in grade school, and it is generally acknowledged that *primary* prevention programs aimed at high school students are equivalent to teaching fish to swim.

## The First Attempts

There are trends in primary prevention programs, just as there are trends in clothing, automobiles, and psychotherapy methods. The earliest programs were based on the entirely reasonable assumption that rational people do not do harmful things to themselves, and that revealing the danger of drugs would be an effective deterrent. Many of us remember seeing programs like these in high school. The presenter showed slides of cancerous lungs, then smoked a cigarette through a handkerchief to display the tars and residue the filter did not remove. Slides of abscesses on the arms of addicts were followed by lurid details of the horrors of drug withdrawal. There may also have been a graphic film of traffic accidents caused by drunken drivers.

Unfortunately, these programs on the dangers of drugs did not work. Furthermore, much of the information presented was inaccurate. The stories of people taking LSD and staring at the sun until they were blinded, hideous murders being perpetrated by "marijuana addicts," and instantaneous death due to heroin overdose were either patently untrue or greatly exaggerated. When the experimental user discovered, through personal experience, that marijuana did not cause permanent insanity, disbelief led to skepticism and the user ignored "advice" on other drugs by these same "experts." After all, it is not irrational to think that if the authorities were wrong about marijuana they were also wrong about heroin.

Many of these programs went so far overboard on the *dangers* of drugs that they produced "overkill." In fact, many experts presently believe that this kind of emphasis only serves to make it more attractive to precisely those who are at greatest risk for developing a pattern of abuse. Young adolescents and preteens often are attracted to the element of danger in any endeavor, and drug use is often seen by them as daring behavior.

Only slightly better than the focus on drug dangers were the *drug education* programs. These were supposedly nonjudgmental discussions of the pros and cons of drug use and of specific drugs. The assumption was that people used drugs because of misconceptions and a lack of knowledge about their effects. Take away the mythology (LSD dissolves the ego and enables you to see God), be honest and correct about the dangers, and the drug problem will disappear.

Consider, however, that very few teachers also are experts in pharmacology, psychology, and medicine. The programs tended to be conducted either in a perfunctory manner (remember your classes on sex education in high school?) or were directed by traveling "road show" experts who went from school to school with one-time one-hour lectures. Somehow these methods were expected to counteract a lifetime of learning, perhaps, misinformation about drugs from adults and peers (Weisheit, 1983).

Imagine the despair of the drug abuse establishment when evaluations of these programs revealed that they may actually have led to an *increase* in drug use (Bernard, Fafoglia, & Perone, 1987). In April 1973 the White House Special Action Office for Drug Abuse Prevention (SAODAP) called a moratorium on the production of all federally-funded drug information material, and eight months later published guidelines for subsequent material. The guidelines called for an end to all scare tactics, stereotyping of drug users, and dogmatic statements, such as "use of drug X always causes problem Y." At the same time they called for excluding information that demonstrated the proper use of illegal drugs (Resnick, 1978).

In all probability the increase in drug use resulting from these programs was in experimental use and did not reflect any basic flaw in the programs. Any discussion of any topic is bound to produce an increase in awareness and often arouse curiosity. If I did not know, for example, that I could get light-headed by sniffing gasoline until I heard about it in class, I might decide to try it the next time I had to mow the lawn. In the late 1960s, there was a brief fad of banana peel smoking. Rational, intelligent people by the thousands scraped the inside of banana skins, baked the result in an oven and smoked it. They were inspired by newspaper reports that smoking banana peels would get you high.

## The Self-Esteem Approach

These first drug abuse prevention programs were replaced by programs that often were so tangentially related to drug use as such that drugs frequently were never mentioned at all! In the late 1970s, the momentum in programs shifted from the drug to the person taking the drug. The philosophy behind these programs came from the humanistic psychology movement and can be explained partly by figure 1. There is a limit to how good you can feel and how much a drug can simulate that feeling. If you already feel good about yourself, then a drug will have little effect. As shown in figure 1, drugs have their greatest effect on those who aren't happy to begin with.

Drug abuse prevention programs following this model focused on develop-

Figure 1

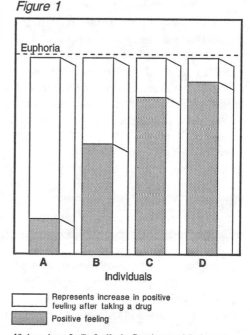

All drugs have "ceiling" effects. People cannot feel more than euphoric. Isn't it reasonable to assume that Individual A will "enjoy" a drug more than Individual D? Perhaps part of the solution is to help people feel better about themselves so that drugs will not affect them as greatly.

ing self-esteem and teaching such skills as coping and communication. Values clarification was a catchword for these programs which, until recently, were quite popular. Of course, most hard-working high school teachers were no more experienced in values clarification than in pharmacology. Usually, high school teachers use a fact-oriented approach to teaching and are less experienced than the elementary school teachers in dealing with small groups and utilizing what is called the affective approach.

Many politically conservative and religious groups objected to values clarification believing that these programs were teaching "moral relativity." Others, although not upset by the humanistic underpinnings of this approach, were critical because they thought that self-esteem was too complex to be altered in programs that probably lasted only an hour or so a week. Perhaps the most difficult problem facing these programs was convincing taxpayers that teaching high school students how to climb mountains or feel good about themselves was going to keep them off drugs, when drugs were never even mentioned. After all, isn't it reasonable to assume that a drug prevention strategy should focus on drugs?

Evaluations of these programs generally showed that they failed to alter drug-taking behavior. Although a few showed some positive effects, the majority of studies failed to support these claims. Furthermore, no program that relied on a values clarification approach could demonstrate that changes in values were related to changes in drug-taking behavior. In short, the critics were right; the *affective* or "feel good" programs did not substantially alter drug use (Polich, Ellickson, Reuter, & Kahan, 1984).

**The New Approaches**
Recently a third type of primary prevention program has been developed. These are based on a "social pressure" model and have a wider focus than previous programs. Rather than looking at drug use as a problem of education or as a result of some psychological deficiency on the part of the user, the programs look at the environmental and social factors involved in drug use. They emphasize the importance of the media and role models, both adult and peers. These programs relate much drug use to the desire of the younger person to appear grown up. Their goal is to provide positive role models for abstinence from drugs.

Nearly everyone remembers the Just Say No program so widespread in the late 1980s, but few understand its theoretical basis. Just Say No and programs like it are based on the theory of "cognitive inoculation," a very influential concept developed by McGuire (1981). This theory and those that have stemmed from it offer an analogy between biological and cognitive inoculation. Because you had smallpox, diphtheria, whooping cough, polio, and other inoculations as a child, your body produces antibodies that make you immune to these diseases. Cognitive inoculation is supposed to work in a similar fashion.

In a variation of the cognitive inoculation theory called *social inoculation* that forms the basis for the Just Say No campaign, students first are taught about the pressures to which they will be exposed to use drugs and then are taught various strategies to resist them. The Just Say No campaign is much more complicated than a simple exhortation to say no to drugs. Students are encouraged to model behavior that precludes drug use, to avoid social situations in which drug and alcohol use is present, and to change the subject or walk away.

Students often are encouraged to make a public commitment not to use drugs. The purpose of this strategy is to fight the "everybody is doing it" mentality and to provide reinforcement for positive nondrug-related behavior. Such public commitments also help change the consensus of those participating to the idea that "everyone is *not* doing it."

The Just Say No program was geared to a much younger group than what was traditionally targeted. The focus of many of these programs is junior high school, since most studies now indicate that seventh and eighth grade is where much experimental drug use begins, especially illicit drug use such as marijuana and cocaine. Even more recently, programs have been developed for elementary schools since attitudes toward licit drugs, such as alcohol and nicotine, are formed quite early.

The Just Say No program has been carefully evaluated and found to have mixed results. It does seem to be effective in reducing smoking, but the strategies that have proved useful for this drug may not transfer to drugs such as cocaine, heroin, or marijuana. Also, the effects seem to be short term with minimal carryover to later years. Finally, the Just Say No campaign is probably most successful with middle-class white populations. Its effectiveness probably does not extend to other segments of the population (U.S. General Accounting Office, 1987).

### One Model Program

A model program for drug prevention has been developed by the United States Department of Education. It incorporates elements of all three approaches previously described and also takes into consideration the cognitive and emotional level of students' development. The program is divided into four objectives:

1. to value and maintain sound personal health, to understand how drugs affect health

2. to respect laws and rules prohibiting drugs

3. to recognize and resist pressures to use drugs and

4. to promote activities that reinforce the positive, drug-free elements of student life (U.S. Department of Education, 1986).

This model program suggests various learning activities for the elementary and secondary school levels. For the elementary schools they tend to be broadly based and do not have a specific focus on illicit drugs or alcohol. One sample topic suggested for elementary schools under objective 1 is: the effects of poisons on the body; the effects of medicine on body chemistry; the wrong drug making a person ill (U.S. Department of Education, 1986). For objective 3, the model recommends a topic on "ways to make responsible decisions and deal constructively with disagreeable moments and pressures."

For secondary schools, the suggested topics focus more on drugs of abuse. For example, one suggested exercise involves examining advertisements for drugs to decide what images are being projected and whether the ads are accurate (objective 3). For objective 4, a suggestion is to form action teams for school improvement with membership limited to students who are drug-free (how to make sure the participants are drug-free is not mentioned). Another suggestion: serving as peer leaders in drug prevention programs. You should be able to recognize elements of the social inoculation, information, and affective approaches in these suggestions.

There are certain inherent drawbacks in any school-based drug education program that limit its usefulness. Such programs are not bad, and few suggest that they should be abandoned, but you should resist thinking that all we need to do to combat drugs is offer a better program in the schools. If such tactics were effective we would not have the problem with teenage pregnancies and sexually-transmitted diseases that, along with the drug epidemic, plague us.

## Problems with School-Based Programs

In addition to teaching academic skills, such as reading, writing, and arithmetic, Americans expect schools to instill patriotic and moral values, foster social justice and the brotherhood of man, and at the same time instill good manners, teach sex education, and beat the Japanese on standardized math tests. Whenever there is a problem in our society, we seek a program in the schools to cure it.

School-based drug prevention programs often set unrealistic goals and do not challenge the unrealistic expectations of society (Bernard, Fafoglia, & Perone, 1987). Prevention programs that seek to eradicate drug use are doomed to failure if they are evaluated on that basis, and yet this is often the expected goal.

Consider the example of alcohol. More than 90 percent of high school seniors report using alcohol, with significant alcohol use beginning *before* junior high school. By seventh grade 22 percent of the girls and 30 percent of the boys in one study admitted to having a "drink" rather than a "sip" within the previous month (Zucker & Harford, 1983). Given the pressure to drink in our society, is it reasonable to expect that any school-based program could eradicate drinking? As one group of researchers suggests:

> "The present societal environment, at least in North America, is permeated with messages about alcohol and drugs (even if only the licit mood-altering kind) that range from tolerance to glamorization. In such an environment, any effort to teach youngsters abstinence from such substances is a little like trying to promote chastity in a brothel!" (Mauss, Hopkins, Weisheit, & Kearney, 1988, p. 59.)

A second problem is that most school-based programs are limited in time and scope. As we saw previously the demands on teacher and student time may preclude spending the hours each week that is necessary to promote self-esteem, work on communication skills, practice on strategies for refusing drugs, and learning factual information about drugs. Furthermore, teachers and administrators often lack an understanding of the complex theoretical model on which contemporary drug abuse prevention programs are based.

Another problem is that school-based programs are limited by the nature of the participants. Not everyone likes school or participates enthusiastically in programs such as these. By the time students are in high school, a significant number have dropped out, so school-based programs do not reach this group at all. The student most likely to get involved in such programs may be the student *least* likely to get into trouble in the first place. Conversely, many of the students most likely to need the program may ignore it or view it with scorn.

Children and adolescents approach school with a wide variety of backgrounds and psychosocial traits. The characteristics that we associate with persons of decreased drug use experience: high self-esteem, good decision-making skills, and an achievement orientation may be the result of factors that are beyond the capacity of drug abuse programs to affect. While drug education programs address things that *ought* to be related to drug use, they may actually contribute very little to the overall determinants of drug use since they cannot create social change or improve mental health (Mauss, Hopkins, Weisheit, & Kearney, 1988).

## Factors Affecting School-Based Programs

In evaluating school-based programs care must be taken to consider the social and cognitive aspects of elementary and secondary school students as well. Elementary students think on a simplistic, concrete, and egocentric level. They might readily interpret the message "If you drink and drive you could get into an accident" into "If you drink and drive, you will die," and be terrified when Dad has a beer and then goes out to the store. On the other hand, secondary school students are capable of more complex levels of thinking. . . .

High school students also are capable of subtle behavior that is not only beyond the capacity of elementary school students but also might raise questions about the sophistication of those who advocate drug prevention programs. In California, for example, May brings graduation and a widespread dissemination of "Sober Graduation" bumper stickers for cars. Some students put these on their cars with the mistaken belief that they will deter police from stopping them. Just for good measure some add a "Don't Drink and Drive" or even a "One Day at a Time" (an AA slogan) sticker.

High school students are quite capable of cynicism as well as subtlety. Given the difficulty of getting into a good college and with an acute awareness of the need to appear to be a "well-rounded student," some students see participation in drug abuse programs as a good extracurricular activity to put on their college entrance application. Their motivation to join these groups is more for ambition than commitment.

On the other hand, just getting students to use these stickers or attend the meetings, for whatever reason, might have some impact. Attendance at meetings might expose the student to role models and authority figures who are opposed to indiscriminate drug use. Moreover, numerous studies of attitude change have found that arguing a position opposite to one's beliefs produces an attitude change. Perhaps some students who make presentations against driving and drinking do so for motives that are less than pure, but the act of doing so may alter their attitude and subsequent behavior.

Realistically, school-based programs must be linked to the world beyond school if they are to be effective, which means that drug prevention programs have to reflect an understanding of the impact of society, especially the influence of parents and peers. The phrase "What you *do* speaks so loudly I cannot hear what you *say*" should be remembered before school boards approve yet another drug abuse program.

# POSTSCRIPT

## Do Drug Education Programs Prevent Drug Abuse?

Before the effectiveness of drug education programs can be determined, it is necessary to determine the goals of drug education. Are the goals of drug education to prevent drug use from starting? To prevent drug abuse? To prevent drug dependency? Perhaps the goal of drug education is to teach young people how to protect themselves and others from harm *if* they are going to use drugs. Without a clear understanding of the goals one wants to achieve in teaching about drugs, it is impossible to determine the effectiveness of drug education.

Before a drug education program can be designed, one needs to address other questions regarding what to include in the drug education curriculum. Should the primary focus be on teaching abstinence or responsible use? Is it feasible to teach abstinence of some drugs and responsible use of other drugs? Almost 90 percent of high school students have drunk alcohol; should we tell them they should not drink at all, or should we teach them how to use alcohol responsibly? Does the age of the children make a difference in what is taught? Do elementary students have the reasoning skills of high school students? Should the goal be for students to engage in a decision-making process or simply to adopt certain behaviors? If you were hired to teach a class of sixth-grade students about drugs and the principal asked you to outline what you would like to accomplish and how you plan to achieve your goals, would you be able to provide an answer? As Baker and Avis point out, too many programs were started without any clear focus. Vague questions yield vague solutions, so such programs were destined to fail.

In the last 10 years there has been a significant reduction in drug use among high school seniors in the United States. In their 1992 publication *Drug Use, Drinking and Smoking: National Survey Results from High School, College and Young Adult Population, 1975–1991*, Johnston, O'Malley, and Bachman report that the percentage of seniors who smoked marijuana within 30 days of the survey declined from 37 percent in 1978 to 14 percent in 1991. How much of this reduction is due to drug education, coincidence, or other factors? Throughout American history drug use has been cyclical—perhaps the United States is currently in a down cycle in terms of drug use.

If drug prevention programs are going to be effective in reducing drug use, schools and other institutions will need to work together. Many young people drop out of school or simply do not attend, so community agencies and religious institutions need to become involved. The media have a great impact on young people. What is the best way to incorporate the media in the effort to reduce drug use?

A good reference that addresses many of the problems with drug prevention programs and offers suggestions on how to improve them is *An Ounce of Prevention: Strategies for Solving Tobacco, Alcohol, and Drug Problems* (Jossey-Bass, 1991), by Don Cahalan. A publication from the Office for Substance Abuse Prevention (OSAP), *Stopping Alcohol and Other Drug Use Before It Starts* (Monograph 1, 1989), stresses the importance of initiating drug education in the elementary grades and provides suggestions for educating young people about drugs. A second OSAP publication, *Research, Action, and the Community: Experiences in the Prevention of Alcohol and Other Drug Problems* (Monograph 4, 1990), describes community projects designed to reduce drug problems. An overview of prevention programs is discussed in *Prevention Plus II: Tools for Creating and Sustaining Drug-Free Communities* (OSAP, 1989).

# ISSUE 12

## Should Tobacco Advertising Be Prohibited?

**YES: Don Cahalan,** from *An Ounce of Prevention: Strategies for Solving Tobacco, Alcohol, and Drug Problems* (Jossey-Bass, 1991)

**NO: John Luik,** from "Government Paternalism and Citizen Rationality: The Justifiability of Banning Tobacco Advertising," *International Journal of Advertising* (vol. 9, 1990)

### ISSUE SUMMARY

**YES:** Don Cahalan, an emeritus professor of public health, discusses the link between tobacco companies advertising to certain audiences and the increase in tobacco use among these populations and argues that such advertising should be restricted.

**NO:** Professor of philosophy John Luik argues that individual autonomy, not advertising campaigns, is responsible for the desire to smoke and that prohibiting tobacco advertisements infringes on freedom of speech.

Scientific evidence clearly indicates that smoking causes numerous adverse health conditions. This debate, however, is not about whether or not tobacco is hazardous, but whether or not tobacco advertising should be prohibited. Several questions need to be considered: Do tobacco advertisements alter the behavior of children and adults? Is banning tobacco advertisements a form of censorship? If tobacco advertisements are prohibited because tobacco products are harmful, should the advertisement of other products that are potentially harmful, such as foods with high fat content, electric blankets, and guns, be prohibited also? Are tobacco companies being unfairly targeted? Does the prohibition of tobacco advertising violate the democratic rights of tobacco companies? How much responsibility does the consumer have for his or her behavior?

In 1970, the Public Health Cigarette Smoking Act was passed, which banned cigarette advertisements from television and radio (advertisements for smokeless tobacco were unaffected). Since that time, cigarette advertisements have become much more prevalent in the print media and on roadside billboards. Over $2 billion each year is spent by tobacco companies to promote their products. Critics contend that many of these advertisements are geared toward target populations, notably adolescents and minorities. For example, the R. J. Reynolds Company created a new cigarette called "Uptown" in 1990. Marketed specifically for African Americans, Uptown evoked much protest and was subsequently withdrawn. Proportionately, there are significantly more cigarette advertisements in magazines targeted to African American readers than in magazines whose readers are predominantly white.

Many critics contend that stricter controls need to be put in place to eliminate the manipulative effects that tobacco advertising campaigns have on target audiences as well as on the general public. There is much concern that tobacco is a gateway drug that paves the way for other, illegal types of drug use, such as marijuana, cocaine, heroin, and LSD. The longer young people wait before they smoke cigarettes, if they even do choose to smoke, the less likely they will be to use other drugs. Many critics argue that to market tobacco products to young people is unconscionable because of the potential long-term effects. Young people often have difficulty internalizing the long-term consequences of their behavior because they are more concerned with meeting their immediate needs.

Supporters of the tobacco industry and advertising executives claim that there is no compelling evidence of a causal link between advertising and smoking initiation and behavior. Moreover, advertisers contend that they do not market their tobacco products to young people. Advertising, they claim, is used to enhance brand loyalty. They also argue that banning advertising violates their right to free speech. It is their contention that advertisers have a constitutional right to disseminate their advertisements and that consumers have the right to view tobacco advertisements.

How much of the responsibility for smoking lies with the consumer? Many people argue that smoking is done under one's own volition. What is the impact of parental smoking? Studies show that children of smokers are more likely to smoke than children who grow up in households where parents do not smoke. Children with older siblings who smoke are also more likely to smoke than those whose immediate family members are all nonsmokers.

Curiosity and experimentation are very common among adolescents. If a young person experiments with cigarettes out of curiosity, can advertising be blamed? Cultural attitudes toward smoking are another factor. There is a growing negative attitude in society with regard to smoking, and smoking rates are declining as a result. What is the effect of nonsmokers' attitudes on the smoking behavior of people around them?

In the following selections, Don Cahalan espouses the view that restricting tobacco advertising is an important first step toward decreasing smoking rates, particularly among young people and minority populations. John Luik argues that the government has no right to proclaim a "health moralism" and that the consumer must be given the freedom to choose the life-style habits that he or she desires.

# YES

Don Cahalan

# REDUCING TOBACCO-CAUSED DEATHS

## PRESSURES AGAINST TOBACCO MARKETING

Turning now to current trends in cigarette advertising and marketing: According to the Federal Trade Commission (Davis, 1987) total cigarette advertising and promotional expenditures reached $2.1 billion in 1984. From 1974 through 1984, total expenditures increased approximately sevenfold, or threefold after adjustment by the consumer price index. In 1985, cigarette advertising expenditures accounted for 22.3 percent, 7.1 percent, and 0.8 percent of total advertising expenditures in outdoor media, magazines, and newspapers, respectively. When *all* products and services were ranked according to national advertising expenditures, cigarettes were first in the outdoor media, second in magazines, and third in newspapers. The proportion of total cigarette advertising and promotional expenditures increased steadily, from 25.5 percent in 1975 to 47.6 percent in 1984.

Several advertising campaigns have targeted women, minorities, and blue-collar workers (Davis, 1987). Evidence that the cigarette industry is targeting the sale of menthol cigarettes to African-American consumers is suggested by a Buffalo study measuring the types of cigarettes smoked by whites and African-Americans. One group consisted of 70 white and 365 African-American adult smokers seen at a Family Medicine Center. The second population included 1,070 white and 92 African-American smokers who called a Stop Smoking Hotline in Buffalo. The results showed that, in both populations, African-Americans were twice as likely to smoke mentholated cigarettes as whites. In an attempt to evaluate the targeting of cigarette ads to African-American smokers as a possible explanation for black-white differences in brand preferences, cigarette ads appearing in magazines targeted to predominantly white or African-American readers were compared. Cigarette ads appearing in seven magazines were reviewed, four directed to predominantly white readers (*Newsweek, Time, People, Mademoiselle*) and three with wide circulation among African-American audiences

From Don Cahalan, *An Ounce of Prevention: Strategies for Solving Tobacco, Alcohol, and Drug Problems* (Jossey-Bass, 1991). Copyright © 1991 by Jossey-Bass, Inc., Publishers. Reprinted by permission. References omitted.

(*Jet, Ebony, Essence*). The results showed that the magazines targeted to African-American readers contained significantly more cigarette ads, and more ads for menthol brand cigarettes, than magazines similar in content but targeted to white readers. However, the study did not attempt to determine whether cigarette advertising is the cause of the differences in preference of cigarette brands between white and African-American smokers (Cummings, Giovino, and Mendicino, 1987).

Smokeless tobacco was not affected by the ban on broadcast advertising of cigarettes that went into effect in 1971, and until 1986 both print and broadcast media were used to advertise it. The approaches used to advertise and promote smokeless tobacco products during the early to mid 1980s included traditional motifs that featured rugged-looking masculine models in sporting and outdoor settings as well as an expanded white-collar appeal. Promotional activities ranged from sponsorship of sporting events to offers for clothing bearing smokeless tobacco product logos. Despite the claims of manufacturers that advertising and promotional efforts were not targeted to youth, smokeless tobacco companies sponsored tobacco-spitting contests with teenage participants, a college marketing program, and college scholarships. Federal legislation was passed in 1986 that banned television and radio advertising of smokeless tobacco products and required manufacturers to include warning labels on their products on the potential health hazards of smokeless tobacco use (Ernster, 1989).

In January 1990, R. J. Reynolds dropped its Philadelphia test marketing of "Uptown," a new cigarette being marketed heavily to African-Americans, a day after

Health and Human Services [Secretary Louis W.] Sullivan (himself African-American) accused Reynolds of trying to create a "culture of cancer." About thirty organizations in Philadelphia had joined in the effort to fight Uptown. In response to a reminder that the U.S. Public Health Service has found that African-American men have a 58 percent higher incidence of lung cancer than white men and that African-Americans lose twice as many years of life as do whites because of smoking-related diseases, the R. J. Reynolds executive vice president of marketing said, "We regret that a small coalition of anti-smoking zealots apparently believes that black smokers are somehow different from others who choose to smoke and must not be allowed to exercise the same freedom of choice available to all other smokers. This represents a loss of choice for black smokers and a further erosion of the free-enterprise system" ("Cigarette Ads for Blacks Dropped," 1990, p. A2).

In an article immediately following the withdrawal of the Uptown cigarettes, which were challenged as being directed toward African-Americans, Cohen (1990) asserted that selling to women through ads in women's magazines is also reprehensible, for lung cancer has passed breast cancer as a cause of death at a time when smoking has diminished among men. The article noted that ads featuring Capri Super Slims and other brands emphasize the "slim" because cigarette makers know that many women are obsessed with their weight, and that those who smoke fear quitting because they will gain weight. Should either group have any qualms about smoking, the ads are there to put them at ease. The models are the epitome of healthfulness, and they are all slim. Cohen thought Dr.

Sullivan should also blast cigarette companies for targeting women.

In the summer of 1989, the National Archives accepted $600,000 from Philip Morris, makers of Marlboro cigarettes, and allowed the company to use the Archives' name in ads celebrating the Bill of Rights. The Archives also agreed to sponsor a joint exhibit on the Bill of Rights and promised that it would use its "best effort" to locate such items as recordings of the voices of past presidents for use in the advertising.

Tobacco industry critics quickly attacked the deal. Sidney Wolfe, head of the Public Citizen Research Group, a Ralph Nader–founded consumer advocacy group, said the advertising "smears the Bill of Rights with the blood of all Americans killed as a result of smoking Marlboro and other Philip Morris cigarets." ("Lawmakers Want," 1990, p. 13.)

A Philip Morris spokesman said the company is not advertising smoking or cigarettes with the ads, but just its corporate image. "We are celebrating the Bill of Rights," said Guy Smith, Philip Morris vice president for corporate affairs. "It is also a way for us to give the company an identity. We hope people will think better of the company ("Lawmakers Want," 1990, p. 13). One Philip Morris advertisement that appeared in *Harper's Magazine* (March 1990, p. 58) carried a photo of President Franklin D. Roosevelt when he designated December 15 as Bill of Rights Day. The advertisement ends saying, "Today, as we approach the bicentennial of the adoption of the Bill of Rights, let us all, as President Roosevelt asked us then, 'rededicate its principles and its practice.' " Readers were invited to call a toll-free number or to write the Bill of Rights department of Philip Morris for a free copy of the Bill of Rights. Could it be

possible that Philip Morris was not only using the prestige of the National Archives, President Roosevelt, and the Bill of Rights to promote its corporate image, but also slyly to remind the readers about the debatable commercial "freedom of speech" in cigarette advertising that it wishes to maintain?

National Council on Alcoholism (now National Council on Alcohol and Drug Dependence) President Hamilton Beazley promptly called the collaboration of Philip Morris and the Archives in the Bill of Rights promotion "appalling" in a letter to the National Archivist. As the letter said, "A Bill of Rights promotion sponsored by Philip Morris, Inc., and Miller beer will be a tremendous disservice to the cause of personal freedom for the millions of Americans for whom the freedom from addiction is a prerequisite for enjoying the basic liberties guaranteed by the Founding Fathers in our remarkable and treasured Bill of Rights." Rep. Luken (D-Ohio) wrote to the Attorney General that "if Philip Morris can circumvent the law prohibiting it from advertising cigarettes [on television] by the transparent device used here, we may as well tear up the Federal Cigarette Labeling and Advertisement Act" (Lewis, 1989, p. 6).

Another frequent anticigarette complaint by public authorities was voiced by Health and Human Services Secretary Louis Sullivan: "An athlete or sports figure should not allow his or her good name, hard-earned image, or integrity to be exploited by the tobacco industry to push a product that, when used as intended, causes death. This blood money should not be used to foster a misleading impression that smoking is compatible with good health." He called on universities and other institutions to refuse to host events sponsored by tobacco companies, and he warned advertisers to "shun the temptation of this tainted money, stained by addiction, disease, and death" ("Athletes Urged to Spurn Tobacco 'Blood Money,' " 1990, p. A1).

Sullivan spoke at a meeting called by a coalition of health groups to protest sponsorship of women's tennis events by Virginia Slims cigarettes, which has been sponsoring such events for two decades. In rebuttal, a Philip Morris spokesperson said that it does not ask players to smoke or endorse smoking, but just to play tennis.

Sullivan also attacked tobacco advertising practices in general, calling on television stations to donate free air time to help educate viewers about the dangers of smoking. He asked hospitals to declare hospitals smoke-free zones and Department of Health and Human Services grantees to prohibit smoking where they work, and has written national convenience stores asking them to enforce laws prohibiting the sale of tobacco to minors.

The growing sentiment against smoking is evident in the results of a 1989 national survey by Peter B. Hart and the Roper Organization, which found that half the nation's adult consumers would support an outright ban on advertising of all alcoholic beverages and tobacco. And 57 percent said cigarette machines should be eliminated so that those below legal age could not get cigarettes so easily (Freedman, 1989, p. B1).

Even *Time* magazine, which has carried so much cigarette advertising, featured an article (Gallagher, 1990) on all the criticism the tobacco business has been getting: R. J. Reynolds's canceling of the Uptown brand directed at African-Americans, Secretary Sullivan's charge that smoking cost the country $52 billion a year ("Cigarettes are the only legal product that when used as intended cause death"), the smoking ban on all domestic flights, and announcements by state and local officials of additional antismoking initiatives.

R. J. Reynolds attempted to rebound with its new cigarette, Dakota, planned to be test marketed in its Project VF (for "virile female"), which describes the typical customer as an entry-level factory worker, eighteen to twenty, who enjoys watching drag races and aspires to "get married in her early 20s and have a family." Health experts and women's groups accused the company of targeting uninformed young women for death: Lung cancer among women has jumped more than fivefold in the past twenty years. The *Time* reporter (Gallagher, 1990, p. 41) noted that "target marketing has taken on an odious reputation as tobacco makers aim for the few groups that have been slow to kick the habit." A sociologist is quoted as saying, "You certainly don't see ads featuring 65-year-olds." A lobbyist for the Tobacco Institute disagreed: "Advertising doesn't get people to smoke. High school kids haven't seen ads for marijuana."

The article (Gallagher, 1990, p. 41) also noted that Congress was considering seventy-two bills to inhibit tobacco use, including Kennedy's proposed $185 billion Center for Tobacco Products, which would have broad powers to regulate the industry.

California is conducting a new $28.6 million advertising war against smoking, designed to counter the marketing efforts of tobacco companies with equally sophisticated television, radio, and newspaper ads. "The goal is to persuade 5 million of the State's 7 million smokers to kick the habit by the end of the decade. Most ironic of all is that the campaign will be financed by smokers through the new 25¢-a-pack cigarette tax. Says Thomas Lauria, a spokesman for the Tobacco Institute, 'Now smokers are paying for their own harassment' " (Castro, 1990, p. 61).

The tobacco companies spent $15 million to defeat this initiative, but failed. Governor Deukmajian tried to distance himself from the antismoking television campaign: His press secretary said, "We weren't aware of the ads. The approach was developed by the Department of Health Services and an advertising agency. Whether or not it is going to work remains to be seen" (Lucas, 1990, p. A1). The antismoking money came from a publicly generated statewide initiative, not through a legislative act. Many legislators receive substantial money from the tobacco and alcohol industry.

One of the thirty-second ads shows an actor portraying a tobacco company executive in a smoke-filled conference room with his employees, saying to them that 3,000 new smokers must be recruited every day to make up for the 2,000 who quit and the 1,000 who die of lung cancer, heart disease, and emphysema. ("We're not in this business for our health!" he concludes with a demonic laugh.) The tobacco interests are complaining that the ads are unfair, but the director of Health Services noted that preliminary statistics from the Federal Trade Commission showed that $3.2 billion was spent nationwide in 1988 to promote smoking, and that the antismoking ads are simply full disclosure, to let the people know that many of their decisions are actually a response to very clever tobacco industry advertising.

The *Time* article by Castro (1990) suggests how California's campaign opens another chapter in the fight against the marketing of alcohol as well as tobacco. New York, Chicago, and Dallas residents have been whitewashing inner-city billboards to obliterate ads for cigarettes and cognac. Secretary Sullivan attacked Virginia Slims for sponsoring tennis matches; the National Collegiate Athletic Association reduced alcohol advertising during postseason games. Congress is working on seventy-two bills to constrain tobacco products, and Senator Albert Gore of Tennessee and Representative Joseph Kennedy of Massachusetts have introduced bills (S. 2439 and H.R. 4493) that would require health warnings on all alcoholic beverage advertisements in television, radio, or print.

Castro's article says the new outcry has spread to Europe also: The French government plans to ban all tobacco advertising by 1993 and to restrict alcohol advertising to print media. "The recent outburst against vice marketing seems motivated by a larger social movement, suddenly abloom at the turn of the decade, in which citizens are demanding more socially responsible behavior from individuals and corporations alike. In a fashion, the war on drugs has carried over to legal but abusable substances" (Castro, 1990, p. 61). But this article in *Time*, which has been an exceptionally heavy carrier of cigarette advertising over the years, could not resist ending with a jab at the California campaign by saying, "To some extent, blaming advertisers for selling products that society has been unable to control by other means is like shooting the messenger" (p. 61).

More economic pressure on the tobacco industry was exerted by John Van de Kamp, then California state attorney general, who called for legislation to end California's tax write-off for tobacco advertising, saying that "this misguided tax subsidy of the tobacco industry will cost California about $15 million over the next 18 months. . . . What does California get for its money? We get to watch 30,000 of our friends and neighbors die painful, premature deaths every year. Plus we get the economic burden of $7 billion a year in lost productivity and extra health care and its costs for smokers." Such antideduction legislation is being written into an anticigarette bill by State Assemblyman Tom Bates (Barabak, 1990, p. A13).

Concerning the responsibilities of the tobacco companies for damage to the public's health, George Will (1990), a prominent conservative columnist, recently observed that democracy rests on three assumptions: personal responsibility, individual rationality, and the efficacy of information. Will said that smoking and attempts to hold cigarette companies liable for its costs show how all three assumptions, although valid as generalities, are problematic when it comes to specifics. Since 1954, 321 suits have been filed against cigarette companies, but none have been forced to pay any damages. One recent case was a New Jersey court's overturning of a $400,000 award to a widower whose wife died at fifty-eight after forty-two years of smoking. At issue was whether, when there were no health warnings prior to 1966, the manufacturer had misled the woman about the risks of smoking. The court found the woman was 80 percent to blame for her condition. Will contends that antismoking advocates want a risk-benefit liability rule, where a jury can find a manufacturer liable because the risk of its use far exceeds its

benefits. Driving the tax up (it would cost at least $2.25 a pack to match the costs) would be politically impossible, but the price also can be driven up by a flood of liability suits. "Cigarette companies are winning in courts, but being routed in the culture. In the mid 1950s about half of all Americans older than 18 smoked. Today about 26 percent do. If liability law ever aligns with the flow of social feeling, the following scandalous numbers will change: America spends $35 billion annually on smoking-related illnesses and suffers $65 billion in lost productivity. Even pessimistic projections for AIDS deaths in the late 1990s amount to one-eighth the annual toll (390,000) from smoking" (Will, 1990, p. 28).

Concerning the influence of cigarette advertising revenues on the media: When the cigarette broadcast advertising ban took effect in 1971, cigarette manufacturers shifted advertising expenditures to the print media. In the last year of broadcast advertising and the first year of the ban, cigarette ad expenditures in a sample of major national magazines increased by 49 and then 131 percent in constant dollars. From an eleven-year period preceding the ban to an eleven-year period following it, these magazines decreased their coverage of smoking and health by 65 percent, an amount that is statistically significantly greater than decreases found in magazines that did *not* carry cigarette ads and in two major newspapers. This finding strongly suggests that media dependent on cigarette advertising have restricted their coverage of smoking and health. This may have significant implications for public health, as well as raising obvious concerns about the integrity of the profession of journalism (Warner and Goldenhar, 1989).

Evidently the mandated requirement of a readable health warning on cigarette advertising billboards is still being flouted. In a study of the readability of the Surgeon General's warning in cigarette advertisements in two outdoor media (billboards and taxicab advertisements) in metropolitan Atlanta under typical driving conditions, observers were able to read the entire health warning on eighteen (46 percent) of thirty-nine street billboards but on only two (5 percent) of thirty-nine highway billboards. In contrast, the content of the ads (that is, brand name, other wording, and notable imagery) could be recognized under the same conditions on more than 95 percent of the billboards. In a similar study of 100 taxicab cigarette ads in New York City, observers were unable to read the health warning in any of the ads but were able to identify the brand name in all ads and notable brand imagery in 95 percent of the ads. The researchers concluded that the Surgeon General's warning is not readable in its current form in the vast majority of billboard and taxicab ads. Factors contributing to unreadability include the small size of the letters, the excessive length of the warnings, the distance between the viewers and the ads, and movement of the viewers in relation to the ads (Davis and Kendrick, 1989).

Another gambit on the part of the cigarette manufacturers to flout tobacco advertising controls is that although the 1970 Public Health Cigarette Smoking Act banned tobacco ads on radio and television, tobacco companies are paying to get exposure in films—"often those aimed at teenagers or even children." Philip Morris paid $150,000 to have Lark cigarettes prominently featured in *License to Kill*, the latest James Bond film, in which the major players light up and a cigarette lighter plays a major part in the plot. Philip Morris also paid $42,500 to have Lois Lane smoke Marlboro cigarettes in *Superman II*, and Liggett paid $30,000 to display Eve cigarettes in *Supergirl*.

Even paid promotion of cigarettes is still common in movies: A recent study found cigarette smoking was shown in 87 percent of PG-rated films. Such movies are seen by little children when they are played on home VCRs. The editor of the *Tobacco and Youth Reporter* comments that "smoking may have been the norm during Hollywood's Golden Age, but today, when smoking is in decline in America, glamorizing smoking is irresponsible. In fact, it's murderous." At the very least, "it is an unfair and deceptive way for tobacco companies to attract children" ("Smoking in Movies . . . ," 1990, p. 3).

Yet the tobacco companies are not about to give up the ghost, because at least they can fight a rearguard action by mobilizing their smokers to fight back. Witness the address by the president of the Retail Tobacco Dealers of America at the association's annual trade show in Chicago in 1989. He said, in part,

> The antismokers are making themselves heard all over the country—from major cities to rural towns. And as we all know, the squeaky wheel gets the grease. So now it's time for us, both as individuals and as retailers who can educate our customers, to speak out—*loud and often.*
>
> I know that you are acutely aware of the general atmosphere concerning tobacco. It might even be appropriate to compare this to the abortion debate—two sides fighting over a highly emotional issue. But if we don't educate smokers about ways to band together to control the governmental beasts of taxa-

tion and regulation, who will? Writing letters to your representative is a great first step, but it is *only* a first step. Talk to the people who come into your shop. Have a sample letter that they can send to their representatives. Most of all, do something, *anything*, to make a difference.

George Bush often talks of a thousand points of light. I'd like to think that those points of light are coming from the glowing ends of cigars, cigarettes, and pipes across the country and symbolize the cornerstone of this nation—tobacco ["Tobacco's Last Gasp," 1990, p. 24].

# NO

John Luik

## GOVERNMENT PATERNALISM AND CITIZEN RATIONALITY: THE JUSTIFIABILITY OF BANNING TOBACCO ADVERTISING

The first assumption [that philosophers bring to any discussion of tobacco advertising] is the primacy of autonomy or individual liberty in a democratic society, a primacy that can normally be overridden only on the basis of two types of demonstration. One is that there is a conjunction of other significant values at issue and that this conjunction serves to diminish the foundational status of freedom in any given context. The other is that we can in fact produce a rational demonstration of the highest order that a course restricting individual autonomy is justified. It is thus not only that there must be a conjunction of other values which in a particular case outweigh freedom, but there must also be a demonstration of the most rigorous kind that the competing values can be secured only through the restriction of autonomy.

A second assumption that follows on from this is that when we speak about the goals for social policy and the justifications for government intervention—the two are not the same but we have, for convenience, conflated them—the only appropriate context in which we can speak of these goals is within the context of the primacy of autonomy. Thus the status of freedom as a basic value is always a legitimate consideration when any sort of social policy issue is at stake.

Having said this, an interesting paradox now emerges: what we are arguing for are two quite different and, one might say, peculiar senses of rationality. On the one hand we want to argue for individual autonomy which may include a large dose of irrational 'choice', and yet at the collective or social level we want to argue that social policies ought only to be undertaken on the most traditionally rational basis of analysis, so that when social policy decisions are being discussed or implemented we have the most stringent guarantees against irrational action. One might think that if one were going to hold society in general to stringent conditions of rationality, one would *not* allow individuals a high degree of eccentric irrationality. I hope that the reasons for this asymmetry will emerge in the course of these discussions.

The third assumption is what might be called the liberal presumption as advocated, for instance, by J. S. Mill in *On Liberty*. Essentially the liberal presumption is characterized by three different claims. The first is that one can make a reasonably clear distinction between actions that affect only oneself and actions that affect others. The second is that the individual is the best judge both of his own ends and the means necessary for the realization of those ends. The third is that government intervention in the life of a genuinely autonomous agent is justified only to prevent harm to others, never to prevent harm to self.

## PATERNALISM AND INDIVIDUAL AUTONOMY

All of those assumptions are open to the objections of what can be described as classical paternalism. Classical paternalism wishes to assert that:

1. A cluster of values, not autonomy alone, assume primacy in a democratic society;

2. A clear distinction between self-regarding and other-regarding action is impossible to sustain;

3. Autonomy is frequently outweighed by other justifiable state interests in furthering happiness and welfare, broadly construed;

4. Individuals often do not understand their interests in the clearest way and often do not appreciate the means best suited to the actualization of those interests;

5. Individuals need to be assisted in furthering their 'real interests' and prevented from embarking on irrational courses of action such as the permanent alienation of the capacity for voluntary action.

Classical paternalism itself can be divided into two categories: strong and weak. The strong paternalist claims that if, for instance, an individual wants to walk across a bridge that he knows to be unsafe, then he is in some sense mentally deficient, if not long term at least temporarily, and we are justified in using the strongest measures—on compassionate grounds, even though they restrict autonomy—in preventing this individual from embarking on this course.

The strong paternalist can thus actually justify infringements on non-insane instances of autonomy (for example, starting to smoke) on what appear to be liberty-enhancing principles: namely, by keeping one alive we enhance one's autonomy. If in fact we allow you to fall off the bridge we allow you ultimately to destroy your autonomy. No one who is dead is autonomous. Therefore, although it appears that we are being paternalistic, what is being done is an action to enhance your long-term autonomy, which you have irrationally chosen to cast aside.

But the paternalist has a weaker sort of case which does not hinge on demonstrably insane action. The weaker paternalist case wants to claim that the State can justifiably intervene to prevent the action of a citizen or subject on two grounds: first, when the individual is about to make an unreasonable choice, not a *prima facie* insane choice but an unreasonable choice; second, when the individual is about to make a non-voluntary choice: that is, when the individual appears to be in the grip of a compulsion over which he has no control.

Here, of course, one encounters a related issue: the extent to which tobacco use is addictive and therefore a non-voluntary action. If in fact the tobacco user could be demonstrated to be non-voluntary, the plausibility of the paternalist argument is enormously strengthened, inasmuch as what one does by beginning to smoke is, it might be said, to surrender a significant degree of autonomy over the rest of one's life in the sense that one takes up a form of behavior which it is very difficult, if not impossible, to break.

Of course, the argument can still be made, despite the best efforts of the surgeon general, that there is no convincing evidence that this is in fact the case, and that there are millions of ex-smokers who can testify that autonomy is not surrendered. Even if that were not the case the autonomist would argue that the real commitment to freedom comes precisely at this point: that one is in fact willing to allow people to use their freedom to extinguish their freedom, in the same way in which democracy allows people to use free speech to campaign against democracy itself. The real test of a commitment to autonomy is precisely the extent to which one allows liberty to argue against itself. For the paternalist, however, tobacco advocacy could be an invitation to involuntary, perhaps unreasonable, action, and the question is, what justification could ever be given to allow someone to make that sort of advocacy? It is to this question—which lies at the heart of the debate over tobacco advertising bans—that we must now turn.

## THE ANTI-PATERNALIST RESPONSE TO TOBACCO ADVERTISING BANS

A large measure of conceptual confusion, not to say controversy, that presently surrounds measures designed to prohibit the advertisement of tobacco products is due to the peculiar melange of empirical and theoretical issues that 'hazardous' product advertising in general and this type of 'hazardous' product advertising in particular generates. On the one hand there are the obviously empirical issues, such as the role of advertising in initiating and sustaining the use of tobacco products and the effectiveness of various measures designed to restrict advertising for such products in terms of reducing aggregate consumption. On the other hand, there are highly contentious theoretical issues about the ethics of hazardous product advertising, the status of commercial speech, and the legitimacy of governmental attempts to restrict certain types of speech and action. The paternalist justification for advertising prohibitions is based in a large measure on what might be called a mixed case argument; that is, an argument that relies on a mixture of empirical and theoretical elements.

Thus, the paradigm paternalist argument justifying tobacco advertising bans involves empirical arguments about the role of advertising in:

1. Establishing a general climate of legitimacy with respect to tobacco use;

2. Initiating new consumers, particularly minors, to tobacco use;

3. Increasing total tobacco consumption, whether aggregate or per capita;

4. Dissuading consumers from considering the health risks of tobacco use and from considering abandoning the products.

These arguments should be considered in harness with theoretical arguments about the merits of government paternalism in situations of non-rational and involuntary individual action. The paradigm paternalist argument is then constructed upon, first, the plausible association between tobacco use and certain forms of ill health; and second, the plausible connection between tobacco use and advertising, inasmuch as the decision to embark on a course of action injurious to health is so far outside the web of rational decision-making that it can only be the product of a factor like advertising that is designed to subvert rational choice. Given that the state has an interest in the health of its citizens, and given further that a particular product is threatening to citizens' health, then the state has a legitimate reason to curtail the use of that product through restricting advocacy on behalf of the product.

Now the anti-paternalist can counter this argument by initially noting that the required connections are not evident because:

1. Tobacco advertisements contain clear warnings about the dangers of tobacco products, warnings which provide a *prima facie* assurance that the users of these products are not ignorant as to the products' health risks;

2. It is not at all clear, given the evidence available, that advertising plays as substantial a role in individual decisions to begin smoking as do other cultural, socio-economic, and psychological factors (Childrens Research Unit, 1987); nor indeed that advertising is directed primarily to non-smokers rather than to existing smokers with a view to retaining or increasing a particular manufacturer's market share.

Without such connections the paternalist's argument is significantly weakened.

## Weak Anti-Paternalism
Anti-paternalism is, however, a general term. As with classical paternalism, we can distinguish two types: weak and strong. The weak anti-paternalist attempts to assess the claim about tobacco and advertising on a strictly empirical basis. The weak anti-paternalist argues that the restriction of advertising and the imposition of bans, whether partial or total, in terms of tobacco products are justified if, and only if, the following conditions obtain.

First, bans are justified only if there is some extraordinarily significant objective at stake, or some important interest which the ban is designed to promote. Usually the implicit assumption is that the significant objective at stake is a reduction in smoking which would improve the overall health of the country, reduce health spending and result in people living longer.

The second condition is that bans are justified only if there is a rationally demonstrable connection between the significant objective, which is specified in the legislation, and the actual method that one is going to employ to achieve that objective. Here we return to the claim specified at the beginning of the essay: namely, that if any social policy issue is to be described as rational and acceptable in a democratic society, it has to meet a strictly defined test of rationality. If the policy could be shown in any sense to be irrational, causally or evidentially, then that would be a good reason to reject the policy. Thus the paternalist must satisfy us that there is a rational connection between the objectives specified, i.e., saving lives by reducing tobacco consumption, and the means chosen, in this case the advertising ban. This point will be discussed later in the article, but it seems clear that there is no decisive published evidence that can establish any rational connection between advertising bans and the objective of reducing tobacco consumption. Bans therefore fail this test and the legislation is by definition *prima facie* unreasonable.

The third condition is that individual autonomy, which we argued was a basic value in a democratic society, must be impaired as little as possible by the ban. In other words one must design a means to meet this objective and choose an instrument that reduces the scope of autonomy as little as possible. Otherwise, given that the autonomy of individual actors is significantly affected (in the case of advertisers it is obliterated by a total advertising ban), one fails to meet the condition that autonomy is impaired as little as possible.

Fourth, advertising bans are justified only if they do not infringe fundamental justice or equity. In other words, they preserve the equity of risk ventures across society. By 'risk ventures' we mean that the paternalistic intervention—in this case the advertising ban—cannot single out one risk venture unless other equally risky ventures are also considered fit candidates for government action. So if the use of tobacco products is relatively far down the list of risky ventures and other more, or equally risky, ventures are left untouched by the legislation, then that legislation is fundamentally unjust, since it has without justification impaired the equity status of risky ventures by prohibiting only one sort of risky venture.

Finally, bans are justified only if there is no other way, short of restricting autonomy, to secure these two objectives. In other words, if it could be rationally demonstrated that there is as much likelihood of achieving a reduction in tobacco use through some other method

rather than a ban on commercial free speech, then it is imperative, if the paternalist case is to succeed, that the necessity of an advertising ban be shown. If you are going to totally eliminate a particular instance of commercial free speech, you have to be able to say, 'this total elimination is necessary because there is no other measure short of the measure that will achieve our necessary objective.'

Now, it is clear, based on the best empirical evidence about the role of advertising in (1) establishing a general climate of legitimacy with respect to tobacco use; (2) initiating new consumers, particularly minors, to tobacco use; (3) increasing total consumption; and (4) dissuading consumers from considering the health risks inherent in tobacco use and considering abandoning the product, that the paternalist argument justifying tobacco advertising bans can never meet conditions two, three, four and five. Whatever the sources, whether studies about adolescent smoking sponsored by the World Health Organisation (certainly no friend of the tobacco industry); studies which suggest that children begin smoking because of peer and parental influence; or comparative studies of smoking rates in countries that have bans (Norway and Finland) and those without bans (Britain and Austria) which suggest that a ban on all forms of tobacco advertising results—depending on which evidence one accepts as definitive—in either a higher consumption of tobacco products than before the ban, or a not significantly lower rate of consumption, there is no compelling evidence that advertising bans reduce smoking and thus save lives. It should also be noted that there is no compelling evidence of a causal link between advertising and smoking initiation and behaviour. Thus, we should not be surprised if there is no connection between advertising bans and reduced smoking. Without such causal links there can be no demonstrable connection between the objective of advertising bans and the means employed to realize that objective.

Moreover, such bans also violate conditions three, four and five in that a total ban, for example in Canada, does not impair autonomy as little as possible and, inasmuch as other equally risky forms of autonomous behaviour are not subjected to similar legislative intervention, the equity of risk venture is not preserved. Finally, even if there were evidence that advertising bans might reduce tobacco consumption, it is still incumbent on the paternalist to demonstrate that banning advertising is the only method whereby this objective can be achieved. Again, much of the evidence suggests that vigorous public education campaigns about the dangers of smoking and certain restrictions on smoking and sales to minors are more effective in reducing tobacco consumption than advertising bans, and they do not infringe autonomy in the unjustifiable ways that advertising bans do (Aaro *et al.*, 1986, Allegrante *et al.*, 1978, Bewley and Bland, 1977, Boddewyn, 1986, Leventhal and Cleary, 1980, Ross, 1973).

### Strong Anti-Paternalism

So far we have spoken exclusively of weak anti-paternalism, but there is a second, perhaps more confident version of anti-paternalism: strong anti-paternalism that justifies tobacco advertising bans solely on the grounds of theoretical considerations. For the sake of the argument let us assume first that there is a demonstrable and universally accepted connection between the initiation and mainte-

nance of juvenile and adult smoking and advertising, so that the empirical support for a ban must be conceded. Secondly, let us concede for the purpose of argument that there is a significant and growing body of literature which shows that advertising bans do in fact work; that they do discourage the recruitment of new smokers; and that they do result in lessened consumption.

Strong anti-paternalists would argue, however, that even if this were the case, advertising bans would be unjustified because free and democratic societies place such a high value on freedom and autonomy that they are willing to risk, and indeed allow, a significant loss of life in order to preserve a value. History is replete with instances where a society places greater value on the continuance of society in a free and democratic way on the saving of individual lives. For instance, this is precisely what happens when society goes to war. We place a higher value on the maintenance of a particular kind of society than on saving individual lives. We may lose no lives if we capitulate but the democratic character of our society would be changed. Thus the first step in the argument is to establish the primacy of autonomy, even with the consequence of some individuals living shorter or less happy lives.

The next step is to demonstrate that any erosion of autonomy—as through an advertising ban—is an unacceptable erosion. This demonstration can be merely provisional. One could construct two different arguments, the first perhaps a little better than the second. The first is that arguments put forward by people who are in favour of restrictions on commercial free speech assume that it is legitimate to curtail commercial expression or commercial advocacy because commercial advocacy is, if not corrupt, then certainly of a much less distinguished character than other sorts of advocacy. In other words, commercial advocacy is about commerce; it is about economics and money-making, and economics and money-making play a peripheral role in society. Freedom of speech, on the other hand, was established to protect not the peripheral, but the important, primarily political, debates over societal issues.

There are several problems with this argument. The first is that, aside from anything, it reflects an extraordinary elitist view about the value of political speech. It is surely an arbitrary assumption that one form of speech can be characterized as peripheral and that commercial speech, precisely because it deals with economic choices, is therefore less important than political speech. This claim represents not merely an elitist, but also an antiquated view about the relative importance of political speech versus economic speech in society. A good argument could be made that the locus of autonomy and individual decision-making hinges for ordinary people far more on individual economic choices, such as the decision to buy certain products and to engage in certain practices, which in turn affect decisions to produce certain things, than on 'exalted political discourse'. A consequence of this argument is that it is necessary to maintain commercial free speech.

In other words the peculiar character of commercial free speech is that it affects the lives of ordinary people in a democracy far more than political free speech. Given the importance of individual economic decisions and their role in a democratic social order, it might be argued that we ought to reverse the traditional distinction and argue that commercial speech is more valuable in many contexts than political speech.

... [I]f one values democracy, then one values a particular form of citizen autonomy, and citizen autonomy is integrally connected with free speech in all of its varieties. When a society decides that certain forms of communications should be banned, it says, in effect, that there are some forms of communication that are too dangerous for a citizen to contemplate because the citizen may embark upon a course of action which society deems to be irrational. What this establishes is a socially defined notion of citizen rationality and a socially approved manner of living one's life. Certain social choices are closed by virtue of the fact that you cannot receive communications about those choices.

What strikes us as so offensive about restrictions of this sort is that they establish a paradigm of social rationality that in fact may be completely at odds with the majority of society. They open the door to a government-imposed definition of what constitutes acceptable risk-taking and unacceptable risk-taking, something that is a fundamentally subversive activity on the part of government in a democratic society. When the government assumes that there is an allowable conception of how one lives one's life in a rational way and a non-allowable conception, and then acts to censure information so that people do not even see other alternatives, then one arguably erodes autonomy in a fundamental sense. As Richard Arneson notes:

This failing is manifest when proposed paternalistic coercion would enhance someone's capacity for rationality by means of uprooting an irrational trait that is prominent in his self-conception or even in his ideal of himself. Consider the project of forcing adult education on a hillbilly who is suspicious of urban ways and identifies himself as a rural character. Somewhat similarly, the wild Heathcliff in *Wuthering Heights* would doubtless find his 'ability to rationally consider and carry out his own decisions' considerably enhanced if psychotherapy coercively administered should extirpate his self-destructive passion for Catherine Earnshaw. Note that no taint of sympathy for rural parochialism or for grotesque romanticism need color the judgment that paternalism is unacceptable in such instances. Rather these examples recall to us the conviction that rationality in the sense of economic prudence, the efficient adaptation of means to ends, is a value which we have no more reason to impose on an adult against his will for his own good than we have reason to impose any other value on paternalistic grounds. A vivid reminder that rationality may sometimes be alien to some humans is the circumstance that persons sometimes self-consciously choose to nurture an irrational quirk at the center of their personalities. Perhaps it is appropriate to deplore such a choice but not to coerce it (Arneson, 1980).

It could of course be argued that some erosion of autonomy is a necessary feature of social living, though the notion of a little erosion of autonomy might be as coherent as the idea of a little pregnancy. More important, however, is the fact that such arguments about autonomy and rationality miss a central feature of democratic life that has emerged over the last three hundred years: namely, the fact that by allowing individuals to shape the course of their lives, for better or worse, the State concedes to them the right to misorder and misshape their lives to a substantial degree. Consider, for instance, the rationale that might be given, and

indeed was traditionally given, for state-enforced religious belief: namely, that the matter of individual salvation, eternal destiny, was far too significant to be left in the hands of the individual citizen. The State had a compelling 'state interest' in securing an individual's assent to religious truth, and in suppressing dissenting presentations of 'truth'.

Today, however, such an intrusion by the State into the rational ordering of an individual's life is universally considered inappropriate. The individual, whatever the cost in rationality and happiness, is left to pursue his own way with respect to his eternal outcome. But what the paternalist wishes to do is to revive state-imposed rationality, not with respect to religious belief, but with respect to health. Health moralism, as we might call it, proclaims that there is but one rational-healthy-moral way to live one's life, and inducements to divergent behaviour, e.g., tobacco advertisements, are not to be permitted. The question can thus legitimately be asked why, having abandoned one form of state-enforced rationality, the rationality of certain forms of religious belief and practice, we should accept, as consistent with autonomy, the imposition of another form of state-enforced rationality, health moralism?

Having once decided that there is an official standard of rationality, an acceptable life plan to which we must all conform, where do we stop? If we cannot trust the rationality of the smoker who concludes that his enjoyment of smoking is worth the risk of a shorter lifetime, can we trust the rationality of the overweight who regularly ignore our pleas to start an exercise programme, or the rationality of the red-meat eater who prefers his steak to the latest embodiments of lean cuisine, or the rationality of the credit-card addict who spends his way into insolvency, or the rationality of the lottery ticket buyer who, ignoring all the odds, still gambles his money? Surely these individuals are just as susceptible to the dangers of free speech that advertising presents as is the smoker.

If individuals wish to make assessments of risk, based on differing life plans and differing judgements of pleasure, then they should be allowed to do so. To put the case more specifically with respect to tobacco: there are no doubt smokers who would prefer to live shorter lives, if that is really the trade-off, in return for the pleasure they receive from smoking.

Free speech is about choices: about idiosyncratic choices and life plans, about the necessity of choices based on a fair hearing of all sides—popular and unpopular, socially condoned and socially condemned—of an issue. Free speech is also about confidence: confidence in autonomy as in the long run the foundational value of society, confidence that we have in ourselves and in others the right to make choices for ourselves, even if those choices are not the culturally approved ones. It is about the confidence that we have that dangers of suppressing certain forms of information and advocacy are always greater than the dangers of missing information and advocacy. And free speech is also about the tolerance that we have that permits all of us the chance to make what might well appear to others to be the wrong, the terribly wrong, choice.

In conclusion, the strong anti-paternalist cares too deeply about people to attempt to protect them against themselves, however attractive such a course of action might appear in the short term. Instead, the strong anti-paternalist turns

to what might be called the paradox of democratic societies: namely, that democracy succeeds only because it allows the vigorous exercise of the very free speech that could destroy it, as the paradox of autonomy. The great compliment of democracy to human dignity is that through it we entrust to ourselves, not to a government, however well-intentioned, the task of ordering—and indeed perhaps misordering—our lives. And that compliment makes all the difference.

## REFERENCES

Aaro, L. E., Wold, B., Kannas, L. & Rimpela, M. (1986) Health behaviour in schoolchildren, a WHO cross-national study. *Health Promotion*, **1**, pp. 17–33.

Allegrante, J. P., O'Rourke, R. W. & Tuncalp, S. A. (1978) Multivariate analysis of selected psychosocial behaviour. *Journal of Drug Education*, **7**, pp. 239–242.

Arneson, R. (1980) Mill versus Paternalism. *Ethics*, **90**, p. 474.

Bewley, B. R. & Bland, J. M. (1977) Academic performance and social factors related to cigarette smoking by schoolchildren. *British Journal of Preventive and Social Medicine*, **32**, pp. 18–24.

Boddewyn, J. (1986) *Tobacco Advertising Bans and Consumption in 16 Countries*. New York: International Advertising Association.

Children's Research Unit (1987) *An Examination of the Factors Influencing Juvenile Smoking Initiation in Canada*. Toronto: Children's Research Unit, Association of Canadian Advertising.

Leventhal, U. & Clary, P. D. (1980) The smoking problem: a review of the research and theory in behavioural risk modification. *Psychological Bulletin*, **88**, pp. 370–405.

Ross, R. (1973) Personality, social influence and cigarette smoking. *Journal of Health and Social Behaviour*. **14**, pp. 279–286.

# POSTSCRIPT

## Should Tobacco Advertising Be Prohibited?

Cahalan refers to "target audiences," particularly young people and minorities, and how advertising increases sales of tobacco products to these groups. A study in the *Journal of the American Medical Association* (vol. 266, 1991) reported that over half of children between ages 3 and 6 were able to identify Old Joe, the mascot for Camel cigarettes. By age 6, as many children were able to recognize Old Joe as readily as Mickey Mouse. Significantly, within four years after the Old Joe campaign was initiated, Camel's share of the youth market escalated from 0.5 percent to 32.8 percent. An estimated 85–90 percent of smokers start smoking before age 20. Tobacco advertisers assert that they do not market to children but that advertising does affect what children know.

Prohibition of tobacco advertising is a highly charged political issue. U.S. senator Tom Harkin (D.-Iowa) recently proposed an amendment to the Senate Tax and Urban Aid Bill to reduce the amount of money tobacco companies could deduct from their taxes for advertising expenses from the current 100 percent down to 80 percent. The additional revenue would go toward public education campaigns to dissuade people from smoking. Industry-supported lobbying against the Harkin amendment is intense. Another fight is being waged in California, where an aggressive effort to discourage smoking and a tax increase of 25 cents per pack resulted in a 17 percent decline in smoking among adults between 1987 and 1990.

From an economic standpoint, the revenue generated by the tobacco industry goes toward state and national treasuries. Also, thousands of people are employed by tobacco companies, and the livelihood of many farmers comes from growing tobacco crops. Should these people be deprived of their livelihoods? Some people assert that if restrictions on tobacco advertising went into effect and fewer people smoked, tax revenue losses would be lessened because federal and state government expenditures for health care costs would likely diminish.

Two articles in *The Economist* (September 1990) discuss the impact of banning tobacco advertisements: "Advertising Under Siege" and "Smoking 'em Out." In "The Marlboro Grand Prix: Circumvention of the Television Ban on Tobacco Advertising," *The New England Journal of Medicine* (March 28, 1991), Alan Blum describes how the ads of cigarette companies are prominently seen on television through the sponsorship of motor races. *World Smoking and Health* (vol. 16, no. 3, 1991), published by the American Cancer Society, is devoted entirely to countering tobacco advertisements.

# ISSUE 13

## Is the "Disease" of Alcoholism a Myth?

**YES: Herbert Fingarette,** from "Alcoholism: The Mythical Disease," *The Public Interest* (Spring 1988)

**NO: William Madsen,** from "Thin Thinking About Heavy Drinking," *The Public Interest* (Spring 1989)

### ISSUE SUMMARY

**YES:** Professor of philosophy Herbert Fingarette asserts that proof for labeling alcoholism a disease is lacking. Heavy drinking is destructive behavior, he argues, but identifying alcoholism as a disease is ultimately a greater disservice to heavy drinkers.

**NO:** Professor of anthropology William Madsen claims that research showing that alcoholics can be moderate drinkers is faulty and that promoting the idea that alcoholics can overcome their condition and drink socially may prove fatal to the problem drinker and to society.

The idea that alcoholism is a disease has become so widely accepted that it is seldom questioned by most people. The general public, health care providers, and various organizations embrace the idea that alcoholism is a disease, and the notion often goes unchallenged. However, in the following debate, Herbert Fingarette does question whether or not alcoholism should be regarded as a disease. William Madsen, in opposition, defends the disease concept. This debate raises two questions: (1) What criteria are used to determine whether or not alcoholism is a disease? and (2) Does it matter if alcoholism is a disease? With regard to the latter issue, both feel that whether or not alcoholism is a disease is quite relevant but for very different reasons.

The basis for determining if a condition is a disease is the presence of some type of pathogen or organism, such as a virus or bacteria, that causes the disease. However, no one organism has been found to cause alcoholism. Using this same criterion, medical conditions like diabetes and schizophrenia would not be labeled as diseases, although they are both medically accepted as diseases. Also, drinking alcohol is a behavior; is it reasonable to call a behavior a disease? Perhaps this depends on whether or not one can exert control over one's behavior.

The disease concept is further muddied because experts cannot determine who will become an alcoholic. Madsen and Fingarette agree that sons of alcoholics have a higher risk of becoming alcoholic than do sons of non-alcoholics. However, their interpretations of the data differ. Fingarette contends that the percentage of sons who become alcoholic is small and inconclusive and that most children of alcoholics do not become alcoholic. Madsen asserts that the percentage is indeed significant. Although he does not dismiss the role of environment in determining alcoholism, Madsen feels that the number of sons of alcoholics who become alcoholic in relation to males who grow up without an alcoholic parent is consequential.

It is clear that sons of alcoholics are more likely to become alcoholic; however, most do not become alcoholic. Although a person may be more biologically vulnerable, does that prove that alcoholism is a disease? Some diseases are more common to some groups than to others: Sickle-cell anemia, for example, is more common among African Americans than among other ethnic groups, and Tay-Sachs disease occurs most frequently among Jews. One might argue that alcoholism is similarly passed on.

Cultural attitudes and social norms regarding alcohol seem to have a strong bearing on rates of alcoholism. Alcoholism is also more prevalent among groups that tolerate drunkenness and heavy alcohol use. On many college campuses, heavy alcohol use is acceptable. Social norms on many campuses actually encourage excessive consumption. Yet, most college students reduce their alcohol use once they move away from the college environment, become employed, and/or assume other responsibilities.

No one questions the devastating effects of chronic, heavy alcohol use: Cirrhosis of the liver is one of the 10 leading causes of death among men; longevity is dramatically reduced; cognitive functioning is impaired; in effect, every organ in the body is affected by heavy drinking. Some people look at the physical effects of heavy drinking and assume that alcohol has a biological basis. Others feel that heavy drinking causes biological harm but that biology does not cause alcoholism.

Whether or not alcoholism is considered to be a disease is legally and morally relevant. One could argue that the disease label absolves alcoholics of responsibility—alcoholics can blame poor behavior on their medical condition. Proponents of the disease model, however, assert that alcoholism is not an excuse for poor drinking behavior. Alcoholics may not have total control over whether or not they become alcoholic, but they can still act in a responsible manner. An important question is whether the disease label enables or inhibits people from receiving help. Alcoholics may be more willing to seek help for a "disease." There is generally no stigma in having a medical condition. However, if alcoholism is viewed as a moral weakness, then one may be less likely to seek help. In the following selections, Herbert Fingarette takes the position that alcoholism is not a disease, while William Madsen points out limitations in Fingarette's arguments.

# YES

Herbert Fingarette

# ALCOHOLISM: THE MYTHICAL DISEASE

The idea that alcoholism is a disease is a myth, and a harmful myth at that. The phrase itself—"alcoholism is a disease"—is a slogan. It lacks definite medical meaning and therefore precludes one from taking any scientific attitude toward it, pro or con. But the slogan has political potency. And it is associated in the public consciousness with a number of beliefs about heavy drinking that do have meaning, and do have important consequences for the treatment of individuals and for social policy. These beliefs lack a scientific foundation; most have been decisively refuted by the scientific evidence.

This assertion obviously conflicts with the barrage of pronouncements in support of alcoholism's classification as a disease by health professionals and organizations such as the American Medical Association [AMA], by the explosively proliferating treatment programs, and by innumerable public-service organizations. So it may seem that a sweeping challenge to the disease concept can only be hyperbole, the sensationalist exaggeration of a few partial truths and a few minor doubts.

To the contrary: the public has been profoundly misled, and is still being actively misled. Credulous media articles have featured so many dramatic human-interest anecdotes by "recovering alcoholics," so many "scientific" pronouncements about medical opinion and new discoveries, that it is no wonder the lay public responds with trusting belief.

Yet this much is unambiguous and incontrovertible: the public has been kept unaware of a mass of scientific evidence accumulated over the past couple of decades, evidence familiar to researchers in the field, which radically challenges each major belief generally associated in the public mind with the phrase, "alcoholism is a disease." I refer not to isolated experiments or off-beat theories but to massive, accumulated, mainstream scientific work by leading authorities, published in recognized journals. If the barrage of "public service" announcements leaves the public wholly unaware of this contrary evidence, shouldn't this in itself raise grave questions about the credibility of those who assure the public that alcoholism has now been scientifically demonstrated to be a disease? . . .

From Herbert Fingarette, *Heavy Drinking: The Myth of Alcoholism as a Disease* (University of California Press, 1988, 1989), of which this selection is a partial summary. Citations have been omitted but are available in the book itself. Reprinted by permission of the author. This article first appeared in *The Public Interest*, no. 91 (Spring 1988).

Use of the word "disease" . . . shapes the values and attitudes of society. The selling of the disease concept of alcoholism has led courts, legislatures, and the populace generally to view damage caused by heavy drinkers as a product of "the disease and not the drinker." The public remains ambivalent about this, and the criminal law continues to resist excusing alcoholics for criminal acts. But the pressure is there, and, of more practical importance, the civil law has largely given in. Civil law now often mandates leniency or complete absolution for the alcoholic from the rules, regulations, and moral norms to which non-diseased persons are held legally or morally accountable. Such is the thrust of a current appeal to the U.S. Supreme Court by two veterans, who are claiming certain benefits in spite of their having failed to apply for them at any time during the legally specified ten-year period after discharge from the army. Their excuse: alcoholism, and the claim that their persistent heavy drinking was a disease entitling them to exemption from the regulations. The Court's decision could be a bellwether.

What seems compassion when done in the name of "disease" turns out, when the facts are confronted, to subvert the drinker's autonomy and will to change, and to exacerbate a serious social problem. This is because the excuses and benefits offered heavy drinkers work psychologically as incentives to continue drinking. The doctrine that the alcoholic is "helpless" delivers the message that he might as well drink, since he lacks the ability to refrain. As for the expensive treatments, they do no real good. Certainly our current disease-oriented policies have not reduced the scale of the problem; in fact, the number of chronic heavy drinkers reported keeps rising. (It is currently somewhere in the range of ten to twenty million, depending on the definitions one uses.)

In the remainder of this discussion I will set out the major beliefs associated with the disease concept of alcoholism, and then summarize the actual evidence on each issue. I will also sketch an alternative perspective on chronic heavy drinking that is warranted by the evidence we have today.

## CONVENTIONAL WISDOM

Science, according to the conventional view, has established that there is a specific disease that is triggered by drinking alcoholic beverages. Not everyone is susceptible; most people are not. But (the argument continues) a significant minority of the population has a distinctive biological vulnerability, an "allergy" to alcohol. For these people, to start drinking is to start down a fatal road. The stages are well defined and develop in regular order, as with any disease, with the symptoms accumulating and becoming increasingly disabling and demoralizing. First comes what looks like normal social drinking, but then, insidiously and inevitably, come heavier and more frequent drinking, drunken bouts, secret drinking, morning drinking, and, after a while, "blackouts" of memory from the night before. It begins to take more and more liquor to get the same effect—physical "tolerance" develops—and any attempt to stop drinking brings on the unbearable and potentially life-threatening "withdrawal" symptoms. Eventually, the crucial symptom develops: "loss of control." At that point, whenever the person takes a drink the alcohol automatically triggers an inability to control the drinking, and drunken bouts become the rule. There follows an inevitable, deepening slavery to alcohol, which wrecks social life, brings ruin, and culminates in death. The only escape—according to this elaborate myth—is appropriate medical treatment for the disease.

The myth offers the false hope that as a result of recent "breakthroughs" in science we now basically understand what causes the disease—a genetic and neurophysiological defect. But fortunately, it is claimed, medical treatment is available, and generally produces excellent results. However, the argument continues, even after successful treatment the alcoholic can never drink again. The "allergy" is never cured; the disease is in remission, but the danger remains. The lifelong truth for the alcoholic is, as the saying goes, "one drink—one drunk." The possibility of a normal life depends on complete abstinence from alcohol. There are no "cured" alcoholics, only "recovering" ones.

That is the classical disease concept of alcoholism. As I have said, just about every statement in it is either known to be false or (at a minimum) lacks scientific foundation.

## ORIGINS OF THE MYTH

... Alcoholics Anonymous [A.A.], founded in 1935, taught that alcohol was not the villain in and of itself, and that most people could drink safely. (In this way the great majority of drinkers and the beverage industry were mollified.) A minority of potential drinkers, however, were said to have a peculiar biological vulnerability; these unfortunates, it was held, are "allergic" to alcohol, so that their drinking activates the disease, which

then proceeds insidiously along the lines outlined earlier.

This contemporary version of the disease theory of alcoholism, along with subsequent minor variants of the theory, is often referred to now as the "classic" disease concept of alcoholism. Like the temperance doctrine, the new doctrine was not based on any scientific research or discovery. It was created by the two ex-alcoholics who founded A.A.: William Wilson, a New York stockbroker, and Robert Holbrook Smith, a physician from Akron, Ohio. Their ideas in turn were inspired by the Oxford religious movement, and by the ideas of another physician, William Silkworth. They attracted a small following, and a few sympathetic magazine articles helped the movement grow.

## ALCOHOLISM AND SCIENCE

What A.A. still needed was something that would serve as a scientific authority for its tenets. After all, the point of speaking of a "disease" was to suggest science, medicine, and an objective malfunction of the body. The classic disease theory of alcoholism was given just such an apparent scientific confirmation in 1946. A respected scientist, E. M. Jellinek, published a lengthy scientific article, consisting of eighty-plus pages impressively filled with charts and figures. He carefully defined what he called the "phases of alcoholism," which went in a regular pattern, from apparently innocent social drinking ever downward to doom. The portrait, overall and in its detail, largely mirrored the A.A. portrait of the alcoholic. Jellinek's work and A.A. proselytizing generated an unfaltering momentum; the disease concept that they promulgated has never been publicly supplanted by the prosaic truth.

Jellinek's portrait of the "phases of alcoholism" was not an independent scientific confirmation of A.A. doctrine. For as Jellinek explicitly stated, his data derived entirely from a sampling of A.A. members, a small fraction of whom had answered and mailed back a questionnaire that had appeared in the A.A. newsletter. The questionnaire was prepared by A.A. members, not by Jellinek; Jellinek himself criticized it, finding it scientifically inadequate. In addition, many A.A. members did not even subscribe to the newsletter, and so had no opportunity to respond. Jellinek obtained only 158 questionnaires, but for various reasons could actually use just 98 of them. This was a grossly inadequate set of data, of course, but it was all Jellinek had to work with. . . .

By the 1970s there were powerful lobbying organizations in place at all levels of government. The National Council on Alcoholism (NCA), for example, which has propagated the disease concept of alcoholism, has been a major national umbrella group from the early days of the movement. Until 1982 the NCA was subsidized by the liquor industry, which had several representatives on its board. The alliance was a natural one: at the cost of conceding that a small segment of the population is allergic to alcohol and ought not to drink, the liquor industry gained a freer hand with which to appeal to the majority of people, who are ostensibly not allergic.

Health professionals further widened the net, and economic incentives came powerfully into play. Federal and local governments began to open their health budgets to providers of alcoholism treatment, and also to alcoholism researchers. Insurance companies are increasingly required to do the same. Today, treatment aimed at getting alcoholics to stop drinking brings in over a billion dollars a year. Alcoholism researchers now rely on what is probably the second largest funding source after defense—government health funds. And by now there are hundreds of thousands of formerly heavy drinkers who feel an intense emotional commitment; they supply a large proportion of the staffs of treatment centers. . . .

## BIOLOGICAL CAUSES?

What does it mean to say that alcoholism is a disease? In public discussions in the news media, it is usually taken to mean that alcoholism has a single biological cause. "I believe [alcoholics] have a genetic predisposition and a certain kind of biochemistry that dooms you to be an alcoholic if you use alcohol." This is a characteristic remark, with what in this domain is a familiar kind of specious authority. The statement was printed in an alcoholism bulletin issued under the aegis of a University of California Extension Division Alcoholism Program. It appears in an interview with Kevin Bellows, a lay activist heading an international organization fighting alcoholism.

Lay activists are not alone in pressing this theme. When I was on a network talk-show recently, the physician on the panel—a man high in government alcoholism advisory councils—devoted most of his time to running through a list of recent research discoveries about the biological peculiarities of alcoholics. His thesis was that alcoholism is unquestionably a disease, and he plainly implied that it has a biological cause. What the lay audience does not realize is that the newly discovered biological phenomena can rarely be regarded as *causes* of chronic heavy drinking; instead, they are merely *associated* with chronic heavy drinking, or with intoxication. Nevertheless, the audience is led to infer that they play a causal role; in fact, we know that there are *no* decisive physical causes of alcoholism.

Long-term heavy drinking is undoubtedly an important contributing cause of bodily ailments—including major organ, nerve, circulatory, and tissue disorders. The illness and mortality rates of heavy drinkers are far higher than those of the population generally. Chronic heavy drinking is rivaled only by habitual smoking as a major contributor to the nation's hospital and morgue populations. But all this is the *effect* of drinking; the drinking behavior itself is the cause. Stop the behavior and you stop its terrible physical effects.

Another abnormal physical condition associated with heavy drinking is the appearance of biological "markers." These metabolic and other physiological conditions—statistically abnormal but not necessarily ailments in and of themselves—may often be present among alcoholics. More significantly, some of them are present in persons who are not and have not been alcoholics, but who have been identified on independent grounds as being at higher-than-average risk of eventually becoming alcoholics. Such "markers" can serve as warning signs for those at higher risk. It has been hypothesized that some of these biological "markers" may play a causal role in bringing about alcoholic patterns of drinking. The question is: What kind and what degree of causality are at issue?

One much discussed metabolic "marker" is the difference in the way those who are independently identified as being at higher risk oxidize alcohol into acetaldehyde and in turn metabolize the acetaldehyde. The toxic effects of acetaldehyde in the brain have led to speculation that it might play a key causal role in inducing alcoholism. Analogous claims have been made about the higher level of morphine-like substances that alcoholics secrete when they metabolize alcohol. As it happens (so often in these matters), there are serious difficulties in measuring acetaldehyde accurately, and the reported results remain inadequately confirmed. But these confirmation problems are problems of technique, and not of fundamental importance.

The substantive point, generally obscured by the excitement of new discovery, is that even if the existence of any such metabolic processes were confirmed, they still would not cause alcoholic behavior, because the metabolism of alcohol takes place only when there is alcohol in the body. Therefore, these metabolic products cannot be present in alcoholics who have not been drinking for a period of time, and in whom the total metabolic process in question is not presently taking place. Yet by definition, these individuals return to drinking and do so recurrently, in spite of the intermittent periods of sobriety. The metabolic phenomena bear only on drinking that is done while in a state of intoxication; the key question about alcoholism, however, is why a sober person, with no significant toxic product remaining in the body, should resume drinking when it is known to have such harmful effects.

The story of biological discoveries concerning alcoholism is always the same: many unconfirmed results are unearthed, but no causal link to repetitive drinking is ever established. There is one exception, however: the recent discoveries in genetics. A study of these, and of how they have been reported to the public, is revealing.

## ALCOHOLISM AND GENES

Several excellently designed genetic studies of alcoholism have recently come up with credible positive results; thus we have been hearing from activists, treatment-center staff members, and physicians that "alcoholism is a genetic disease." The reality—as revealed by the data—is very different from what this slogan suggests.

The course followed in these recent "decisive" studies has been simple: find children who were born of an alcoholic mother or father, who were put up for adoption very shortly after birth, and who thus spend little time with their biological parents. Then see whether this group of children shows a higher rate of alcoholism in later life than a comparable group of adoptees whose biological parents were not alcoholics. Controlling all other relevant conditions so that they are the same for both groups, one can infer that any eventual differences in the group rates of alcoholism is attributable to their heredity, the one respect in which they differ. In all these studies, the prevalence of alcoholism was significantly greater among the biological sons of alcoholics, especially the sons of alcoholic fathers. Doesn't this suggest that alcoholism is hereditary?

To answer this question, let us consider the first of these reports, a 1973 article by Donald Goodwin and his colleagues. They concluded that about 18 percent of the biological sons of an alcoholic parent themselves became alcoholics, whereas only 5 percent of the

biological sons of non-alcoholic parents become alcoholics—a statistically significant ratio of almost four to one, which in all probability is ascribable to heredity. This is what we typically hear about in the media, with or without the precise numbers.

Now let's look at the same data from a different angle, and in a more meaningful context. As simple arithmetic tells us, if 18 percent of the sons of alcoholics do become alcoholics, then 82 percent—more than four out of five—do not. Thus, to generalize from the Goodwin data, we can say that the odds are very high—better than four to one—that the son born of an alcoholic parent will *not* become an alcoholic. Put differently, it is utterly false, and perniciously misleading, to tell people with a parental background of alcoholism that their heredity "dooms" them to become alcoholics, or even that their heredity makes it probable that they will become alcoholics. Quite the contrary. Their alcoholic heredity does make it more probable that they'll become alcoholics than if they had non-alcoholic parents, but the probability is still low. This is to say that life circumstances are far more important than genes in determining how many people in any group will become heavy drinkers.

There is yet another important implication: since 5 percent of the sons of non-alcoholic parents become alcoholics, and since there are far more non-alcoholic parents than alcoholic ones, that 5 percent ends up representing a far larger total number of alcoholic sons. This is consistent with what we know anyway—the great majority of alcoholics do not have alcoholic parents.

The most recent (and influential) adoptee genetic study, reported by Cloninger and his colleagues, concludes with these words: "The demonstration of the critical importance of sociocultural influences in most alcoholics suggests that major changes in social attitudes about drinking styles can change dramatically the prevalence of alcohol abuse regardless of genetic predisposition."

Given the possibly dramatic effect of social attitudes and beliefs, the media emphasis on genes as the cause of alcoholism has a pernicious, though unremarked, effect. As we have noted, only a minority of alcoholics have an alcoholic parent. Emphasis on heredity as the "cause" of alcoholism may give a false sense of assurance to the far greater number of people who are in fact in danger of becoming alcoholics, but who do not have an alcoholic parent. These potential alcoholics may feel free to drink heavily, believing themselves genetically immune to the "disease."

The Special Committee of the Royal College of Psychiatry put the matter in perspective by saying the following in its book-length statement on alcoholism: "It is common to find that some genetic contribution can be established for many aspects of human attributes or disorders (ranging from musical ability to duodenal ulcers), and drinking is unlikely to be the exception."

## CAUSES OF ALCOHOLISM

There is a consensus among scientists that no single cause of alcoholism, biological or otherwise, has ever been scientifically established. There are many causal factors, and they vary from drinking pattern to drinking pattern, from drinker to drinker. We already know many of the predominant influences that evoke or shape patterns of drinking. We

know that family environment plays a role, as does age. Ethnic and cultural values are also important: the Irish, Scandinavians, and Russians tend to be heavy drinkers; Jews do not. The French traditionally drank modest amounts at one sitting, but drank more regularly over the course of the day. Cultural norms have changed in France in recent decades and so have drinking styles.

We have interesting anthropological reports about the introduction of European styles of drinking into non-European tribal societies. Among the Chichicastenango Indians of Guatemala, for example, there are two different ways of drinking heavily. When drinking ceremonially, in the traditional way, men retain their dignity and fulfill their ceremonial duties even if they have drunk so much that they cannot walk unassisted. When they drink in the bars and taverns where secular and European values and culture hold sway, the men dance, weep, quarrel, and act promiscuously.

The immediate social setting and its cultural meaning are obviously important in our own society. The amount and style of drinking typically vary according to whether the drinker is in a bar, at a formal dinner party, a post-game party, or an employee get-together. It is known that situations of frustration or tension, and the desire for excitement, pleasure, or release from feelings of fatigue or social inhibitions, often lead people to drink. Much depends on what the individual has "learned" from the culture about the supposed effects of alcohol, and whether the person desires those particular effects at a particular moment.

But does any of this apply to alcoholics? The belief in a unique disease of alcoholism leads many to wonder whether the sorts of influences mentioned above can make much of a difference when it comes to the supposedly "overwhelming craving" of alcoholics. Once one realizes that there is no distinct group of "diseased" drinkers, however, one is less surprised to learn that no group of drinkers is immune to such influences or is vulnerable only to other influences.

## DO ALCOHOLICS LACK CONTROL?

. . . [W]hen alcoholics in treatment in a hospital setting, for example, are told that they are not to drink, they typically follow the rule. In some studies they have been informed that alcoholic beverages are available, but that they should abstain. Having decided to cooperate, they voluntarily refrain from drinking. More significantly, it has been reported that the occasional few who cheated nevertheless did not drink to excess but voluntarily limited themselves to a drink or two in order to keep their rule violation from being detected. In short, when what they value is at stake, alcoholics control their drinking accordingly.

Alcoholics have been tested in situations in which they can perform light but boring work to "earn" liquor; their preference is to avoid the boring activity and forgo the additional drinking. When promised money if they drink only moderately, they drink moderately enough to earn the money. When threatened with denial of social privileges if they drink more than a certain amount, they drink moderately, as directed. The list of such experiments is extensive. The conclusions are easily confirmed by carefully observing one's own heavy-drinking acquaintances, provided one ignores the stereotype of "the alcoholic." . . .

## A USEFUL LIE?

Even if the disease concept lacks a scientific foundation, mightn't it nevertheless be a useful social "white lie," since it causes alcoholics to enter treatment? This common—and plausible—argument suffers from two fatal flaws.

First, it disregards the effects of this doctrine on the large number of heavy drinkers who do not plan to enter treatment. Many of these heavy drinkers see themselves (often correctly) as not fitting the criteria of "alcoholism" under some current diagnostic formula. The inference they draw is that they are therefore not ill, and thus have no cause for concern. Their inclination to deny their problems is thus encouraged. This can be disastrous, since persistent heavy drinking is physically, mentally, and often socially destructive.

Furthermore, since most people diagnosable as alcoholics today do not enter treatment, the disease concept insidiously provides an incentive to keep drinking heavily. For those many alcoholics who do not enter treatment and who (by definition) want very much to have a drink, the disease doctrine assures them that they might as well do so, since an effort to refrain is doomed anyway.

Moreover, a major implication of the disease concept, and a motive for promoting it, is that what is labeled "disease" is held to be excusable because involuntary. Special benefits are provided alcoholics in employment, health, and civil-rights law. The motivation behind this may be humane and compassionate, but what it does functionally is to reward people who continue to drink heavily. This is insidious: the only known way to have the drinker stop drinking is to establish circumstances that provide a motivation to stop drinking, not an excuse to continue. The U.S. Supreme Court currently faces this issue in two cases before it. And the criminal courts have thus far resisted excusing alcoholics from criminal responsibility for their misconduct. But it's difficult to hold this line when the AMA insists the misconduct is involuntary.

The second flaw in the social "white lie" argument is the mistaken assumption that use of the word "disease" leads alcoholics to seek a medical treatment that works. In fact, medical treatment for alcoholism is ineffective. Medical authority has been abused for the purpose of enlisting public faith in a useless treatment for which Americans have paid more than a billion dollars. To understand why the treatment does no good, we should recall that many different kinds of studies of alcoholics have shown substantial rates of so-called "natural" improvement. As a 1986 report concludes, "the vast majority of [addicted] persons who change do so on their own." This "natural" rate of improvement, which varies according to class, age, socioeconomic status, and certain other psychological and social variables, lends credibility to the claims of success made by programs that "treat" the "disease" of alcoholism. . . .

A British report concludes that "it seems likely that treatment may often be quite puny in its powers in comparison to the sum of [non-treatment] forces."

The more pessimistic reading of the treatment-outcome data is that these elaborate treatments for alcoholism as a disease have no measurable impact at all. In a review of a number of different long-term studies of treatment programs, George Vaillant states that "there is com-pelling evidence that the results of our treatment were no better than the natural history of the disease." . . .

## NEW APPROACHES

In recent years, early evaluation studies have been reexamined from a non-disease perspective, which has produced interesting results. For example, it appears that the heaviest and longest-term drinkers improve more than would be expected "naturally" when they are removed from their daily routine and relocated, with complete abstinence as their goal. This group is only a small subset of those diagnosable as alcoholics, of course. The important point, though, is that it is helpful to abandon the one-disease, one-treatment approach, and to differentiate among the many different patterns of drinking, reasons for drinking, and modes of helping drinkers.

Indeed, when we abandon the single-entity disease approach and view alcoholism pluralistically, many new insights and strategies emerge. For example, much depends on the criteria of success that are used. The disease concept focuses attention on only one criterion—total, permanent abstinence. Only a small percentage of alcoholics ever achieve this abolitionist goal. But a pluralistic view encourages us to value other achievements, and to measure success by other standards. Thus, marked improvement is quite common when one takes as measures of success additional days on the job, fewer days in the hospital, smaller quantities of alcohol drunk, more moderate drinking on any one occasion, and fewer alcohol-related domestic problems or police incidents. The Rand Report found that about 42 percent of heavy drinkers with withdrawal symptoms had reverted to somewhat more moderate drinking with no associated problems at the end of four years. Yet, as non-abstainers, they would count as failures from the disease-concept standpoint.

The newer perspective also suggests a different conception of the road to improvement. Instead of hoping for a medical magic bullet that will cure the disease, the goal here is to change the way drinkers live. One should learn from one's mistakes, rather than viewing any one mistake as a proof of failure or a sign of doom. Also consistent with the newer pluralistic, non-disease approach is the selection of specific strategies and tactics for helping different sorts of drinkers; methods and goals are tailored to the individual in ways that leave the one-disease, one-treatment approach far behind.

Much controversy remains about pluralistic goals. One of the most fiercely debated issues is whether so-called "controlled drinking" is a legitimate therapeutic goal. Some contend that controlled drinking by an alcoholic inevitably leads to uncontrolled drinking. Disease-concept lobbies, such as the National Council on Alcoholism, have tried to suppress scientific publications reporting success with controlled drinking, and have excoriated them upon publication. Some have argued that publishing such data can "literally kill alcoholics." Authors of scientific studies, such as Mark and Linda Sobell, have been accused of fraud by their opponents (though expert committees have affirmed the scientific integrity of the Sobells' work). Attacks like these have been common since 1962, when D. L. Davies merely reviewed the literature and summarized the favorable results already reported in a number of published studies—and was severely criticized for doing so. But since that time hundreds of similar reports have appeared. One recent study concludes that most formerly heavy drinkers who are now socially adjusted become social drinkers rather than abstainers.

In any case, the goal of total abstinence insisted upon by advocates of the disease concept is not a proven successful alternative, since only a small minority achieves it. If doubt remains as to whether the controversy over controlled drinking is fueled by non-scientific factors, that doubt can be dispelled by realizing that opposition to controlled drinking (like support for the disease concept of alcoholism) is largely confined to the U.S. and to countries dominated by American intellectual influence. Most physicians in Britain, for example, do not adhere to the disease concept of alcoholism. And the goal of controlled drinking—used selectively but extensively—is widely favored in Canada and the United Kingdom. British physicians have little professional or financial incentive to bring problem drinkers into their consulting rooms or hospitals. American physicians, in contrast, defend an enormous growth in institutional power and fee-for-service income. The selling of the term "disease" has been the key to this vast expansion of medical power and wealth in the United States.

What should our attitude be, then, to the long-term heavy drinker? Alcoholics do not knowingly make the wicked choice to be drunkards. Righteous condemnation and punitive moralism are therefore inappropriate. Compassion, not abuse, should be shown toward any human being launched upon a destructive way of life. But compassion must be realistic: it is not compassionate to encourage drinkers to deny their power to change, to assure them that they are helpless and dependent on others, to excuse them legally and give them special government benefits that foster a refusal to confront the need to change. Alcoholics are not helpless; they can take control of their lives. In the last analysis, alcoholics must *want* to change and *choose* to change. To do so they must make many difficult daily choices. We can help them by offering moral support and good advice, and by assisting them in dealing with their genuine physical ailments and social needs. But we must also make it clear that heavy drinkers must take responsibility for their own lives. Alcoholism is not a disease; the assumption of personal responsibility, however, is a sign of health, while needless submission to spurious medical authority is a pathology.

# NO
William Madsen

# THIN THINKING
# ABOUT HEAVY DRINKING

The conflict between the moral and medical approaches to alcoholism is being revived. The newest champion of the moral cause is Herbert Fingarette, who has argued in *The Public Interest* (Spring 1988) that "the idea that alcoholism is a disease" is a "myth" that is being pawned off on a gullible public by a coalition of avaricious doctors, cynical providers of ineffective "treatment," public officials eager to shirk their duties and millions of alcoholics who wish to avoid taking personal responsibility for their actions. Those who perpetuate the myth, Fingarette suggests, do so for the most venal reasons: physicians "defend an enormous growth in institutional power and fee-for-service income"; researchers seek government funds; legislators, judges, and bureaucrats lighten their work loads by compelling heavy drinkers to enter costly but ineffective treatment programs, as a show of addressing the social problems posed by alcohol abuse.

The perpetration of the myth that alcoholism is a disease, Fingarette further charges, has required that the public be "kept unaware of a mass of scientific evidence accumulated over the past couple of decades, evidence familiar to researchers in the field, which radically challenges each major belief generally associated in the public mind with the phrase, 'alcoholism is a disease.' "

But Fingarette's attempt to share the scientific truth with the heretofore deluded public is badly misconceived, because he himself—a layman in the field, lacking all scientific credentials—has completely misunderstood the medical issues and badly misrepresented the pertinent scientific literature. In what follows I will point out only a few of the most glaring defects in his arguments.

FINGARETTE'S CLAIM THAT ALCOHOLISM IS NOT A DISEASE IS SUPPOSEDLY BASED NOT on "isolated experiments or off-beat theories," but on "massive, accumulated, mainstream scientific work by leading authorities, published in recognized journals." But the hard scientific evidence from biology and medicine offered by Fingarette is tiny and insignificant. His portrayal of the findings of psychology and sociology as hard scientific fact is unpersuasive, but constitutes practically all of the evidence for his erroneous arguments.

Thus Fingarette fails to recognize the obvious inadequacy of much experimentation done on alcoholics under highly artificial laboratory conditions. These experiments are based on simplistic models of "rat research" in laboratories in which all variables can supposedly be controlled. But as animal researchers realized long ago, laboratory research must be supplemented by observations of the behavior of animals in their normal environment. Fingarette accepts the results of these lab experiments as proof that alcoholics do not experience uncontrollable "craving" for a drink; he deduces that alcoholics can willfully control their drinking behavior, which in turn disproves the disease concept of alcoholism. One of these studies showed that when alcoholics are "promised money if they drink only moderately, they drink moderately enough to earn the money." Another demonstrated that if the alcoholic had to do something boring—like pushing a lever—to get a drink, the alcoholic would "avoid the boring activity and forgo the additional drinking." But it is ludicrous to think that data from such contrived experiments will bear any resemblance to the behavior of alcoholics in a normal environment. Outside a laboratory, alcoholics have been known to lie, steal, break into liquor stores, and even threaten to kill to obtain alcohol when they really craved it.

By fiat Fingarette then rejects the claim that alcoholism is a disease, claiming instead the "heavy drinkers" drink for reasons "that are not results of alcohol's chemical effect." He further tries to justify his dismissal of alcoholism as a disease by asserting that since drinking habits range from abstinence to chronic abuse, it is impossible to establish distinct categories of drinking. By this reasoning we should throw out the concept of "puberty" in growth studies, because the onset and termination of that condition are hard to mark and vary widely from individual to individual. Or perhaps because there is debate today over the demarcation between life, brain death, and biological death, the concept of death is invalid. Death would be for Fingarette a fabrication foisted on the public by money-mad morticians and by cadavers trying to avoid their responsibilities to the living. Fingarette's refusal to classify alcoholism as a disease rests on his opinion and nothing else.

Fingarette knows little about what constitutes a disease. Since no single cause has been discovered for alcoholism, he believes that it cannot be a disease. But by this standard many medically accepted diseases would be denied their classification, such as diabetes, chronic obstructive pulmonary disease, eczema, psoriasis, Alzheimer's disease, and schizophrenia.

Fingarette also seems to have trouble understanding that diseases are not static, but progress through a course. He is extremely critical of Jellinek's claim that the disease of alcoholism goes through "phases." It is true that Jellinek's claim was not completely supported by later studies. Nevertheless, Fingarette's critique is unpersuasive. In the first place, no individual case of a disease follows a generic model perfectly. Jellinek's research, moreover, was the first to produce a useful description of the disease's course, and subsequent progress has been based on his work.

Some scientific evidence is too strong for Fingarette to ignore, and so he dismisses it as irrelevant. The evidence derives from genetics: Fingarette admits that 18 percent of the sons of alcoholic parents become alcoholics, but sees little significance in this, since this means that 82 percent of them "do *not*." Fingarette would do well to consider the implications of Mendel's classic pea-flower experiments. Seventy-five percent of his cross-bred flowers were red, but this does not mean that genetic factors played no role in causing 25 percent to be white. Fingarette has also ignored the vast and significant literature on genetics and personality. Of particular importance here is the research of neuropsychologist Ralph Tarter at the University of Pittsburgh School of Medicine, which indicates that there are six inherited "temperaments" that seem to predispose individuals to alcoholism.

Fingarette's sampling of the alcoholism literature, then, has been very limited. He ignores most of the significant biological research, such as that on alcoholic abnormalities in the P3 wave and in enzymes. The material he does cite was chosen prejudicially, and he lacks the background to discuss the physical aspects of the disease.

FINGARETTE ASSUMES THAT THE AMERICAN Medical Association [AMA] ratified the diagnosis of alcoholism as a physiological disease. Had he bothered to check the facts, he would have found that the AMA pronouncement in fact supports his own stance, rather than establishing the physiological model of alcoholism that he attacks. As Dr. Joseph Beasley pointed out in his book *Wrong Diagnosis, Wrong Treatment,* the AMA's official statement describes alcoholism primarily as a mental condition—the behavioral outcome of both conscious and unconscious psychological forces. In other words, the AMA recognizes alcoholism as a behavioral disorder. Furthermore, a behavioral model, as Dr. Margaret Bean demonstrates, is "often a disguised variant of the moral model." Thus, had he read widely enough in the literature, Fingarette could have claimed that the AMA supported his position. Although Fingarette denies that "punitive moralism" directed at the alcoholic is an appropriate response, he still strongly advocates the moral model. As Dr. Bean states, "The moral model assumes that alcoholism is a result of voluntarily chosen behavior (excessive drinking) which results from either immorality (not knowing or caring that one's behavior is bad) or defective will power (knowing but not behaving well) because of poor self-discipline or impulse control." Dr. Beasley cites Bean's work and other evidence to demonstrate that in fact the biological aspects of the disease of alcoholism have until recently been largely ignored. He concludes that alcoholism is a real disease, but "not a behavioral one." Thus Fingarette, who claims to be attacking an antiquated model of alcoholism as a physiological disease, is actually attacking a rather recent one, which has yet to be ratified by the AMA, but which is fully accepted by physicians today.

Having "disproved" the concept of "craving" (and the related concept of "loss of control") by misinterpreting their meaning and drawing on the results of slipshod research projects, Fingarette attempts to pursue his attack on the disease concept. He lets us in on the ultimate secret held back by proponents of the disease theory: "controlled drinking" (as opposed to total abstinence) is a legitimate therapeutic goal for alcoholics.

Although he claims that "hundreds of . . . reports" confirm this view, he never identifies them. He does refer to the 1962 work of D. L. Davies, who first reported successful "controlled drinking" that was accomplished without his knowledge, endorsement, or training. Fingarette does not mention that this "success" involved only seven individuals out of a sample of ninety-one. Had he really read the report, I do not see how he could think that even these seven had returned to normal drinking. One, for example, regularly relied on Antabuse when he had to be sure that no unpredictable drinking binge would interrupt some important activity. Nor does Fingarette mention that Davies strongly urges abstinence as the only valid therapeutic goal for alcoholics.

FINGARETTE CHIEFLY RESTS HIS CASE ON THE 1972 report of Linda and Marc Sobell. Two ambitious graduate students with comparatively little experience, the Sobells were eager to arouse the interest of alcoholism researchers. Knowledgeable professionals with vast experience have rejected their study as a fraud. Whether or not this is the case, an evaluation of the evidence casts substantial doubt upon the study's validity.

The original grant that funded the Sobells' research was made to Dr. Halmuth Schaefer, then Chief of Research at Patton State Hospital in California. Schaefer had to leave for New Zealand and turned the grant over to the Sobells. They grossly enlarged Schaefer's original goals for the project and set out to make gamma alcoholics—that is, those who are biologically addicted—into "controlled drinkers."

The experimental subjects in the research were exposed to movies of themselves after drinking and were counseled. Seated at a realistic bar, they were free to order drinks as they pleased, but received a slight electric shock in one finger if they ordered straight liquor or drank too fast. Finally the subjects "graduated"; each was given an identity card stating that the bearer had been "trained as a SOCIAL DRINKER." These were signed by Marc Sobell as project director. Follow-up studies by the Sobells and by Glen Caddy and his associates announced that the experiment had been a success.

In 1982, however, *Science* published an article based primarily on a review of the Sobell evidence. The study was extremely difficult to do and the investigators are to be congratulated for overcoming obstacles put in their way by the Sobells. Irving M. Maltzman, one of the authors, has stated that these obstacles were "to my knowledge unprecedented within the scientific enterprise." The editor of *Science* also noted the Sobells' totally unprofessional attempts to block publication of the article. Maltzman openly accused the Sobells of fraud. Because of the seriousness of the charge, the Committee on Ethics of the American Psychological Association censured Dr. Maltzman; but the censure was withdrawn after a hearing in which Maltzman presented some of the evidence for his charges. As Maltzman says, "The Ethics Committee found that I had a reasonable basis for my beliefs." Nor was the *Science* report the only significant source to question the veracity of the claims made by the Sobells. Dr. Schaefer, who had originally turned the project funds over to the Sobells, demanded that his name be withdrawn from any association with the project, stating that "the data clearly show that social drinking is not an acceptable alternative."

The *Science* article, which was meticulous in its quest for accuracy, depicts anything but a successful experiment. Only sixteen of the twenty subjects were classified as gamma alcoholics when the project began. Of these, thirteen were hospitalized again within a year for alcohol-related complaints. Two others were using alcohol destructively during the same period. The sixteenth appeared to be drinking socially, but because of further research, Maltzman now believes that this person may not have been a genuine gamma alcoholic. Of the four experimental subjects who were alpha alcoholics (that is, psychologically dependent but not addicted), three reportedly drank to excess, were arrested on drunk-driving charges, and abused drugs other than alcohol. At best, then, one (possible) gamma alcoholic ended up drinking responsibly.

In 1983 a "60 Minutes" report concluded that the Sobell experiment failed tragically. By 1983 five of the experimental subjects had died alcohol-related deaths, all before reaching forty-two years of age. These facts point to grave ethical and legal problems. The Sobells encouraged individuals to ingest a substance that could and did prove lethal to them, while claiming the imprimatur of science. Their action was negligent and culpable in the extreme.

Fingarette blithely discounts the deaths following the Sobell experiment. In his book (*Heavy Drinking: The Myth of Alcoholism*, University of California Press, 1988) he claims that six subjects died in ten years in the control group that received abstinence-oriented psychotherapy. From

this he concludes that controlled drinking "may prove to be a significantly more successful method than abstinence for at least some drinkers." It is true that psychotherapeutic approaches to alcoholism are seldom successful. I know from my experience as a consultant that abstinence programs run by psychotherapists can be disastrous. Once this is recognized, Fingarette's argument amounts to the claim that one inadequate program was successful because fewer experimental subjects died in it than in another inadequate program—odd reasoning at best.

FINALLY, FINGARETTE DISREGARDS ACCUMULATED scientific research suggesting that no more than 1.6 percent of treated alcoholics can ever return to normal drinking. To urge alcoholics to try for a goal with a demonstrated failure rate of 98.4 percent is madness. Even the Sobells recommended abstinence as the primary goal in treating alcoholics. Despite Fingarette's claims, controlled drinking has been so disastrously ineffective as therapy that professionals in this country have totally abandoned it. Fingarette's critique of "the myth of alcoholism" comes tumbling down like a house of cards.

Fingarette's diatribe against Alcoholics Anonymous [AA] is also unpersuasive. Treatment programs based on AA principles, such as the Betty Ford Center, the Navy Alcohol Recovery Program, and the Employment Assistance Programs, have recovery rates up to 85 percent. It is true that AA reaches only a small percentage of alcoholics and is far from successful with all who join. But it is the best approach we have today; it merits support rather than attack from Fingarette and other self-designated "authorities."

When Fingarette criticizes the philosophical foundations of Alcoholics Anonymous, he lapses into caricature. Alcoholics Anonymous realizes quite as well as Fingarette that alcoholism has "psychological, social, cultural, economic, and even spiritual dimensions." In fact, every suggestion that Fingarette makes in his book for helping alcoholics recover is endorsed by Alcoholics Anonymous—with the lethal difference that AA recommends abstinence, while Fingarette advocates controlled drinking with tolerated binges. Although the members of AA believe that one drink may compel them to have another, they otherwise see alcoholism in the same terms as Fingarette—a fact Fingarette understandably chooses to disregard. In his excellent book, *The Alcoholics Anonymous Experience*, Milton Maxwell states that "AA sees alcoholism as an illness, symptomatic of a personality disorder. Its program is designed to get at the basic problem, that is, to bring about a change in personality." Years earlier, Bill Wilson, cofounder of AA, wrote that "anyone who knows the alcoholic personality by first-hand contact knows that no true 'alky' ever stopped drinking permanently without undergoing a profound personality change."

Finally, and perhaps most importantly, Fingarette's emphasis on the alcoholic's need to accept personal responsibility is platitudinous. "Alcoholics are not helpless; they can take control of their lives. In the last analysis, alcoholics must *want* to change and *choose* to change." Who would disagree? Not the medical profession and certainly not Alcoholics Anonymous—even though Fingarette accuses them of sanctioning the drinking of alcoholics by proclaiming their total lack of responsibility for their actions. Here again, Fingarette overwhelms the reader by his ability to misrepresent the truth.

DOCTORS ALWAYS EXPECT THAT PATIENTS who are not totally psychotic or comatose will take due responsibility for their own cures. Likewise, far from freeing alcoholics from accountability, Alcoholics Anonymous stresses that they must take full responsibility for their behavior. Alcoholics, far from being freed of responsibility for past performance, whether drunk or sober, are expected to make amends for the wrongs of the past. While the AA group gives all the help it can to each member, one of its most important sayings is, "We will walk with you but we can't walk for you." If Fingarette had simply made this valid and important point about public policy—that alcoholism should not serve as a legal defense in either civil or criminal actions—he would have discovered that virtually all recovering alcoholics agree with him. The AMA specifically states that alcoholism is properly not a valid defense for civil and criminal violations of the law.

Fingarette has no trouble demanding responsibility of others, both alcoholics and nonalcoholics. He claims in his book that private hosts "should be encouraged to assume some responsibility, moral if not legal, in serving alcohol to their guests." Do crusades like his, which seem to urge alcoholics to drink, show any responsibility at all? While claiming that alcoholism is a myth, Fingarette does concede that "alcoholism is . . . profoundly harmful, both to the drinkers themselves and to others." I am convinced that his crusade will increase the damage to which he rightly points.

# POSTSCRIPT

## Is the "Disease" of Alcoholism a Myth?

The implications of whether or not alcoholism is a disease are many. If alcoholism were viewed as a moral weakness, then health care personnel and alcohol treatment facilities would lose a considerable amount of income and researchers who receive funds to study the genetic basis of alcoholism would likely be in jeopardy of losing funding. If alcoholism were viewed as a disease, then there would be less stigma attached to it and people would be less hesitant to seek help.

There appears to be a trend to label many undesirable behaviors, such as excessive alcohol use, as medical diseases. Eating disorders, as well as compulsive gambling, sex, and shopping, have been identified as addictions requiring medical treatment. Is the autonomy of alcoholics and others who exhibit compulsive behavior undermined by calling their problems medical conditions? Rather than deeming these addictions as medical or behavioral, is it possible for them to be both medical *and* behavioral? What may start out as unhealthy or inappropriate behavior may become an obsession that requires medical intervention.

Although most people stop their abusive behaviors on their own without any formal treatment program, several factors have been shown to help people overcome alcoholism and drug abuse: Having a strong supportive social system is essential; meaningful employment is helpful; and the desire to change behavior is important. Some people do not change their life-styles until they reach a low point. Others simply mature out of alcohol and drug use—they find that they no longer want or need to use drugs. In essence, it may not matter if people have the disease of alcoholism. What matters is whether or not they deal with their alcoholism.

The question of whether or not alcoholism is hereditary or environmental is explored in Constance Holden's article "Probing the Complex Genetics of Alcoholism," *Science* (January 11, 1991). Two studies examining the genetic basis of alcoholism are Andrew Heath and Nicholas Martin's "Teenage Alcohol Use in the Australian Twin Register: Genetic and Social Determinants of Starting to Drink," *Alcoholism* (December 1988) and "Genetic Influences on Use and Abuse of Alcohol: A Study of 5638 Adult Finnish Twin Brothers," *Alcoholism* (August 1987), by Jaakko Kaprio and others. Support for a chemical basis for drug addiction is found in Marguerite Holloway's "Rx for Addiction," *Scientific American* (March 1991), in which she reviews research in which addictive behavior is chemically controlled. And an overview of Alcoholics Anonymous and how it has changed in recent years is described in Nan Robertson's "The Changing World of Alcoholics," *The New York Times Magazine* (February 21, 1988).

# ISSUE 14

# Should Alcohol Advertising Be Limited?

**YES: Patricia Taylor,** from Statement Before the Subcommittee on Transportation and Hazardous Materials, Committee on Energy and Commerce, U.S. House of Representatives (March 1, 1990)

**NO: Harold Shoup and Christine Dobday,** from "Alcohol Advertising Restrictions Without Due Cause," in Ruth C. Engs, ed., *Controversies in the Addiction's Field, Volume One* (Kendall/Hunt, 1990)

## ISSUE SUMMARY

**YES:** Patricia Taylor, director of the Alcohol Policies Project of the Center for Science in the Public Interest, argues that banning alcohol advertisements aimed at youths and minorities is an important initial step for eliminating alcohol-related health problems.
**NO:** Harold Shoup and Christine Dobday, executives of the American Association of Advertising Agencies, contend that research does not support singling out advertising as a major controlling cause of alcohol abuse and that advertising does not affect alcohol consumption habits.

Television, magazines, and billboards are replete with advertisements about alcohol. In movies and television programs, the alcohol industry pays to have actors and actresses shown drinking alcoholic beverages with the labels prominently displayed. The public is reminded that with alcohol one can have fun at any time and in any place. Some advertisements imply that alcoholic beverages will improve one's sex appeal. People are told that if they work hard and play hard, then they deserve certain alcoholic products; hence, alcohol is depicted as a reward. Whether or not these advertisements for alcoholic products have any effect on alcohol-related behavior and whether or not the advertising of these products should be limited are relevant questions.

To what extent, if any, does alcohol advertising contribute to alcohol-related problems? To suggest that alcohol problems originate from alcohol advertisements negates the influence of parents, peers, and social attitudes. Alcohol advertisements have become a scapegoat for alcohol problems. By blaming advertising, people can absolve themselves of their roles and responsibilities if they, their children, or their partners have troubles due to alcohol. One could reason that if people were taught to be better consumers—to develop reasoning skills and to make informed decisions—many problems would disappear.

Alcohol advertising and alcohol-related problems have resulted in the formation of organizations like Mothers Against Drunk Driving (MADD) and Students Against Driving Drunk (SADD), which are especially concerned about alcohol and its relationship to automobile fatalities. Groups like MADD and SADD believe that advertisements for alcohol glamorize the drug and link alcohol to athletic and sexual prowess. To mediate the influence of alcohol advertisements, they propose that an equal amount of time be allocated in the media for health and safety messages. They also suggest that alcohol advertisements be limited, especially at rock concerts and sporting events, which attract large numbers of youths. They advocate restricting promotional activities on college campuses and requiring mandatory health and safety warnings on alcohol advertisements.

The advertising industry opposes restricting alcohol advertisements for a number of reasons: Restricting alcohol advertising has little effect on decreasing consumption habits (as seen in other countries); there is no compelling evidence showing a connection between viewing advertisements and increasing alcohol consumption; and the First Amendment rights of advertisers to disseminate information regarding their products and of consumers to receive such information are violated by such restrictions. In addition, the alcohol industry states that it does not advertise to underage drinkers and that, as long as alcohol is legal for people age 21 and over, the industry's freedom to advertise should not be restricted.

One problem identified by people who advocate restricting alcohol advertisements is that the alcohol industry spends billions of dollars promoting its products. The budgets to counter alcohol advertisements are minuscule in comparison. According to Jean Kilbourne, a leading proponent for limiting alcohol advertising, the advertising budget just for Budweiser beer is greater than the entire federal budget for research on alcoholism and alcohol abuse. Kilbourne contends that the alcohol industry has a vested interest in promoting overconsumption. The alcohol industry sends out the message that people should not drive after drinking. However, this message does not say that one should not overdrink—only that drinking and driving is a bad combination.

In the following selections, Patricia Taylor argues that because alcohol advertising is pervasive and alcohol problems are rampant, restrictions are necessary. Harold Shoup and Christine Dobday claim that advertising is geared toward promoting brand loyalty and that restricting advertisements violates policies that are fundamental to government and the economy.

# YES

Patricia Taylor

## STATEMENT OF PATRICIA TAYLOR

### ALCOHOL AND TOBACCO: DIFFERENCES AND SIMILARITIES

[Alcohol and tobacco] are responsible for far more harm, both in loss of life and societal cost, than all other drugs combined. And when alcohol and tobacco are used together, their impact can be even more devastating. There are, however, some important differences between these two products.

One is the rate at which individuals using the products become addicted to them. For alcohol, 10–15 percent of drinkers become dependent on alcohol. Alcohol is used by more Americans than any other drug, including cigarette tobacco. According to the U.S. Department of Health and Human Service's 7th Report to Congress on Alcohol and Health, released last month, 18 millions Americans suffer from alcohol problems, with a projected increase of almost one million more Americans who will exhibit symptoms of alcohol dependence by 1995.

Another critical difference between these two products is *when* the negative impacts occur. Alcohol-related problems can result immediately, even after short-term use, unlike tobacco, which causes long-term adverse effects. For example, I know of no cases of acute nicotine poisoning resulting in death, whereas acute alcohol poisoning is a far too common occurrence. Drinking, unlike smoking, is also linked with violent crime, suicide, spousal and child abuse, and drinking and driving crashes—the leading cause of death for young Americans.

And, contrary to what the alcoholic beverage companies would have members of Congress and the public believe, the majority of alcohol-related problems are *not* caused by heavy drinkers—but by light to moderate drinkers, according to a report issued by the Institute of Medicine in January, 1990.

A third important distinction between these products is the fact that alcoholic beverage producers spent over $1 billion last year advertising their products on radio and TV, compared to no broadcast expenditures for cigarettes. According to New York University professor Neil Postman and

From U.S. House of Representatives. Committee on Energy and Commerce. Subcommittee on Transportation and Hazardous Materials. *Tobacco Issues (Part 2): Targeting of Minorities by Alcohol and Tobacco Advertising.* Hearing, March 1, 1990. Washington, DC: Government Printing Office, 1990. (H361-50.)

his colleagues in "Myths, Men, and Beer," a report funded by the AAA Foundation for Traffic Safety, young people see tens of thousands of television commercials for beer alone before they reach the legal drinking age of 21. . . .

Despite the differences between alcohol and tobacco, there are also some interesting parallels. Both of these drugs, presumably because they are manufactured legally, are excluded from President Bush's drug control strategy and Drug Czar Bennett's mandate. Both alcohol and tobacco are excluded from the Media Partnership for a Drug-Free America campaign. That campaign claims to be a $365 million a year effort, counting donated messages in the print and electronic media. While the campaign uses the best minds of the advertising community to inform Americans about drugs, it is no coincidence that it only includes the drugs that are not advertised on radio and TV.

There are powerful economic and political interests—agencies, broadcasters, and alcohol producers—doing everything they can to keep alcohol and tobacco removed from what is on the minds of the majority of Americans—curbing drug problems. Many of the "Partners" are getting rich off of the sale of alcohol and tobacco products, and it is certainly to their benefit to oppose the competition from illegal drugs.

In the alcohol area, producers talk about their products in "creative"—and misleading—ways. Wine trade associations and producers promote wine as an agricultural product—they're even trying to move jurisdiction over wine from the Bureau of Alcohol, Tobacco, and Firearms to the Department of Agriculture. Noticeably absent from these debates are the nation's health agencies, including the Department of Health and Human Services.

Brewers have even taken to writing stockholders, claiming that their products are totally different from illicit drugs, and certainly shouldn't be part of the nation's anti-drug campaign. Alcohol may not be as addictive as crack cocaine, but it certainly is a drug and it certainly can be addictive. And even beer companies would be hard-pressed to dispute the fact that alcohol costs our society far more than all other drugs combined, including tobacco—over $100 billion each year. Finally, alcoholic beverages *are* illicit for people under 21.

## ALCOHOL ADVERTISERS AND YOUTH

. . . At the Center for Science in the Public Interest, we have conducted two surveys of young people, to learn more about the influence of alcohol advertising on youth. In one survey of 4th and 5th graders in metropolitan Washington, D.C., we found that the average 8 to 12 year old child could name 5.2 alcoholic beverages, but only 4.8 presidents. And they didn't just know the brand names, they could spell them remarkably well also. One 11-year-old boy who spelled Matilda Bay, King Cobra, and Bud Light correctly, couldn't do any better than presidents "Nickson" and "Rosselvet." We suspect that much of this brand awareness is due to billboards, TV and radio commercials, and other forms of advertising.

Last year, we conducted another survey, this time of teenagers, asking them to name their favorite TV ads. Once again, we found that kids are attracted to these clever, well-produced ads. Boys cited beer ads more often than any other type of ad as their favorite. The 40 percent of the boys who named one or more beer ads as their favorite, put beer ahead of ads for fast foods, cars, running shoes, and even soft drinks. . . .

America's largest brewer, Anheuser-Busch, helps finance all U.S. Major League baseball teams, 20 of the 28 NFL teams, more than 300 college teams, and about 1,000 other sporting events. The alcoholic beverage industry may give lip service to their concerns about underage drinking, but high school coaches, who work with young athletes, are worried. They view alcohol as the main threat to high school athletes. In a *USA Today* survey of 798 high school coaches conducted in October 25–31, 1989, 88% of coaches identified alcohol as the greatest threat to their athletes. Only 6% identified crack-cocaine, and even fewer, 3%, identified marijuana.

But the alcoholic beverage industry's sponsorship of athletic events belies these problems and promotes a dangerously misleading myth among youth—that drinking is linked to athletic success. They certainly don't let under-age drinkers know that alcohol is a drug, that it may be addictive, or that drinking can in fact lead to serious health problems that undermine athletic prowess. . . .

## TARGETING MINORITIES

Some Americans are changing their drinking habits, partly in response to the health information that has been provided by Dr. Koop and other prominent health officials. But, to maintain sales, the $90 billion a year alcoholic beverage industry spent over $2 billion on advertising and promotions last year. That money lines the pockets of ad agencies and media that are only too willing to

testify on behalf of the First Amendment rights of some of their best customers.

This $90 billion a year industry is also investing in Congress—over the last two election cycles, the alcoholic beverage industry stuffed over $4 million in PAC, honoraria, and individual contributions into Congressional pockets. The broadcasters and their allies also gave generously, as did the outdoor advertisers who are responsible for the billboards littering our inner cities with messages promoting drinking and smoking. I'm sure that these facts are all too familiar to critics of smoking, because the methods and strategies of alcohol producers are similar to those of tobacco producers.

Both industries selectively target certain segments of our population with various products. Malt liquors are clearly targeted at minorities. Blacks account for only about 10 percent of sales of regular beer, but about 30 percent of sales of malt liquor, according to *Impact*, an alcohol trade publication. And, while regular beer contains about 4.6 percent alcohol, malt liquors range in alcohol content from 5.6 percent to a whopping 10.9 percent. Four cans of malt liquor have as much alcohol as five to eight cans of regular beer.

Despite the beer industry's written, voluntary policy of not touting the potency of their products, producers have named or advertised these brews specifically to imply high potency. Names like Schlitz Malt Liquor, with its bull crashing through a wall; Elephant; Midnight Dragon; and Turbo 1000 convey the impression that these beers are higher octane than regular beer.

But there's more to the story than the high alcohol content and the advertisements that connote strength and power. Ads for these products are explicitly targeted to Blacks and Latinos. I have here promotional materials, available in English and Spanish, for Pabst's Olde English 800. Provocatively dressed Black and Latina models, posing as "Lady and the Tiger," are accompanied by the slogan, "It's the Power." Most telling is the back page of a sales brochure that states, " . . . brewed for relatively high alcohol content (important to the Ethnic market!)." In another ad, this one for something called Midnight Dragon malt liquor, a seductively dressed woman sits backward on a chair, saying, "I could suck on this all night."

A coalition of 22 Black, Latino, and health organizations joined together to protest this marketing formula. They stressed that these aggressive marketing campaigns undermine the nation's anti-drug programs.

According to Dr. Walter Faggett, representing the National Medical Association, "The War on Drugs is doomed to failure when slick ads for Colt 45 and other malt liquors tell young men that drinking is the key to fun and sexual success. Not only are malt liquor products harmful themselves, but they're 'gateway' drugs that could pave the way to crack-cocaine and other illegal drugs." The groups called unsuccessfully on Secretary of HHS Dr. Louis Sullivan and Treasury Secretary Nicholas Brady to demand that the companies stop targeting Blacks and Latinos and that they limit the alcohol content of malt liquor to 5 percent.

I would like to submit for the record a copy of a report that we released in 1987, "Marketing Booze to Blacks," which explores in greater detail many of the marketing themes and targeting practices utilized by alcohol producers to target Blacks.

In addition to particular products, alcohol and tobacco producers also utilize selected advertising techniques to reach minority markets. One advertising medium, billboards, has been under growing attack by citizen activists and elected officials across the country. Billboards target inner-city neighborhoods with 24-hour-a-day messages to smoke and drink. Last week, Scenic America and the Center for Science in the Public Interest released a report, "Citizens' Action Handbook on Alcohol and Tobacco Billboard Advertising." . . .

Alcohol and tobacco companies haven't restricted their targeting practices to billboards or to Black communities. In a report we issued in October, "Marketing Disease to Hispanics," Representative Matthew Martinez underscored the growing concern about the escalating cancer rates among Hispanics: more Hispanics are smoking, and smoking more cigarettes than in the past. Meanwhile alcohol-related problems, which had been limited almost exclusively to men, are now spreading to Latina women, who traditionally drank little.

According to Representative Martinez, "Many factors obviously play a role, but one clear contributor is the slick advertising campaigns that alcohol and tobacco companies have aimed at Hispanics for years. The glamorous images in the ads, which are particularly enticing to young people, saturate Hispanic neighborhoods across the country." "Marketing Disease to Hispanics" examines the pervasive influence of the alcohol and tobacco industries in the Hispanic community and the impact this influence is having on health.

I would like to cite one example of the differences in how alcoholic beverages are marketed to the majority population compared to Hispanics. There has been a long-standing voluntary restraint on the part of liquor producers from advertising on television, as you know. In 1988, we were informed by a Spanish-language TV viewer that similar restraint was not being exercised on Spanish-language TV. As a matter of fact, not only were ads being aired, but ads for one particular product even had a man drinking on a boat from a gallon-sized bottle and then jumping in the water, while a gaggle of admiring, bikini-clad women, also drinking, admired his exploits from a nearby boat. We, along with a number of Hispanic and public health organizations, were eventually successful in persuading Telemundo and Univision to halt the airing of ads for hard liquor. . . .

## NEED FOR ALCOHOL ADVERTISING REFORMS

Which gets us back to the heart of the problem—how is it that alcohol and tobacco aren't part of the nation's anti-drug effort? Part of the problem clearly lies in the powerful pro-drinking messages that fill our airwaves. In response to public criticism about these messages, the alcoholic beverage industry has appointed itself the purveyor of so-called moderation messages, which are oftentimes nothing more than an extension of their advertising, creating a "Good Guy" image and geared to undermine demands for governmental action.

Have you thought about what Spuds McKenzie telling your 10 year old to "Know When To Say When" really means? First, your child is getting a pro-drinking message. "Know When To Say When" assumes that someone has started drinking, and the only question that

needs to be answered is, how much? There certainly is no information about the fact that it is illegal for your 10 year old to purchase alcoholic beverages before reaching the age of 21, or that alcohol is a drug or that alcohol can be deadly. The very image that Anheuser-Busch uses to advertise their products, in this case one with great appeal to young people, is carried over into these so-called "moderation messages."

Second, and very disturbing for organizations concerned about preventing alcohol-related problems, the companies that produce these products are setting themselves up as deliverers of a health message at the same time they are dependent upon sales of their products to people with alcohol problems. Over 50 percent of the alcoholic beverages sold each year are bought by the 10 percent of drinkers with the most severe alcohol problems. The American public deserves and needs more than a subtle pro-drinking message in sheep's clothing from beer barons worried that the public is catching on to the fact that their product is America's leading drug problem. . . .

In an article headlined "Beer ad ban won't hurt nets," L. F. Rothschild . . . described networks even more dependent on beer advertising than today—18% of network sports revenues in 1983 were derived from beer and wine advertising, compared with 15% today. Further, according to Mr. Rothschild, an imposed ban would severely crimp the marketing efforts of beer advertisers, not the revenues of the networks. That's because the networks obtained sports advertising revenues from a broad variety of sources, including companies like General Motors, Ford, and IBM. Clearly there will be a period of adjustment to any changes in alcohol advertising policies, but the draconian nature predicted is simply inconceivable.

And what about the alcohol advertising policies of some of the cable networks that make the advertising/media business today so different from what it was 20 years ago when tobacco ads left the nation's airwaves? Nick-at-Night doesn't allow ads for alcoholic beverages before 10:00 p.m. The Family Channel doesn't allow any alcoholic beverage advertising at all. Even MTV says that generally they don't allow beer ads during the day. Alcoholic beverage producers are understandably concerned about advertising controls. The American public is fed up with all of their ads. In a November, 1989 poll for the *The Wall Street Journal*, 60% of those surveyed favored requiring equal time for health and safety messages; almost half of those polled wanted to ban them altogether, along with the retired athletes and other celebrity pitchmen. When it comes to warnings, 67% favored requiring warnings about the dangers of drinking.

When the Roper organization asked if alcoholic beverages should be advertised on TV, 63% favored restricting beer advertising, 33% to after 9:00 p.m., and 30% favored eliminating it altogether. The Bureau of Alcohol, Tobacco and Firearms conducted its own public opinion survey on warning labels for a report to Congress and found that nearly one-half of those surveyed felt that alcoholic beverage advertising greatly influences under-age people to drink alcoholic beverages.

When Dr. Koop issued his recommendations on curbing drinking and driving crashes, he stated, "certain advertising and marketing practices for alcoholic beverages clearly send the wrong messages about alcohol consumption to the wrong audiences . . . they send the message that drinking is a normal and glamorous activity without negative consequences."

The marketing practices of alcoholic beverage producers are the best their money can buy. For the sake of our nation's health, the policies that regulate those marketing practices should also be the best that we can muster. Obviously, reforming alcohol advertising practices alone will not eliminate all of the health problems associated with drinking and smoking. For alcohol, we need a comprehensive program that includes sharp increases in alcohol excise taxes, expanded prevention and treatment programs, and better consumer information about legal drugs.

# NO

Harold Shoup and<br>Christine Dobday

# ALCOHOL ADVERTISING RESTRICTIONS WITHOUT DUE CAUSE

## INTRODUCTION

Alcoholism and drunk-driving gained national awareness as two of society's primary ills during the tenure of the former United States Surgeon General C. Everett Koop. Alcohol advertising was condemned as the alleged root of these evils by those who subscribe to a simple, lineal theory: alcohol advertising increases alcohol abuse which increases drunk-driving. But the theory has a basic flaw: it's wrong. It is not supported by research data, empirical evidence, or previous studies. Despite the compelling evidence, country after country has tried to affect alcohol consumption by limiting alcohol advertising; and has found such restrictions to have little, if any effect. In the United States, the fallacies surrounding alcohol advertising persist much to the detriment of the consumer. Although the movement to combat alcohol abuse is admirable, the measures undertaken must be proven effective when the freedom of commercial speech is at risk.

## AD RESTRICTIONS DO NOT SOLVE THE PROBLEM

A study conducted by the Federal Trade Commission determined that " . . . a review of the literature regarding the quantitative effect of alcohol advertising on consumption and abuse found no reliable basis to conclude that alcohol advertising significantly affects consumption, let alone abuse" (Crawford, 1985).

The University of Texas at Austin reinforced these findings. Over a twenty-one year period from 1964 to 1984, they examined the effect of alcohol advertising expenditure level on alcoholic beverage consumption in the U.S. "The findings indicate that advertising expenditure levels have no important relationship with aggregate consumption" (Wilcox, 1986). Anti-alcohol interests would have the public believe that alcohol advertising

From Harold Shoup and Christine Dobday, "Alcohol Advertising Restrictions Without Due Cause," in Ruth C. Engs, ed., *Controversies in the Addiction's Field, Volume One* (Kendall/Hunt, 1990). Copyright © 1990 by The American Council on Alcoholism, Inc. Reprinted by permission.

*Figure 1*

**Advertising and Consumption 1970-1988**

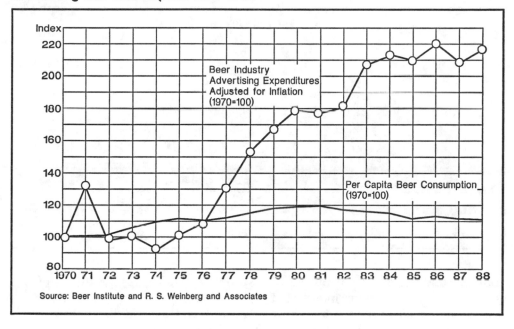

Source: Beer Institute and R. S. Weinberg and Associates

plays a major role in prompting abusive behavior but the statistics prove otherwise.

In British Columbia and Manitoba, Canada and the U.S.A. the effects of alcoholic beverage restrictions showed no substantial link between advertising and consumption (Waterson, 1983; Smart and Cutler, 1976; Ogbourne and Smart, 1980). In France, imports of whiskey actually rose from 157,000 proof gallons in 1957—the year whiskey advertising was banned—to 6,294,000 proof gallons in 1979. The ban, having proven ineffective, was then lifted (Waterson, 1983). This lack of a correlation cannot be overlooked when the dissemination of information on a legal product is in jeopardy.

Over the past few years, alcohol advertising expenditures have increased; however, alcohol-related traffic fatalities have decreased. (see Figure 2).

Thus, the evidence indicates that other factors, such as society's intolerance of alcohol abuse, stronger law enforcement, educational programs, and public service initiatives are responsible for the decline in alcohol abuse and that the volume of product advertising is irrelevant.

The statistics are equally impressive among teenage drivers. In the 16–19 year old range, fatal crashes involving teenage drivers declined to 18.7% in 1987, down from 21% in 1986, and 28.4% in 1982. (Federal Register, 1988). These significant decreases were achieved with no restrictions on commercial speech.

## THE ROLE OF ALCOHOL ADVERTISING

It may seem illogical or counter-intuitive that alcohol advertising does not significantly affect overall consumption of the

*Figure 2*
**Alcohol Involvement in Fatal Traffic Crashes**

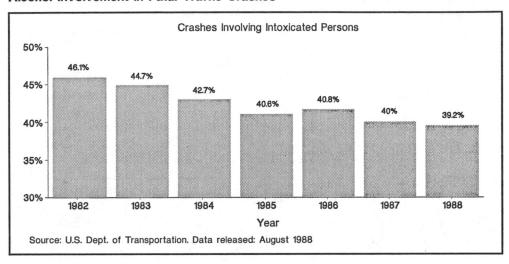

Source: U.S. Dept. of Transportation. Data released: August 1988

product. However, a careful review of the data reflects an intense inter-brand rivalry, not an attempt to attract new drinkers to that product. Alcohol is a "mature" product category, which means that consumers are aware of the product and its basic characteristics; therefore, the overall level of consumption is not affected significantly by the advertising of specific brands.

In this latter regard, it is significant to note that the Health and Human Services Department in its *Seventh Special Report to the U.S. Congress on Alcohol and Health* (1990), concluded that "research has yet to document a strong relationship between alcohol advertising and alcohol consumption." This same report also makes no recommendation to ban or restrict alcohol advertising.

Marketing strategists in mature product categories realize that the over-riding objective of advertising is to promote brand loyalty and encourage brand switching. In the same way that manufacturers of laundry detergent and tooth paste

promote their brands, producers of alcoholic beverages advertise their brands to protect and expand their share of the available market.

The domestic annual retail market for beer is roughly $40 billion. Thus, an advertising campaign that would gain just one point of additional market share would produce $400 million in increased sales for the brewer advertising the product. On the other hand, if total beer consumption increased one percent (and that would be a quantum leap forward for this relatively static category), a brand with a 10% share would only gain $40 million in sales.

Attempts by any one brand to "grow" the total market simply don't make sense. The potential return for any single brand would be in the approximate proportion to its existing share of the market. Small wonder, then, that brand managers target their advertising dollars on established consumers of their products in an effort to reinforce brand loyalty or encourage trial by users of other

*Table 1*

**Money Differences Between Increasing Total Market Versus Increasing Market Share**

| *Scenario I: Increase Total Market* | |
|---|---|
| Total beer market is: | $40,000,000,000 |
| Brand A's share is 10 percent, or: | $ 4,000,000,000 |
| Total market increases by one percent to: | $40,400,000,000 |
| Brand A's 10 percent share is now: | $ 4,040,000,000 |
| | |
| *Scenario II: Increase Market Share* | |
| Total beer market remains flat at: | $40,000,000,000 |
| Brand A's share increases by one percent, or: | $ 400,000,000 |
| Brand A's 11 percent share is now: | $ 4,400,000,000 |

brands. Brand managers realize that the name of the game is share of market, not size of market.

## THE CONSTITUTIONAL RIGHT TO ADVERTISE

It is also illogical and inappropriate to deny consumers access to truthful information that helps them make informed purchase decisions. Approximately two-thirds of Americans consider themselves drinkers according to the U.S. Surgeon General (Press conference, May 31, 1989). For the consumer, advertising plays an important role in providing information about alcoholic beverages. It communicates information on new products such as wine coolers and low-alcohol beer, as well as information on pricing and packaging. Just as alcohol producers have the right to distribute information via advertising, the consumer has the right to receive it. In this sense, it is fundamental

to both our government and our economy that people can be trusted to make wise decisions if they have access to all relevant information. Proposed restrictions to limit commercial speech have a resultant diminution of the First Amendment rights of both alcoholic beverage advertisers and consumers.

Recognizing this fundamental danger, the Supreme Court has ruled that such restrictions on commercial speech must advance a specific government interest and be narrowly tailored in its method of doing so. (Central Hudson, 1980) Thus, freedom of commercial speech cannot be swept aside by advertising bans and restrictions that would have an unsubstantiated effect on product abuse and simultaneously deprive responsible consumers of their right to truthful information.

## CONCLUSION

The problems of alcohol abuse are complex and cross all sections of society. The only successful way to address alcoholism is to confront the socio-economic, psychological, and possibly genetic factors which can be directly linked to the behavior. The subjective and arbitrary singling out of advertising as a major controlling cause of abuse is unsupported by research. Alcohol advertising already is regulated heavily by the government. Before further regulations are imposed they should be supported by facts and not by assumptions. Such a dangerous precedent ignores the legitimate interest of both producers and consumers of a legal product.

## REFERENCES

*Central Hudson Gas and Electric Corp. vs. Public Service Commission* 447 U.S. 557 (1980) 561–562.

Crawford, C. T. and Gramm, W. L. (1985). Writing in the cover memo to *Omnibus Petition for Regulation of Unfair and Deceptive Alcoholic Beverage Advertising and Marketing Practices* (Docket No. 209–46). Federal Trade Commission, p. 2 (March 6).

Ogbourne, A. C. and Smart, R. G. (1980). Will restrictions on alcohol advertising reduce alcohol consumption? *The British Journal of Addiction,* 75 296–298.

Presidential Document (1988). Proclamation 5918 of December 5, 1988, cited in the *Federal Register,* 53 (235) 49287–49288 (December 7).

*Seventh Special Report to the U.S. Congress on Alcohol and Health* (1990). U.S. Department of Health and Human Services. Public Health Service. Drug Abuse and Mental Health Administration. National Institute of Alcohol Abuse and Alcoholism: Rockville, MD.

Smart, R. G. and Cutler, R. E. (1976). The alcohol advertising ban in British Columbia: Problems and effects on beverage consumption, *The British Journal of Addiction,* 7 13–21.

Surgeon General C. Everett Koop's Press Conference, May 31, 1989.

Waterson, M. J. (1983). *Advertising and Alcohol Abuse,* a report published by the Advertising Association, p. 10.

Wilcox, G. B., Franke, G. R., and Vacker, B. (1986). Alcohol beverage advertising and consumption in the United States: 1964–1984. *Department of Advertising Working Paper,* The University of Texas: Austin, p. III (January).

# POSTSCRIPT

## Should Alcohol Advertising Be Limited?

Taylor mentions how alcohol advertisers target specific groups, such as inner-city youth. She cites Dr. Louis Sullivan, secretary of Health and Human Services and an outspoken critic of the alcohol advertising industry, who objects to beer companies aiming ads for malt liquor (malt liquor has a higher alcohol content than regular beer) at African Americans and Latinos. In a study of 2,015 billboards in Baltimore, for example, the Abell Foundation reported that 70 percent of billboards were located in inner-city neighborhoods and that more than three-fourths of these billboards advertised either alcohol or tobacco.

People who argue for limiting alcohol advertisements do not necessarily oppose alcohol use. In a survey conducted for the Roper Organization, Peter Hart found that "alcohol and cigarettes have turned into vices that people want to preserve—but not promote." Hart noted that the general public does not want alcohol or tobacco use prohibited but that half would like to see advertisements for alcohol and tobacco banned.

The Association of National Advertisers is a powerful lobbying group in Washington. They have effectively attacked legislation, such as two bills proposed in Congress in 1984 and 1985 that would have required equal air time for health and safety messages regarding alcohol use. They also oppose warning labels on alcohol products and advertisements because of the onerous burden that warning labels would make for advertisers.

In "Advertising Addiction: The Alcohol Industry's Hard Sell," *Multinational Monitor* (June 1989), Jean Kilbourne criticizes the alcohol advertising industry as a large contributor to alcohol-related problems. In *Drug Abuse Update* (National Families in Action, 1992), a background paper by the Anheuser-Busch and Adolph Coors companies argues that agencies in the federal government, especially the Office of Substance Abuse Prevention, have overstepped their boundaries by trying to make public policy rather than carrying out public policy. The paper states that "no responsible member of the alcoholic beverage industry disputes the need to combat irresponsible drinking."

In recent years, alcohol advertising has become more specialized. An article in *Advertising Age* (March 16, 1992) describes how the Miller Brewing Company is targeting its beer products to women. And in "Coalition Charges Malt Liquor Pitched to Blacks/Hispanics," *Alcoholism Report* (1989), Lewis discusses the marketing of beer with relatively higher alcohol content to inner-city residents.

# ISSUE 15

## Are Drug Addicts Always in Control of Their Addiction?

**YES: Jeffrey A. Schaler,** from "Drugs and Free Will," *Society* (September/October 1991)

**NO: Craig Nakken,** from *The Addictive Personality: Understanding Compulsion in Our Lives* (Hazelden Foundation, 1988)

### ISSUE SUMMARY

**YES:** Psychotherapist Jeffrey A. Schaler contends that addicts always have control over their addiction and that they must therefore assume responsibility for their behaviors. Addiction, he says, is not a disease over which people have no control but a matter of the addict's free volition.
**NO:** Lecturer and certified chemical dependency therapist Craig Nakken argues that addiction results when a person repeatedly seeks relief from unpleasant feelings or situations through avoidance and develops unhealthy and unnatural ways of coping with emotions. Once an addictive personality has been established, the addict has no control over his or her addiction.

A fundamental issue is whether drug addiction is caused by an illness or disease or whether it is caused by inappropriate behavioral patterns. This distinction is extremely important because it has legal and medical implications. Should people be held legally accountable for behaviors that stem from an illness over which they have no control? For example, if a person cannot help being an alcoholic and hurts or kills someone as a result of being drunk, should that person be treated or incarcerated? Likewise, if an individual's addiction is due to lack of self-control rather than to a disease, should taxpayer money go to pay for that person's treatment?

It can be argued that the disease concept of drug addiction legitimizes or excuses behaviors. If addiction is an illness, then blame for poor behavior can be shifted to the disease and away from the individual. Moreover, if drug addiction is incurable, can people *ever* be held responsible for their behavior?

Jeffrey A. Schaler contends that addicts should be held responsible for their behavior and that loss of control is not inevitable. Schaler refutes the idea of addiction as a disease, and he supports his belief with Alan Marlatt's finding that "the ability of alcoholics to stop drinking alcohol is not determined by a physiological reaction to alcohol." It has also been shown that many cocaine and heroin users do not lose control while using these drugs. In their study of U.S. service personnel in Vietnam, epidemiologist Lee N. Robins and colleagues showed that most of the soldiers who used narcotics regularly during the war did not continue using them once they returned home. Many service personnel in Vietnam reportedly used drugs because they were in a situation they did not want to be in. Moreover, without the support of loved ones and society's constraints, they were freer to gravitate toward behaviors that would not be tolerated by their families and friends.

Attitudes toward treating drug abuse are affected by whether it is perceived as an illness or as an act of free will. The disease concept implies that one needs help in overcoming addiction. By calling drug addiction a medical condition, the body is viewed as a machine that needs fixing; character and will become secondary. Also, by calling addiction a disease, the impact of society in causing drug addiction is left unexplored. What roles do poverty, crime, unemployment, inadequate health care, and poor education have in drug addiction? Schaler contends that psychological and environmental factors account for drug addiction.

Craig Nakken argues that drug addicts cannot exert control over their lives. Addiction, whether it is to drugs, sex, food, exercising, gambling, or shopping, is a way of life for certain individuals. Addiction offers addicts the illusion of fulfillment and provides relief from unpleasant situations or relationships. Drug addicts mistakenly believe that drugs help them, so they develop a relationship with drugs. According to Nakken, overcoming drug addiction is beyond the capabilities of drug addicts, who lack the requisite skills to help themselves, so outside intervention is necessary.

According to the disease perspective, an important step for addicts to take in order to benefit from treatment is to admit that they are powerless against their addiction. They need to acknowledge that their drug addiction controls them and that addiction is a lifelong problem. The implication of this view is that addicts are never cured. Addicts must therefore abstain from drugs for their entire lives. This view is contradictory to Schaler's free will model, which states that drug addicts can moderate their use of drugs when they want to.

Does personality cause addiction, or are there other factors that cause addiction? How much control do drug addicts have over their use of drugs? In the following selections, Jeffrey A. Schaler argues that drug use is a matter of free will. Craig Nakken, in describing the addictive personality, claims that addiction comes from one's relationship with drugs.

# YES                          Jeffrey A. Schaler

## DRUGS AND FREE WILL

"That was the disease talking . . . I was a victim." So declared Marion Barry, 54, mayor of the District of Columbia. Drug addiction is the disease. Fourteen charges were lodged against him by the U.S. attorney's office, including three counts of perjury, a felony offense for lying about drug use before a grand jury; ten counts of cocaine possession, a misdemeanor; and one count of conspiracy to possess cocaine.

Barry considered legal but settled for moral sanctuary in what has come to be known as the disease-model defense. He maintained that he "was addicted to alcohol and had a chemical dependency on Valium and Xanax." These are diseases, he asserted, "similar to cancer, heart disease and diabetes." The implication: It is as unfair to hold him responsible for drug-related criminal behavior as it is to hold a diabetic responsible for diabetes.

The suggestion was that his disease of addiction forced him to use drugs, which in turn eroded his volition and judgment. He did not voluntarily break the law. According to Barry, "the best defense to a lie is truth," and the truth, he contended, is that he was powerless in relation to drugs, his life unmanageable and "out of control." His behaviors or acts were purportedly the result, that is, symptomatic, of his disease. And jail, say those who agree with him, is not the answer to the "product of an illness."

This disease alibi has become a popular defense. Baseball's Pete Rose broke through his "denial" to admit he has a "gambling disease." Football's Dexter Manley claimed his drug use was caused by addiction disease. Addiction treatment professionals diagnosed televangelist Jimmy Swaggart as having "lost control" of his behavior and as being "addicted to the chemical released in his brain from orgasm." They assert that Barry, Rose, Manley and Swaggart all need "twelve-step treatment" for addiction, the putative disease that, claims the multimillion-dollar addiction treatment industry, is reaching epidemic proportions and requires medical treatment. To view addiction-related behaviors as a function of free will, they often say, is cruel, stigmatizing and moralistic, an indication that one does not really understand the disease.

Others are more reluctant to swallow the disease model. After testing positive for cocaine in 1987, Mets pitcher Dwight Gooden said he could moderate his use of the drug and was not addicted. This is heresy according to disease-model proponents, a sign of denial, the salient symptom of the disease of addiction and considered by some to be a disease itself. There is no such thing as responsible drug taking or controlled drinking for an addict or an alcoholic, they assert.

The tendency to view unusual or questionable behavior as part of a disease process is now being extended, along with the characteristic theory of "loss of control," to include all sorts of "addictive" behaviors. We are currently experiencing the "diseasing of America," as social-clinical psychologist Stanton Peele describes it in his recent book of the same name (1989). The disease model is being applied to any socially unacceptable behavior as a means of absolving people of responsibility for their actions, criminal or otherwise. "The practice is justified on this basis: Drug use constitutes an addiction. Addiction is a disease. Acts stemming from the disease are called symptoms. Since the symptoms of a disease are involuntary, the symptoms of drug addiction disease are likewise involuntary Addicts are thus not responsible for their actions.

Is this analogizing of drug addiction to real diseases like diabetes, heart disease and cancer scientifically valid? Or is the word "disease" simply a misused metaphor? Does drug use truly equal addiction? Are the symptoms of drug addiction really involuntary?

## LOSS OF CONTROL

At the heart of the idea that drug use equals addiction is a theory known as "loss of control." This theory may have originated among members of Alcoholics Anonymous "to denote," as described by researcher E. M. Jellinek in his book *The Disease Concept of Alcoholism* (1960), "that stage in the development of [alcoholics'] drinking history when the ingestion of one alcoholic drink sets up a chain reaction so that they are unable to adhere to their intention to 'have one or two drinks only' but continue to ingest more and more—often with quite some difficulty and disgust—contrary to their volition."

Loss of control also suggests that addictive drugs can start a biochemical chain reaction experienced by an addict as an uncontrollable physical demand for more drugs. Drug addicts are people who have allegedly lost their ability to control their ingestion of drugs.

In a speech in San Diego two years ago, National Drug Policy Director William Bennett explained that a drug "addict is a man or woman whose power to exercise . . . rational volition has . . . been seriously eroded by drugs, and whose life is instead organized largely—even exclusively—around the pursuit and satisfaction of his addiction."

Yet, there is a contradiction in Bennett's point of view. If an addict's power to exercise rational volition is seriously eroded, on what basis does the addict organize life "largely even exclusively around the pursuit and satisfaction of his addiction"? An act of organizing is clearly a volitional act, an act of will. . . .

It may be helpful to look at how the term "addiction" has developed. Its use in conjunction with drugs, disease, loss of control, withdrawal and tolerance developed out of the moralistic rhetoric of the temperance and anti-opium movements of the nineteenth century, not through scientific inquiry. Such a restrictive use of the word served multiple purposes according to psychologist Bruce Alexander of Simon Fraser University in British Columbia, lead author of an article on the subject. Linking addiction to drugs and illness suggested it was a medical problem. It also helped to scare people away from drug use, a tactic that became increasingly important with anti-opium reformers. Etymologically, the word "addiction" comes from the Latin "dicere" (infinitive form) and, combined with the preposition "ad," means "to say yes to," "consent." Consent implies voluntary acceptance.

The idea of choice, volition or voluntariness inherent in the meaning of the word "addiction" is significant to [free-] will model proponents because the concept of addiction as a disease depends so much on the loss-of-control theory. Most people think of addiction with the element of volition decidedly absent. Studies of alcoholics and cocaine and heroin addicts conducted over the past twenty-six years appear to refute this claim, however.

## THE MYTH OF LOSS OF CONTROL

In 1962 British physician and alcohol researcher D. L. Davies rocked the alcoholism field by publishing the results of a long-term follow-up study of patients treated for alcoholism at the Maudsley Hospital in London. Abstinence, long considered the only cure for alcoholism, was seriously questioned as the only form of treatment when seven out of ninety-three male alcoholics studied exhibited a pattern of normal drinking. Physiological differences purportedly present in alcoholics did not seem to affect their ability to control drinking.

Four years later, *The Lancet* published an important study by British psychiatrist Julius Merry that supported Davies's findings. Alcoholics who were unaware they were drinking alcohol did not develop an uncontrollable desire to drink more, undermining the assertion by supporters of the disease model that a small amount of alcohol triggers uncontrollable craving. If alcoholics truly experience loss of control, then the subjects of the study should have reported higher craving whether they believed their beverages contained alcohol or not.

According to the loss-of-control theory, those with the disease of alcoholism cannot plan their drinking especially when going through a period of excessive craving. Yet, psychologist Nancy Mello and physician Jack Mendelson, leading alcoholism researchers and editors of the *Journal of Studies on Alcohol*, reported in 1972 that he found alcoholics bought and stockpiled alcohol to be able to get as drunk as they wanted even while undergoing withdrawal from previous binges. In other words, they could control their drinking for psychological reasons; their drinking behavior was not determined by a physiologically uncontrollable force, sparked by use of alcohol.

As Mello and Mendelson wrote in summary of their study of twenty-three alcoholics published in *Psychosomatic Medicine:* "It is important to emphasize that even in the unrestricted alcohol-access situation, no subject drank all the alcohol available or tried to 'drink to oblivion.' These data are inconsistent with predictions from the craving hypothesis so often invoked to account for an alcoholic's perpetuation of drinking. No empirical support has been provided for the notion of craving by directly observing alcoholic subjects in a situation where they can choose to drink alcohol in any volume at any time by working at a simple task. There has been no confirmation of the notion that once drinking starts, it proceeds autonomously."

A significant experiment conducted by Alan Marlatt of the University of Washington in Seattle and his colleagues in 1973 supported these findings by showing that alcoholics' drinking is correlated with their beliefs about alcohol and drinking. Marlatt successfully disguised beverages containing and not containing alcohol among a randomly assigned group of sixty-four alcoholic and social drinkers (the control group) asked to participate in a "taste-rating task." One group of subjects was given a beverage with alcohol but was told that although it tasted like alcohol it actually contained none. Subjects in another group were given a beverage with no alcohol (tonic) but were told that it did contain alcohol.

As Marlatt and co-authors reported in the *Journal of Abnormal Psychology*, they found "the consumption rates were higher in those conditions in which subjects were led to believe that they would consume alcohol, regardless of the actual beverage administered." The finding was obtained among both alcoholic and social drinker subjects. Marlatt's experiment suggests that according to their findings the ability of alcoholics to stop drinking alcohol is not determined by a physiological reaction to alcohol. A psychological fact—the belief that they were drinking alcohol—was operationally significant, not alcohol itself.

Similar findings have been reported in studies of cocaine addiction. Patricia G. Erickson and her colleagues at the Addiction Research Foundation in Ontario concluded, in their book *The Steel Drug*

(1987), after reviewing many studies on cocaine that most social-recreational users are able to maintain a low-to-moderate use pattern without escalating to dependency and that users can essentially "treat themselves." They state, "Many users particularly appreciated that they could benefit from the various appealing effects of cocaine without a feeling of loss of control."

Erickson and co-authors cite in support a study by Spotts and Shontz (1980) that provides "the most in-depth profile of intravenous cocaine users to date." They state: "Most users felt a powerful attachment to cocaine, but not to the extent of absolute necessity. [A]ll agreed that cocaine is not physically addicting . . . [and] many reported temporary tolerance."

In a study by Siegel (1984) of 118 users, 99 of whom were social-recreational users, described by Erickson et al. as the only longitudinal study of cocaine users in North America, "all users reported episodes of cocaine abstinence."

These results thus further support the hypothesis that drug use is a function of psychological, not physiological, variables. Even the use of heroin, long considered "the hardest drug," can be controlled for psychological and environmental reasons that are important to heroin addicts. A notable study of 943 randomly selected Vietnam veterans, 495 of whom "represented a 'drug-positive' sample whose urine samples had been positive for opiates at the time of departure" from Vietnam, was commissioned by the U.S. Department of Defense and led by epidemiologist Lee N. Robins. The study shows that only 14 percent of those who used heroin in Vietnam became re-addicted after returning to the United States. Her findings, reported in

1975, support the theory that drug use is a function of environmental stress, which in this example ceased when the veterans left Vietnam. Veterans said they used heroin to cope with the harrowing experience of war. As Robins and co-authors wrote in *Archives of General Psychiatry*:

> . . . [I]t does seem clear that the opiates are not so addictive that use is necessarily followed by addiction nor that once addicted, an individual is necessarily addicted permanently. At least in certain circumstances, individuals can use narcotics regularly and even become addicted to them but yet be able to avoid use in other social circumstances. . . . How generalizable these results are is currently unknown. No previous study has had so large and so unbiased a sample of heroin users.

The cocaine and heroin studies are important for several reasons. They challenge the contention that drug addiction is primarily characterized by loss of control. Moreover, these and similar studies support the idea that what goes on outside of a person's body is more significant in understanding drug use, including alcoholism, than what goes on inside the body.

Consider for a moment how a person enters and exits drug use. While disease-model proponents such as Milam, Ketcham and Gold, claim that abstinence is the only cure for this "special disease," implying that strength of will is irrelevant, we must recognize drug use, and abstinence from it, for what they really are—volitional acts. . . .

## DISEASE VS. BEHAVIOR

According to professor of psychiatry Thomas Szasz at the State University of New York in Syracuse, a disease, as textbooks on pathology state, is a phenomenon limited to the body. It has no relationship to a behavior such as drug addiction, except as a metaphor. Szasz argues against the disease model of addiction on the basis of the following distinction between disease and behavior. In *Insanity: The Idea and Its Consequences* (1987) he writes:

> [B]y behavior we mean the person's 'mode of conducting himself' or his 'deportment' . . . the name we attach to a living being's conduct in the daily pursuit of life. . . . [B]odily movements that are the products of neurophysiological discharges or reflexes are not behavior. . . . The point is that behavior implies action, and action implies conduct pursued by an agent seeking to attain a goal.

The products of neurophysiological discharges or reflexes become behavior when they are organized through intent, a willful act. Drug-taking behavior is not like epilepsy. The former involves intentional, goal-seeking behavior. An epileptic convulsion is an unconscious, unorganized neurophysiological discharge or reflex, not a behavior.

In another example, smoking cigarettes and drinking alcohol are behaviors that can lead to the diseases we call cancer of the lungs and cirrhosis of the liver. Smoking and drinking are behaviors. Cancer and cirrhosis are diseases. Smoking and drinking are not cancer and cirrhosis. . . .

Many advocates of the disease model cite as further evidence for their view the results of genetic studies involving the heritability of alcoholism. Recently, the dopamine $D_2$ receptor gene was found to be associated with alcoholism. A study by Kenneth Blum and co-authors, published in the *Journal of the American*

*Medical Association,* suggests that this gene confers susceptibility to at least one form of alcoholism. The goal of this and similar studies is to identify the at-risk population in order to prevent people from becoming alcoholics and drug addicts.

What such studies do not tell us is why people who are not predisposed become alcoholics and why those who are predisposed do not. It seems more than reasonable to attribute this variance to psychological factors such as will, volition and choice, as well as to environmental variables such as economic opportunity, racism and family settings, to name just a few. Experimental controls accounting for genetic versus environmental influences on alcoholic behavior are sorely lacking in these studies.

The basis upon which people with alleged alcoholism disease are distinguished from mere heavy drinkers is arbitrary. No reliable explanation has yet been put forth of how the biological mechanisms theoretically associated with alcoholism and other forms of drug addiction translate into drug-taking behavior. Moreover, Annabel M. Bolos and co-authors, in a rigorous attempt to replicate the Blum findings, reported higher frequencies of the $D_2$ receptor gene found in their control population than in the alcoholic population in the same journal seven months later.

## TREATMENT

Finally, the contribution of treatment to exposing the myth of addiction disease warrants mention. Since his arrest at the Vista Hotel in Washington, D.C., Marion Barry has undergone treatment for alcohol addiction and chemical dependency at the Hanley-Hazelden clinic in West Palm Beach, Florida, and at the Fenwick Hall facility near Charleston, South Carolina. Barry said he needs treatment because he has "not been spiritual enough." His plan is to turn his "entire will and life over to the care of God . . . using the twelve-step method and consulting with treatment specialists." He said he will then "become more balanced and a better person."

The twelve-step program Barry is attempting to follow is the one developed by Alcoholics Anonymous (AA), a spiritual self-help fellowship. AA is the major method dealing with alcoholism today. All good addiction treatment facilities and treatment programs aim at getting the patient into AA and similar programs such as Narcotics Anonymous. Yet several courts throughout the United States have determined that AA is a religion and not a form of medicine, in cases involving First Amendment violations, most recently in *Maryland v. Norfolk* (1989). Anthropologist Paul Antze at York University in Ontario has written extensively on AA and describes the "point-by-point homology between AA's dramatic model of the alcoholic's predicament and the venerable Protestant drama of sin and salvation."

Successful treatment from this perspective is dependent upon a religious conversion experience. In addition, patients are required to adopt a disease identity. If they do not, they are said to be in denial. But such an approach is a psychologically coercive remedy for a moral problem, not a medical one. And here—in their concepts of treatment—is where the disease model and moralistic model of addiction seem to merge.

With so much evidence to refute it, why is the view of drug addiction as a disease so prevalent? Incredible as it may seem, because doctors say so. One leading alcoholism researcher asserts that alcoholism is a disease simply because people go to doctors for it. Undoubtedly, addicts seek help from doctors for two reasons. Addicts have a significant psychological investment in maintaining this view, having learned that their sobriety depends on believing they have a disease. And treatment professionals have a significant economic investment at stake. The more behaviors are diagnosed as disease, the more they will be paid by health insurance companies for treating these diseases.

Most people say we need more treatment for drug addiction. But few people realize how ineffective treatment programs really are. Treatment professionals know this all too well. In fact, the best predictor of treatment success, says Charles Schuster, director of the National Institute on Drug Abuse, is whether the addict has a job or not.

George Vaillant, professor of psychiatry at Dartmouth Medical School, describes his first experience, using the disease model and its effectiveness in diagnosing alcoholism, in *The Natural History of Alcoholism* (1983):

" . . . I learned for the first time how to diagnose alcoholism as an illness. . . . Instead of pondering the sociological and psychodynamic complexities of alcoholism. . . . [A]coholism became a fascinating disease. . . . [B]y inexorably moving patients into the treatment system of AA, I was working for the most exciting alcohol program in the world. . . . After initial discharge, only five patients in the Clinic sample never relapsed to alcoholic drinking, and there is compelling evidence that the results of our treatment were no better than the natural history of the disease."

This is important information because the definition of who an alcoholic or drug addict is and what constitutes treatment as well as treatment success can affect the lives of people who choose not to use drugs as well as those who choose to. For example, Stanton Peele has written extensively on how studies show that most people arrested for drinking and driving are directed into treatment for alcoholism disease, yet the majority are not alcoholics. Those receiving treatment demonstrate higher recidivism rates, including accidents, driving violations, and arrests, than those who are prosecuted and receive ordinary legal sanctions.

Furthermore, in a careful review of studies on treatment success and follow-up studies of heroin addicts at the United States Public Health Service hospital for narcotics addicts at Lexington, Kentucky, where "tens of thousands of addicts have been treated," the late Edward M. Brecher concluded in *Licit & Illicit Drugs* (1972) that "[a]lmost all [addicts] became readdicted and reimprisoned . . . for most the process is repeated over and over again . . . [and] no cure for narcotics addiction, and no effective deterrent, was found there—or anywhere else."

Brecher explained the failure of treatment in terms of the addictive property of heroin. Vaillant suggested that tuberculosis be considered as an analogy. Treatment, he said, rests entirely on recognition of the factors contributing to the "resistance" of the patient. And here is the "catch-22" of the disease model. Addiction is a disease beyond volitional control except when it comes to treatment failure, wherein "resistance" comes into play.

Neither Brecher nor Vaillant recognized that treatment does not work because there is nothing to treat. There is no medicine and there is no disease. The notions that heroin as an addictive drug causes addicts not to be treated successfully, or that "resistance" causes alcoholics to be incurable, are mythical notions that only serve to reinforce an avoidance of the facts: Addicts and alcoholics do not "get better" because they do not want to. Their self-destructive behaviors are not disturbed. They are disturbing.

All of this is not to suggest that the people we call addicts are bad, suffering from moral weakness and lack of willpower, character or values. Drug addicts simply have different values from the norm and often refuse to take responsibility for their actions. Public policy based on the disease model of addiction enables this avoidance to continue by sanctioning it in the name of helping people. As a result, criminals are absolved of responsibility for their actions, drug prevention and treatment programs end up decreasing feelings of personal self-worth and power instead of increasing them, and people who choose not to use drugs pay higher taxes and health insurance premiums to deal with the consequences of those who do.

Drug use is a choice, not a disease. Still, our current drug policies give the drug user only two options: treatment or jail. But if the drug user is sick, that is, is not responsible for his behavior, why should he go to jail for his illness? And if the drug user is someone who chooses to use drugs because he finds meaning in doing so, why should he be forced into treatment for having unconventional values? "Unconventional values" is not a disease.

"Treatment" for drug addiction is a misnomer. Education is a more appropri-ate term. In this modality a drug addict is given psychological and environmental support to achieve goals based on an identification of values and behavior-value dissonance. Behavioral accountability is stressed insofar as people learn about the consequences of their actions.

The legal arguments set forth to exculpate criminals because of addiction disease do not seem to be supported by scientific findings. Quite to the contrary, research suggests that drug addiction is far from a real disease. And as long as drug addiction can be blamed on a mythical disease, the real reasons why people use drugs—those related to socioeconomic, existential and psychological conditions including low self-esteem, self-worth and self-efficacy—can be ignored.

# NO

Craig Nakken

# THE ADDICTIVE PROCESS: THE CREATION OF AN ADDICTIVE PERSONALITY

Addiction must be viewed as a continuum because of its progressive nature. Some people teeter on a thin line between abuse and addiction for a long time; all objects or events that produce a positive, pleasurable mood change can be used and abused as part of an addiction. Addiction is different than periodic or even frequent abuse. This difference will become much more clear in the following pages where I'll discuss the addictive personality: the different changes that occur to addicts, their world, and the people who surround them.

Addiction is a set of experiences that indicates a specific movement in a specific direction, bringing a series of changes that takes place within a person. It is through the commonalities of these experiences and changes that we are able to describe addiction.

As addiction develops, it becomes a way of life. Rather than being rigid, addiction is continually changing. As it changes, it inflicts changes on the person suffering from the addiction. . . .

## THE ADDICTIVE CYCLE

The true start of any addictive relationship is when the person repeatedly seeks the illusion of relief to avoid unpleasant feelings or situations. This is nurturing through avoidance—an unnatural way of taking care of one's emotional needs. At this point, addicts start to give up natural relationships and the relief and healing they offer. They replace these relationships with the addictive relationship.

Consequently, addicts seek serenity through an object or event. This is the beginning of the addictive cycle. If one were to diagram addiction there would be a downward spiraling motion with many valleys and plateaus.

This cycle causes an emotional craving that results in mental preoccupation. For an addict, the feeling of discomfort becomes a signal to act out, not a signal to connect with others or with oneself. The amount of mental

## The Addictive Cycle

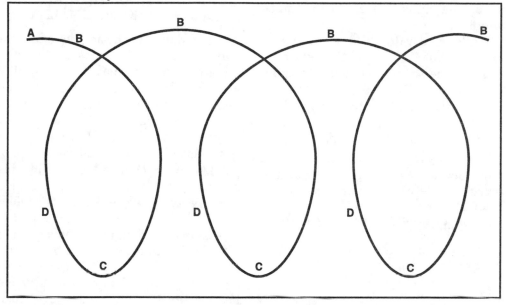

A=pain; B=feel the need to act out; C=act out, start to feel better; D=pain resulting from acting out; B=feel the need to act out; C=act out, start to feel better.

obsession is often an indication of the stress in the addict's life. Some addictions produce physical dependency that creates physical symptoms upon withdrawal (as with alcohol and other drugs). Many other types of recovering addicts—sex addicts, addictive gamblers, and addictive spenders—also report physical symptoms when they stop acting out. Whether this is part of the grief process in ending an addictive relationship or actual withdrawal symptoms is unclear—it's probably a combination of both. Addicts who have stopped acting out report feeling edgy and nervous, and these symptoms can last up to a few months.

## THE ADDICTIVE PERSONALITY

. . . The reason the idea of the addictive personality is so important to under-stand is that eventually a person forms a dependent relationship with his or her own addictive personality.

Once an addictive personality created by the addictive process is established within a person, the specific object or event takes on less importance. When an addictive personality is firmly in control, addicts can (and often do) switch objects of addiction as preferences change or when they get into trouble with one object. Addicts who switch objects of addiction know it's a good way to get people off their backs.

The addictive personality is very important for recovering addicts to under-stand because the addictive personality will stay with them for life. On some level, this personality will always be searching for an object or some type of event to form an addictive relationship. On some level, this personality will always give the person the illusion that there is an object or event that can nurture them.

The term "dry drunk" describes a person whose life is being controlled by an addictive personality without any drug being present. Dry drunks still trust in the addictive process and cut themselves off from the natural relationships they need in order to be nurtured.

> People in a recovery program for alcohol addiction need to clearly understand that they are prone to form a possible addictive relationship with another object or event—food, for example. For these people, sobriety acquires a new dimension: instead of only monitoring their relationship with alcohol, they also need to learn how to monitor the addictive part of themselves.

I am using the example of alcohol and food here because it's common for a recovering alcoholic to become a food addict. I've met persons who, within three or four years of leaving an alcoholism treatment center, have gained 40 or 50 pounds and are as unhappy and emotionally isolated as they were the day they entered treatment. To quote one such person, "I now find myself eating for all the same reasons I drank: I'm lonely, I'm afraid." Many of these people attend A.A. [Alcoholics Anonymous] regularly, are working good recovery programs, and their lives are much better, but something stands in their way of serenity—another addiction.

It's in understanding the addictive personality, even in recovery, that the words, "cunning, baffling, powerful!" show their true meaning. It's the addictive relationship inside oneself that the recovering addict will need to break, not just the relationship with an object. This is when total recovery takes place.

## DEVELOPMENT OF AN ADDICTIVE PERSONALITY

The foundation of the addictive personality is found in all persons. It's found in a normal desire to make it through life with the least amount of pain and the greatest amount of pleasure possible. It's found in our negativism and our mistrust of others and the world, whether our pessimism is big or small, valid or not valid. There is nothing wrong with this part of us; it's natural for all of us to have these beliefs to some degree. It's when these beliefs control one's way of life, as it does in addiction, that people get into trouble. There are persons who are more susceptible to addiction. These are persons who don't know how to have healthy relationships and have been taught not to trust in people. This is mainly because of how they were treated by others while growing up, and they never learned how to connect.

If you were raised in a family where closeness was just a word, not a reality, you are much more prone to form an addictive relationship. This is for two reasons. First, you were taught to distance yourself from people instead of being taught to connect with them. Second, growing up in this type of family left you with a deep, lonely emptiness that you've wanted to have filled. Addiction offers the illusion of fulfillment. If you were raised in a family where people were treated as objects rather than as people, you have already been taught addictive logic. The sad part for many of these people is that many of them struggle hard in recovery; for them, recovery is not a return to a healthier self, but needing to develop a new personality.

Addiction is an active belief in and a commitment of oneself to a negative lifestyle. Addiction begins and grows when a person abandons the natural ways of getting emotional needs met, through connecting with other people, one's community, one's self and spiritual powers greater than oneself. The repeated abandonment of oneself in favor of the addictive high causes the addictive personality to develop and gradually gain power.

The development of an addictive personality is similar to a person who gets up each morning and throughout the day says to himself, "Why bother? Life is hard." The more people tell themselves this, the more they will develop the lifestyle and personality of someone who has given up on life. Every time addicts choose to act out in an addictive way, they are saying to themselves one or more of the following:

- "I don't really need people."
- "I don't have to face anything I don't want to."
- "I'm afraid to face life's and my problems."
- "Objects and events are more important than people."
- "I can do anything I want, whenever I want, no matter who it hurts."

This type of thinking forms a pattern in which a person continually supports and reinforces an addictive belief system found inside oneself. A subtle personality change starts to take place. The fact that in most cases these changes are subtle and gradual over long periods of time adds to the seductiveness of addiction.

## Shame

As time goes on and a person continues to act out and is preoccupied and emotionally distant from others, the addictive personality starts to assert more control over the person's internal life. At this stage, the person suffering from addiction will start to feel a "pull" inside. This may come in the form of emotional restlessness or pangs of conscience.

Addiction now starts to produce a by-product—shame. This happens both consciously and unconsciously to addicts, but mostly on an unconscious level. The more addicts seek relief through addiction, the more shame they'll start to experience and the more they will feel a need to justify the addictive relationship to themselves.

Shame creates a loss of *self*-respect, *self*-esteem, *self*-confidence, *self*-discipline, *self*-determination, *self*-control, *self*-importance, and *self*-love. In the beginning, this shame may be a general uneasiness. It's the first cost an addict pays for the addictive relationship. The person starts to feel shame about the signs of loss of control that are beginning to appear within. There may be an occasional incident of behavioral loss of control, but the major forms of loss of control happen on the emotional, thinking level. The person is more apt to feel bad about the internal withdrawal from others. For as the person slowly starts to become more committed to an object or event, there is a gradual emotional withdrawal from intimate relationships with people or a Higher Power.

## Where the Addictive Personality Emerges

Addiction starts to create the very thing the person is trying to avoid—pain. In creating pain, the process also creates a need for the continuation of the addictive relationship. *The addict seeks refuge from the pain of addiction by moving further into the addictive process.* The addict seeks happiness and serenity in the high, but because the addict has started to withdraw from self and others, the addict can't see that the pain he or she feels is created by acting out.

Long before episodes of being out of control behaviorally appear, the person has fought and lost many battles with his or her Addict on the emotional level, where the addictive personality gains control. An addictive personality starts its development here, at the emotional level. This is the first part of one's personality that becomes controlled by the addictive process.

Addicts act like kids—if it feels good, they do it. They explore; they follow their emotional impulses. Emotions are at the very core of most people's being. This is easily understood when we remember emotions existed long before we had words to describe them or words to help us understand them.

At this stage, the person emotionally feels uneasy, restless, and guilty. These are some of the internal warning signals that one may feel, but part of the addictive process is learning how to deny these warning signals. Addiction is also a process of denial—denial of reality, but mainly denial of the Self. This denial must be accomplished for the addiction to progress.

"Talk therapy" hasn't proven very effective in treating addicts, for the core of the illness exists on an emotional level, not on a thinking level.

### How the Addictive Personality Gains Control

Much of an addict's mental obsession results from denial or refusing to recognize the loss of control that is happening on the emotional level. Avoiding the reality of the situation allows the creation of more pain, which will eventually create the need to explain to oneself what is happening. This will evolve into obsessive thoughts or preoccupation and rationalizations. The obsessive thoughts occur more often and consist of constant questioning: *Why?* Preoccupation has to do with acting out and creating a mood change. We've all heard the saying, "Just change your thoughts and you'll feel better." No one knows this better than addicts. If practicing addicts don't like the way they're feeling, they'll think about acting out and a subtle mood change occurs. Each time this happens, the person loses a small piece of control that is transferred to the addiction.

We are starting to see how the gradual loss of the Self occurs in addiction, and how the addictive personality slowly gains more and more control. *The decrease in the Self causes an increase in the addictive personality.*

In addiction, there is an almost constant internal conflict between the Self and the Addict. In this struggle, the Addict wins. This is what is meant by "loss of control." The longer the struggle, the more control the addictive personality gains and establishes. Each time the Self struggles against the addiction, the Addict becomes stronger. To fight and struggle against something that has more power than you drains your energy. For each defeat there is some loss of self-esteem. This is why in recovery people are taught to surrender. It is through accepting that one can't conquer his disease that the person finds strength to start connecting with others. . . .

The addictive relationship is an internal relationship based on the interaction between the Self and the Addict; it is a one-to-one relationship; it is based on emotional logic; it creates an inward focus and isolation; it is sustained by the mood change produced by acting out in the addictive process. The longer the inter-action between the Self and the Addict, the stronger the addictive personality becomes; the longer the interaction, the more developed the addictive relationship within becomes. In addiction, the Addict becomes the dominant personality.

People and family members often desperately ask themselves and others, "Why does he act like this? Doesn't he care about us anymore?" The truth is that the Addict within doesn't care about them. What it cares about is acting out, getting the mood change. The Addict doesn't care about the Self either. A statement such as, "At least if you won't stop for me, stop for yourself!" falls on deaf ears. The person who suffers from an addiction often asks the same question long before anyone else: "Why do I act this way? Don't I care?"

I've seen many families gather together in tears, realizing it's the Addict, the illness, the addiction they all hate and fear, not the person. It's often a great relief for people suffering from an addiction to realize that they are not "bad people," as they believed, that their addictive personality is not all of them, but only a part of them, having grown as a result of the illness.

# POSTSCRIPT

## Are Drug Addicts Always in Control of Their Addiction?

There is no question that drug addiction is a problem. Addressing the causes of drug addiction and what to do about people who are addicted is especially relevant. The causes of drug addiction are divergent. Because drug abuse can be viewed as a matter of free will (Schaler) and as a disease (Nakken), there are also different views on how society should deal with drug abuse and how drug abuse should be treated.

One could argue that free will and the concept of disease both apply to drug addiction. For example, what may start out as a matter of free will may turn into an illness. People do not choose to become addicted but people often choose to use drugs. For example, a person may use alcohol for social purposes, but his or her use may develop into a chronic pattern—one that the person cannot easily overcome. Initially, one can stop using alcohol without too much discomfort. As time passes, however, and drinking becomes heavier, stopping becomes difficult.

In their book *The Truth About Addiction and Recovery: The Life Process Program for Outgrowing Destructive Habits* (Simon & Schuster, 1991), Stanton Peele and Archie Brodsky claim that addictions are not diseases and that formal treatment is unnecessary to overcoming addiction. In *Diseasing of America: Addiction Treatment Out of Control* (Lexington Books, 1989), Stanton Peele argues that the disease concept has led to the uncontrolled growth of drug treatment facilities. Another author who argues against the disease concept is David Musto. In *The American Disease: Origins of Narcotic Control* (Yale University Press, 1987), Musto explains how drugs have been used prominently throughout American history. Rather than calling chronic drug use an addiction, people traditionally referred to it as a bad habit.

Nakken's approach to treating drug addiction follows many of the precepts of Alcoholics Anonymous (AA). Part of AA's 12-step model of recovery includes admitting to having no control over one's addiction. Abstinence is also a prerequisite for staying drug free because AA sees drug addiction as an incurable disease. In "Allelic Association of Human Dopamine D2 Receptor Gene in Alcoholism," *Journal of the American Medical Association* (April 18, 1991), Kenneth Blum and others claim to have found a gene responsible for alcoholism. This provides support for the disease concept. In her article "Rx for Addiction," *Scientific American* (March 1991), Marguerite Holloway writes that pharmaceutical drugs are currently being explored as treatment for drug addiction. If drugs can be used to treat drug addiction, then overcoming drugs may entail more than simply deciding not to use drugs.

# ISSUE 16

## Do Alcoholics Have to Maintain a Lifetime of Abstinence?

**YES: Ray Hoskins,** from *Rational Madness: The Paradox of Addiction* (TAB Books, 1989)

**NO: Harry H. Avis,** from "Beyond AA: Rational, Secular Recovery," in Arnold S. Trebach and Kevin B. Zeese, eds., *New Frontiers in Drug Policy* (Drug Policy Foundation, 1991)

### ISSUE SUMMARY

**YES:** Ray Hoskins, an alcoholism and drug abuse counselor, advocates total abstinence for the successful treatment of addiction, and he argues that controlling addiction through moderation is impractical.

**NO:** Harry H. Avis, a professor of psychology, criticizes the 12-step model of Alcoholics Anonymous and other self-help groups because it is not applicable to many addicts. Avis feels that many addicts moderate their behavior on their own and that, for others, alternatives to lifelong recovery need to be explored in helping people deal with their addictions.

There are an estimated 10 million alcoholics in the United States. Cocaine addicts number between 250,000 and 1 million, according to government figures. Eating disorders, sexual addictions, compulsive gambling, excessive spending, and compulsive working affect millions more people. Knowing the best way to help people who engage in these compulsive or addictive behaviors is difficult. One way to control addictive behavior is to abstain from it. However, is abstention the best or only viable treatment goal?

Ray Hoskins and Harry H. Avis approach the concept of helping people with addictions from opposing perspectives. Hoskins takes the view that addiction occurs when people lose control over their addictive behavior. Moreover, there is always some kind of reward or payoff that fuels one's addictive behavior. The benefit may be security, sensation, or power, but as long as one or more of these benefits are experienced, people will not stop their behavior. Hoskins does not feel that everybody needs to abstain from unhealthy behaviors; only those people whose behaviors have reached the addictive stage. With some potentially addictive behaviors, such as eating or work, it is impossible to abstain. However, with behaviors that are not necessary for survival, like alcohol consumption, abstention is, to Hoskins, the only path to follow.

If addiction leaves people powerless, as Hoskins maintains, then the only way to gain personal power and control is through abstention. If alcoholics are powerless against alcohol, then they cannot drink simply for the enjoyment of alcohol; they will invariably drink to excess. Furthermore, abstinence does not come naturally but must be learned. People need to learn to abstain each time they feel the urge to drink.

The abstinence model is currently the most popular approach for treating addiction. Abstinence is included in the 12-step model promoted by Alcoholics Anonymous (AA) and other self-help groups. Elements of this model include admitting to being powerless over one's addiction, accepting a higher power, and restructuring one's life. Avis argues that this approach is not suitable for everyone and that it has not been proven effective. The idea of placing faith in a higher power, for example, is inconsistent with the values of many people, especially those who do not believe in the concept of a higher power. Another problem is that programs like AA claim to be effective based on the testimonies of people who are in it. However, because of the anonymity of people who attend or have attended AA meetings, follow-up studies are negligible.

Avis notes that most people who stop addictive behavior do so on their own. Heroin addicts who quit using heroin generally do not go through any type of formal treatment. Likewise, the majority of individuals who quit smoking also stop without an organized program. It is unlikely that heroin addicts and tobacco users stop because they develop a belief in a higher spiritual power. Factors contributing to spontaneous remission are not well understood. Avis feels that people stop self-destructive behaviors once they "hit bottom."

In recent years alternative self-help groups to Alcoholics Anonymous have appeared. The Secular Organization for Society is one such group for alcoholics, but it does not have the same emphasis on a belief in a higher power. There is also Women for Sobriety/Men for Sobriety, which does not accept AA's disease model of addiction. Abstinence is a prominent aspect of this group, but overcoming alcoholism is based on self-acceptance and the role of love in relationships. A third type of program is Rational Recovery (RR), which is modeled on the principles of rational emotive therapy developed by Albert Ellis. Unlike the other models, RR accepts moderate alcohol use. As the name implies, this approach encourages people to exert control over their cognitive processes.

In the selections that follow, Ray Hoskins makes the case for abstinence as the only viable approach for overcoming addictions, especially alcoholism. Harry H. Avis highlights several limitations of the traditional approach to treating alcoholism and discusses several alternatives for treatment.

# YES

**Ray Hoskins**

## ABSTINENCE

*Abstinence and the ability to have a happy life are not the same thing. As one man said, "Abstinence is like standing up at the starting line. The race hasn't started yet, but at least you are standing up rather than lying down."*

—Earnie Larsen

Each of us can best begin recovery by beginning abstinence from all power-level addictions and from all unnecessary security and sensation-level addictive behaviors. This will provide the stability needed to chip away at the rest of life. It will also prevent the failure which occurs when one merely drops one addiction and switches to other addictions in one's menu. In using the self-help group language, it is also helpful to recognize that one's life is unmanageable and will be that way as long as one does not abstain.

### WHY IS THIS NECESSARY?

As one of my clients pointed out, he couldn't think of any other way to know whether he had recovered than to quit. Yet addicts usually go through years of trying to control their addictions rather than practicing abstinence. This points out some controversies about whether addictions can be controlled, or whether an addict must be abstinent from his addictions. In spite of years of research and experience to the contrary, there are still those who believe it isn't necessary to abstain from addictions in order to recover. Unfortunately, some of them are health professionals.

### ABSTINENCE VERSUS CONTROL

Throughout the history of the addiction sciences, there has been this ongoing debate about whether abstinence or control should be the goal of treatment and recovery. Recent evidence comes down hard on the side of abstinence. For example, some professionals have consistently tried to teach alcoholics to control their drinking. At this stage of the research and of our clinical experience, this attempt is irresponsible, and seems to reflect the control addictions of the professionals rather than the clinical realities of alcoholism.

Whenever we encourage an addict to control his addiction, we are setting him up to progress from a sensation addiction to a power addiction. We need to avoid this at all costs.

Once an addictive behavior has progressed to the addiction level, it can't be controlled. If it can, then it isn't an addiction. In most cases, if the person attempts to control it, he will only succeed in making sure the behavior progresses to the addiction and then disease levels. In addition, such attempts are power-based and interfere with the goal of making serenity, rather than power, the top goal of recovery.

Mind you, I am not saying that persons with solely enhancement or infrequent addictive behavior patterns must abstain from those behaviors. I am referring to those persons whose addictive behaviors have reached at least the regular addictive behavior stage. All these people might benefit from abstinence, but for the persons using addictive behavior as a regular coping option, this is critical.

There are differences between truly occasional use of enhancement or addictive behavior and the regular use of such behavior to cope with life. For example, people who have not progressed to addictions to alcohol, drugs, food, or sex do not control those behaviors. They don't have the desire to abuse them! A "social drinker" doesn't want twenty-five beers in a night, at least not more often than on one, crazy night. The fact that you have ever felt a need to control a behavior in and of itself is the best indicator that you have an addiction going or developing.

## PREFERENCES AND ABSTINENCE

In his *Handbook To Higher Consciousness*, Ken Keyes gives some very sound advice. He advises that if an addictive behavior is not necessary for survival, abstain from it. In the case of substances, it is never necessary to drink alcohol to survive. Therefore, alcoholics should quit drinking. They should do so for several reasons, one of which is that their drinking will keep them from enjoying more important things in life. Keyes also talks about upgrading addictions which are necessary for survival, such as eating, having relationships, and loving sex to "preferences."

. . . [A]ddictions are the attempts of a person to stay happy by coping with external realities by focusing on emotional states. It reflects a core belief that we can feel the way we want to feel, regardless of our problems or the level of responsibility for our behavior. In this manner, it is self-spoiling. It is also self-deluding.

Because of this, the addict in recovery should treat himself in much the same manner that a parent should treat a spoiled child whom he is trying to retrain. He should ask which of his addictive behaviors are necessary for survival, and plan on changing those behaviors from addictions to preferences. Sometimes this will be difficult. He should also decide to abstain from those addictive behaviors which are not necessary for survival, and from those parts of necessary addictive behaviors, such as eating massive amounts of sweets within food addiction, which are detrimental to him. His ability to upgrade addictions to preferences will depend greatly on whether his primary pleasure within the addiction is a security, sensation, or power-centered pleasure. He needs to look at this closely.

[For] example:

| Security | Sensation | Power |
|----------|-----------|-------|
| *work* | *cocaine* | *sex* |

There are three addictions in this complex. Using the first rule of which addictions are necessary for survival, only work qualifies. The client will have to upgrade his work addiction to a preference to recover. In both of the other addictions, he needs to learn abstinence from the addictive behavior. If this does not occur, the progression will continue.

Security addictions can usually be changed to preferences. We can, for example, change from feeling a desperate need for love to preferring to be loved by certain people. We can prefer to have money, but not commit suicide if we don't. We can stop drinking to fit in with a crowd, and base the decision to drink or not to drink on other factors. We can decide to eat to survive, not survive to eat.

Mild sensation addictions can sometimes be upgraded to preferences. Sex addiction, as long as it is in the security or sensation level of progression, can be changed to a preference by most people. Eating for sensation can sometimes be changed in the same way. *As a general rule, the recommendation is to upgrade those addictions which are centered on behaviors necessary for survival to preferences, while learning to abstain from those which are not.*

This is a fine line, which should not be applied to chemical addictions. Chemicals, especially most addictive chemicals, are almost never necessary for survival.

Once an addiction has become primarily a search for power, the addict's first choice should be abstinence. This is very consistent with clinical experience, that true pedophiles and violent rapists are rarely able to return to limiting themselves to normal sexuality. It is also consistent with the accepted standard that physically addicted (powerless) alcoholics should learn to be abstinent from alcohol. Giving up the behavior is often the only way to escape the struggle a power-level addiction creates. This is true of sadomasochistic, abusive relationships, totally power-centered work addiction (he should change to a different line of work), materialism addicts who constantly abuse credit, and extreme gambling addiction in which the gambler risks becoming powerless in society or becoming injured if he loses.

The only addictions which are truly necessary for an individual's survival regardless of progression are eating and working. Everyone needs to eat, and few people do not need to work at some level to survive.

Overeaters Anonymous and other groups which help the food addict recognize the limits on the need to eat, help the overeater change preferences for which foods to eat. This is an excellent approach, but it is far more difficult for most advanced overeaters to do this than it is for most other addicts to abstain from unnecessary addictions.

Work addiction is also very insidious because the ingrained belief system is supported by almost all of society and recovery depends on a total shift of preferences which is not sanctioned by society.

## PREVENTING FURTHER PROGRESSION

Perhaps the most important reason for learning abstinence from your unneeded addictive behaviors is to prevent further progression from the current stage of the behavior to addiction and disease. In some addictive behaviors, this will almost always happen. Let's review the earlier example:

| Security | Sensation | Power |
|----------|-----------|-------|
| *work* | *cocaine* | *sex* |

In this example there is a good likelihood that the system will shift in the near future unless abstinence from cocaine occurs immediately. The complex will probably soon look like this:

| Security | Sensation | Power |
|----------|-----------|-------|
| *work* | | *sex* |
| | | *cocaine* |

This shift will occur because of the rapidity with which cocaine users become powerless in their relationship with the drug. For this reason, the person encountering this client during the earlier pattern would have been wise to follow my proposed guidelines and recommend abstinence from cocaine while it remained at the sensation level. Further damage would have been prevented if abstinence had occurred.

## OTHER CONSIDERATIONS

In some addictions, abstinence is also necessary for physical reasons. Alcohol and drugs, for example, produce physical dependence and a physical inability to control their use. In order to even begin to think rationally, the person addicted to these substances must spend significant time in abstinence from them.

In food addiction it is impossible to abstain from all food and still survive. It is possible, however, to identify those foods which set off addictive cravings and eating patterns, and to eat other foods instead. Overeaters Anonymous and Weight Watchers are two organizations which are very good at helping people learn to change the foods they eat.

At this time there are, to my knowledge, no self-help groups for the work-addict. This presents a slight problem, but as work addicts usually have other addictions too, they can often simply apply the steps from a self-help program for another addiction to their work addiction.

## IT'S NO FUN ANYMORE

Another point in abstaining from power-level addictions is that the addict can never expect to return successfully to those behaviors, without returning to the addiction. The reasons for this have nothing to do with willpower, or any other such illusion. They have to do with physical and psychological progression. Once we go so far in our addictions, they are simply no fun to practice at a less advanced level.

There have been several movies lately about this phenomena in sexual addiction. The theme of out-of-control sexuality leading to the inability to enjoy less-controlled sexual experiences is common, *and real*. I have had several cases in which a couple experimented with sexual swinging, to have the husband or wife eventually become unable to get excited without others being present. Needless to say, this created some problems with their intimacy.

As an addiction progresses from security to sensation to power levels, the person loses the ability to get any pleasure out of practicing the addiction at the previous level. He builds a psychological, and sometimes physical, tolerance.

For example, when my alcoholic clients come in for diagnosis, I ask them how much alcohol it takes for them to achieve the feeling they want. We then compare their answers to blood alcohol levels they produce, and assess the security, sensation, or power levels regarding that addiction.

If a person drinks with friends, and only drinks two drinks to get his effect, he is drinking at security levels, and, if he is telling the truth, is probably not alcoholic. He is not, as common wording has it, "controlling his drinking." He simply desires to drink a small amount and does so. This is true at every level. People do not control drinking. Some people merely want more than others.

If he drinks with friends, and drinks four to six beers to get his effect, he is operating at the sensation and security levels and may or may not be alcoholic.

If he drinks with friends or alone, and drinks eight or more drinks and maintains a level well above the level of .10 blood alcohol content to get the effect he wants, he is drinking at the sensation and power/powerless levels, and needs to quit.

If you notice, the focus is on the amount it takes for the alcoholic to achieve the feeling he wants to achieve, and whether this feeling is security, sensation, or power related. The reason for this is simple. Once a person has progressed in an addiction from security to sensation or to power levels, he will not be able to enjoy addiction at the lower levels again.

If he drank for complete intoxication, there will be minimal satisfaction in drinking for a mild buzz and the addict will increase his drinking eventually to create the desired feelings of intoxication because he gets no pleasure from drinking moderately, in spite of the anticipation that he will.

There are both physical and psychological reasons for this response. Alcoholics seem to have different physical responses to alcohol than nonalcoholics. For example, they have different tolerance levels to alcohol than others have. This tolerance in most cases first climbs quite high, then later, if drinking continues, becomes very low. Another difference seems to be in how pleasurable the alcohol-affected state seems to be. The pleasure from being drunk for an alcoholic is, or at least was, very pleasureful. Both the tolerance and pleasure factors seem to be genetically related, and complement the psychological factors.

If I know a client has more than one addiction, I will explore the other addictions as well because this rule is true in all the addictions. In sex addiction, for example, once a person gets to a point where he can only get completely turned on by dominance, or group sex, or by children, he will not be able to return to casual sex and enjoy it for an extended period, without seeking the type of sex that turns him on the most. He may or may not be able to experience intimate sex in a loving relationship, but that is usually a separate issue from his addictive sexuality.

Just as the alcoholic will experience an intense desire to drink, regardless of the quality of his love relationships, the sex addict will experience an intense desire for casual sex, regardless of the quality of the sexuality within his marriage or primary relationship. In extreme cases, however, it seems that any sexual relationship whatsoever will trigger urges for addictive sexuality, even the sexuality within an intimate relationship.

Work addicts tends to drive themselves to greater and greater levels of achievement in order to achieve those early feelings of power and freedom they had when they began their careers. Since work addiction and addiction to material items are complements, early work addiction has, as its foundation, fantasies of material things and power which are going to make the addict and those close to him happy. Since everyone fails to be happy as the result of the addiction, whether or not the addict achieves his goals, the work addict looks for more powerful positions from which to continue to feed self and family with possessions. He does this in order to make up for the poor emotional quality in the family. He can no longer enjoy the smaller things in life, and doesn't see how the family members are puppets to his addiction.

So you see, all addiction is a gamble, with the stakes going up as the addiction progresses. Once an addict has experienced the intensity of the power-level practice of an addiction, he will not be satisfied with playing for lower stakes.

### ONE-DAY-AT-A-TIME

I need to point out that it is impossible for a power-level addict to commit to abstinence from an addiction for any long period of time. This is not to say he cannot be abstinent for long periods of time, he just can't predict that he can. The ability to be abstinent is a skill, or set of skills, he will have to learn. In the self-help groups, he learns that he can only stay abstinent "one-day-at-a-time." This is actually too long a time span for him to attack. He can only stay abstinent from his addictions in each here-and-now situation. He can stay abstinent now, but he may risk relapse this afternoon.

### MISGUIDED SYMPATHY

Most of us feel sympathy for persons who must be completely abstinent from their addictive behaviors, and sometimes we help them convince themselves this is not necessary. This is extremely misguided, and may be reflective of our own denial of our inability to control our own addictions.

I have known alcoholics who died because they couldn't believe abstinence was necessary. I have also known an abused wife who was killed by a second abusive husband after leaving a first one when she created a new power-level addictive relationship. I have known several people who have filed for bankruptcy more than once because they attempted to control their use of credit. In most cases, this sympathy for the power-level addict is misguided. Abstinence from a power-centered addiction provides far more freedom for the recovering person than he would achieve by trying to continue controlling his behavior.

In fact, abstinence from unnecessary security and sensation level addictions can also offer more freedom than trying to hang on to them. We just can't know this until we upgrade them to preferences and then find we no longer prefer them.

The only addiction in which I feel sympathy for those who must stay abstinent is the sexual addicts who can only be excited by violent dimensions in their sexuality. My sympathy is for their inability to enjoy normal, loving sexuality, and our lack of a method to help them, rather than for their having to give up raping people.

While abstinence from sex is uncomfortable, sex which must entail coercion or violence to be enjoyable is simply not acceptable in civilized society. And abstinence is better than humiliating or killing others and being incarcerated or killed. For this reason, as well as many others, the more power-level addictions addicts have, the more help they need in their recovery. They need to make new friends and learn about reality. They can't do it alone.

These guidelines are hard for some addicts to accept, but usually no addict will be in a situation in which he has no historical addictions to upgrade to preferences. Those will remain sources of pleasure during his recovery, and he will be able to discover more meaningful coping methods.

### PEOPLE DO CHANGE!

Unless we being recovering from our addictions, we will gradually spend more and more of our time in our combined addictions, until we find another way to cope. As I have said, some of our addictions will have to be completely abandoned. Others can be "upgraded," in Keyes' terminology, to preferences. There are several factors which are relevant to the decision to abandon or upgrade an addiction.

People do move away from an addictive lifestyle. Depending on the addictive configuration, the addict will be able to slowly adopt less addictive coping, once the hangover phenomena overcome the ability to lie to self about the behavior. Once this occurs, he has "hit bottom," and is ready to begin learning other coping means.

When we are practicing addictions, we are practicing a most obvious self-delusion. We tell ourselves we receive pleasure when we don't. If we have an addiction to any behavior at a power level, we are extremely dedicated to that behavior and the inherent selfishness and dishonesty it represents. We have to shed this skin before we can grow another. The only way to begin this shedding is abstinence from any addictive behavior which is not required for survival.

# NO                          Harry H. Avis

# BEYOND AA: RATIONAL, SECULAR RECOVERY

As we approach the 21st century, we are faced with a challenge unprecedented in the history of civilization. Ideologies no longer hold our unthink-
ing allegiance, political and economic boundaries that have defined our
world for the last century are collapsing, and we are being forced to re-
examine virtually every "given" that makes up the matrix of our culture.
Even in the narrow sphere that is the topic of this paper, a revolution is
imminent. Our understanding of the reasons for drug taking, the nature of
abuse and addiction, and the complex issues involved in recovery and
relapse, is finally reaching beyond such simplistic concepts as the deviance
model for use, and the disease model for both addiction and treatment.

In the specific area of drug abuse treatment, the 21st century will almost
undoubtedly be born with a cry for help. Wherever there is social destabiliz-
ation, political chaos and economic uncertainty, drug abuse seems to increase. Taking as a rough estimate, the often repeated statistic that
approximately 10 percent of users of a given drug will experience problems
with that drug means that hundreds of millions of people are currently in
need of some help and that number is certain to increase. Those needing
help come from many religious backgrounds (or none at all), have different
political and philosophical perspectives, and are almost definitely lacking
private health insurance that will guarantee $12,000 for a six-week package
at the New World Order Clinic for Alcohol and Other Drug Abuse.

What is needed to help as many as need assistance is a pluralistic
approach to drug abuse treatment that incorporates as many diverse points
of view as possible. The current model, known in the United States as the
Minnesota model, must be either abandoned or greatly modified and
expanded. Perhaps the part of the model that needs change the most is the
dominance of the Alcoholics Anonymous approach to treatment. In order to
understand where I feel we must go, it is essential to understand how we got
where we are. We must also examine why the AA approach may not be
applicable to the world wide problem of drug abuse. Finally, we must look

From Harry H. Avis, "Beyond AA: Rational, Secular Recovery," in Arnold S. Trebach and Kevin
B. Zeese, eds., *New Frontiers in Drug Policy* (Drug Policy Foundation, 1991). Copyright © 1991 by
The Drug Policy Foundation, 4455 Connecticut Ave., NW, Suite B500, Washington, DC 20008.
Reprinted by permission.

with a fresh viewpoint at recovery from drug abuse without the tacit assumptions that come from adherence to one approach. Just as Freudian concepts have so pervaded our everyday thinking that we are often unaware that many of them are unproven or even disproved, even professionals in the field of drug abuse fail to acknowledge their debt to a specific and very narrow view of the causes and treatment of drug abuse.

## THE DOMINANCE OF ALCOHOLICS ANONYMOUS IN MODERN TREATMENT

A word about terminology is appropriate here. AA is, of course, Alcoholics Anonymous and while many members of AA have other drug problems, AA devotes itself exclusively to dealing with alcoholism. The 12-step approach is a term that will be used to describe self-help groups that adhere to basic principles developed by AA, namely admission of powerless-[ness], acceptance of a higher power as a requirement for change, testimony as a means of preventing relapse, and a dedication to restructuring one's life.

Since most of the literature on self-help group treatment focuses on AA itself, this paper will do the same. The criticisms and suggestions apply to other 12-step programs as well, however.

## THE BIRTH AND 'SUCCESS' OF ALCOHOLICS ANONYMOUS

Ever since the birth of Alcoholics Anonymous in Akron, Ohio, in 1935, AA has been helping alcoholics gain and retain sobriety. So dominant has it become that most laymen and many professionals see it as being the only self-help group in existence. It has spawned hundreds of

12-step programs to help people overcome everything from overeating to sexual "addiction," and has imbedded itself in the psyche of America. So successful has it been that many of its precepts are taken as absolutes even by those who should know better. Millions of people owe their lives to AA and its influence extends throughout the treatment industry.

Even the most ardent fans of AA admit, however, that it doesn't work for everyone. It seems to work best for those who share the basic values of American culture. Some would claim that fewer than 10 percent of those seeking help from AA actually "succeed."[1] Of course, the same characteristics that define AA, its guaranteed anonymity, its dogged lack of structure and antipathy toward record keeping also make it impossible to accurately evaluate its effectiveness. The huge numbers of those with alcohol and other drug problems also guarantee that even if only a small percentage of alcohol abusers are helped by AA, that percentage translates into hundreds of thousands, if not millions of success stories.

Anyone retaining any semblance of contact with the real world of drugs and sex, as opposed to the artificial reality imposed by the drug war and its elite guard, the Office of Substance Abuse Prevention, must have pondered at least three questions when contemplating recovery from alcohol and drug addiction: (a) did people get well before AA?—they did; (b) do people get well without AA?—they do; and (c) are there people who don't need groups?—there are. The purpose of this paper is to examine these questions and suggest a course of action for future research into recovery and treatment. In addition this paper hopes to demonstrate a need for a pluralistic approach to drug treatment.

## RECOVERING FROM ALCOHOL/ DRUG ABUSE ON YOUR OWN

Taking the third question first, it is fascinating to note that "spontaneous recovery," "maturing out" or simply quitting are phenomena that have been widely documented but virtually ignored. For example, the former U.S. Surgeon General C. Everett Koop declared 90 percent of cigarette smokers stop without outside help even though in the same report nicotine addiction was equated with heroin addiction! With heroin addiction, the story is the same, the National Institute of Drug Abuse Treatment Research Report determined that the average addiction career of a heroin user was 9.5 years and only 41 percent of those surveyed said they ever exceeded two years of continuous daily use.[2] Treatment was considered a small element of the decision to quit and the overall impression was that the addicts stopped using because it became too much hassle, a phenomenon that was reported many years earlier by Brecher.[3] Peele and Brodsky,[4] in a recent book for the lay public, summarized the evidence and found that the majority of abusers of all drugs manage to abstain or moderate their behavior without resorting to any program.

Several recent studies have examined a related phenomenon, the cessation (or quiet moderation) of the experimental drug use that occurs for most adolescent users with the attainment of what passes in our society for maturity.[5,6] Reading these and other studies a picture emerges of a group of basically stable, adventuresome, creative adolescents experimenting with various drugs and giving them up in their twenties when the demands of society and lack of social support for continued drug use make maintaining their habits inconvenient.

If so many people have managed to control their use and abuse in recent years, it follows that at least as many succeeded before AA gained ascendancy. If (as virtually every anti-drug message in the media pounds into public consciousness) "you can't do it alone," how did all these millions of people over all those thousands of years manage to do just that? Is it simply that they, in the words of the folk song "gave up their dreams when they cut off their hair?"

One study looked for common elements of spontaneous recovery from alcohol, opiates, tobacco and food abuse and found that in most cases, the pathway was the same;[7] the first element was a "psychic change," often brought about by a "significant accident" similar to "hitting bottom" in AA literature or the "epiphany" of Peele and Brodsky. A psychic change involved a change in the individual's self perception from that of being a user/abuser to being a non-user. The significant accident or epiphany is not always extremely dramatic or life threatening, but is seen by the spontaneous recoverer as being somehow particularly important. This cognitive reevaluation leads the individual to the second element of enlisting the support of others and finally to the third element of stabilizing a new identity. If studies were to find that a majority of cancer patients experienced spontaneous recovery, billions of dollars would immediately be allocated to determine how. In contrast, the fact that most drug users stop without help has virtually been ignored.

Compared to the vast literature on treatment methods, the literature on spontaneous recovery is minuscule. In this regard, the field of drug treatment is like that of developmental psychology. Until recently, adolescence was seen as an inevitable period of stress and turmoil, because those adolescents who were having problems were going for therapy and thereby drew attention to themselves. More recent studies focusing on a wider range of teenagers have indicated that adolescence is not a period of major upheaval for the majority of adolescents. Those who manage to recover on their own and normal adolescents do not come to the attention of professionals and must be sought out. We need to know more about the strategies that the spontaneous recoverers have used and especially how they managed the crucial first few weeks of recovery.

The first message for those who think they may have a drug or alcohol problem should be "many people can do it on their own and here is how they succeeded." Of course, in order to provide this information, we must first unearth it. At the same time, we must avoid stigmatizing those who seek help. To have to admit that you are powerless over a drug and require the help of a group of other failures, makes going to some 12-step programs the modern equivalent of wearing the letter "A" on your forehead. That AA groups glory in their weakness, helps the non-AAers not at all.

For those who feel the need for organized social support, the 12-step programs (NA and AA primarily) are the most famous. The problem is that although the 12 Steps may translate into other languages they may not translate into other cultures. They assume the existence of basic elements of human nature that are not recognized as valid in many societies. They also take as given certain precepts which can then become self-fulfilling prophecies.

Addressing the issue of spontaneous recovery specifically, AA does not deny in theory that drinkers can overcome their abusive pattern. In practice, however, they maintain that those who do were not really alcoholics to begin with. They use the terms "dry drunk" and "white knuckler" to disparage those who attempt to stop without the help of AA. These people may not be drinking but they are not dealing with their alcoholism. The problems of everyday life that we all face are due directly to this inability to admit that they are alcoholic. Should the person relapse (and relapse rates are, of course, high) this is taken as proof of the original belief. Should the person remain a lifelong teetotaller, then the only logical conclusion is that they were either not truly alcoholic to begin with, or are lifelong dry drunks.

## THE RELIGIOUS ROOTS OF ALCOHOLICS ANONYMOUS

AA has deep roots in a religious point of view that is much stronger in the United States than in most other cultures. Although much is made in the AA literature of the connection between AA and William James and Carl Jung, it appears that this contribution is limited to the fact that Jung told one of the seminal figures in AA that his problem was beyond the help of the medical profession and that a spiritual conversion might be helpful and to read James' book *Varieties of Religious Experience*. On the other hand, little is said about the connection between AA and the Oxford Group, an evangelical movement that later became known as Moral ReArmament, but much of AA's philosophy and strategy stems from this group,

The Oxford group was an attempt to return to what it saw as primitive Christianity. It was nondenominational, theologically conservative and evangelical. It had many elements that are seen in only slightly different terms in AA: (a) men are sinners, (b) men can be changed, (c) confession is a prerequisite to change, and (d) those who change must change others. Change the word sinners to alcoholics and the basic similarities are obvious. Also the Oxford Group stressed the undervaluation of intelligence and emphasized confession through story telling. These elements are paralleled in AA by its rejection of professional guidance and the famous "drunkalogues." Several of the founders of AA were deeply involved in the Oxford group, although AA split from them.

Certain other characteristics that AA shares with evangelical Christianity further point out its limitations in a more secular world. Evangelical Christianity holds that man's nature is essentially depraved, that all good comes from God. Therefore no one should take pride in their own accomplishments lest they think that they are as good as God. It is only through total submission to God that man gains salvation. AA holds that the alcoholic is powerless over alcohol, that the basic problem that the alcoholic has is pride and the belief that they are God. Alcoholics must admit they are "not God" and that it is only through submission and the public acknowledgment of their own weakness that they gain strength. The strict Jesus and God of evangelism was replaced by a "higher

power," in part to permit agnostics, Catholics and non-Christians to accept the ideas.

The concept of "sober alcoholic" is also essential to AA and has its parallel in the evangelical idea of man being an eternal sinner. According to AA, the problem drinker is "both-and," both alcoholic and sober, just as in fundamental Christianity man has a sinful and a spiritual nature that are always at war. This concept is so fundamental to AA that it forces the idea that alcoholism is an incurable disease. The analogy is often made to the disease of diabetes. The diabetic may have a normal blood sugar level but can never again eat sugar normally. Recovery is, of course, impossible and it is only through lifelong acceptance of the 12 Steps, and attendance at AA meetings, that the alcoholic may remain sober. I suppose that AA is to the alcoholic what insulin is to the diabetic.

For those within the American culture who do not ascribe to the underlying philosophy of evangelical Christianity AA can be a difficult pill to swallow. AA has even recognized this with the motto "Fake it 'til you make it." Many who attend AA meetings do so in the belief that AA is the only group available and never become "converted." AA, of course, has a motto for this, "take the best, leave the rest." The fact is that AA meetings are a powerful force for teaching the problem drinker how to play the role of "alcoholic" and the reinforcement of group approval often, if not usually, persuades the problem drinker to accept this new identity and restructure their past experiences in conformity with AA dogma.

For those from a different culture, AA must seem even more incomprehensible. It is hard to imagine how an East German, for example, steeped in materialism and Hegelian dialectics, would take to Steps One and Two. Even if you throw in a vague Catholic upbringing, it is hard to imagine Dieter believing that he has to take a fearless moral inventory of himself and make amends to all he has hurt specifically because he is an alcoholic with an incurable disease.

The rates of alcohol and other drug abuse are reported to be phenomenally high in Eastern Europe and Russia and inpatient treatment centers are luxuries that not only are prohibitively expensive, but probably not needed. Accepting as a premise that recovery from alcohol and drug abuse is not that difficult for most abusers but that some will want to seek out like minded individuals, we come to the next question. Are there any other groups that have a different emphasis that may be more amenable to those who cannot accept the concepts of AA?

A few do exist and differ with AA to varying degrees. Their similarities and differences will be explored by examining seven issues that I feel make up the core of a treatment schema. The issues are: (a) abstinence orientation, (b) acceptance of disease concept, (c) the possibility of "recovery," (d) incorporation of religious concepts, (e) role of professionals, (f) locus of control, that is, whether the problem lies with the drug or with the person, and (g) position on drugs other than alcohol.

## SECULAR ORGANIZATIONS FOR SOBRIETY

Secular Organizations for Sobriety was begun in 1986 by Jim Christopher. It now is reported to have several hundred chapters throughout the United States. Of the groups, it is most similar to AA.

While clearly abstinence oriented it takes no official stand on the various theories of alcoholism although it seems to accept the disease concept. SOS denies the need for a belief in a higher power for sobriety, but does not restrict its membership to the irreligious. It has no specific plan for recovery, such as the 12 Steps, nor does its literature take any position on the necessity for continued meetings. It is nonprofessional in nature, and is headed by a group leader. It accepts the idea that each individual is responsible for their own sobriety. It is open to those with drug as well as alcohol problems. AA ideas such as "one day at a time" also are incorporated in SOS.

## WOMEN FOR SOBRIETY/ MEN FOR SOBRIETY

Women for Sobriety/Men for Sobriety was founded by Jean Kirkpatrick. It was originally formed because the founder felt that AA did not address the needs and psychological perspective of women. There is now a Men For Sobriety organization with the same principles. It is abstinence oriented but does not accept the disease concept as wholeheartedly as AA or SOS. SOS feels that people drink to solve problems or for any number of reasons and only then eventually become physically addicted. Recovery is possible and the members are encouraged to leave the group when they feel they have solved the problems that led them to drink. WFS takes its philosophy from the Unity Church which has a transcendental orientation, rather than being evangelical. Instead of the 12 Steps, there are 13 Principles which focus on self acceptance and the role of love in relationships. Its groups are led by a certified leader who has had experience in the principles of WFS. Its locus of control is internal, meaning that the person accepts control for their own recovery and focuses on "recovery" rather than alcohol itself, so seems open to those with problems other than alcohol.

## RATIONAL RECOVERY

Rational Recovery, founded by Jack Trimpey, is the group most adamantly and conscientiously different than AA. Founded in 1990, its principles derive from Rational Emotive Therapy, a form of therapy developed by Albert Ellis which stresses the individual's rational cognitive control over behavior. Like the other two (and AA, of course) it is abstinence oriented but at least accepts the possibility of controlled drinking and welcomes those attempting to moderate either alcohol or drug use. It seems ambivalent toward the disease concept but is dogged in its attack on alcoholism. According to the "Small Book" the RR equivalent of the "Big Book" of AA, alcoholism is a set of beliefs, and a person who does not subscribe to those beliefs can no more be an alcoholic than a person who doesn't believe in Catholicism can be a Catholic.[8]

The concept of recovery is essential to RR. Not only is recovery from "alcoholism" possible but should take less than a year. Individuals who have not been drinking and seemed to have solved the basic issues of why they drank in the first place are encouraged to leave the group. They are told, in essence, to put that sorry time of their life behind them and get on with the rest of it. Like SOS, it shuns the need for a spiritual approach to sobriety, and feels that reliance on such a power simply substitutes a dependence on alcohol or drugs with a

dependence on a higher power. It encourages participation by trained mental health professionals, who need not even be abusers themselves. Its attitude toward personal responsibility and an internal locus of control is directly opposite from that of AA. Rather than admit to powerlessness, RR emphasizes the abusers' own personal strength and power to change their own lives permanently and relatively easily.

RR's attitude toward "one day at a time" epitomizes the differences between RR and AA. RR has a "big plan," which is simply to stop drinking or doing drugs, forever. According to RR, "one day at a time" is counterproductive and leads to a poor self image. If after 10 years of sobriety, a person is still doing it one day at a time, he/she is still dependent, not on alcohol, but on the group or on the belief of alcoholism. The common element of all drug abuse is dependence, so alcoholics and other drug abusers are equally welcome.

Of all of the groups, RR seems to be the best counterpoint to AA and its philosophy deserves a wider dissemination. It has its limitations, in that like most forms of psychotherapy, it probably works best with those who are verbal, logical and insight oriented, but the Rational Emotive Therapy principles that form its basis are relatively simple and easily applied. Its opposition to AA is understandable in the United States, but may be less comprehensible elsewhere and certain details of its approach may need modification to appeal to those in other cultures. Its biggest problem may be organizational, however. In the 1950s cars were designed to fall apart after a few years, guaranteeing a new car market. The opposite problem seems to apply with RR and like groups that encourage short term treatment and discourage long term group involvement. It is difficult to see how RR groups can remain stable for more than a short period of time without a cadre of "believers" who carry the message. This is precisely the advantage of AA. With its evangelical zeal to proselytize and its insistence that recovery is a life long process AA assures itself of at least a few old timers to carry the torch. It is difficult to see how a group can remain in existence if it turns over completely every few months. In short, RR may be doomed by its own success.

## CONCLUSION

In this paper, I have tried to take the point of view of the loyal opposition to accepted treatment practices. Looking at facts rather than ideology, the majority of drug abusers moderate their behavior on their own and for those that can't, the predominant self-help group in the United States, is effective with a very small percentage. In spite of this, the AA model is viewed by many as the most effective form of treatment available. If so, it is because until recently, it was the only one available. Now that others are emerging, we must look at all of them objectively. No one method of recovery will work with everyone and each must be equally valued and equally available. To do anything else borders on the criminal.

## NOTES

1. Fingarette, Herbert, *Heavy Drinking: The Myth of Alcoholism as a Disease*, University of California Press, 1988.
2. "Addiction Careers: Summary of studies based on the DARP 12-year follow up," National Institute on Drug Abuse Treatment Research Report, U.S. Department of Health and Human Services, 1986.
3. Brecher, James, *Licit and Illicit Drugs*. Little, Brown and Company, 1972.
4. Peele, Stanton, and Brodsky, Archie, *The Truth About Addiction and Recovery*, Simon and Schuster, 1991.
5. Shedler, Jonathan, and Block, Jack, "Adolescent Drug Use and Psychological Health: A Longitudinal Inquiry," *American Psychologist*, 45, 612–630, 1990.
6. Kandel, Denise, and Raveis, Victoria, "Cessation of Illicit Drug Use in Young Adulthood," *Archives of General Psychiatry* 46, 109–116, 1989.
7. Stall, Robb and Biernacki, Patrick, "Spontaneous remission from the problematic use of substances: An inductive model derived from comparative analysis of the alcohol, opiate, tobacco and food/obesity literature," *The International Journal of the Addictions*, 2, 1–23, 1986.
8. Trimpey, Jack, *Rational Recovery from Alcoholism: The Small Book*, Lotus Press, 1990.

# POSTSCRIPT

## Do Alcoholics Have to Maintain a Lifetime of Abstinence?

The fundamental question here is, Must alcoholics totally abstain from alcohol use or can they learn to drink in moderation? This issue was raised in the 1970s when Linda and Mark Sobell presented research showing that alcoholics who were taught to drink socially were less likely to relapse than people who were told to abstain from alcohol. (This study was subsequently criticized for its methodology.) In another study supported by the RAND Corporation in the 1970s, it was found that the majority of alcoholics who went through formal treatment were drinking moderately or occasionally up to 18 months after treatment. Most did not resume their abusive use of alcohol. A criticism of this study was that it did not follow those in treatment long enough—a 4-year follow-up revealed that many had relapsed.

Many people who attempt to completely stop addictive behaviors fail. If a person tries several times to abstain from drinking alcohol (or other self-destructive behaviors) and cannot stop, perhaps other forms of treatment may be worth pursuing. However, moderation as a treatment goal may not prove to be productive because alcohol—the central element to the addiction—is still present in the alcoholic's life.

Rather than trying to identify the one best type of treatment, it may be more logical to match people with the type of treatment that is best for them. It may be shortsighted to think that one form of treatment is best for all addicts. One advantage of Alcoholics Anonymous (AA) over other forms of treatment is expense. In "Typical Patterns and Costs of Alcoholism Treatment Across a Variety of Populations and Providers," *Alcoholism: Clinical and Experimental Research* (April 1991), Harold Holder and James Blose report that the average stay for inpatient alcohol treatment lasts 22 days and costs $4,665. In contrast, there is no cost to be a member of AA.

An older, excellent essay that reviews the efficacy of alcohol treatment is William Miller and Reid Hester's "The Effectiveness of Alcoholism Treatment: What Research Reveals," in William Miller and Nick Heather, eds., *Treating Addictive Behaviors: Processes of Change* (Plenum Press, 1986). In "Maintaining Sobriety: Stopping Is Starting," *International Journal of the Addictions* (August 1991), Priscilla Mackay and G. Alan Marlatt describe how the relapse rate of alcoholics is high because too much emphasis is put on drinking cessation and not enough on maintaining sobriety. And in an article in *Behavior Therapy* (Winter 1992) titled "Problem Drinkers' Perceptions of Whether Treatment Goals Should Be Self-Selected or Therapist-Selected," Mark Sobell and others assert that almost two-thirds of problem drinkers would be more likely to achieve a goal they had set for themselves, while one-third prefer having a therapist establish the goal.

# ISSUE 17

## Are the Dangers of Steroids Exaggerated?

**YES: Virginia S. Cowart,** from "Support Lags for Research on Steroid Effects," *Journal of the American Medical Association* (November 10, 1989)

**NO: National Institute on Drug Abuse,** from "Anabolic Steroids: A Threat to Body and Mind," a NIDA Research Report Series, U.S. Department of Health and Human Services (1991)

### ISSUE SUMMARY

**YES:** Medical writer Virginia S. Cowart asserts that the long-term consequences of anabolic steroid use has yet to be determined because this type of research has not been systematically and scientifically conducted.
**NO:** The National Institute on Drug Abuse, the lead federal agency for research into the problems and treatment of drug abuse, identifies many short-term physical and psychological problems and potential long-term problems linked to the nonmedical, unregulated, and illicit use of anabolic steroids.

Anabolic steroids are synthetic derivatives of the male hormone testosterone. Although they have legitimate medical uses, steroids are increasingly being used by individuals as a way to quickly build up muscle and increase personal strength. Concerns over the potential negative effects of steroid use seem to be justified: An estimated 500,000 Americans under age 18 use anabolic steroids. Anabolic steroid users span all ethnic groups, nationalities, and socioeconomic groups. The emphasis on winning has led many athletes to take risks with steroids that are potentially destructive. Despite the widespread belief that anabolic steroids are primarily used by athletes, up to one-third of users are nonathletes, who use these drugs to improve their physiques and self-images.

Society places much emphasis on winning, and to come out on top, many individuals are willing to make sacrifices—sacrifices that may entail compromising their health. Some people will do anything for the sake of winning. In an article in *Sports Illustrated* prior to his death, professional football player Lyle Alzado spoke out not against the use of steroids but against the way he used steroids. The message was not necessarily that steroids were bad but that they can be used badly.

The short-term consequences of anabolic steroid use are well documented. Some possible short-term effects among men include testicular atrophy, sperm count reduction, impotency, baldness, difficulty in urinating, and breast enlargement. Among women, some potential effects are deepening of the voice, breast reduction, menstrual irregularities, and clitoral enlargement. Both sexes may develop acne, swelling in the feet, reduced HDL levels (which is the "good" cholesterol), hypertension, and liver damage. Also related to steroid use are psychological changes, such as mood swings, paranoia, and violent behavior. The short-term effects of steroid use have been thoroughly researched; however, their long-term effects have not been substantiated.

The problem with identifying the long-term effects of anabolic steroid use is that there are virtually no systematic, scientific long-term studies. Most of the information regarding steroids' long-term effects comes from personal reports, not well-conducted, controlled studies. Personal stories or anecdotal evidence is often accepted as fact. For example, anabolic steroids have been implicated with the development of liver tumors. Yet, there are only three documented cases of liver tumors among steroid users. It is difficult to know if the effects from anabolic steroids are exaggerated.

The American Medical Association opposes stricter regulation of anabolic steroids on two grounds: First, anabolic steroids have been medically used to improve growth and development and for certain types of anemia, breast cancers, endometriosis, and osteoporosis. By imposing stricter regulations, people who may medically benefit from these drugs will have more difficulty acquiring them. Second, the problem of illicit use of these drugs will not disappear merely by banning them. By maintaining legal access to these drugs, studies into their long-term consequences can be determined. One of the lessons of drug education is that information needs to be accurate when it comes to drugs. There is a lack of credibility when unsubstantiated claims are made.

In the following selections, Virginia S. Cowart discusses the need for long-term studies into the effects of anabolic steroids, but she maintains that current reports on the long-term consequences of steroid use may be exaggerated. The National Institute on Drug Abuse examines an aggregate of various studies dealing with steroids and argues that steroids do have proven and potential negative effects. The institute then calls for greater regulation.

# YES

Virginia S. Cowart

## SUPPORT LAGS FOR RESEARCH ON STEROID EFFECTS

Efforts to gain international agreement on drug testing in sports continue, with the latest developments emerging from a world congress in the Soviet Union.

A charter covering areas of international agreement on drug testing and sanctions was developed at a 1987 meeting in Ottawa, Canada. That charter, which has nine annexes and covers what is currently believed by its authors to be right and wrong in sports in this regard, was approved by the International Olympic Committee in Seoul, South Korea, in September 1988.

### NEXT: NORWAY

The goal of the latest meeting, in Moscow, has been to develop specific points on out-of-competition testing, education, and the rights and responsibilities of athletes and other members of the sports community. Agreement on additional specifics is expected to be the focus of the next world congress, set for 1991 in Oslo, Norway.

Andrew Pipe, MD, who chairs the National Advisory Committee on Drug Abuse in Amateur Sports, Sports Medicine Council of Canada, summed up the Moscow meeting this way: "I would have to say that the conference was useful. It permitted people to come together and discuss the problems and to recognize that everybody is singing from the same hymn book, even if they may not be on the same verse."

The United States and the Soviet Union are trying to sing the same verse, having signed a bilateral agreement for athlete drug testing. Work on standardization of the IOC-approved laboratories in Moscow and at the University of California at Los Angeles continues. But there is, as yet, no starting date for the actual testing of athletes.

From Virginia S. Cowart, "Support Lags for Research on Steroid Effects," *Journal of the American Medical Association,* vol. 262, no. 18 (November 10, 1989), pp. 2500–2502. Copyright © 1989 by The American Medical Association. Reprinted by permission.

## MAYBE IN 1990s

Pipe says he believes it will be possible to achieve a workable international accord sometime in the next decade. He notes that athletes themselves are eager to deal with drug use in sports.

A number of athletes attended the Moscow meeting. Pipe says they were "quite outspoken" in calling for lifetime suspension from competition for athletes who have drug tests with positive results, even if it is the first offense. "It became clear to me," he says, "that we need to involve athletes in developing strategy much more than we have."

One recommendation to be made to the International Olympic Committee as a result of the Moscow meeting is that its charter be amended. The amendment would provide that only athletes who agree to be tested for drugs will be eligible for competition.

## SCHEDULE II?

The US effort to contain the spreading use of anabolic steroids moved to the political arena with the introduction this fall of proposed federal legislation that would place them on Schedule II under the Controlled Substances Act. This bill would establish an interagency coordinating council charged with developing a comprehensive national steroid strategy, and it also directs the Office for Substance Abuse Prevention to create programs targeted at secondary schools.

"We have a chance to stop steroids before they become as uncontrollable as cocaine," says the bill's sponsor, Rep Mel Levine (D, Calif). He acknowledges the lack of research, particularly on long-term health effects of steroids, but says: "I think we clearly know enough about how harmful steroids can be to have a social interest in trying to stop their use except for legitimate medical purposes."

The American Medical Association (AMA) opposes, as a matter of principle, congressional rescheduling of drugs, in the belief that this shortcut undermines the utility of the regular scheduling process. Also, there is no documentation that scheduling will have an impact on the problem, an AMA spokesperson said, particularly since about 80% of steroids used for performance enhancement do not come through medical channels. Historically, for example, cocaine is a controlled substance; yet it is widely available in the United States on the black market.

The spokesperson said the AMA also fears that the government will seize on scheduling the drug as a substitute for dealing with the problem in more effective ways. Merely making it a controlled substance will not necessarily make money available for enforcement, it was pointed out.

The bill is being cosponsored by Rep Henry Waxman (D, Calif) and Rep Ben Gilman (R, NY). Waxman, who is chair of the Subcommittee on Health and the Environment, notes that an estimated half million high-school boys have used steroids and says: "This is a national tragedy. It is a tragedy for young people who may have done permanent damage to their bodies. It is a tragedy of leadership in the high schools, where coaches turn a blind eye to obvious evidence of steroid use. It is a tragedy that the fruits of biomedical research could be put to uses that are harmful, unethical, and illegal."

## JOHNSON CAVEAT

Joining the congressmen at a press conference in Washington was Ben Johnson, the Canadian sprinter who lost his Olympic gold medal because of his use of steroids. Johnson said that if steroids had been a controlled substance in Canada before the 1988 Olympics, it would not have deterred his use of them.

Also appearing at the press conference were Gary Wadler, MD, clinical associate professor of medicine at Cornell University Medical College, New York, NY, and coauthor of *Drugs and the Athlete* (Philadelphia, Pa: FA Davis Co Publishers; 1989) and Alan D. Rogol, MD, a pediatric endocrinologist at the University of Virginia, Charlottesville.

Wadler noted that as many as 30% of steroids used by students and athletes are obtained from health professionals. He says that placing steroids on the controlled substance list parallels similar action with amphetamines, which were widely abused, but warns that controlling production is not the sole answer.

"We must be mindful that controlling the production of pharmaceutical grade anabolic androgenic steroids carries with it the risk of increasing the availability of illicitly manufactured drugs," Wadler said. "As with cocaine, the demand must be decreased as well as the supply."

## FOLKLORE VS 'FACTLORE'

Many physicians and steroid researchers have become concerned that the folklore about steroids appears to be outstripping the "factlore". As public worry grows about unsupervised use of these drugs, which cause fundamental derangements of body chemistry, a great deal of anecdotal information has been accepted as completely valid. For example, although liver tumors are believed to be a common result of steroid use, there are only three documented cases in the medical literature.

Moreover, it still is virtually impossible to get funding for research studies, these investigators say. "It is frustrating," says Charles Yesalis, ScD, professor of epidemiology at Pennsylvania State University, Hershey, about his 6-year effort to get funding for a study of long-term effects in a group of former steroid users. He has just received a "priority scare" that appears to preclude funding in the near future.

Yesalis and William E. Buckley, PhD, would like to repeat a study they coauthored (*JAMA.* 1988;260:3385–3544) that found 6.6% use of anabolic steroids among high-school students. They propose to use the same 46 schools and look at what changes have occurred during the past 3 years.

Like some other steroid experts, Yesalis says steroid use may be more an ethical problem than a health problem in that many of the deleterious short-term effects appear to be reversible. This seems to be the case in men, at any rate, Yesalis says, particularly if they have not used the extremely high doses that some steroid users now take and if they have taken them for a relatively brief period.

## ABOUT TO CHANGE?

Speaking of research funding, Richard Strauss, MD, observes: "Until recently, I don't know of anybody who was willing to even consider looking at funding any studies on the health effects of anabolic steroids in athletes."

Strauss is an associate professor of preventive medicine and internal medicine and a team physician at Ohio State University, Columbus, and editor in chief of *The Physician and Sportsmedicine.* He is studying men and women to look at the short-term health effects of steroids.

"A few of us have done studies," he says, "but it was basically unfunded research, accomplished by using volunteer, unpaid participation," and he likens it to astronomy." "We are looking at a population taking anabolic steroids in whatever way they wish, and studying those effects in a relatively haphazard way, like making observations of what is happening in another world."

Strauss says the point is that the potential problems have not been clearly identified in the user group. For example, although some short-term health effects have been identified, this is complicated by the fact that some users take multiple drugs in very high doses.

## LONG-TERM EFFECTS?

He predicts that, as the problem of steroid abuse becomes recognized, more research will be conducted, but he warns that physicians will have to keep an open mind. "There may or may not be serious long-term effects," he says.

One area that many observers suggest should have top priority in funding and time is the psychological effect of steroids. Researchers say that it appears some steroid users who are in legal trouble would like to explore this as an avenue of defense.

Harrison Pope, MD, associate professor of psychiatry at Harvard Medical School, Boston, Mass, coauthored the only study regarding the psychiatric effects of steroids (*Am J Psychiatry.* 1988;145:487–490). Since it appeared, several attorneys have con-

tacted Pope and David Katz, MD, and the two physicians have interviewed several steroid users while the latter were in jail. An article on homicide and near homicide by steroid users is in press (*J Clin Psychiatry*). There were 42 subjects in their first study and Pope agrees that it is not possible to know whether the prevalence rates are representative of the population as a whole.

"We can argue that people with psychological problems would have been more likely to come forward to be interviewed by us," he says, "or the opposite could be true. The only conclusion for the moment is that clearly there are some people—and probably a fair number—with prominent psychiatric effects from steroids."

Support for that position comes from a paper in press in which two Yale University psychiatrists, Kenneth B. Kashkin, MD, and Herbert D. Kleber, MD, conclude that some anabolic steroid abusers may develop "a previously unrecognized sex steroid hormone-dependence disorder."

Pope says that doing the study that should be done is impossible because approval would never be given to administer massive doses of as many as seven kinds of drugs to test subjects. He and Katz are planning to study 150 bodybuilders, but Pope says the larger sample size alone will not answer some of the questions.

## CONTROVERSIAL ADVICE

Contrary to some, Pope advises physicians whose adolescent patients may be interested in using steroids (in preparation for athletic competition) to acknowledge that steroids may be effective for some of these purposes and that serious medical problems so far appear to be rare. By doing this, he says, physicians will keep their credibility. Then, Pope suggests, physicians will be able to tell young athletes that the psychiatric effects of steroids are insidious and potentially more common and dangerous than the physical effects.

Moreover, there is no way to predict who might become uncharacteristically aggressive as a result of taking steroids, Pope says. "Acne will go away and testicles will return to normal size, but if you're in jail for 20 years because of steroids, that's a pretty serious effect in itself," he says.

## PUBLIC PERCEPTION

Public opinion about the use of anabolic steroids has become more negative, reflecting a stricter stance with regard to all drug use. David Musto, MD, professor of psychiatry and the history of medicine at Yale University, New Haven, Conn, says he recognizes a pattern he has seen before.

"If history is a guide," Musto says, "and if we look back to our last epidemic of illicit drug use in the 1920s and 1930s, the strict and punitive attitude with regard to the use of these drugs will only become stronger. There probably will not be any swaying back of the pendulum for a long time."

Musto says that, in his view, the general hardening of tolerance toward those who use drugs is related to concern about what humans take into their bodies.

"In the 1960s," he says, "the attitude was that if you were careful and knew how much to use, drugs would help you be more than you could be otherwise. But, in the last 15 years, there has been a fundamental shift toward seeing drugs in any amount as wrong."

In summary, moves are in progress, in the United States and internationally, to control and regulate anabolic steroids. Most experts believe that research funding will continue to be tight for the foreseeable future, although there are many aspects of these drugs that clearly need more systematic research.

# NO National Institute on Drug Abuse

# ANABOLIC STEROIDS: A THREAT TO BODY AND MIND

## THE PRICE OF PERFECTION

Shock waves went through the sports world when Canadian track superstar Ben Johnson was denied his gold medal at the 1988 Olympics after tests showed he had taken anabolic steroids. The incident called international attention to the use of anabolic steroids among world-class athletes to gain competitive advantage.

Still, athletes and nonathletes alike persist in taking them. Teenagers are taking anabolic steroids not just to excel in sports but to enhance their self-images by perfecting their physiques. There are even reports of male adults in physically demanding professions like law enforcement using them to appear tougher and more formidable.

As the drug grows in popularity so does awareness of the serious side effects it may cause. One of the most alarming is the threat of AIDS. HIV—human immunodeficiency virus—can be transmitted if shared needles are used to inject the drug.

But potential harm to physical and psychological health is only one aspect of this troubling trend.

### A Question of Values

The nonmedical use of anabolic steroids raises more ethical and moral issues. Engaging in steroids use is illegal. Users are likely to find themselves acquiring these drugs through illicit—and expensive—channels. The heavy demand for anabolic steroids has given rise to a black market, with sales estimated at as much as $400 million a year. Moreover, supplies, which are often illegally manufactured and do not meet established standards, may be contaminated.

Athletes who use these drugs are cheating. They gain an unfair advantage over opponents and violate the ban on steroids imposed by most major sports organizations.

From National Institute on Drug Abuse, "Anabolic Steroids: A Threat to Body and Mind," a NIDA Research Report Series, U.S. Department of Health and Human Services. Rockville, MD: National Institute on Drug Abuse, 1991.

### Another Addictive Substance?

Can anabolic steroids be added to the list of addictive drugs? Early signs point to addictive patterns among users. At the very least, users demonstrate an unwillingness to give up anabolic steroids even in the face of possibly dire consequences to their health.

### Stopping the Trend

As the health risks of anabolic steroids become more apparent, efforts to curtail their use—through education, legislation, and medical practices—are intensifying.

For those already hooked, kicking the steroids habit is the best chance to escape devastating side effects. For potential users, the solution, of course, is to never take the drug at all. There are other ways to be a winner athletically and socially without harming health and without cheating.

## USING ANABOLIC STEROIDS

### Valid Medical Uses

Steroids are drugs derived from hormones. Anabolic steroids comprise one group of these hormonal drugs. In certain cases, some may have therapeutic value.

The U.S. Food and Drug Administration has approved the use of selected anabolic steroids for treating specific types of anemia, some breast cancers, osteoporosis, endometriosis, and hereditary angioedema, a rare disease involving the swelling of some parts of the body. Some medical specialists believe that anabolic steroids can improve the appetite and improve healing after surgery, but the FDA has withdrawn approval for such uses since the claims are vague and largely unsubstantiated.

### What Are Anabolic Steroids?

Anabolic steroids—or more precisely, anabolic/androgenic steroids—belong to a group known as ergogenic, or so-called "performance-enhancing," drugs. They are synthetic derivatives of testosterone, a natural male hormone.

"Anabolic" means growing or building. "Androgenic" means "masculinizing" or generating male sexual characteristics.

Most healthy males produce between 2 and 10 milligrams of testosterone a day. (Females do produce some testosterone, but in trace amounts.) The hormone's anabolic effects help the body retain dietary protein, thus aiding growth of muscles, bones, and skin.

The androgenic characteristics of testosterone are associated with masculinity. They foster the maturing of the male reproductive system in puberty, the growth of body hair and the deepening of the voice. They can affect aggressiveness and sex drive.

### Do They Really Work?

Anabolic steroids are designed to mimic the bodybuilding traits of testosterone while minimizing its "masculinizing" effects. There are several types, with various combinations of anabolic and androgenic properties. The International Olympics Committee to date has placed 17 anabolic steroids and related compounds on its banned list.

Athletes who have used anabolic steroids—as well as some coaches, trainers, and physicians—do report significant increases in lean muscle mass, strength, and endurance. But *no* studies show that the substances enhance performance.

Anabolic steroids do not improve agility, skill or cardiovascular capacity. Some athletes insist that these substances aid in recovery from injuries, but no hard data exists to support the claim.

## A BRIEF HISTORY

### Winning Through Doping
The drive to compete—and to win—is as old as humankind. Throughout history, athletes have sought foods and potions to transform their bodies into powerful, well-tuned machines.

Greek wrestlers ate huge quantities of meat to build muscle, and Norse warriors—the Berserkers—ate hallucinogenic mushrooms to gear up for battle.

The first competitive athletes believed to be charged with "doping"—taking drugs and other nonfood substances to improve performance—were swimmers in Amsterdam in the 1860s. Doping, with anything from strychnine and caffeine to cocaine and heroin, spread to other sports over the next several decades.

### Enter Anabolic Steroids
The use of anabolic steroids by athletes is relatively new. Testosterone was first synthesized in the 1930's and was introduced into the sporting arena in the 1940's and 1950's. When the Russian weightlifting team—thanks, in part, to synthetic testosterone—walked off with a pile of medals at the 1952 Olympics, an American physician determined that U.S. competitors should have the same advantage.

By 1958 a U.S. pharmaceutical firm had developed anabolic steroids. Although the physician soon realized the drug had unwanted side effects, it was too late to halt its spread into the sports world.

Early users were mainly bodybuilders, weightlifters, football players, and discus, shot put, or javelin throwers—competitors who relied heavily on bulk and strength.

During the 1970's demand grew as athletes in other sports sought the competitive edge that anabolic steroids seemed to provide.

By the 1980's, as nonathletes also discovered the body-enhancing properties of steroids, a black market began to flourish for the illegal production and sale of the drugs for nonmedical purposes.

## ABUSING ANABOLIC STEROIDS

### Who Takes Them—and Why?
Today it is not only the college football player or the professional weightlifter or the marathon runner who may use anabolic steroids.

It may be an 18-year-old who loathes his skinny body. Or a 15-year-old in a hurry to reach maturity.

Or a policeman who wants more muscle power on the job.

And the use of anabolic steroids is not confined to males. Professional and amateur female athletes—track and field competitors, swimmers, bodybuilders—feel the pressure to triumph, too.

Increasing numbers of adolescents are turning to steroids for cosmetic reasons. In a 1986 survey, as many as 45 percent of 200 high school users cited appearance as a primary reason for taking steroids.

Young people who use steroids defy easy categorizing. They come from cities and rural areas, from poor families and wealthy ones. They are of all races and nationalities. The common link among them is the desire to look, perform and feel better— at almost any cost. Users— and especially the young—are apt to

---

**A GLOSSARY OF TERMS**

Drug and steroids use in sports has spawned a glossary of its own:

*Blending.* Mixing different drugs.

*Bulking up.* Increasing muscle mass through steroids.

*Cycling.* Taking multiple doses of steroids over a specified period of time, stopping for a time and starting again.

*Doping.* Using drugs and other non-food substances to improve athletic performance and prowess.

*Ergogenic drugs.* Performance-enhancing substances.

*Megadosing.* Taking massive amounts of steroids, by injection or pill.

*Plateauing.* When a drug becomes ineffective at a certain level.

*Roid rages.* Uncontrolled outbursts of anger, frustration or combativeness that may result from using anabolic steroids.

*Shotgunning.* Taking steroids on a hit-or-miss basis.

*Stacking.* Using a combination of anabolic steroids, often in combination with other drugs.

*Tapering.* Slowly decreasing steroids intake.

---

ignore or deny warnings about health risks. If they see friends growing taller and stronger on steroids, they want the same benefits. They want to believe in the power of the drug.

**How Prevalent Is Use?**

Surveys and anecdotal evidence indicate that the rate of nonmedical steroids use may be increasing.

In 1990, a NIDA survey of high school seniors showed that nearly 3 percent—5 percent of males and 0.5 percent of females—reported using steroids at some time in their lives.

The same survey showed that steroids were used within the last year by nearly as many students as crack cocaine and by more students than the hallucinogenic drug PCP.

Use among college females appears to have increased somewhat. A study of 11 universities in 1984 found that steroids

users were reported in only one women's sport—swimming—at a rate of 1 percent. In a follow-up survey in 1988, 1 percent of women in track and field and basketball also reported taking steroids.

Use among adult or professional athletes has not been well documented, although anecdotal evidence clearly supports the suggestion that anabolic steroids have enjoyed popularity among football players, weightlifters, wrestlers, and track and field competitors, among others.

**MEGADOSING**

Anabolic steroids are usually taken in pill form. Some that cannot be absorbed orally are taken by injection. The normal prescribed daily dose for medical purposes usually averages between 1 and 5 milligrams.

Some athletes, on the other hand, may take up to hundreds of milligrams a day, far exceeding medically recommended dosages.

Operating on the erroneous more-is-better theory, some athletes indulge in a practice known as "stacking." They take many types of steroids, sometimes in combination with other drugs such as stimulants, depressants, pain killers, anti-inflammatories, and other hormones.

Many users "cycle," taking the drugs for 6 to 12 weeks or more, stopping for several weeks and then starting another cycle. They may do this in the belief that by scheduling their steroids intake, they can manipulate test results and escape detection. It is not uncommon for athletes to cycle over a period of months or even years.

## HEALTH HAZARDS

### Raising a Red Flag

Although controlled studies on the long-term outcome of megadosing with anabolic steroids have not been conducted, extensive research on prescribed doses for medical use has documented the potential side effects of the drug, even when taken in small doses. Moreover, reports by athletes, and observations of attending physicians, parents, and coaches do offer substantial evidence of dangerous side effects.

Some effects, such as rapid weight gain, are easy to see. Some take place internally and may not be evident until it is too late. Some are irreversible.

### The Dangers

#### ... to Men

Males who take large doses of anabolic steroids typically experience changes in sexual characteristics. Although derived from a male sex hormone, the drug can trigger a mechanism in the body that can actually shut down the healthy functioning of the male reproductive system. Some possible side effects:

- Shrinking of the testicles
- Reduced sperm count
- Impotence
- Baldness
- Difficulty or pain in urinating
- Development of breasts
- Enlarged prostate

#### ... and to Women

Females may experience "masculinization" as well as other problems:

- Growth of facial hair
- Changes in or cessation of the menstrual cycle
- Enlargement of the clitoris
- Deepened voice
- Breast reduction

#### ... and to Both Sexes

For both males and females, continued use of anabolic steroids may lead to health conditions ranging from merely irritating to life-threatening. Some effects are:

- Acne
- Jaundice
- Trembling
- Swelling of feet or ankles
- Bad breath
- Reduction in HDL, the "good" cholesterol
- High blood pressure
- Liver damage and cancers
- Aching joints
- Increased chance of injury to tendons, ligaments, and muscles

### Special Dangers to Adolescents

Anabolic steroids can halt growth prematurely in adolescents. Because even small doses can irreversibly affect growth, steroids are rarely prescribed for children and young adults, and only for the severely ill.

The Office of the Inspector General in the U.S. Department of Health and Human Services has gathered anecdotal evidence that preteens and teens taking steroids may be at risk for developing a dependence on the drugs and on other substances as well.

### The Threat of AIDS

People sometimes take injections of anabolic steroids to augment oral dosages, using large-gauge, reusable needles normally obtained through the black market. If needles are shared, users run the risk of transmitting or contracting the HIV infection that can lead to AIDS.

### The Psychological Effects

Scientists are just beginning to investigate the impact of anabolic steroids on the mind and behavior. Many athletes report "feeling good" about themselves while on a steroids regimen. The downside, according to Harvard researchers, is wide mood swings ranging from periods of violent, even homicidal, episodes known as "roid rages" to bouts of depression when the drugs are stopped.

The Harvard study also noted that anabolic steroids users may suffer from paranoid jealousy, extreme irritability, delusions, and impaired judgment stemming from feelings of invincibility.

### ARE ANABOLIC STEROIDS ADDICTIVE?

Evidence that megadoses of anabolic steroids can affect the brain and produce mental changes in users poses serious questions about possible addiction to the drugs.

While investigations continue, researchers at Yale University have found that long-term steroids users do experience many of the characteristics of classic addiction: cravings, difficulty in ceasing steroids use and withdrawal symptoms.

Pennsylvania State University researchers studied a group of high school seniors who had developed a psychological, if not physical, dependence on anabolic steroids. Adolescent users exhibit a prime trait of addicts—denial. They tend to overlook or simply ignore the physical dangers and moral implications of taking illegal substances.

Certain delusional behavior that is characteristic of addiction can occur. Some athletes who "bulk up" on anabolic steroids are unaware of body changes that are obvious to others, experiencing what is sometimes called reverse anorexia.

### SUPPLY AND DEMAND: THE BLACK MARKET

Many users maintain their habit with anabolic steroids acquired through a highly organized black market handling up to $400 million worth of the drugs a year.

Until recently most underground steroids were legitimately manufactured pharmaceuticals that were diverted to the black market through theft and fraudulent prescriptions. More effective law enforcement coupled with greater demand forced black marketers to seek new sources.

Now black-market anabolic steroids are either made overseas and smuggled into the United States or are produced in clandestine laboratories in this country. These counterfeit drugs may present greater health risks because they are manufactured without controls and thus may be impure, mislabeled, or simply bogus.

Sales are made in gyms, health clubs, on campuses, and through the mail. Users report that suppliers may be drug dealers or they may be trainers, physicians, pharmacists, or friends. It's not hard for users to buy the drugs or to learn how to use them. Many of them rely on an underground manual, a "bible" on steroids that circulates around the country.

## SAFE—AND HEALTHY— ALTERNATIVES

Anabolic steroids may have a reputation for turning a wimp into a winner or a runt into a hulk, but the truth is that it takes a lot more to be a star athlete.

Athletic prowess depends not only on strength and endurance, but on skill and mental acuity. It also depends on diet, rest, overall mental and physical health, and genes. Athletic excellence can be, and is, achieved by millions without reliance on dangerous drugs.

## FIGHTING BACK

### Testing

The major national and international sports associations enforce their ban against anabolic steroids by periodic testing. Testing, however, is controversial.

Some observers say the tests are not reliable, and even the International Olympic Committees tests, considered to be the most accurate, have been challenged. Athletes can manipulate results with "masking agents" to prevent detection, or they can take anabolic steroids that have calculable detection periods.

Despite the problems, testing remains an important way of monitoring and controlling the abuse of steroids among athletes. Efforts are underway to make testing more accurate.

### Treatment

Treatment programs for steroids abusers are just now being developed as more is learned about the habit.

Medical specialists do find persuasion is an important weapon is getting the user off the drug. They attempt to present medical evidence of the damage anabolic steroids can do to the body. One specialist notes that medical tests, such as those that show a lowered sperm count, can motivate male athletes to cease usage.

One health clinic considers the anabolic steroids habit as an addiction and structures treatment around the techniques used in traditional substance abuse programs. It focuses on acute intervention and a long-term follow-up, introducing nonsteroids alternatives that will maintain body fitness as well as self-esteem.

### Legislation

Both Federal and State governments have enacted laws and regulations to control anabolic steroids abuse.

In 1988, Congress passed the Anti-Drug Abuse Act, making the distribution or possession of anabolic steroids for nonmedical reasons a Federal offense. Distribution to minors is a prison offense.

In 1990, Congress toughened the laws, passing legislation that classifies anabolic steroids as a controlled substance. The new law also increases penalties for steroids use and trafficking. To halt diversion of anabolic steroids onto the black market, the law imposes strict production and recordkeeping regulations on pharmaceutical firms.

Over 25 states have passed laws and regulations to control steroids abuse, and many others are considering similar legislation.

## Education
Prevention is the best solution to halting the growing abuse of anabolic steroids. The time to educate youngsters is *before* they become users.

Efforts must not stop there, however. Current users, as well as coaches, trainers, parents, and medical practitioners need to know about the hazards of anabolic steroids. The young need to understand that they are not immortal and that the drugs can harm them. An education campaign must also address the problem of covert approval by some members of the medical and athletic communities that encourages steroids use.

The message needs to be backed up by accurate information and spread by responsible, respected individuals.

# POSTSCRIPT

## Are the Dangers of Steroids Exaggerated?

The cultural values in any society are often reflected in its heroes; heroes embody those qualities deemed desirable. For many people, athletes are their heroes. However, stories of professional and college athletes as well as Olympic athletes using anabolic steroids are rampant. What is the message? If our heroes use drugs to enhance performance, then using steroids is okay.

There are several reasons why long-term research on anabolic steroid use is lacking. The problems are with the conduct of long-term research itself. First, it is unethical to give drugs to people that may prove harmful, even lethal. Also, the amount of steroids given to subjects in a laboratory setting may not replicate what illegal steroid users take. Some users take more than 100 times the amount of steroids that are clinically used.

Second, to determine the true effects of drugs, double-blind studies should be done. This means that the researcher as well as the people receiving the test drugs do not know whether the subjects are receiving the real drug or a placebo (an inert substance). This is not practical with steroids because subjects can always tell if they received the steroids or the placebos. The effects of steroids could be determined by following up with people who are known steroid users. One problem with this is that if physical or psychological problems appear, it cannot be determined whether the problems are due to the steroids or to other drugs the person may have been using. Also, the type of person who uses steroids may be the type of person who has emotional problems in the first place.

Although the black-market trade in anabolic steroids is estimated to be over $400 million a year, one could argue that steroids are a symptom of a much larger problem. Society emphasizes appearance and performance. We are told to either starve ourselves or pump ourselves up (or both) in order to satisfy the cultural ideal of beauty. If we cannot achieve these cultural standards through exercising, dieting, or drugs, we can turn to surgery or to steroids. Steroid use fits into a much larger problem of people who cannot accept themselves and their limitations.

For an account of the black-market trade in steroids, read Stanley Penn's "Muscling In: As Ever More People Try Anabolic Steroids, Traffickers Take Over," *The Wall Street Journal* (October 4, 1988). In the *Journal of the American Medical Association* (December 8, 1989), see Kenneth Kashkin and Herbert Kleber's "Hooked on Hormones? An Anabolic Steroid Addiction Hypothesis." And, in the 1990 NIDA Research Monograph, the potential effects of steroids are discussed in "Reappraisal of the Health Risks Associated With the Use of High Doses of Oral and Injectable Androgenic Steroids," by Karl Friedel.

# CONTRIBUTORS
# TO THIS VOLUME

## EDITOR

**RAYMOND GOLDBERG** has been a professor of health education at the State University of New York College at Cortland since 1981. He received a B.S. in health and physical education from Pembroke State University in 1969, an M.Ed. in health education from the University of South Carolina in 1971, and a Ph.D. in health education from the University of Toledo in 1981. He is the author or coauthor of many articles on health-related issues that have appeared in such publications as *Wellness Perspectives, Health Education,* and *Journal of Drug Education,* among others. The president of both the Cortland County American Cancer Society and the Cortland County Health Systems Council and the chairperson of the New York State Division of the American Cancer Society, he has received over $500,000 in grants for his research in health and drug education.

## STAFF

Marguerite L. Egan   Program Manager
Brenda S. Filley   Production Manager
Whit Vye   Designer
Libra Ann Cusack   Typesetting Supervisor
Juliana Arbo   Typesetter
David Brackley   Copy Editor
David Dean   Administrative Assistant
Diane Barker   Editorial Assistant

# AUTHORS

**HARRY H. AVIS** is a professor in the Department of Psychology at Sierra College in Rocklin, California. He has taught at the University of California Medical School, San Francisco, and at Antioch University, and is the author of the textbook *Drugs and Life* (Wm. C. Brown, 1990).

**FALCON BAKER** is the director of delinquency programs for the Louisville, Kentucky, school district.

**ROBERT E. BROCKIE** is a physician with the Presbyterian Hospital of Dallas.

**ARCHIE BRODSKY** is a senior research associate in the Program in Psychiatry and the Law at the Massachusetts Mental Health Center, Harvard Medical School. A professional writer and health care activist, he is a coauthor of numerous books, including *Sexual Dilemmas for the Helping Professional* (Brunner/Mazel, 1991), with Jerry Edelwich.

**DON CAHALAN** is a professor emeritus of public health at the University of California, Berkeley. He has directed national and regional studies of drinking behavior and problems for more than 20 years, and he has published more than 40 articles and publications on alcohol use and abuse, including *Understanding America's Drinking Problem: How to Combat the Hazards of Alcohol* (Jossey-Bass, 1987).

**GRAHAM COLDITZ** is an associate professor of medicine at Harvard Medical School and an associate professor of epidemiology at the Harvard School of Public Health in Boston, Massachusetts. He received a D.P.H. in epidemiology from the Harvard School of Public Health.

**VIRGINIA S. COWART,** a medical writer who specializes in the field of sports medicine, was one of the first to write in depth about androgenic anabolic steroids in a series of articles that appeared in the *Journal of the American Medical Association* and *The Physician and Sportsmedicine*. She is the coauthor, with James E. Wright, of *Anabolic Steroids/Altered States* (Brown Benchmark Press, 1990).

**CHRISTINE DOBDAY** is affiliated with the Washington, D.C., office of the American Association of Advertising Agencies.

**ROBERT L. DuPONT,** former director of the National Institute on Drug Abuse, is a clinical professor of psychiatry at the Georgetown University School of Medicine in Washington, D.C. He is also the president of the Institute for Behavior and Health and the vice president of Bensinger, DuPont, and Associates, a management consulting firm dealing with workplace substance abuse.

**HERBERT FINGARETTE** is a professor emeritus of philosophy at the University of California, Santa Barbara. He has also served as an alcoholism and addiction consultant to the World Health Organization.

**EDWARD GIOVANNUCCI** is a physician with the Department of Epidemiology at the Harvard School of Public Health in Boston, Massachusetts.

**LEONARD H. GLANTZ,** associate director of the School of Public Health at Boston University, is a professor of public health, specializing in health law, and a professor of sociomedical sciences and community medicine in the School of Medicine at Boston University. He is also on the board of directors for the Center for Drug Development at Tufts University in Boston.

**RICHARD J. GOEMAN** is a continuing graduate student in health sciences and physical therapy at Indiana University in Bloomington, Indiana, where he has also taught as a graduate assistant. He holds a master's degree in public health education.

**DIEDERICK E. GROBBEE** is a professor of clinical epidemiology and the chairperson of the Cardiovascular Epidemiology Group in the Department of Epidemiology at Erasmus University Medical School in Rotterdam, the Netherlands. He is also chairperson of the Division of Clinical Epidemiology of the Cardiovascular Research Institute at Erasmus University, Rotterdam.

**DAVID J. HANSON** is a professor of sociology at the State University of New York at Potsdam and the

president of the New York State Sociological Society. He has received research grants from federal, state, and private sources and has authored over 250 publications.

**RAY HOSKINS** is an alcoholism and drug abuse counselor at Prevention, Intervention, and Treatment Services, located in Indianapolis, Indiana. His work in the addictions field has involved student assistance programs, drug abuse prevention, treatment of opiate addicts, and inpatient and outpatient alcoholism and drug addiction programs. He is a member of the National Association of Alcoholism and Drug Abuse Counselors.

**GARY L. HUBER** is the director of the nutrition unit in the Department of Medicine at the University of Texas at Tyler and a professor of medicine at the University of Texas Health Science Center in Tyler, Texas. He is a member of the American Association for the Advancement of Science and a member of the American Medical Association.

**RAY IRIZARRY** is a recovered drug addict who has been a drug counselor for over 20 years. Previously the outreach coordinator of Project COPE, an AIDS prevention project targeted to injection drug users, he is now a drug counselor for the Connecticut Halfway House, Inc.

**JOHN C. LAWN** was an officer with the Federal Bureau of Investigation for 15 years, and he also served as deputy administrator and then administrator of the Drug Enforcement Administration. He received numerous awards during his law enforcement career, including the President's Medal for Distinguished Service. Although he currently serves as vice president, chief of operations for the New York Yankees, he continues to be involved with drug education and prevention, and he serves on numerous advisory committees.

**PAUL A. LOGLI** is the state's attorney for Winnebago County, Illinois, and a lecturer with the National College of District Attorneys. A member of the Illinois state bar since 1974, he is a nationally recognized advocate for prosecutorial involvement in the issue of substance-abused infants.

**JOHN LUIK** is a senior associate of the corporate values and ethics programs at the Niagara Institute in Canada, and he has served as an ethics consultant to a number of governmental institutions, professional organizations, and corporations. He was educated on a Rhodes scholarship at the University of Oxford, and he has taught philosophy at the University of Oxford and the University of Manitoba.

**WILLIAM MADSEN** is a professor of anthropology at the University of California, Santa Barbara. His specialties include primitive religion, psychological anthropology, and addiction, and he is an Honorary Life Member of the Board of Directors for the National Council on Alcoholism–Santa Barbara chapter.

**VIJAY K. MAHAJAN** is a physician with St. Vincent's Hospital–Medical College of Ohio. He is the coauthor, with Jerry Wind, of *New Product Models: Practice, Shortcomings, and Desired Improvements* (Marketing Science Institute, 1991).

**ALIDA V. MERLO** is a professor in the Department of Criminal Justice at Westfield State College in Westfield, Massachusetts.

**JAMES F. MOSHER** is the program director for the Marin Institute for the Prevention of Alcohol and Other Drugs Problems in San Rafael, California.

**ETHAN A. NADELMANN** is an assistant professor of politics and public affairs at the Princeton University Woodrow Wilson School of Public and International Affairs. He was a founding coordinator of the Harvard Study Group on Organized Crime and has been a consultant to the Department of State's Bureau of International Narcotics Matters. He is an assistant editor of the *Journal of Drug Issues*.

**CRAIG NAKKEN** is a certified chemical dependency practitioner with the Family Therapy Institute in St. Paul, Minnesota, and a summer lecturer at the Rutgers School of Alcohol Studies in Piscataway, New Jersey.

**NATIONAL INSTITUTE ON DRUG ABUSE**, established in 1974, is one of the three institutes that form the Alcohol, Drug Abuse, and Mental Health Administration and is the lead federal agency for research into the problems and treatment of drug abuse. In addition to research, it is given a broad mandate in managing national drug abuse programs, including developing and overseeing a nationwide network of treatment, prevention, research, and training programs.

MAE NUTT, a Michigan mother, is an advocate for legalizing marijuana use for medicinal purposes. She has testified to this effect before the Michigan Senate Judiciary Committee and the House Committee on Public Health.

OFFICE OF NATIONAL DRUG CONTROL POLICY was created by the Anti–Drug Abuse Act of 1988 to advise the president of the United States on a national drug control strategy, a consolidated drug control budget, and other management and organizational issues. Its principal purpose is to establish policies, priorities, and objectives for the United States' drug control program.

STANTON PEELE is a social and clinical psychologist and an international lecturer on addiction. He has written several highly influential books on the nature of addiction and on treatment efficacy and social policy with respect to substance abuse, including *Diseasing of America: Addiction Treatment Out of Control* (Lexington Books, 1989).

ERIC B. RIMM received a doctorate in epidemiology from the Harvard School of Public Health in 1990 and has since been practicing there as a research associate. He also serves as project director of the Health Professionals Follow-up Study, which is designed to investigate the nutritional etiologies of chronic disease among U.S. men. He has coauthored over 30 scientific publications.

JEFFREY A. SCHALER, a doctoral candidate in human development at the University of Maryland, is a psychotherapist in Silver Spring, Maryland. He also lectures on drugs, alcoholism, and society in the Department of Justice, Law, and Society at American University in Washington, D.C.

JEAN J. SCHENSUL is the executive director of the Institute for Community Research and an associate professor of anthropology at the University of Connecticut. She is the coprincipal investigator of Project COPE and an organizer of the AIDS Community Research Group.

RICHARD G. SCHLAADT is the director of the University of Oregon Substance Abuse Prevention Program. Active in the health education area as an officer in several health organizations, he is the author of over 50 professional journal articles and 5 textbooks. He received a Ph.D. in education from Oregon State University.

SECRETARY OF HEALTH AND HUMAN SERVICES of the Department of Health and Human Services (HHS) advises the president of the

United States on health, welfare, and income security policies of the U.S. federal government. HHS is the principal agency for protecting health and providing essential human services to Americans. Administering some 250 separate programs, HHS provides services that protect and advance the quality of life for all Americans.

**HAROLD SHOUP** is the executive vice president and director of the Washington Office of the American Association of Advertising Agencies. His many professional and public service activities include serving as chairperson of the National Advertising Agency Network and as president of the Cleveland Advertising Club.

**MERRILL SINGER** is a member of the graduate faculty of the University of Connecticut and serves as the deputy director of the Hispanic Health Council in Hartford. The author of over 70 articles and 2 books, he also serves as the chairperson of the American Anthropological Association Task Force on AIDS and as a steering committee member of the AIDS and Anthropology Research Group.

**MEIR STAMPFER** is an associate professor of epidemiology at the Harvard School of Public Health, and he holds appointments at the Harvard Medical School and at the Brigham and Women's Hospital. He received an M.D. from New York University School of Medicine and a Ph.D. in epidemiology from Harvard University. His current research focuses on the influence of diet and exogenous hormones on health.

**PATRICIA TAYLOR** is the director of the Alcohol Policies Project of the Center for Science in the Public Interest, a nonprofit organization dedicated to promoting the public's health. The organization works to promote public policies to prevent the devastation caused by drinking.

**WALTER WILLETT** is a trained physician and a professor in the Department of Nutrition at the Harvard School of Public Health. He is the author of *Nutritional Epidemiology* (Oxford University Press, 1990).

**JAMES Q. WILSON** is the James Collins Professor of Management and Public Policy at the University of California, Los Angeles, where he has been teaching since 1985. He is also the chairperson of the board of directors of the Police Foundation and a member of the American Academy of Arts and Sciences. He has published numerous books on crime, government, and politics, including *Politics of Regulation* (Basic Books, 1982).

**JANIS A. WORK** is a free-lance writer in Minneapolis, Minnesota.

**KAREN L. YANAGISAKO** is a training coordinator for the Marin Institute for the Prevention of Alcohol and Other Drugs Problems in San Rafael, California.

# INDEX